Drivers of Innovation

DRIVERS OF INNOVATION

ENTREPRENEURSHIP, EDUCATION, AND FINANCE IN ASIA

Edited by Yong Suk Lee and Fei Yan

Stanford | Walter H. Shorenstein
Asia-Pacific Research Center
Freeman Spogli Institute

ROWMAN & LITTLEFIELD
Lanham • Boulder • New York • London

Shorenstein APARC addresses critical issues affecting the countries of Asia, their regional and global affairs, and U.S.-Asia relations. As Stanford University's hub for the interdisciplinary study of contemporary Asia, we produce policy-relevant research, provide education and training to students, scholars, and practitioners, and strengthen dialogue and cooperation between counterparts in the Asia-Pacific and the United States.

The Walter H. Shorenstein Asia-Pacific Research Center
Freeman Spogli Institute for International Studies
Stanford University
Encina Hall
Stanford, CA 94305-6055
http://aparc.fsi.stanford.edu

Walter H. Shorenstein Asia-Pacific Research Center, 2023.

Published by Rowman & Littlefield
An imprint of The Rowman & Littlefield Publishing Group, Inc.
4501 Forbes Boulevard, Lanham, MD 20706
www.rowman.com

86–90 Paul Street, London EC2A 4NE, United Kingdom

First printing, 2023
ISBN 978-1-5381-7779-2 (paper)
ISBN 978-1-5381-7778-5 (cloth)

Library of Congress Control Number: 2022931368

Contents

Tables and Figures

Tables

Figures

Abbreviations

A*STAR	Agency for Science, Technology and Research
AAD	Academy of Arts and Design (Tsinghua)
AI	artificial intelligence
AYUSH	ayurveda, yoga, naturopathy, unani, siddha, and homeopathy
CSIR	Council of Scientific and Industrial Research
CSRC	China Securities Regulatory Commission
CVC	corporate investment by a strategic partner
ESD	Education for Sustainable Development
ESV	estimated shell value
GCP	Globis Capital Partners
GDP	gross domestic product
GERD	gross expenditure on research and development
GII	Global Innovation Index
GP	general partner
GPS	global positioning system
GSF	Graduate School of Finance (Tsinghua)
GVC	government-led private equity/venture capital funds
HSAHP	Hang Seng Stock Connect China AH Premium Index
ICT	information and communication technology
IIT	Indian Institute of Technology
IP	intellectual property
IPO	initial public offering
IT	information technology
JAFCO	Japan Associated Finance Co., Ltd.
KED	Kyoto Enterprise Development
KFoF	Korea Fund of Funds
KODIT	Korea Credit Guarantee Fund
KONEX	Korea New Exchange

KOTEC   Korea Technology Finance Corporation
KRIVET   Korea Research Institute for Vocational Education and Training
KVIC   Korea Venture Investment Corporation
LCGF   local credit guarantee foundation
LP   limited partner
M&A   merger and acquisition
MAR   major asset restructuring
MB   market-to-book ratio
MITI   Ministry of International Trade and Industry
MoE   Ministry of Education
MSIT   Ministry of Science, Information, Communication, and
         Technology
MSS   Ministry of SMEs and Start-ups
NED   Nippon Enterprise Development
NEEQ   National Equities Exchange and Quotations
NSF   National Science Foundation
NSTB   National Science and Technology Board
NTEFS   New Technology Enterprise Financial Support Act
NUS   National University of Singapore
NUSP   national university science park
NVCC   Nippon Venture Capital Co., Ltd.
ODM   original design manufacturer
OECD   Organisation for Economic Co-operation and Development
OEM   original equipment manufacturer
PISA   Programme for International Student Assessment
R&D   research and development
RM   reverse merger
ROA   return-on-assets
SBIR   Small Business Innovative Research
SDG   Sustainable Development Goal
SEM   School of Economics and Management (Tsinghua)
SIGS   Tsinghua Shenzhen International Graduate School
SMBA   Small and Medium Business Administration
SMBF   Small and Medium Business Fund
SME   small- and medium-sized enterprise
SMESS   Small and Medium-Size Enterprise Start-up Support Act
SMTE   small and medium technology-based enterprise
SOE   state-owned enterprise/entity
STEM   science, technology, engineering, and mathematics
TGER   gross enrollment in tertiary education
TLO   technology licensing organization
TSE   Tokyo Stock Exchange
TUEF   Tsinghua University Education Foundation

UICC	University-Industry Cooperation Committee (Tsinghua)
UTEC	University of Tokyo Edge Capital
VC	venture capital
VCPE	venture capital and private equity
WCU	world-class university
WiL	World Innovation Lab

Contributors

HE SOUNG AHN is an assistant professor at Myongji University, teaching strategy and international business. She received her PhD in management with a concentration in strategy and organizational studies at Korea University, an MSc in management from the London School of Economics and Political Science and a BA in economics from Korea University. Her main research interests include corporate governance, strategic leadership change/CEO succession, strategic decision-making, and entrepreneurship.

LIN WILLIAM CONG is the Rudd Family Professor of Management, an associate professor of finance, and the founding faculty director of the FinTech Initiative at Cornell University. He is also a Kauffman Foundation Junior Faculty Fellow, Poets & Quants World Best Business School Professor, and serves on the editorial boards of leading journals such as *Management Science*. He was previously a faculty member at the University of Chicago Booth School of Business, a George Shultz scholar, and a doctoral fellow at the Stanford Institute for Innovation in Developing Economies.

Cong's research spans financial economics, information economics, big data and AI, and entrepreneurship. Widely recognized as the world's leading expert on FinTech, Cong has received the International Centre for Pension Management Research Award, AAM-CAMRI-CFA Institute Prize in Asset Management, CME Best Paper Award, and Finance Theory Group Best Paper Award, among other accolades. He has been invited to speak at or advise universities, venture funds, technology startups, investment shops, and government agencies including the International Monetary Fund, Asset Management Association of China, Blackrock, and federal reserve banks. He received his PhD in finance and MS in statistics from Stanford, and AM in physics jointly with an AB in math and physics from Harvard.

RAFIQ DOSSANI is director of the RAND Center for Asia Pacific Policy, a senior economist at the RAND Corporation, and a professor at the Pardee RAND Graduate School. He works on education, finance, regional development, security, trade, and technology issues. Recent projects include security in the Korean Peninsula, the Belt and Road Initiative, Track II diplomacy between the United States and China, and Asia's democratization. Previously, Dossani was director of Stanford University's Center for South Asia and a senior research scholar at Stanford University's Institute for International Studies. He holds a PhD in finance from Northwestern University, an MBA from the Indian Institute of Management, Calcutta, and a BA in economics from St. Stephen's College, Delhi.

CHARLES (CHUCK) EESLEY is an associate professor and W.M. Keck Foundation Faculty Scholar in the Department of Management Science and Engineering at Stanford University. As part of the Stanford Technology Ventures Program, his research focuses on the role of the institutional and university environment in high-growth, technology entrepreneurship. His research focuses on rethinking how the educational and policy environment shapes the economic and entrepreneurial impact of university alumni. His field research spans China, Japan, Chile, Bangladesh, Thailand, and Silicon Valley, and has received awards from the Schulze Foundation, the Technical University of Munich, and the Kauffman Foundation. He is a faculty affiliate at the Stanford Center for International Development, the Woods Institute for the Environment, and the Stanford King Center on Global Development. He is also a member of the editorial board for the *Strategic Management Journal*. Before coming to Stanford, Eesley completed his PhD at the MIT Sloan School of Management. He has also been an advocate and mentor for immigrants and historically underrepresented groups in STEM, academia, and the tech sector via programs such as Diversifying Academia, Recognizing Excellence (DARE), Global Innovation through Science and Technology (GIST), and SURF, among others.

YUTA FUKUDOME is a research assistant who worked on the JST-RISTEX "Star Scientists and Innovation in Japan" and KAKENHI (18H00840) projects. He was in charge of bibliographic analysis, using a large database of articles and patents, and network analysis.

TAKEO HOSHI is dean of the Graduate School of Economics and professor at the University of Tokyo. His research area includes corporate finance, banking, monetary policy, and the Japanese economy. Hoshi is also co-chairman of the Academic Board of the Center for Industrial Development and Environmental Governance (Tsinghua University). His past positions include Henri and Tomoye Takahashi Senior Fellow at the Freeman Spogli Institute for International Studies at Stanford University and Pacific Economic Cooperation Professor in International Economic Relations at University of California, San Diego. He received the 2015 Japanese Bankers Academic Research Promotion Foundation Award, the 2011 Reischauer International Education Award of Japan Society of San Diego and Tijuana, the 2006 Enjoji Jiro Memorial Prize of Nihon Keizai Shimbun, and the 2005 Japan Economic Association-Nakahara Prize.

Hoshi's books include *Corporate Financing and Governance in Japan: The Road to the Future* (MIT Press, 2001; co-authored with Anil Kashyap), which received the Nikkei Award for the Best Economics Books; *The Japanese Economy*, 2nd Edition (MIT Press, 2020; co-authored with Takatoshi Ito); and *The Political Economy of the Abe Administration and Abenomics Reforms* (Cambridge University Press, 2021; co-edited with Phillip Lipscy). Other publications include "Zombies, Again? The COVID-19 Business Support Programs in Japan" (joint with Daiji Kawaguchi and Kenichi Ueda), forthcoming in the *Journal of Banking and Finance*; "Will the U.S. and Europe Avoid a Lost Decade? Lessons from Japan's Post Crisis Experience" (joint with Anil K Kashyap), *IMF Economic Review*, 2015; and "Zombie Lending and Depressed Restructuring in Japan" (joint with Ricardo Caballero and Anil Kashyap), *American Economic Review*, December 2008. Hoshi received his BA from the University of Tokyo in 1983 and a PhD in economics from the Massachusetts Institute of Technology in 1988.

DAVID H. HSU is the Richard A. Sapp Professor of Management at the Wharton School of the University of Pennsylvania. His research and teaching are in the fields of entrepreneurship, innovation, and strategy. Hsu received his undergraduate degree in economics and political science from Stanford, his master's degree in public policy from Harvard, and his PhD in management from the Massachusetts Institute of Technology Sloan School of Management.

MOHAN KANKANHALLI is the Provost's Chair Professor of Computer Science at the National University of Singapore (NUS). He has also been the dean of the NUS School of Computing since July 2016. Before that, he was the NUS vice provost of graduate education (2014–16) and associate provost (2011–13). Kankanhalli obtained his BTech from IIT Kharagpur and MS and PhD from the Rensselaer Polytechnic Institute. His current research interests are in multimedia computing, information security & privacy, image/video processing and social media analysis. He has made many contributions in the area of multimedia content processing—image and video understanding, data fusion, visual saliency as well as in multimedia security—content authentication and privacy, and multi-camera surveillance. He directs the NUS Centre for Research in Privacy Technologies, which conducts fundamental research to help holistically protect the privacy of individuals and organizations. He is on the editorial boards of several journals, including *ACM Transactions on Multimedia, Springer Multimedia Systems Journal, IEEE Multimedia*, and *Springer Journal on Big Data*. He is an IEEE fellow.

DOHYEON KIM is a professor at Kookmin University Business School, teaching entrepreneurship and strategy. Originally with a PhD in aerospace engineering from Seoul National University, he began his career designing the optimal trajectory of launch vehicles. Then he deviated from the trajectory toward the world of business. He has gained practical experience in strategy and M&A at consulting firms and investment banks such as the Boston Consulting Group and has a history of a failed startup. Seeking refuge in academia, he received his second PhD in entrepreneurial strategy from the Warwick Business School. Currently, he takes advisory roles with VCs, large corporations, startups, and non-profit organizations in Korea, the United States, and France. His most recent research on these topics has been published in journals such as *Entrepreneurship Research Journal* and the *Journal of Innovation and Entrepreneurship*.

HICHEON KIM is a professor of strategy and entrepreneurship and a former associate dean at the Korea University Business School (KUBS). He is a founding director of the KUBS Startup Institute, whose mission ranges from startup acceleration to entrepreneurship education and research. Kim's research interests include startup strategy and ecosystem, corporate entrepreneurship, business groups, and corporate governance. His work has appeared in leading journals such as *Academy of Management Journal, Strategic Management Journal, Organization Science,* and the *Journal of International Business Studies.* One of his articles, published in *Academy of Management Journal* in 1997, has been recognized as one of the top 25 most-cited articles in global strategy research.

Kim is a former senior editor of the *Asia Pacific Journal of Management* and has served on the editorial boards of the *Journal of Management, Journal of Management Studies,* and *Corporate Governance: An International Review.* Kim received his BBA from Korea University, MS from the Korea Advanced Institute of Science and Technology, and PhD from Texas A&M University.

JIN-YEONG KIM is a professor of economics at Konkuk Universitiy in Seoul. His BA in economics is from Seoul National University, and he received the PhD in economics from the University of Rochester. Before joining Konkuk University's faculty in 2002, he worked at the Korea Institute of Public Finance. Kim's main research area is the economics of education, public finance, and labor economics. His research interests include educational programs and policy evaluation, the effect of private tutoring, public grants for college students, the early labor market performance of college graduates, and income mobility in Korea. He has served on many editorial boards and has been the editor of the *Korean Journal of Labor Economics,* the *Korean Journal of Applied Economics,* and the *Korean Journal of Public Finance.* He was president of the Korean Association of Applied Economics from 2020 to 2021. Kim has advised and worked closely with many government organizations such as the Ministry of Economy and Finance, Ministry of Education, and Ministry of Employment and Labor. In 2018, Kim was a member of the Special Committee on Fiscal Reform, a presidential advisory body.

KENJI E. KUSHIDA is a senior fellow at the Carnegie Endowment for International Peace. He directs Japan programming and research focused on innovative, global, and technology related areas, and he leads the Japan–Silicon Valley Innovation Initiative @ Carnegie. He is also an International Research Fellow at the Canon Institute for Global Studies (CIGS) and nonresident senior fellow at the Tokyo Foundation for Policy Research (TKFD). He was previously a research scholar at the Japan Program at the Shorenstein Asia-Pacific Research Center at Stanford University. He holds a PhD in political science from the University of California, Berkeley, an MA in East Asian studies, and BAs in economics and East Asian studies, all from Stanford University.

His research streams include (1) information technology innovation, (2) Silicon Valley's economic ecosystem, (3) Japan's startup ecosystem and its political economic transformation since the 1990s, and (4) the Fukushima nuclear disaster. He has published several books and numerous articles in each of these streams, including "The Politics of Commoditization in Global ICT Industries," "Japan's Startup Ecosystem," and "Cloud Computing: From Scarcity to Abundance."

CHARLES M. C. LEE is the Moghadam Family Professor of Management and Professor of Accounting at Stanford University. His research focuses on the effect of human cognitive constraints on market participants and other factors that impact the efficiency with which market prices incorporate information. He has published extensively in leading academic journals on topics including behavioral finance, financial statement analysis, equity valuation, market microstructure, quantitative investing, and security market regulation. He was previously the director of the Parker Center for Investment Research at Cornell University, and the managing director at Barclays Global Investors (now Blackrock) and led the team to manage over $300 billion in active equity assets.

Lee has received numerous honors and awards, including twelve school-wide or national-level Teaching Excellence awards and the Notable Contribution to Accounting Literature Prize. His recent honors include the Q Group's 2018 Roger F. Murray Prize, the Stanford Asian American Faculty Award for Outstanding Achievements and Service to the Asian community, and the 2017 AAA Innovation in Financial Accounting Education Award. Lee received his BMath from the University of Waterloo (1981), and his MBA (1989) and PhD (1990) from Cornell University.

YONG SUK LEE is assistant professor of technology, economy, and global affairs at the Keough School of Global Affairs at the University of Notre Dame. Lee's research focuses on new technologies, such as artificial intelligence and robotics, in relation to labor economics, entrepreneurship, and urban economics. His current research focuses on how artificial intelligence and robotics affect labor, and the governance and ethical issues related to these new technologies. Lee also focuses on the application of machine learning to examine socioeconomic questions, such as bias, urban inequality and change, and the demand for skill. Lee's research also examines aspects of technology education and entrepreneurship, e.g., education and mobility, and entrepreneurship and economic growth. Prior to joining the University of Notre Dame, Lee was Stanford University faculty member as the SK Center Fellow at the Freeman Spogli Institute for International Studies. Prior to Stanford, he was an assistant professor of economics at Williams College. He received his PhD in economics from Brown University, a Master of Public Policy from Duke University, and bachelor's and master's in architecture from Seoul National University. Lee also worked as a real estate development consultant and architecture designer as he transitioned from architecture to economics.

JIZHEN LI is a professor of innovation and entrepreneurship at Tsinghua University's School of Economics and Management (SEM). Li is also the associate dean of Tsinghua SEM. His research interests include the management of technological innovation, strategic management, and project management. His research has appeared in *Industry and Innovation, Information and Management,* the *International Journal of Technology Management, Journal of Management, Research Policy, R&D Management,* and *Strategic Management Journal.*

KANETAKA M. MAKI is an associate professor at the Waseda Business School (WBS). He also serves as a visiting associate professor at the Rady School of Management, University of California San Diego. Maki's research interests involve the fields of the socioeconomics of innovation and entrepreneurship, science policy, and university-industry technology transfer. He has three streams of research contributions: (1) the institutional design of entrepreneurship at research universities; (2) methods to improve startup success rates; and (3) quantitative research of star scientists particularly comparing the United States and Japan.

Prior to joining WBS, Maki worked at the National Graduate Institute for Policy Studies, Stanford University, the University of California

San Diego, and Keio University. In both the United States and Japan, he has been actively involved in designing and implementing university innovation systems. In Japan, he is a committee member in national and local governments working to create effective innovation policy.Maki received his PhD in management from the University of California San Diego. He received a master's in media and governance and BA in environmental information, both from Keio University.

DINSHA MISTREE is a research fellow in the Program on Strengthening US-India Relations at the Hoover Institution and a research fellow in the Rule of Law Program at Stanford Law School. Mistree studies the relationship between governance and economic growth in developing countries. His scholarship concentrates on the political economy of legal systems, public administration, and education policy, with a special focus on India. Recent and forthcoming scholarship has appeared or is forthcoming at *Stanford Law Review*, *Social Science and Medicine*, *Public Administration Review*, and *Comparative Politics*. Mistree holds a PhD and an MA in politics from Princeton University, along with an SM and an SB from the Massachusetts Institute of Technology. He previously held a postdoctoral fellowship at Stanford's Center on Democracy, Development, and the Rule of Law and was a visiting scholar at IIM-Ahmedabad.

HIROMI SAITO NAGANE is a professor in Chiba University's Graduate School of Social Sciences. She earned the PhD in economics. Her research interests are health economics, the economics of innovation, science and technology policy, and industry-academia collaboration. She has published on a wide range of topics and using a variety of methods, including: welfare analysis of healthcare regulation using Contingent Valuation Method (CVM); the relationship between firm performance and industry-university collaboration using panel data; cross-industry comparisons of firms' evaluations for basic research by universities and public research institutions; analysis of article productivity using large-scale article data; development of measures of interdisciplinary research; and text mining analysis of researcher interviews. Her basic method is empirical analysis, but she also uses qualitative analysis such as interview surveys, and emphasizes the careful collection of facts in the field that do not appear in the data.

Nagane received a category award for her article about science and technology policy from the Japan Society of Mechanical Engineers in

2020, and a best paper award from Asialics international conference in 2015. She also holds the post of visiting scholar at the National Institute of Science and Technology Policy in the Ministry of Education, Culture, Sports, Science and Technology.

YUANYU QU is an associate professor of finance at the School of Banking and Finance, University of International Business and Economics. He also serves as a research fellow at the National Institute of Financial Research, Tsinghua University, and was a consultant at the Asian Development Bank. He received a PhD in finance from Tsinghua University.

Qu's research interests encompass the area of empirical asset pricing, mutual funds, and corporate governance, with a specialization in the Chinese financial markets. He has published in the *Journal of Financial and Quantitative Analysis, Journal of Corporate Finance, Financial Management, Management World* (in Chinese), and the *Journal of Financial Research* (in Chinese). He is a principal investigator at the National Natural Science Foundation of China. He is a recipient of the China Financial Research Conference Best Paper Award, the China Decision Science Annual Meeting Best Paper Award, and Best Thesis Advisor of Beijing.

TATSUO SASAKI is an adjunct researcher at the Institute for Business and Finance at Waseda University, and a member of the professional staff at Science for RE-Designing Science, Technology and Innovation Policy Center, at the National Graduate Research Institute for Policy Studies (GRIPS). His work focuses on science, technology, and innovation policy in Japan, with a focus on university-industry research collaboration. He is a member of the JST-RISTEX: "Star Scientists and Innovation in Japan" project, along with with Kanetaka M. Maki and Hiromi Saito Nagane. Currently, Sasaki has started a new project to investigate the impact of Japan's science and technology innovation policy on interdisciplinary research, using bibliometric methods.

TAO SHEN is an associate professor of finance at Tsinghua University's School of Economics and Management and a research fellow at the Tsinghua University Institute for Industrial Innovation and Finance. He also serves as the coordinator of undergraduate programs at the School of Economics and Management.

His research spans corporate investment, capital structure, and financial markets, with a specialization in Chinese financial market development. He has published a dozen articles in both English and Chinese in academic journals such as the *Journal of Financial Economics*, the *Journal of Financial and Quantitative Analysis*, *Management World* (in Chinese), and the *Journal of Financial Research* (in Chinese).

Shen is a principal investigator at the National Natural Science Foundation of China and participates in several of the foundation's projects. He is the recipient of the China Financial Research Conference Best Paper Award, the China Decision Science Annual Meeting Best Paper Award, and numerous Teaching Excellence awards at Tsinghua University. Shen received a PhD in finance from the University of Minnesota Twin Cities and two master's degrees in economics and statistics from Georgia Institute of Technology. He earned his BA in finance from Nankai University.

YOU (WILLOW) WU is an assistant professor in the Department of Management at the Chinese University of Hong Kong. She holds a PhD in management science and engineering from Stanford University, where she received the Stanford Graduate Fellowship and the King Center Graduate Student Fellowship on Global Development. She holds a bachelor's degree in environmental sciences and a bachelor's degree in economics from Peking University in China, where she received a National Scholarship and a China Economic Research Scholarship.

Wu's research examines technology entrepreneurship and entrepreneurial strategies in nascent markets, using econometric and machine learning methods. She is particularly interested in how institutional environment influences entrepreneurial strategies. Her dissertation won the Academy of Management Best Paper Award and was nominated for the Strategic Management Society PhD Paper Prize. She has published papers in the *Strategic Entrepreneurship Journal*, *Regional Studies*, and the *Quarterly Journal of Management*.

FEI YAN is an associate professor of sociology at Tsinghua University. He received his PhD from the University of Oxford and a master's from Stanford University. Prior to joining Tsinghua, he was a visiting research fellow and a postdoctoral fellow at the Walter H. Shorenstein Asia-Pacific Research Center, Stanford University. His research focuses on historical sociology, political sociology, and the sociology of development. Yan has published numerous refereed articles at top international journals, including *Social Science Research*, *Sociological Re-*

view, *Urban Studies*, *Social Movement Studies*, *Oxford Bibliographies in Sociology*, *Development Policy Review*, *China Quarterly*, *Modern China*, *China Information* and *China: An International Journal*. He was awarded the Graduate Student Best Paper Prize by the Association for Asian Studies in 2015. Currently, he serves as the vice-chair of the Department of Sociology, Tsinghua University.

BERNARD YEUNG is the Stephen Riady Distinguished Professor in Finance and Strategic Management at the National University of Singapore Business School. He is also the president of the Asian Bureau of Finance and Economic Research. Yeung was dean of NUS Business School from June 2008 to May 2019. Before joining NUS, he was the Abraham Krasnoff Professor in Global Business, Economics, and Management at New York University's Stern School of Business and the director of the NYU China House. He has previously taught at the University of Michigan (1988–99) and at the University of Alberta (1983–88). He has published widely in top-tier academic journals covering topics in finance, economics, and strategy, and has more than 27,000 citations.

Yeung was awarded the Public Administration Silver Medal (2018) in Singapore, Irwin Outstanding Educator Award (2013) from the Academy of Management, and is an elected Fellow of the Academy of International Business. He has served as a member of the Economic Strategies Committee in Singapore (2009), the Social Science Research Council in Singapore (2016–18), and the Financial Research Council of the Monetary Authority of Singapore (2010–13). Yeung received his BA in economics and mathematics from the University of Western Ontario and his MBA and PhD from the Graduate School of Business at the University of Chicago.

CHAO ZHANG is an associate professor at Tsinghua University, where he obtained his PhD from the university's Department of Automation. He is the director of the Career Development Center at Tsinghua University. He established the "Zhang Chao Studio" for students who are interested in working in the public sector, and has provided career guidance for nearly a thousand such individuals. He also serves as a committee member on Tsinghua University Student Affairs System Teaching Committee, and deputy chairman and secretary general of the Graduate Career Development Education Committee of the Chinese

Society of Academic Degrees and Graduate Education. He won first prize in Tsinghua University's Outstanding Teaching Award in 2012, 2016, and 2019, and one of his articles was given the Annual Impact Paper Award by University Counselors in 2016.

ZHOU ZHONG is an associate professor at the Institute of Education at Tsinghua University, where she has worked since 2006. She graduated from Peking University with a BA in English language and literature and received an MSc and DPhil in comparative and international education from the University of Oxford. Zhong's research interest lies in comparative, international and interdisciplinary studies of higher education innovation. She has a special interest in integrating the teaching, research, and practice of teaching and learning innovation and in promoting global mobility for students and scholars. Her recent research projects focus on university global strategy, higher education internationalization studies, and teaching and learning innovation.

LIJIE ZHOU is a software engineer in Silicon Valley. Her expertise is in cloud infrastructure and cyber security. She has been witness to numerous innovations and technology changes by working at companies at different sizes and phases, including Gusto, Facebook and McAfee. Previously, she was an entrepreneur in China working on an education startup. Zhou holds master's degrees in both linguistics (University of Toledo) and computer science (San Francisco State University).

Preface

Innovation is pivotal to the future course of economic development. Recognizing the importance of innovation for the future development of East Asia and beyond, the Walter H. Shorenstein Asia-Pacific Research Center at Stanford University launched the Stanford Asia-Pacific Innovation Project to produce academic and policy research from comparative and regional perspectives, looking into how Asian nations are responding to the imperative to develop the skills, competencies, long-term health, and systems for innovation in the twenty-first century.

This volume is based on the papers presented at the conference at Tsinghua University in Beijing. We convened scholars from the United States and Asia in various research areas to examine human capital and education policies that can help develop a more entrepreneurial and innovative workforce in East Asia, as well as on financial policies that can promote innovation financing and entrepreneurship in the region. This volume will serve as a valuable reference for scholars, educators, and policymakers working to develop human capital and policy interventions for innovation in Asia.

We would like to extend our appreciation for the productive discussions we have had with colleagues in Asia, Europe, and the United States. Special thanks to Gi-wook Shin, who led this long-term project, and James Chen, the founding director of D&C Think in Beijing for his generous financial support. We also would like to thank Takeo Hoshi and Karen Eggleston for their academic support and Kristen Lee for her administrative assistance. Ultimately, it is George Krompacky, our amazing editor at the Walter H. Shorenstein Asia-Pacific

Research Center, who deserves our greatest gratitude for helping us get this book to the finishing line. We hope that the book will be able to contribute to some of the most pressing questions and discussions on innovation and entrepreneurship during this rapidly changing time.

Yong Suk Lee
University of Notre Dame
Fei Yan
Tsinghua University

Drivers of Innovation

1 Educating Entrepreneurs and Financing Innovation in Asia

Fei Yan, Yong Suk Lee, Lin William Cong, Charles Eesley, and Charles M. C. Lee

Innovation and entrepreneurship rank highly on the strategic agendas of most countries today. In response, Stanford University's Walter H. Shorenstein Asia-Pacific Research Center embarked on a series of collaborative research projects on innovation and entrepreneurship policy for future economic growth, with a focus on Asia. Many countries in the region have pursued catch-up economic growth by importing new technologies, using them efficiently, and exporting to the world. Many firms in these countries have caught up to the frontiers of technology and are now seeking new ways to innovate and sustain growth (Lee, Hoshi, and Shin 2020). The series of conferences and collaborative research projects on innovation and entrepreneurship led by Shorenstein APARC has culminated in three book volumes, with the first volume examining national innovation policies and regional cluster policies (Lee, Hoshi, and Shin 2020) and the second volume examining innovation policies in an aging world (Eggleston, Park, and Shin 2021).

As global economic competition intensifies, many national policymakers recognize the central importance of entrepreneurship education and the building of financial institutions to promote long-term innovation, entrepreneurship, and economic growth. This book, the third and last of the series, brings together scholars from the United States and Asia to explore those education and finance policies that might be conducive to accelerating innovation and developing a more entrepreneurial workforce in East Asia. We focus on five innovative Asian countries, namely, China, the Republic of Korea, Japan, Singapore, and India. Government-led industrial policy and strong administrative guidance continue to leave a long shadow of government intervention in promoting innovation and entrepreneurship. While the major concern for China and India might be bureaucratic inertia that obstructs creativity and distorts the investment environment, Korea and Japan have to deal with monopolistic corporations that intrinsically fear change and resist new entrants. China has the world's largest state investment in innovation, yet also overly cautious regulations, which exact a high price in terms of social capital participation and the soundness of the nation's stock markets. Similar problems exist in Korea, where innovation is mainly financed by the government and regulations forbid large corporations from funding innovative start-ups. Bureaucratic inefficiency also troubles India, where government-funded national research institutes are far less productive than research universities that operate independent of the government. Indeed, Japan is no exception, as it faces the adverse effects of a monopoly shaped by the dominance of large banks, many of which are reluctant to finance unprofitable start-ups even if their innovative capability is high. Despite these problems, one silver lining is the rapid emergence of digital infrastructure, business artificial intelligence (AI), and fintech innovations in these countries. The rise of these useful, general-purpose digital technologies is a decidedly positive sign for the entrepreneurs and innovators in these economies.

In this introduction we first discuss key themes surrounding the education of entrepreneurs and financing of innovation by drawing upon the relevant literature. In doing so we consider the specific challenges faced by the countries examined in this book. We then discuss how each chapter contributes to a better understanding of these topics and how countries can make progress in training entrepreneurs and financing innovation.

The Mechanisms of Entrepreneurship Education

Growth in the number of entrepreneurial firms has been linked to greater real economic growth (Lee 2017). Innovation and entrepreneurship scholars have long been interested in the question of why some people transition to being entrepreneurs, and look in particular at the impact of entrepreneurial behavior on economic growth and productivity (Schumpeter 1934). One set of answers posits that individuals with lower opportunity costs or with better access to financing are more likely to become entrepreneurs (Amit, Muller, and Cockburn 1995; Iyigun and Owen 1998). For example, those with higher incomes or parents with greater levels of wealth are likely to have easier access to the funding needed to start a firm and, as expected, are more likely to become founders (Dunn and Holtz-Eakin 2000; Blau 1987).

A second set of answers emphasizes cognitive differences between entrepreneurs and non-entrepreneurs (Mitchell et al. 2000). Individuals with relatively less aversion to risk, a greater need for independence, and less of a tendency toward counterfactual thinking and regret are more likely to become entrepreneurs (Douglas and Shepherd 2000; Baron 2000).

Third, demographic factors have been shown to predict who transitions to entrepreneurship. These factors include religious background (McClelland 1961), age (Levesque and Minniti 2006), and entrepreneurial parents (Dunn and Holtz-Eakin 2000; J. Sørensen 2007). Having entrepreneurial parents has been found to increase the probability of becoming an entrepreneur oneself by about 60 percent (Lindquist, Sol, and Van Praag 2015).

A final set of explanations centers on university training and education, the focus of this volume. Baumol (2005) argues that there are differences between the type of education needed to identify entrepreneurial opportunities and that required for technical mastery. For example, Lazear (2005) shows that, among a set of Stanford business school alumni, those who undertook a greater variety of coursework and jobs were more likely to become founders. Universities, as a source of knowledge spillovers as well as social norms and exposure to entrepreneurship, are increasingly cited as a factor in generating entrepreneurs (Bramwell and Wolfe 2008; Dahlstrand 1997; Oliver 2004; Hsu, Roberts, and Eesley 2007; Guerrero, Cunningham, and Urbano 2015).

While entrepreneurship education has proliferated, high-quality research on its impacts is still nascent (Cumming and Fischer 2012; Vesper and Gartner 1997). Some work shows a positive link between this brand of education and attitudes or intentions toward entrepreneurship or entrepreneurial activity (Souitaris, Zerbinati, and Al-Laham 2007). Entrepreneurship programs may encourage students to increase their entrepreneurial self-efficacy, especially for those with weak intentions ex ante (Peterman and Kennedy 2003). Von Graevenitz, Harhoff, and Weber (2010) find that while the average effects of an entrepreneurship course on intentions are negative, the effects are not uniform. Also, the effects are not well known; as the same authors observe, "While entrepreneurship education has been introduced and promoted in many countries and at many institutions of tertiary education, little is known at this point about the effect of these courses" (2010, 103).

Eesley and Lee (2020) propose that entrepreneurship programs may perform two functions, with differential predictions for the rates and success of ensuing entrepreneurship. One, such programs may help participants form more accurate beliefs around their true individual entrepreneurial ability. Two, they may improve participants' entrepreneurial skills or ability. The authors consider a set of Stanford University alumni and find that program participation is positively associated with entrepreneurial activities. Yet, when the self-selection of innately entrepreneurial individuals into these programs is taken into account, the impacts become nonpositive. From these findings, we can generalize that the effects of human capital policies that aim to promote entrepreneurship will differ depending on the extent of two mechanisms: improved ability, and improved perception of fit with ability. Of course, additional mechanisms can be at work, especially social networks, and the net effects would ultimately influence entrepreneurship rates and entrepreneurial performance. Moreover, the degree to which each mechanism is at work will differ by institution and population.

Lee and Eesley (2018) examine the persistence and differences in entrepreneurship among Stanford alumni by ethnicity and nationality. While the authors find that Asian Americans have a higher rate of entrepreneurship than white Americans, when further disaggregating subgroups of the Asian population (again, among Stanford alumni), they find that Indians have the highest rate of entrepreneurship, and Koreans and Japanese the lowest rates. Moreover, when the authors further disaggregate the Asian Stanford alumni population, they find a lower rate of entrepreneurship among Asian immigrant alumni relative to Asian American alumni. A low level of parental entrepreneurship and high degree of intergenerational correlation in entrepreneurship among Asian immigrant alumni likely result in their lower level of entrepreneurship and participation in university entrepreneurship programs relative to their Asian American counterparts. These findings underscore the importance of institutional contexts in the successful implementation of human capital policies that aim to promote entrepreneurship. University programs across countries will likely differ in how much they improve entrepreneurial ability. Also, students from different countries and universities may differ in the degree to which they overestimate their entrepreneurial abilities. Thus, human capital policies that promote entrepreneurship are very much context dependent, as we will see in the chapters of this volume. What works in India will be different from what works in South Korea. The Chinese model of promoting entrepreneurship may be less pertinent to the Japanese or Singaporeans.

With an understanding that education can increase entrepreneurial skill, and that the effects will differ based on institutional and demographic factors, the chapters in this book take a flexible approach to studying how entrepreneurship can be promoted through university education.

The Economic Underpinnings of Financing Entrepreneurs and Innovation

The financing of innovation-based projects gives rise to three important classes of economic problems that have been widely studied in the literature. First and foremost are the challenges arising from the non-rival nature of the outputs. Innovation and experimentation are costly undertakings whose payoffs often come in the form of knowledge, which is a non-rival good (Schumpeter 1942; Arrow 1962). While the innovator and her funding partners bear the risks and costs associated with a project, much of the benefit derived from the undertaking can accrue to others, through knowledge spillovers. Problems associated with the incomplete appropriability of investment returns are a key reason why innovations can be difficult to finance with capital from sources external to the innovator or entrepreneur. These problems can be partially mitigated through public policies, for example those governing intellectual property protection, government subsidies, or tax incentives. Nevertheless, even with such policies in place, other factors that affect an innovator's ability to capture profits generated by an innovation can still have a significant effect on incentives for innovation in an economy. Over the past decades, the increasing reliance of innovation on big data that are non-rival may further fuel the need for adaptive policies and regulations on privacy and data usage (Cong, Xie, and Zhang 2021).

A second set of challenges arises from the risky nature of the process. Innovation and experimentation are speculative activities, and the associated payoffs often involve a high level of uncertainty that is difficult to quantify ex ante. As the risk of a venture increases, investors' ability to manage these problems through purchase discounts alone becomes increasingly limited. In highly speculative ventures with imperfect information, a host of agency issues and hold-up-related problems can arise (Stiglitz and Weiss 1981; Ewens, Rhodes-Kropf, and Strebulaev 2016; Hochberg, Ljungqvist, and Vissing-Jørgensen 2013), requiring investors to revisit the terms of the agreement. This has given rise to more complicated contracts in the domain of venture investing, often featuring contingency claims. By making the extent of a manager's control and access to capital contingent on performance, such claims can help mitigate agency concerns that increase with issuer risk. Of course, to the extent that such risk-sharing problems cannot be fully resolved through contingent contracts, a certain amount of under-investment in innovative activities will still result.

A third set of challenges arises from the agency conflicts between entrepreneurs and investors, in the form of information asymmetry (Akerlof 1970; Leland and Pyle 1977) and moral hazard problems (Jensen and Meckling 1976). These agency- and information-related issues are particularly salient for young, small firms, and in developing countries such as China or India where the financial markets are not fully developed and the regulatory landscape is complex. In such settings, providers of capital need to acquire a certain minimal level of expertise in the innovative activities at hand. This applies to both private investors and public entities that seek to finance the project. But of course, innovation-based projects are, by nature, more difficult to evaluate, leading potentially to the suboptimal allocation of resources.

A large body of literature has been devoted to how financial intermediaries, especially venture capital (VC) firms, can help overcome the aforementioned challenges and thus facilitate innovation. Prior studies indicate how VC firms can improve efficiency through the active monitoring and advice provided (Hellmann 1998), screening mechanisms employed (Chan 1983), incentives to exit (Berglöf 1994), proper syndication of the investment (Admati and Pfleiderer 1994; Lerner 1994), superior investment staging prior to exit (Sahlman 1990; Gompers 1995; Bergemann and Hege 1998), or better governance once a firm becomes public (Lerner 1995; Hochberg 2011). Overall, theory and evidence to date indicate that VC firms can improve monitoring and help start-ups in professionalizing their businesses (Hellmann and Puri 2002; Rajan 2012), thereby improving outcomes and potentially encouraging more innovation (Kortum and Lerner 2000; Bernstein, Giroud, and Townsend 2016).

A related line of research examines designs that better align the incentives of entrepreneurs and financiers, and thus mitigate agency problems. The specific mechanisms studied include security design, experimentation, as well as manager compensation and style (Cornelli and Yosha 2003; Manso 2011; Tian and Wang 2011). Several studies also examine mechanisms for mitigating the hold-up problem in VC financing settings (Ewens, Rhodes-Kropf, and Strebulaev 2016; Hochberg, Ljungqvist, and Vissing-Jørgensen 2013). Most recently, Azarmsa and Cong (2020) explore how a combination of information design and security design can generate more information for both investors and entrepreneurs in relationship lending and venture capital.

In addition to considering the social value of innovation, it is also important to understand the economic incentives for venture investing from the perspective of financiers and entrepreneurs. Toward this end, many studies consider the risk-return trade-offs in venture investing (Korteweg and Sorensen 2017; Cochrane 2005; Gompers and Lerner 2000). One set of these focuses on evaluating the persistence of investment performance at the level of the fund (Kaplan and Schoar 2005; Harris et al. 2020), individual partner (Ewens and Rhodes-Kropf 2015), or deal (Nanda, Samila, and Sorenson 2020). Recent debates have centered on luck versus skill in VC performance, taking into consideration the endogenous nature of deal flows (M. Sørensen 2007), and the interaction of flows with fund manager contracts (Cong and Xiao 2022). Overall, related studies find persistent outperformance in the VC industry, with managerial skill and endogenous deal flows both playing a role. However, debates continue concerning whether venture capital outperforms other asset classes after adjusting for risk. Relatively less explored is the value proposition of ventures from an entrepreneur's perspective.

To better understand the returns to financing innovation and how financiers add value beyond capital provision, researchers have investigated what exactly venture capitalists do. A key early study is that of Kaplan and Strömberg (2004), who focus on contracting-related benefits. More recent studies have discussed the decision-making process of a typical VC fund (Gompers et al. 2020), as well as valuation issues that venture capitalists often face (Gornall and Strebulaev 2020).

One particularly important decision for financiers is the design of their exit strategy. It is well known that younger VC firms have a tendency to rush the incubation period and thus underprice the initial public offerings (IPOs), in order to build their reputation and improve prospects for future fundraising (this phenomenon is described in the literature as "grandstanding"; see, e.g., Gompers 1995; Grenadier and

Malenko 2011). Equally interesting is the process by which venture firms gradually transfer public shares to their investors (Gompers and Lerner 2000). On balance, alternative exit strategies and reasons for failure are relatively understudied areas of venture investing, with Puri and Zarutskie (2012) being a notable exception.

Private VC firms are not the only source of VC funding for early and mid-stage entrepreneurs. A few papers contrast VC to other alternative funding sources such as bank lending (Landier 2003) and angel investors (Chemmanur and Chen 2014; Kerr, Lerner, and Schoar 2014; Prowse 1998). Another increasingly important funding source is corporate VC by more established firms. Corporate VC allows for strategic venture investing and often brings the benefits of vertical integration (Hellmann 2002). It can also help attract and retain talent (De Bettignies and Chemla 2008). Gompers and Lerner (2000) provide an overview of early corporate VC efforts. Government VC, meanwhile, most often finances social projects and encourages innovation, especially in developing economies (Zhang and Mayes 2018). Other forms of crowd-based entrepreneurial financing are also emerging (e.g., Cong, Li, and Wang 2021; Cong, Tang, Xie, and Miao 2021), but are subject to regulatory uncertainty.

In sum, three key forces shape the economics of entrepreneurial innovation and financing: (1) the non-rival nature of the output, (2) the high degree of uncertainty associated with the process, and (3) the large potential for agency conflicts between the entrepreneur and financier, arising from information asymmetry and moral hazard issues. Many existing regulations on patent protection, government subsidies, and tax incentives can be seen as efforts to mitigate negative externalities (market failures) associated with these economic forces. Likewise, the rise of the modern-day VC fund, with its focus on general partners who possess deep entrepreneurial expertise, can be viewed as a natural market response to the challenges engendered by these forces. Finally, although not the focus of this book, the advancement of digital infrastructure, big data analytics, and financial technology also offers novel perspectives and potential solutions concerning these issues (Huang et al. 2019; Cong, Ponticelli, Yang, and Zhang 2020).

Institutions, Entrepreneurship, and Innovation

In this book, we first emphasize the crucial role of institutions in affecting innovation and entrepreneurship. Some pivotal institutional themes concerning innovation include market freedom versus government regulation in promoting innovation and entrepreneurship, the market-oriented model versus state-driven model, lab studies versus more commercial research, how to raise innovative human capital through education, good public policies to support innovation, the creation of an innovation-friendly social environment, and how to mitigate loss induced by technological changes.

Another significant theme of this book hinges on the university, innovative human capital, and the transfer of knowledge from lab to industry. The countries we examine are all eager to develop entrepreneurial universities in which the human and other resources of industry, research labs, firms, and investors are closely integrated. These universities are also responsible for accelerating the process of innovation, from research findings to commercial applications, as well as for offering entrepreneurship programs that train college graduates to become better future innovators. This book presents a case study of Tsinghua University in China to exemplify the nation's endeavors to establish globally leading entrepreneurial hubs. Starting in 1995, Japan launched a series of policies and intellectual property reforms to encourage preeminent scientists to cooperate or even partner with entrepreneurs. Interestingly, these three countries share Confucian social values of obeying authority and respecting traditions. Data from Korea show that even within such social cultures, the economic returns to innovative thoughts and creativity in the labor market increase over time. Nevertheless, the strong presence of public-sector and monopolistic, large corporations in Korea are shown to reduce innovation.

This book also discusses the role of public policies in promoting innovation, especially those focused on human capital, innovation financing, and educational systems. Differences in policies' focus and regulatory intensity could easily affect the growth pattern and composition of industrial innovation. Many authors in this volume share a pro-market stance on innovation and warn readers of the potential unintended effects of interventions. One author urges regulators to notice each venture's strategies for entering the market and impose fewer limits on its subsequent scaling choices. To make social environments conducive to innovation, policies should intervene less and foster different kinds of human capital: cultivating the creativity of select managerial talent and raising the technology literacy of the general labor force should be given equal significance. Last but not least, several authors agree that government regulations should be loosened or more carefully designed to license innovative start-ups more easily and to grant new capital easier access to markets. Such reforms would allow entrepreneurs to succeed through acquisition or IPO, and to gracefully fail if necessary.

Innovation in Asia

This book contains three parts, discussing the major forces driving entrepreneurial innovation in Asia. The first part explores the foundations of innovation. In chapter 2, Charles Eesley, Lijie Zhou, and You (Willow) Wu argue that technological innovation is mainly driven by market competition and new entrants that challenge the status quo in terms of market share, ideas, and organizational structure. The authors explain how institutions, both physical and normative, can alter a part of the overall market structure and in turn spur innovation. Beyond this, the authors challenge some often misleading conventional wisdom concerning innovation, such as the view that the only way to promote innovation is to lower barriers to entry. Instead, market mechanisms and creative education systems are the main drivers of innovation, dwarfing the achievements of both state and corporate-driven innovation models. In particular, an institutional approach involving formal social institutions such as research universities, innovative industries, and tech firms is indispensable for innovation. Meanwhile, the business environment, government constraints, policies, financial regulations, and partnerships also spur or impede innovation. Changes in relevant institutions might lead to incentives, opportunities, cooperation, and open access. Interestingly, the authors compare the market-oriented innovation model of Silicon Valley with that of China, which shows clear signs of a planned economy and leaves little room for the private sector. This chapter offers a good start to understanding the intricate relationships between innovation, institutions, and entrepreneurship.

In chapter 3, David H. Hsu argues that for a growing venture to proliferate and expand without being hampered, improving its products is not enough. Strategies employed to enter the market will also affect how ventures choose to further expand their business. Based on a critical examination of previous theories on venture scaling and case studies of Foxconn, Amazon, Uber, and Netflix, Hsu identifies two entry strategies, cooperative and competitive. Ventures opting for a cooperative strategy will work together with incumbent firms to innovate, usually adding value to existing products. Spawning partnered innovation requires support from public policies to protect intellectual property and business secrets. In contrast to a cooperative strategy, entering the market through a competitive strategy will very likely disrupt incumbent firms' original plan for innovation, in that latecomers' new technologies are very likely to exceed the efficiency and quality of their predecessors. However, if barriers or prices for entering incumbent industries are too high, entrants might divert to less explored fields. Thus, strategies of market entry decide scaling directions across three dimensions: expand within the original industry, expand outside the original industry, and reach out geographically to another country/area. Government policies are mediators of this process, as policy interventions can easily make a difference in the supply of managerial talent for firms seeking to scale as well as in potential investors' value assessment of ventures in this area. Overall, this chapter confirms the power of ventures' market entry strategies in determining their later scaling paths. Two critical recommendations are offered to policymakers seeking to promote entrepreneurial development: respect the variability of scaling directions and cultivate more managerial talent. A typology of entry strategies is another important contribution of this chapter, and the author sorts out related concepts like disruptive and greenfield entry.

The second part of the book has five chapters, examining entrepreneurship education in Asia. In the fourth chapter, Tatsuo Sasaki, Hiromi S. Nagane, Yuta Fukudome, and Kanetaka M. Maki consider the fruits of Japan's innovation policies launched in and after 1995. These aimed to institutionalize collaboration between industry and academia, give more autonomy to national universities in their innovative research projects, and grant college-based scientists rights to obtain patents. The authors propose that analyzing publications and citations alone is not enough to trace all the technology transfers from labs to companies, so they use a new data set to depict the network connections between outstanding university-based scientists who significantly contribute to business, corporate researchers, and collaborators from research institutes. They find that Japan's innovation policies successfully attracted far more private capital influx in frontier research, and star scientists became more active in transferring knowledge to industries and establishing university-originated start-ups. Japan's key star scientists mainly come from physical and biological sciences; very few are computer scientists. This unbalanced development points to the challenges faced by innovative firms, which are dissected in chapter 9.

In the fifth chapter, Jin-Yeong Kim examines the matrix of factors that might affect Korean college graduates' innovative human capital, measured by a self-evaluation of their ability to find new ways of solving problems or raising new questions. Korean society is widely known as valuing collectivism, discipline, and hierarchy. The inculcation and reinforcement of these values not only happen in school curriculums; workplaces, too, are very eager to turn young graduates into reliable and conforming workers. When the engine of economic growth shifts from imitation to innovation, the importance of educational reforms cannot be underrated. But armed with a data set involving different cohorts, Kim is able to go beyond education level to point out the continuity from college choice, to first job, to occupational type, to later stages of career development. In this sense, the educational and labor markets are both taken into account and given equal importance in the analysis. In sum, the author has two major findings: (1) the cohort effect suggests that economic returns on creativity grow as Korean college graduates stay longer in the labor market, though this relationship is not visible at the beginning of their careers; and (2) self-evaluation of one's creativity is positively related to research and teaching jobs, higher degrees, and negatively related to public sector jobs and larger firm size.

In chapter 6, Zhou Zhong, Fei Yan, Chao Zhang, and Jizhen Li propose a new concept of entrepreneurial university education in Asia through a case study of Tsinghua University in Beijing. Compared with traditional universities, entrepreneurial universities connect more seamlessly with industry and government, shaping a self-strengthening ecosystem conducive to innovation. Centered on the university, people in this network of innovation and entrepreneurship can share resources, exchange ideas, raise funding, start companies, speed career development, and so on. As a result, the distance from lab to campus to market to innovative community is significantly shortened. Detailed examples in the middle of this chapter will show readers how advanced theories of the entrepreneurial university materialized into burgeoning school projects and enterprises, cultivating the next generation of entrepreneurs and supporting them in their efforts to create and grow new companies with financial, legal, managerial, and technical services.

In the seventh chapter, Rafiq Dossani proposes an economic growth theory that manufacturing and service sectors are mutually reinforcing, both bolstered by the openness of an economy and the size of its professional workforce. Specifically, Dossani notices that India's growth in manufacturing has not kept step with its rise in the service sector. Employing macroeconomic data from the World Bank, the author explains why India's underperforming services such as banking and telecommunications lack innovation and added value. Overlooking the importance of the service sector for decades, India still falls short in subsectors such as banking and logistics, whereas it has created a globally enviable information technology industry. Its service sector growth has fallen far behind other Asian countries such as China and Japan. The peculiarity lies in India's low-quality human capital, which arises from fragmentation and imbalances in its educational system engendered by longtime wresting between the federal government and states. India's remarkable research universities, directly sponsored by New Delhi, cannot cover up the failures of its tattered pre-college education delivered by individual states. The author also draws a comparison between India and its competitive neighbor China, whose high-end service sector took off after foreign investors transferred their knowledge to Chinese partners in the 1990s. Dossani finds that China's unprecedented growth in the high-end service sector is also made possible by its well-developed physical infrastructure, export-oriented manufacturing, and reliable human capital, none of which India possessed before the late 1990s. Considering the dilemma of India's service sector, Dossani offers a few suggestions for policymakers on how to direct the manufacturing and service sectors to become better drivers of India's economic growth. Overall, this chapter contributes to academic interest in India's economic development and helps us understand the mutually reinforcing relation between manufacturing and services.

In chapter 8, Mohan Kankanhalli and Bernard Yeung share their views on social changes brought by cutting-edge artificial intelligence and provide practical suggestions for corporations, educational institutes, and governments to better adapt to societies where humans and AI coexist. First of all, the authors agree that AI significantly outperforms humans in mechanistic and repetitive work that involves no cognitive functions such as emotions and creativity. Although AI at its current stage can easily imitate human biases or cognitive errors, there is consensus that it can greatly optimize the decision-making process and reduce costs. The authors suggest that corporations not only develop a collective AI culture but also try to avoid misuse that might contaminate corporate culture, especially in large, data-intensive corporations. To generate a more AI-savvy workforce in the future, government and business owners are responsible for promoting data and technology literacy among employees without sacrificing their innovative and leadership thinking, which are usually trade-offs in the process of acquiring machine intelligence. The case of Singapore is used to illustrate how public policies could well respond to the brave new world of AI. As a country embracing cultural diversity, Singapore carefully balances the government's regulatory and leadership roles with market autonomy in technology development. In face of economic anxiety that AI might cause massive unemployment, the Singaporean government strives to foster an innovative social culture and support its citizens to develop lifelong learning habits to embrace technological changes.

The third part contains four chapters, analyzing financing policies for entrepreneurship and innovation enterprises in Asia. In chapter 9, Takeo Hoshi and Kenji Kushida present their findings from a study of abundant data retrieved from industry reports, academic papers, and government policy documents. These data, in tandem with their meticulous analysis, show the vicissitudes of Japan's VC market. Japan is traditionally viewed as one of the most innovative countries, with tech companies that are ideal targets for investors. But in this chapter, the authors reveal the largest challenge facing the financing of radical innovation in Japan, which is the dominance of large banks in its financial order. The reliance on collateralization prevents these banks from taking a risk on start-ups, which are rarely profitable. Despite this restriction, Japan's VC firms are steadily growing and have developed several characteristics distinct from their American counterparts in Silicon Valley. Among these, the authors point to the increasing number of independent VCs not controlled by large firms, the flourishing university-based VCs, and an emerging start-up equity market that serves as a gateway to the formal stock market. This chapter informs us how far-reaching path dependence in industrial policies could affect this country's financial order and innovation.

In the tenth chapter, Hicheon Kim, Dohyeon Kim, and He Soung Ahn delineate the overall picture of Korea's innovative market. Like its economic growth model, Korea's innovation is mainly driven and financed by several government departments. While government investment corrects some market failures in research and development, it has also resulted in cumbersome bureaucracy, overly stringent regulation, and too-generous subsidies to inefficient firms. Besides these institutional factors, *chaebols*—large corporations that rose rapidly during Korea's economic take-off—control excessive market and social resources. The vigilant government imposes strict regulations on large corporations' acquisitions of start-ups as well as their participation in

VC investments. As a result, large corporations are unwilling to inject capital in the country's start-up ecosystem or even promote innovation by themselves. The lethargy of large corporations has negative spillover effects, as new generations are more likely to spend their careers in these corporations than take the risk of starting something themselves. This chapter is a must-read piece to understand how a government's regulation of corporate finance and the capital market could obstruct the growth of innovative entrepreneurship.

In chapter 11, Lin William Cong, Charles M. C. Lee, Yuanyu Qu, and Tao Shen examine the Achilles' heel of innovation and entrepreneurship in China: that is, the difficulty of financing them. The authors first note two central characteristics of the Chinese capital market, the incomplete nature of its markets and the prominence of government. In particular, overly rigorous IPO regulations hamper the formation of a healthy investment environment for innovative entrepreneurship and favor those enterprises with more political capital and ability to navigate red tape. Nevertheless, the authors also point out the quick regulatory adjustments and the promising side of China's innovative private technology firms, given the sheer volume of VC funding in them. Overall, this chapter is a gateway to policy analysis of Chinese IPO regulation. The authors give a thorough and exhaustive review of the existing literature on the subject and base their conclusions on rich data sources. Their comparison of China's internal stock market and the performance of Chinese firms in overseas stock markets is thought-provoking.

In the last chapter, Dinsha Mistree uses a national economic survey of India to illustrate the inefficiency of its research funding system. The author points out the dilemma of India's government research laboratories: every year, their patents and publications are dwarfed by those of universities, which receive far less government funding. Government researchers, meanwhile, are very unlikely to cooperate with researchers affiliated with nongovernmental institutes. Due in part to this inefficiency, India has certainly fallen behind other emerging innovative economies in Asia, such as Korea and Singapore. And reforms are never easy, as the government has to face backlash from stakeholders with strong vested interest in government labs, as well as hard-line nationalists who vehemently oppose adopting the American, merit-based evaluation system. Mistree suggests that the Indian government try to encourage more collaborative research between different sectors and adopt Western models in such a way as to mitigate cultural conflict.

Interestingly, the author discusses Chinese and Indian forms of traditional herbal medicine to illuminate the heated clash in both countries between traditional values and modernization initiatives.

References

Admati, Anat R., and Paul Pfleiderer. 1994. "Robust Financial Contracting and the Role of Venture Capitalists." *Journal of Finance* 49 (2): 371–402.

Akerlof, George. 1970. "The Market for Lemons: Quality Uncertainty and the Market Mechanism." *Quarterly Journal of Economics* 84 (3): 488–500.

Amit, Raphael, Eitan Muller, and Iain Cockburn. 1995. "Opportunity Costs and Entrepreneurial Activity." *Journal of Business Venturing* 10 (2): 95–106.

Arrow, Kenneth. 1962. "Economic Welfare and the Allocation of Resources for Invention." In *The Rate and Direction of Inventive Activity: Economic and Social Factors*, edited by Universities-National Bureau Committee for Economic Research, Committee on Economic Growth of the Social Science Research Council, 609–26. New Jersey, NY: Princeton University Press.

Azarmsa, Ehsan, and Lin William Cong. 2020. "Persuasion in Relationship Finance." *Journal of Financial Economics* 138 (3): 818–37.

Baron, Robert A. 2000. "Counterfactual Thinking and Venture Formation: The Potential Effects of Thinking about 'What Might Have Been'." *Journal of Business Venturing* 15 (1): 79–91.

Baumol, William J. 2005. "Education for Innovation: Entrepreneurial Breakthroughs versus Corporate Incremental Improvements." In *Innovation Policy and the Economy*, vol. 5, edited by Adam B. Jaffe, Josh Lerner, and Scott Stern, 33–56. Cambridge, MA: MIT Press.

Bergemann, Dirk, and Ulrich Hege. 1998. "Venture Capital Financing, Moral Hazard, and Learning." *Journal of Banking and Finance* 22 (6–8): 703–35.

Berglöf, Erik. 1994. "A Control Theory of Venture Capital Finance." *Journal of Law, Economics, and Organization* 10 (2): 247–67.

Bernstein, Shai, Xavier Giroud, and Richard Townsend. 2016. "The Impact of Venture Capital Monitoring." *Journal of Finance* 71 (4): 1591–622.

Blau, David M. 1987. "A Time-Series Analysis of Self-Employment in the United States." *Journal of Political Economy* 95 (3): 445–67.

Bramwell, Allison, and David A. Wolfe. 2008. "Universities and Regional Economic Development: The Entrepreneurial University of Waterloo." *Research Policy* 37 (8): 1175–87.

Chan, Yuk-Shee. 1983. "On the Positive Role of Financial Intermediation in Allocation of Venture Capital in a Market with Imperfect Information." *Journal of Finance* 38 (5): 1543–68.

Chemmanur, Thomas J., and Zhaohui Chen. 2014. "Venture Capitalists versus Angels: The Dynamics of Private Firm Financing Contracts." *Review of Corporate Finance Studies* 3 (1–2): 39–86.

Cochrane, John H. 2005. "The Risk and Return of Venture Capital." *Journal of Financial Economics* 75 (1): 3–52.

Cong, Lin W., and Yizhou Xiao. 2022. "Persistent Blessings of Luck: Theory and an Application to Venture Capital." *Review of Financial Studies* 35 (3):1183–1221.

Cong, Lin W., Danxia Xie, and Longtian Zhang. 2021. "Knowledge Accumulation, Privacy, and Growth in a Data Economy." *Management Science* 67 (10): 6480–92.

Cong, Lin W., Ye Li, and Neng Wang. 2021. "Token-Based Platform Finance." *Journal of Financial Economics*. Published ahead of print, October 12, 2021. https://doi.org/10.1016/j.jfineco.2021.10.002.

Cong, Lin W., Jacopo Ponticelli, Xiaohan Yang, and Xiaobo Zhang. 2020. "Impact of Digital Platforms on Entrepreneurship and Industrialization: Evidence from E-Commerce Expansions in China" Working paper.

Cong, Lin W., Ke Tang, Danxia Xie, and Qi Miao. 2021. "Asymmetric Cross-Side Network Effects on Financial Platforms: Theory and Evidence from Marketplace Lending." Working paper. http://dx.doi.org/10.2139/ssrn.3461893.

Cornelli, Francesca, and Oved Yosha. 2003. "Stage Financing and the Role of Convertible Securities." *Review of Economic Studies* 70 (1): 1–32.

Cumming, Douglas, and Eileen Fischer. 2012. "Publicly Funded Business Advisory Services and Entrepreneurial Outcomes." *Research Policy* 41: 467–81.

Dahlstrand, Åsa Lindholm. 1997. "Growth and Inventiveness in Technology-Based Spin-Off Firms." *Research Policy* 26 (3): 331–44.

De Bettignies, Jean-Etienne, and Gilles Chemla. 2008. "Corporate Venturing, Allocation of Talent, and Competition for Star Managers." *Management Science* 54 (3): 505–21.

Douglas, Evan J., and Dean A. Shepherd. 2000. "Entrepreneurship as a Utility Maximizing Response." *Journal of Business Venturing* 15 (3): 231–51.

Dunn, Thomas, and Douglas Holtz-Eakin. 2000. "Financial Capital, Human Capital, and the Transition to Self-Employment: Evidence from Intergenerational Links." *Journal of Labor Economics* 18 (2): 282–305.

Eesley, Charles, and Yong Suk Lee. 2020. "Do University Entrepreneurship Programs Promote Entrepreneurship?" *Strategic Management Journal* 42 (4): 833–61.

Eggleston, Karen, Joon-Shik Park, and Gi-Wook Shin. 2021. *Demographics and Innovation in the Asia-Pacific*. Stanford, CA: Shorenstein Asia-Pacific Research Center.

Ewens, Michael, and Matthew Rhodes-Kropf. 2015. "Is a VC Partnership Greater than the Sum of Its Partners?" *Journal of Finance* 70 (3): 1081–113.

Ewens, Michael, Matthew Rhodes-Kropf, and Ilya Strebulaev. 2016. "Insider Financing and Venture Capital Returns." Research Paper No. 16-45, Stanford University Graduate School of Business, Stanford, CA.

Gompers, Paul A. 1995. "Optimal Investment, Monitoring, and the Staging of Venture Capital." *Journal of Finance* 50 (5): 1461–89.

Gompers, Paul A., and Josh Lerner. 2000. "The Determinants of Corporate Venture Capital Success: Organizational Structure, Incentives, and Complementarities." In *Concentrated Corporate Ownership*, edited by Randall Morck, 17–50. Chicago, IL: University of Chicago Press.

Gompers, Paul A., Will Gornall, Steven N. Kaplan, and Ilya A. Strebulaev. 2020. "How Do Venture Capitalists Make Decisions?" *Journal of Financial Economics* 135 (1): 169–90.

Gornall, Will, and Ilya A. Strebulaev. 2020. "Squaring Venture Capital Valuations with Reality." *Journal of Financial Economics* 135 (1): 120–43.

Grenadier, Steven R., and Andrey Malenko. 2011. "Real Options Signaling Games with Applications to Corporate Finance." *Review of Financial Studies* 24 (12): 3993–4036.

Guerrero, Maribel, James A. Cunningham, and David Urbano. 2015. "Economic Impact of Entrepreneurial Universities' Activities: An Exploratory Study of the United Kingdom." *Research Policy* 44 (3): 748–64.

Harris, Robert S., Tim Jenkinson, Steven N. Kaplan, and Rüdiger Stucke. 2020. "Has Persistence Persisted in Private Equity? Evidence from Buyout and Venture Capital Funds." Fama-Miller Working Paper, Chicago Booth, Chicago, IL.

Hellmann, Thomas. 1998. "The Allocation of Control Rights in Venture Capital Contracts." *RAND Journal of Economics* 29 (1): 57–76.

———. 2002. "A Theory of Strategic Venture Investing." *Journal of Financial Economics* 64 (2): 285–314.

Hellmann, Thomas, and Manju Puri. 2002. "Venture Capital and the Professionalization of Start-Up Firms: Empirical Evidence." *Journal of Finance* 57 (1): 169–97.

Hochberg, Yael V. 2011. "Venture Capital and Corporate Governance in the Newly Public Firm." *Review of Finance* 16 (2): 429–80.

Hochberg, Yael V., Alexander Ljungqvist, and Annette Vissing-Jørgensen. 2013. "Informational Holdup and Performance Persistence in Venture Capital." *Review of Financial Studies* 27 (1): 102–52.

Hsu, David, Edward Roberts, and Charles Eesley. 2007. "Entrepreneurs from Technology-Based Universities: Evidence from MIT." *Research Policy* 36 (5): 768–88.

Huang, Yi, Harald Hau, Hongzhe Shan, and Zixia Sheng. 2019. "Fintech Credit, Financial Inclusion and Entrepreneurial Growth." Working paper. https://efmaefm.org/oefmameetings/efma%20an nual%20meetings/2018-Milan/phd/001.pdf.

Iyigun, Murat, and Ann Owen. 1998. "Risk, Entrepreneurship and Human Capital Accumulation." *American Economic Review* 88 (2): 454–57.

Jensen, Michael C., and William H. Meckling. 1976. "Theory of the Firm: Managerial Behavior, Agency Costs and Ownership Structure." *Journal of Financial Economics* 3 (4): 305–60.

Kaplan, Steven N., and Per Strömberg 2004. "Characteristics, Contracts, and Actions: Evidence from Venture Capitalist Analyses." *Journal of Finance* 59 (5): 2177–210.

Kaplan, Steven N., and Antoinette Schoar. 2005. "Private Equity Performance: Returns, Persistence, and Capital Flows." *Journal of Finance* 60 (4): 1791–823.

Kerr, William R., Josh Lerner, and Antoinette Schoar. 2014. "The Consequences of Entrepreneurial Finance: A Regression Discontinuity Analysis." *Review of Financial Studies* 27 (1): 20–55.

Korteweg, Arthur, and Morten Sorensen. 2017. "Skill and Luck in Private Equity Performance." *Journal of Financial Economics* 124 (3): 535–62.

Kortum, Samuel, and Josh Lerner. 2000. "Assessing the Contribution of Venture Capital to Innovation." *RAND Journal of Economics* 31 (4): 674–92.

Landier, Augustin. 2003. "Start-Up Financing: From Banks to Venture Capital." Working paper. https://pages.stern.nyu.edu/~alandier/pdfs/bank_vc.pdf.

Lazear, Edward P. 2005. "Entrepreneurship." *Journal of Labor Economics* 23 (4): 649–80.

Lee, Yong Suk. 2017. "Entrepreneurship, Small Businesses, and Economic Growth in Cities." *Journal of Economic Geography* 17 (2): 311–43.

Lee, Yong Suk, and Charles Eesley. 2018. "The Persistence of Entrepreneurship and Innovative Immigrants." *Research Policy* 47 (6): 1032–44.

Lee, Yong Suk, Takeo Hoshi, and Gi-Wook Shin. 2020. *Shifting Gears in Innovation Policy: Strategies from Asia.* Stanford, CA: Shorenstein Asia-Pacific Research Center.

Leland, Hayne E., and David H. Pyle. 1977. "Informational Asymmetries, Financial Structure, and Financial Intermediation." *Journal of Finance* 32 (2): 371–87.

Lerner, Josh. 1994. "Venture Capitalists and the Decision to Go Public." *Journal of Financial Economics* 35 (3): 293–316.

———. 1995. "Venture Capitalists and the Oversight of Private Firms." *Journal of Finance* 50 (1): 301–18.

Levesque, Moren, and Maria Minniti. 2006. "The Effect of Aging on Entrepreneurial Behavior." *Journal of Business Venturing* 21 (2): 177–94.

Lindquist, Matthew J., Joeri Sol, and Mirjam Van Praag. 2015. "Why Do Entrepreneurial Parents Have Entrepreneurial Children?" *Journal of Labor Economics* 33 (2): 269–96.

Manso, Gustavo. 2011. "Motivating Innovation." *Journal of Finance* 66 (5): 1823–60.

McClelland, David. 1961. *The Achieving Society.* Princeton, NJ: Van Nostrand.

Mitchell, Ronald K., Brock Smith, Kristie W. Seawright, and Eric A. Morse. 2000. "Cross-Cultural Cognitions and the Venture Creation Decision." *Academy of Management Journal* 43 (5): 974–93.

Nanda, Ramana, Sampsa Samila, and Olav Sorenson. 2020. "The Persistent Effect of Initial Success: Evidence from Venture Capital." *Journal of Financial Economics* 137 (1): 231–48.

Oliver, Amalya. 2004. "Biotechnology Entrepreneurial Scientists and Their Collaborations." *Research Policy* 33 (4): 583–97.

Peterman, Nicole E., and Jessica Kennedy. 2003. "Enterprise Education: Influencing Students' Perceptions of Entrepreneurship." *Entrepreneurship Theory and Practice* 28 (2): 129–44.

Prowse, Stephen. 1998. "Angel Investors and the Market for Angel Investments." *Journal of Banking and Finance* 22 (6–8): 785–92.

Puri, Manju, and Rebecca Zarutskie. 2012. "On the Life Cycle Dynamics of Venture-Capital and Non-Venture-Capital Financed Firms." *Journal of Finance* 67 (6): 2247–93.

Rajan, Raghuram. 2012. "Presidential Address: The Corporation in Finance." *Journal of Finance* 67 (4): 1173–217.

Sahlman, William A. 1990. "The Structure and Governance of Venture-Capital Organizations." *Journal of Financial Economics* 27 (2): 473–521.

Schumpeter, Joseph A. 1934. *The Theory of Economic Development: An Inquiry into Profits, Capital, Credit, Interest, and the Business Cycle*, Vol. 55. New Jersey, NY: Transaction Publishers.

———. 1942. *Capitalism, Socialism and Democracy*. New York: Harper and Brothers.

Sørensen, Jesper B. 2007. "Closure and Exposure: Mechanisms in the Intergenerational Transmission of Self-Employment." In *The Sociology of Entrepreneurship*, edited by Martin Ruef and Michael Lounsbury, 83–124. Bingley, UK: Emerald Group Publishing Limited.

Sørensen, Morten. 2007. "How Smart Is Smart Money? A Two-Sided Matching Model of Venture Capital." *Journal of Finance* 62 (6): 2725–62.

Souitaris, Vangelis, Stefania Zerbinati, and Andreas Al-Laham. 2007. "Do Entrepreneurship Programmes Raise Entrepreneurial Intention of Science and Engineering Students? The Effect of Learning, Inspiration and Resources." *Journal of Business Venturing* 22 (4): 566–91.

Stiglitz, Joseph E., and Andrew Weiss. 1981. "Credit Rationing in Markets with Imperfect Information." *American Economic Review* 71 (3): 393–410.

Tian, Xuan, and Tracy Yue Wang. 2011. "Tolerance for Failure and Corporate Innovation." *Review of Financial Studies* 27 (1): 211–55.

Vesper, Karl H., and Wiliam B. Gartner. 1997. "Measuring Progress in Entrepreneurship Education." *Journal of Business Venturing* 12 (5): 403–21.

Von Graevenitz, Georg, Dietmar Harhoff, and Richard Weber. 2010. "The Effects of Entrepreneurship Education." *Journal of Economic Behavior and Organization* 76 (1): 90–112.

Zhang, Yuejia, and David Geoffrey Mayes. 2018. "The Performance of Governmental Venture Capital Firms: A Life Cycle Perspective and Evidence from China." *Pacific-Basin Finance Journal* 48 (April): 162–85.

I. Foundations of Innovation

2 Fostering Entrepreneurship and Innovation

Education, Human Capital,
and the Institutional Environment

Charles Eesley, Lijie Zhou, and You (Willow) Wu

This chapter focuses on the role of education and the regulatory environment in fostering innovation and entrepreneurship. The main message is that innovation originates from education and research, and is driven by market competition and also the threat of competition from new start-up entrants. Competition, in turn, is made possible by a cluster of laws and financial regulations. Thus, creative education, innovative research, legal institutions, and financial regulations function together to enable a highly dynamic and innovative economy.

The flow of this chapter is as follows. First, we discuss institutional support of innovative education and research. More specifically, we analyze the roles of collaborative knowledge building, flexibility, improvisation, and action learning in education. Government funding for research and development (R&D), the tenure system, and technology transfer are vital for innovative research. Then we discuss the kind of institutional environment that supports entrepreneurship and innovation with high-level human capital.

Education for Innovation

The entrepreneurial environment is shaped by a variety of institutions, among which educational institutions play a key role. It is widely acknowledged that a core input into innovation is knowledge, and accordingly the key task for educators is to prepare learners for innovative thinking (OECD 2000). In recent years, the burgeoning entrepreneurial centers, courses, and programs seen in universities the world over attach greater importance to entrepreneurial education. However, the specific mechanisms involved in entrepreneurship education and the impact of such training on subsequent rates of entrepreneurship or entrepreneurial performance are only beginning to be systematically studied (Eesley and Lee 2021).

Collaborative knowledge building

Innovation is not a result of individual inventions but more often of collaborative creation by teams of people working together. Scholars have discovered that the most important innovative insights typically come from collaborative teams (Farrell 2001; John-Steiner 2000; Sawyer 2003). That is partly a result of the complexity in society, where the most pressing problems (e.g., poverty, pollution, etc.) and unmet user needs are often out of the capacity of any one individual to solve. Empirical study shows that even single firms frequently innovate with some form of outside help (OECD 2000). For example, innovative ideas occur during teamwork or brainstorming. Companies often collaboratively come up with ideas and coordinate them in creating a single product. Customers and suppliers interact with companies to support such innovation.

While functionally diverse founding teams tend to exhibit higher performance, this may not be universally true. We find that diverse teams are likely to achieve high performance in a competitive commercialization environment. On the other hand, technically focused founding teams are aligned with a cooperative commercialization environment (Eesley, Hsu, and Roberts 2014). The findings also suggest that ventures cannot ignore founding team composition and expect to later professionalize top management teams to align with their strategy and environment.

Flexibility and improvisation

Institutional flexibility in education promotes individual interests, independent thinking, and entrepreneurial intentions, which are crucial for innovation. Flexibility is defined as the characteristics of institutions to permit choices. Universities provide a wide range of resources and allow the selection of a variety of courses to promote institutional flexibility. The emergence of online courses further promotes flexibility by providing more course choices. NovoEd, Coursera, and Udacity are examples of massive open online course platforms that provide a wide variety of courses for people around the world.

Flexibility in course selection promotes innovation and entrepreneurship for three main reasons. First, this flexibility helps students explore their interests in multidisciplinary studies and recombine knowledge to form innovative ideas. Second, exposure to a variety of courses fosters the habit of questioning underlying assumptions, which is crucial for unfolding alternative possibilities. Finally, giving choices to students implies confidence in their decision-making, which builds their self-efficacy and further inspires them to pursue their entrepreneurial intentions (Chen, Greene, and Crick 1998).

Flexibility in the education system may be extended from course selection to course design, in which improvisation plays a key role in fostering innovation. Research has demonstrated that unstructured group discussion or improvisation tends to promote group creativity and understanding (Sawyer and Berson 2004). Unstructured improvisation leads to constructive learning for understanding, rather than memorization of facts (Bransford, Brown, and Cocking 2000). Constructive learning lays the foundation for innovation and entrepreneurship. Improvisational exercises are used in several professional development programs for teachers in the United States (Sawyer 2006). We also find that an entrepreneur mentor increases the likelihood of a student's decision to join a start-up, and this mentor effect is significantly stronger for students whose parents are not entrepreneurs (Eesley and Wang 2017). This is an important finding since intergenerational correlation in entrepreneurship is an often persistent driver of patterns of inequality in access to opportunities (Lee and Eesley 2018).

Action learning

Action learning is a combination of collaboration and improvisation. More specifically, action learning is a "continued process of learning and reflection with the support of a group of colleagues working on real issues" (McGill and Brockband 2003). By that definition, action learning shares similarities with "learning by doing," but differs in that it is a social process characterized by recognized ignorance. In other words, team members recognize that no one knows the answer but are all obliged to find it, and so they start to learn with one another (Pedler 2011). Action learning may also be regarded as a special form of learning by doing, or "learning by posing fresh questions" (Pedler 2011) rather than copying existing knowledge. This reflects the reality of entrepreneurship: often the surrounding situation is unknown and uncertain to all members of a venture.

Educational systems promote mastery of received knowledge, but also support exploration of the unknown (Baumol 2004). Action-learning methods have been popular in U.S business schools. One example is a mixed-team action-learning class at MIT, called the "Entrepreneurship Laboratory," or E-Lab, where students from all departments, ranging from management to science and engineering, form teams to deal with real-world problems in entrepreneurial organizations (Roberts and Eesley 2011). Students select from the problems presented by early-stage companies and each team works on "a problem that keeps the CEO up late at night" (Roberts and Eesley 2011) for an entire semester. While in class, students communicate, work on project analysis, client relationships, and market research, and share reports of ongoing progress with one another. In the process of action learning, the problems are new to everyone, and solutions arise among team members.

Innovative Research

David and Hall (2000) divide up the mechanisms flowing from public to private R&D according to three dimensions. First, they note that there are direct and indirect effects of public R&D. Direct effects include shifts in the demand and supply of tangible inputs used in the R&D process (scientists, engineers, and research tools). Indirect effects involve the intangible results of the R&D process. The indirect effects stem from the knowledge generated as a result of public R&D and the effects that knowledge has on the expected costs of privately funded R&D. Broadly, these are the "knowledge spillovers" that have spawned a large literature. To avoid crowding out private R&D funding, government funds should focus on basic science—the type of R&D in which companies are most likely to underinvest.[1]

---

[1] The direct and indirect effects are not mutually exclusive. For instance, knowledge spillovers will have an influence on the prices of inputs into the research process and new knowledge can become embedded in research tools.

Government funding for R&D

The second dimension is the mechanism through which public R&D expenditures are disbursed. When grant R&D is given, at least in U.S. practice, it is typically for exploratory research in university labs or national institutes. At the other end of the spectrum is contract R&D, which is often given to private firms or government labs, and typically for a more defined mission of one of the public agencies (Department of Energy, Department of Defense, etc.). Contract R&D, in the sense that it transfers funds from the government to private firms, relaxes financial constraints on firms; however, the government may not act in the same way or with the same expertise expected of profit-seeking financial intermediaries. Thus, it is more likely to be wasted on bad projects, generate excess capacity, and crowd out private investment than is grant R&D.

Third, the effects of public R&D expenditures may be felt in different ways according to different lags. For example, the contemporaneous effects of increased public R&D funding may be to increase the demand for scientists (or other research inputs) in a certain specialty, increasing their salaries and thus the labor costs to private firms (Goolsbee 1998). The short-term effect could be that private firms react to higher labor costs by decreasing the number of scientists hired. However, with a longer lag, supply will catch up with the increased demand and salaries may fall, particularly if public demand subsequently decreases or shifts to new areas. In addition, the knowledge generated by these scientists may (with a lag) increase the productivity of more applied private R&D, resulting in private R&D funding increases. David and Hall (2000) walk through several examples of the complex interactions between short-run and more dynamic effects along the three dimensions. For instance, public R&D could also be interpreted by firms as a signal of future demand, resulting in contemporaneous increases in private R&D to build absorptive capacity and to take advantage of future demand (Cohen and Levinthal 1990). The overall message is a cautionary one, both in terms of the net impacts and also whether public R&D is likely to stimulate or crowd out private R&D funding. Nonetheless, the analysis supports the idea that if complementary effects are to be found, it most likely in grant-based R&D and with a considerable lag. Contract-based public R&D funding for specific technologies or industries (i.e., "picking winners") is often a very poor choice, and should be reserved for use only when it is clearly in the national interest.

Academic intellectual freedom and the tenure system

Created by contract and implemented by institutional regulations (Byrne 1989), the tenure system defends academic freedom (Brown and Kurland 1990) and therefore propels innovative research. Brewster (1972) describes tenure as "a guarantee of appointment until retirement age." Van Alstyne (1971) proposes that tenure only prevents "dismissal without adequate cause" after a specified lengthy period of probationary service. During six years as a junior faculty member, an assistant professor usually works to meet the criteria for the granting of tenure. Among the key criteria are success in publishing research findings in journals judged by academic peers and the ability to teach undergraduate and graduate students. In top research universities, the criteria are heavily weighted toward research publications and teaching loads are typically light, with junior faculty teaching two to three courses that they are permitted to "stack" into a single semester to enable greater time to focus on research the rest of the year. Committee work is also kept to a minimum.

Although its efficiency remains disputable, the tenure system promotes independent thinking. The 1940 Statement of Association of American Colleges (Van Alstyne 1971) proclaims that tenure is a "means to certain ends" (Van Alstyne 1971), and specifically promotes (1) a sufficient degree of economic security and (2) freedom in teaching and research. First, as a social contract (Bowen and Schuster 1986, 35–44), tenure provides lifelong employment so that faculty can get on with their work without much interference. It is presumed that, after receiving tenure, a professor's intrinsic interest will continue to motivate further work. Second, the tenure system is essential to innovation. Carmichael (1988) argues, "without tenure, incumbents would never be willing to hire people who might turn out to be better than themselves." In sum, the assurance of economic stability, the mechanism of dynamic renewal, and long-term incentives result in academic freedom. Freedom of thinking is the foundation of innovative research.

Technology transfer

Technology transfer helps describe the bond between innovative research and high-tech startups. It also partly explains the success of some companies (e.g., Google) that build close ties with research universities. The mechanism of technology transfer is based on the interaction of research and industry. On one hand, university research is sometimes, though not always, motivated by a practical or scientifically challenging problem of industry. Chemical engineering, for example, originated from the problems that puzzled the early petroleum industry. On the other hand, industry benefits from the achievement of scientific research. Through faculty consulting or industrial affiliate programs, research results find their way to commercial application.

Institutions that promote technology transfer play a key role in bridging the gap between scientific research and commercial products. For example, the current MIT Technology Licensing Office website describes its mission as "to benefit the public by moving results of MIT research into societal use via technology licensing, through a process which is consistent with academic principles, demonstrates a concern for the welfare of students and faculty, and conforms to the highest ethical standards." Similarly, Stanford's Office of Technology Licensing outlines several proposals of best practices related to technology transfer as follows (Eesley and Miller 2018):

- Keep the technology transfer process close to the faculty.
- Transfer new technology to as many companies as possible.
- Negotiate agreements with long-term relationships in mind.
- Improve access to information for staff and inventors to expedite technology transfer.
- Encourage collaboration with other institutions by minimizing use of material transfer agreements.
- Manage the licensing process to lessen potential conflicts of interest.
- Facilitate the licensing of Stanford engineering inventions to high-tech companies.
- Assist other nonprofit organizations with licensing.

Institutions that facilitate technology transfer create an entrepreneurial ecosystem, which enables the flow of knowledge from research to industry. Technology transfer begins with an invention that may have commercial impact and an invention disclosure with a technology licensing office. For the inventions that are both patentable and have commercial potential, the office will judge the optimal route to commercialization. Basically, the decision between licensing to an existing firm or developing a start-up is grounded in both the characteristics of the technology and the inclination of inventors. When licensing to an existing firm, information is circulated, often through personal interactions that may include a corporate lab visit, faculty consultation, or the hiring of graduate candidates. For start-ups, both initial funding and mentoring are crucial for success. Universities may support these start-ups with equity investment, and faculty or alumni entrepreneurs may provide assistance in mentoring.

Innovation and entrepreneurship

Most scholars accept that entrepreneurial firms are more likely to introduce radical innovations (products and processes) than are large incumbents, and there is a large literature that reports on the innovation capacity of small compared with large firms. One research line focuses on the relationship between a company's size or age and its innovation capacity. The "incumbent's curse" (Chandy and Tellis 2000) is a common perception in the field of innovation. Huergo and Jaumandreu (2003) examine the impact of firm age on innovation (as reflected in productivity growth). Using plant-level productivity data, they find that "newborn firms tend to show higher rates of productivity growth which tend to converge to common growth rates." Balasubramanian and Lee (2008) draw similar conclusions based on the patents of public firms: their findings show that firm age is negatively related with technical quality; each additional year reduces the impact of a 10 percent increase in R&D intensity on firms' market value by over 3 percent.

Another research line focuses on the interplay between entry by new, more productive firms, on the one hand, and innovations and productivity improvements by existing firms, on the other. Evidence suggests that this interplay is important for productivity growth. Bartelsman and Doms (2000) document that the entry of new establishments/plants accounts for about 25 percent of average total factor productivity growth (which is thought to be mainly due to innovation) at the industry level, with the remaining productivity improvements accounted for by incumbent establishments. Aghion et al. (2005) examine how firms respond to the threat of competition from new entrants. Their findings show that technologically advanced firms and those located in regions with pro-business institutions are more likely to respond to the threat of entry by investing in new technologies and production processes. This further improves productivity across the entire industry.

Based on past research, we can conclude that entrepreneurial firms are important both because they tend to create radical new innovations themselves, and also because the competitive pressure they introduce forces incumbents to innovate. That is why we cannot talk about innovation without talking about policies to encourage the emergence of innovative entrepreneurial firms.

Chandy and Tellis (2000) point out that U.S. innovators are expected to differ from those in Japan and Western Europe. In the United States, small firms and new entrants are most likely to break ground. For one thing, U.S. popular culture celebrates the risk-taker: succeeding after a series of failures tends to enhance the glory of the U.S. entrepreneur. Beyond this, Chandy and Tellis argue that financial institutions play an important role in encouraging radical innovations among less-well-established firms in the United States, and more so than in Japan and Western Europe. Saxenian (1994) also argues that the United States has a more active venture capital market, which makes financing easier to obtain for less-established firms in the United States than in many other countries.

Acemoglu et al. (2013) determine that industrial policy that subsidizes either the R&D or the continued operation of incumbents reduces growth and welfare. For example, a subsidy of incumbent firms' R&D equivalent to 5 percent of gross domestic product reduces welfare by about 1.5 percent because it deters the entry of new and more innovative start-ups. By contrast, substantial improvements are possible if the continued operation of incumbents is taxed while R&D is subsidized. They further argue that subsidies to incumbents encourage the survival and expansion of these firms at the expense of potential high-tech entrants, and suggest that optimal policy encourages the exit of low-tech firms and supports the R&D of high-tech incumbents and new entrants.

State-driven innovation, rare in the United States, has been attempted in Japan and Western Europe in the past (Eberhart, Eesley, and Eisenhardt 2017; Eberhart and Eesley 2018). Fitzroy and Kraft (1991) find that government policies in Japan and Western Europe have traditionally favored technological innovation by large, established firms over small firms. Large incumbents in these countries enjoy financial and technological support that is unavailable to similar firms in the United

States (Magaziner and Patinkin 1989). Similarly, Chandy and Tellis (2000) reexamine the "incumbent's curse" using a historical analysis of a relatively large number of radical innovations. Their findings suggest that the "incumbent's curse" is less prevalent in recent times and, increasingly, incumbents are introducing more radical new products. One important reason may be that such firms have organizational climates that resemble those of small firms. The implication of their studies is that policymakers may encourage the dynamic organizational structure and strong technological capability required to keep large, incumbent organizations nimble and innovative. A state and corporate-driven model may fit more closely with the current institutional context in China. Nonetheless, it still requires a strong, market-based institutional environment that allows entry of entrepreneurial firms, protection of intellectual property, an independent judicial system, and contract enforcement. The state-driven model has a poor track record of success relative to the U.S. Silicon Valley model.

Innovation and institutions

The fundamental mechanism driving innovation is competition in the market. Over time, competition drives prices down and excess profits toward zero, requiring firms to innovate to differentiate their products from competitors. They thus offer new products and services that do not suffer (initially) from competition from other firms. The overarching model of the process of innovation is referred to as the linear model. Vannevar Bush, after the conclusion of World War II, is known for bringing the language of the linear model to the forefront of America's science and technology policy (Bush 2020). The linear model states that innovation begins with basic research, often in universities and government labs designed to create fundamental inventions and breakthroughs. This knowledge gained from basic R&D is then developed further via applied R&D (typically within companies) and once sufficiently developed is commercialized as products and services in the market. A relatively recent model of the innovation process is known as "user innovation," a term that highlights the fact that many innovations are actually first developed by users before being picked up by companies that then improve on the users' designs to manufacture a new product. The United States has a long history of independent inventors and entrepreneurs (Dahlin, Taylor, and Fichman 2004). The legal environment that supports innovation must foster their involvement in the processes of market competition, basic and applied R&D, and user innovation.

Entrepreneurship and institutions

Only relatively recently has entrepreneurship become a topic of policy debate. Much of this emphasis can be attributed to the internet boom in the Silicon Valley of the late 1990s. Before this, U.S. entrepreneurs were seen as needing neither official financial support nor specially designed regulation. Subsequently, opinions changed. Entrepreneurs needed to be regulated and restrained since they might disturb competitive equilibrium or harm consumers through low-quality products; and they needed to be offered financial support through programs such as those administered by the Small Business Administration since they were often capital constrained (Audretsch and Thurik 2004). Yet, with the technology boom in Silicon Valley and elsewhere, entrepreneurship came to be seen as closely linked to economic growth and as a driver of innovation and productivity improvements (Hwang and Powell 2009; Acs and Audretsch 1988; Oliner and Sichel 2000).

The replacement of old firms by new, more efficient and productive ones was found to be more important for the dynamism of the economy and for growth than were the improvement and upgrading of existing firms (Foster, Haltiwanger, and Syverson 2008; Carree and Thurik 2005). In particular, policymakers became more interested in entrepreneurship due to its role in increasing employment (Haltiwanger, Jarmin, and Miranda 2010). Yet, it is important to note that most of this increase in employment comes through young firms (start-ups) rather than through small firms (small and medium enterprises), and government policy often misses this important distinction.

The conventional wisdom now is that entrepreneurship is highly important; it is tightly linked to innovation, yet the risks involved lead to lower levels of entrepreneurship than are socially optimal and therefore it merits encouragement from policies. Around the world, policymakers seek to reduce the barriers, costs, and steps involved in starting new firms. Examples are easy to find and include Start-up Chile, Startup America, the Jobs Act in the United States, Skolkovo in Russia, Gründerland Deutschland in Germany, and Vinnova in Sweden. Many of these programs have two assumptions in common: first, that more entrepreneurship is better; and second, that subsidizing and simplifying the process of starting a firm is the best way to foster entrepreneurship.

Recent research casts serious doubt on these assumptions. And my own work and that of others suggests that alternative policy measures may be more effective. For example, in the process of comparing firms in and outside science parks in Beijing and across China, it becomes clear that institutional intermediaries are effective in helping entrepreneurs pursue government funding in developing economies (Armanios et al. 2017; Armanios and Eesley 2021).

Recent scholarship casts doubt on the effectiveness of many government efforts to foster entrepreneurship in the United States (Haltiwanger, Jarmin, and Miranda 2010; Reedy and Strom 2012) Even more disheartening, some evidence suggests that efforts to support entrepreneurship may actually result in poorly performing ventures (Shane 2009). It is also important to point out that there is no single model that governments can copy from one case to another. National and regional differences, which could be explained by the interactive influence of formal and informal institutions, may result in different policies at the implementation level (Eesley et al. 2018).

Entrepreneurial Environment

What many of these government efforts have in common is the (misguided) notion that the only way to spur more entrepreneurship is to lower the barriers to entry. Two notable barriers to entry are the (plethora of) steps necessary to register a business and the initial capital requirements.

Barriers to entry

The World Bank evaluates the potential for entrepreneurship in countries around the world by the number of steps necessary to establish and register a firm. A study of the procedures required for firms to obtain licenses and permits before operating across European countries found that the greater the number of steps to officially register a business, the lower the rate of entrepreneurship (Klapper, Laeven, and Rajan 2006).

There are also good reasons to expect that entrepreneurs are capital constrained and that raising sufficient funding to get started is an important barrier to entry. For example, wealthy individuals are consistently found to be more likely to found firms (Holtz-Eakin, Joulfaian, and Rosen 1994). This expectation has led many governments to attempt to spur entrepreneurship by providing funding to entrepreneurs directly or by subsidizing venture capital. Many of these programs have failed for various reasons (Lerner 2009). Recent work that carefully evaluates the influence of financial constraints on founding rates (using a policy reform in Denmark) determined that lowering the financial burden of starting a firm does increase entrepreneurship rates. However, individuals who were encouraged to found firms as a result were also likely to shut down their firms soon after getting started. Moreover, wealthy individuals—who were most likely to found firms because they lack constraints on initial capital—were also more likely to found businesses that fail to survive and grow. Thus, lowering barriers to entry may increase the "churn" of new business creation, but it often increases failure and the exit of these new businesses as well.

Barriers to growth

Recently, a growing stream of work examines the influence of the external environment on entrepreneurship. Specifically, scholars investigate the types of environments that encourage the founding of high-growth, technology-based firms. Regarding entrepreneurship in China and the United States, there are two seemingly incompatible innovation models (Wu, Eesley, and Eisenhardt 2020). The first is the Silicon Valley style of entrepreneurial innovation, which is supported by the policies outlined above. The second is the state- and corporate-led innovation model, which is somewhat similar to the current institutional environment in China. Findings in this stream demonstrate that institutions matter and effective institutional change influences who starts firms and what strategies lead to success, not just how many firms are started (Eesley 2016; Wu, Eesley, and Yang 2021). This suggests a new framework in which, as well as barriers to entry, we should also consider barriers to the growth of new firms. In addition, recent research calls into question the dogma that more entrepreneurship is always better. Using data from a survey of Tsinghua University alumni finds that lowering barriers to entry appears to increase entrepreneurship, but among less talented, "lower-human-capital" individuals, resulting in lower-quality and low-growth firms (Eesley 2016). On the other hand, lowering barriers to *growth* increases entrepreneurship among more talented, more educated individuals who are more likely to innovate and to create high-growth firms. Thus, policymakers must be attentive to which type of entrepreneurship their policies are stimulating: more small businesses or more high-growth, innovative start-ups? This is an important distinction and one that merits further investigation.

What are barriers to growth? They are elements in formal, regulatory policies or in the culture of a society that inhibit entrepreneurs from expanding their businesses into quickly growing profitable and successful large firms. Many people mistakenly believe that the creation of a start-up is the goal. But a start-up is meant to be a temporary organization. Once it has demonstrated a profitable, scalable new business model, the goal of the organization is to scale up as rapidly as possible and to become a large, established firm. In our enthusiasm over start-ups and entrepreneurship, we often focus on the first part, neglecting the vitally important role of the latter phases of the complete process. A plethora of barriers get in the way of successfully turning a start-up into a successful, large, established firm. Let's examine a few examples.

The first barrier to growth is an unlevel playing field for competition between established incumbents and start-ups. Anti-trust laws were established in the United States several decades ago to limit the power of large monopolistic firms to obstruct competition from new entrants. In many economies, large incumbents capture the regulatory process through campaign contributions or outright corruption and bribery. They use their influence with regulators and policymakers to erect regulations that either amount to barriers to entry or barriers to growth for start-ups. During the beginning stages of the commercial internet in the United States, the Federal Communications Commission (FCC) was at the heart of one such battle. Large telecommunications companies owned the phone lines and other infrastructure behind the nascent internet. These incumbents wanted to profit from the emerging internet industry by charging internet service providers and other fledgling start-ups for the use of their phone lines to transmit data. However, at the time, the FCC wisely recognized that such charges would effectively tax the nascent internet start-ups and resisted pressure from the incumbent telecommunications companies to allow them to charge fees. Even today, we see similar battles playing out, as the incumbent hotel industry seeks regulation to limit the competitive threat from start-ups like Airbnb. Similarly, in many developing economies, business groups and state-owned enterprises represent powerful economic actors that may be able to stake out advantaged competitive positions and inhibit the growth of start-up firms and their emergence as a competitive threat, even if they cannot prevent their entry in the first place.

For most start-up firms, success is defined as being acquired by a larger company or completing an initial public offering (IPO). Thus, some of the most important barriers to growth may be the laws regulating mergers and acquisitions and IPOs. If these regulations create undue burdens or constrain such liquidity events for entrepreneurs and their investors, the effect is to inhibit the growth of start-ups and creating a chilling effect on the entire entrepreneurship ecosystem.

But the effects of IPO reforms can be subtle and complex, so caution is warranted. In a recent analysis of IPO reform in Japan, a student and I analyzed over 16,000 start-up firms over a 10-year period both before and after the reform. We found that reducing requirements to make IPOs easier had an unanticipated effect of concentrating investment in the technology sector and reducing overall returns and growth in that sector due to overinvestment (Eberhart, Eisenhardt, and Eesley 2014). This occurred despite the larger number of IPOs that were enabled after the reform. Nonetheless, we must recognize that IPOs are important opportunities for entrepreneurs and investors to turn their private stock holdings into tradable public securities. IPOs also represent an important source of growth capital for young firms. Indeed, prior work finds that U.S. regions where there was greater IPO activity around biotechnology ventures subsequently saw greater start-up activity due to the resources and funding available after the IPO to investors and new entrepreneurs.

To the extent that lack of skills or skilled labor represents a barrier to growth for firms, universities have an important role to play. One of the growth strategies for start-ups is to pursue innovation via R&D to produce new products or to manufacture existing products more cheaply, enabling growth. Thus, science and technology policies play a role in supporting high-growth start-ups. In Silicon Valley, many firms have difficulties growing due to the challenges in finding and recruiting engineers and technical talent. The situation is even worse, and often extends to managerial talent, in other parts of the country. Universities can also play a role in patterns of regional migration, which may have an impact on entrepreneurial growth via the impact on the geographic distribution of human capital (Wu and Eesley 2021).

In China, we examined the impact of Project 985 (Eesley, Li, and Yang 2016), a university reform meant to increase the innovation capacity and quality of technological research and education in Chinese universities. We expected that students attending the Project 985 universities would be exposed to new technologies and would be more likely to create high-tech start-ups. The results bore out this result, and we found graduates from 985 universities were more likely to start innovative firms and to express a belief in the importance of innovation and intellectual property (IP). However, unexpectedly, we found that the financial performance of these firms was significantly lower when compared with less innovative start-ups and to firms started by non-985 university graduates. We believe part of the explanation is that there are other institutional barriers to growth in the environment (lack of IP protection, lack of entrepreneurship education, lack of early-stage capital, and competition from state-owned enterprises) that create difficulties for the commercialization of innovations. A final role for universities in lowering barriers to growth may be in educating future entrepreneurs and providing them with the human capital that has been shown to be integrally associated with higher-growth firms.

Barriers to failure

Bankruptcy laws and other "barriers to failure" represent a third pillar of policies that are important for high-growth, innovative entrepreneurship. Bankruptcy law is important because the most likely outcome for a new entrepreneur is that his or her firm will go out of business. Countries vary in the protection offered to investors compared with entrepreneurs during the bankruptcy process. Many creditors (investors) argue that they need a greater ability to recover their resources in the event of a bankruptcy. Without such protections, they would need to raise interest rates (investment returns), which could inhibit entrepreneurship due to the higher cost of capital. Yet, a talented (and wealthy) individual who is contemplating founding a risky, but potentially high-growth, venture is likely to be deterred if a bankruptcy event could result in the loss of a significant share of his or her personal wealth.

Personal liability protection was introduced in a bankruptcy reform that the coauthors and I studied in Japan. We found that a reform to the bankruptcy laws to make them more "entrepreneur friendly" had the effect of increasing bankruptcies in the country. However, it also resulted in more entrepreneurship among highly educated individuals. Due to the entry of this higher-quality group of entrepreneurs, start-up growth rates increased as a result of the reform, meaning that the performance of the average start-up firm was better (Eberhart, Eesley, and Eisenhardt 2017). Thus, lowering the barriers to failure is important to allow under-performing firms to fail and to enable highly talented individuals to take the risk of entrepreneurship because such individuals tend to start more innovative and higher-growth firms.

Conclusion

In the end, we want to carefully compare the entrepreneurship models between China and Silicon Valley across the dimensions of the educational system, entrepreneurial environment, barriers to entry, and innovation (table 2.1).

In conclusion, potential entrepreneurs, especially highly talented individuals with many career options, look carefully at the outcomes of friends and former colleagues who chose to go down the entrepreneurial path. When those efforts fail or when those entrepreneurs struggle to grow their firms, such individuals may be deterred from starting a new venture and choose the safer path of working in established companies or in the government or academia. Where barriers to entry, growth, and failure are low, then potential entrepreneurs are more likely to see their friends and former colleagues enjoying success as entrepreneurs and growing wealthy in the process. This creates confidence and optimism that they also might succeed beyond their wildest dreams.

Institutions matter for innovation. It is clear from work in institutional economics that the level of innovative activity in a place is affected by the surrounding institutions (Busenitz, Gomez, and Spencer 2000). Institutions can help alter the structure of incentives in a society to direct self-interested behavior toward more or less economically productive activities (Baumol 1996; Nee 1996). New opportunities open up as emerging economies undertake the shift from redistributive bureaucracy to open markets (Nee 1996). The environment for entrepreneurship, along with differences in technological opportunities, the characteristics of economic spillovers between universities and private firms, as well as cultural factors, can affect the level of entrepreneurial activity.

TABLE 2.1 Comparison of Chinese and Silicon Valley entrepreneurship models

	Silicon Valley	China
	Entrepreneurial innovation model	State- and corporate-led innovation model
Educational system	Strong public and private research and teaching universities support the ecosystem by acting as a magnet for talent and supplier of human capital, technology, and social norms as well as networks around high-tech entrepreneurship. The academic system incentivizes academic freedom and faculty-driven basic research.	Starting from the second half of the 2000s, China has been second only to the United States in research and development (R&D) by many measures, such as R&D spending as a share of GDP and number of academic research papers. Applied research funding is driven not by academic freedom and tenure but by corporate and government sources and metrics.
Entrepreneurship environment	Start-ups are supported to a limited extent by policies. Policymakers have a very limited role in the entrepreneurial environment.	Government plays a significant, leading role in the entrepreneurial environment. Private sources follow the lead of the government in setting resource priorities.
Barriers to entry	Very low barriers.	Government is trying to lower barriers to entry; however, there are still high barriers to some government-controlled areas.
Funding	Led by independent venture capital firms.	Led by corporate venture capital and government-backed subsidies.
Barriers to growth	Very low barriers at all stages.	Barriers exist still, especially in less-developed western provinces and at the initial public offering stage. Large tech firms (Tencent, Alibaba, and Baidu) dominate, facing little competition internally or from foreign competitors due to market protections.
Innovation	The fundamental mechanism driving innovation is market-based competition. State and corporate-driven innovation is rare except at the mergers and acquisitions stage.	The Chinese government chooses priority areas and subsidizes them heavily. Other funding sources follow this lead. Priority areas are getting closer to the technological frontier in areas such as electronics, automobiles, and high-speed trains. China is driving technological innovation in emerging areas, such as new and renewable energy, big data and artificial intelligence, robotics, etc. There are many government initiatives for innovation in key sectors, resulting in start-ups that compete heavily in overlapping technologies.
Potential advantages	Largely decentralized model dependent on entrepreneurial talent. Likely to produce unexpected, disruptive ideas.	Largely centralized and dependent on entrepreneurial government leaders. Can potentially achieve policy aims alongside financial returns.
Potential disadvantages	Coordinating large, long-term investments is difficult. Boom-and-bust cycles are common.	Potentially more prone to herding behavior, nonfinancial incentives, and investment bubbles.

SOURCE: Authors.

References

Acemoglu, Daron, Ufuk Akcigit, Harun Alp, Nicholas Bloom, and William Kerr. 2013. *Innovation, Reallocation and Growth*. Cambridge, MA: National Bureau of Economic Research (NBER).

Acs, Zoltan J., and David B. Audretsch. 1988. "Innovation in Large and Small Firms: An Empirical Analysis." *American Economic Review* 78 (4): 678–90.

Aghion, Philippe, Robin Burgess, Stephen Redding, and Fabrizio Zilibotti. 2005. "Entry Liberalization and Inequality in Industrial Performance." *Journal of the European Economic Association* 3 (2–3): 291–302.

Armanios, Daniel Erian, and Charles E. Eesley. 2021. "How Do Institutional Carriers Alleviate Normative and Cognitive Barriers to Regulatory Change?" *Organization Science* 32 (6): 1415–38.

Armanios, Daniel Erian, Charles E. Eesley, Jizhen Li, and Kathleen M. Eisenhardt. 2017. "How Entrepreneurs Leverage Institutional Intermediaries in Emerging Economies to Acquire Public Resources." *Strategic Management Journal* 38 (7): 1373–90.

Audretsch, David B., and A. Roy Thurik. 2004. "A Model of the Entrepreneurial Economy." *International Journal of Entrepreneurship Education* 2 (2): 143–66.

Balasubramanian, Natarajan, and Jeongsik Lee. 2008. "Firm Age and Innovation." *Industrial and Corporate Change* 17 (5): 1019–47.

Bartelsman, Eric J., and Mark Doms. 2000. "Understanding Productivity: Lessons from Longitudinal Microdata." *Journal of Economic Literature* 38 (3): 569–94.

Baumol, William J. 1996. "Entrepreneurship: Productive, Unproductive and Destructive." *Journal of Business Venturing* 11 (1): 3–22.

———. 2004. "Education for Innovation: Entrepreneurial Breakthroughs vs. Corporate Incremental Improvements." NBER Working Paper 10578, National Bureau of Economic Research, Cambridge, MA.

Bowen, Howard R., and Jack H. Schuster. 1986. *American Professors: A National Resource Imperiled?* Oxford: Oxford University Press.

Bransford, John D., Ann L. Brown, and Rodney R. Cocking. 2000. *How People Learn*. Vol. 11. Washington, DC: National Academy Press.

Brewster, Kingman. 1972. "On Tenure." *AAUP Bulletin* 58 (4): 381–83.

Brown, Ralph S., and Jordan E. Kurland. 1990. "Academic Tenure and Academic Freedom." *Law and Contemporary Problems* 53 (3): 325–55.

Busenitz, Lowell W., Carolina Gomez, and Jennifer W. Spencer. 2000. "Country Institutional Profiles: Unlocking Entrepreneurial Phenomena." *Academy of Management Journal* 43 (5): 994–1003.

Bush, Vannevar. 2020. *Science, the Endless Frontier*. Princeton, NJ: Princeton University Press.

Byrne, J. Peter. 1989. "Academic Freedom: A Special Concern of the First Amendment." *Yale Law Journal* 99 (2): 251–340.

Carmichael, H. Lorne. 1988. "Incentives in Academics: Why Is There Tenure?" *Journal of Political Economy* 96 (3): 453–72.

Carree, Martin A., and A. Roy Thurik. 2005. "Understanding the Role of Entrepreneurship for Economic Growth." Papers on Entrepreneurship, Growth and Public Policy 2005-10, Planck Institute of Economics, Entrepreneurship, Growth and Public Policy Group.

Chandy, Rajesh K., and Gerard J. Tellis. 2000. "The Incumbent's Curse? Incumbency, Size and Radical Product Innovation." *Journal of Marketing* 64 (3): 1–17.

Chen, Chao C., Patricia Gene Greene, and Ann Crick. 1998. "Does Entrepreneurial Self-Efficacy Distinguish Entrepreneurs from Managers?" *Journal of Business Venturing* 13 (4): 295–316.

Cohen, Wesley M., and Daniel A. Levinthal. 1990. "Absorptive Capacity: A New Perspective on Learning and Innovation." *Administrative Science Quarterly* 35 (1): 128–52.

Dahlin, Kristina, Margaret Taylor, and Mark Fichman. 2004. "Today's Edisons or Weekend Hobbyists: Technical Merit and Success of Inventions by Independent Inventors." *Research Policy* 33 (8): 1167–83.

David, Paul A., and Bronwyn H. Hall. 2000. "Heart of Darkness: Modeling Public-Private Funding Interactions inside the R&D Black Box." *Research Policy* 29 (9): 1165–83.

Eberhart, Robert N., and Charles E. Eesley. 2018. "The Dark Side of Institutional Intermediaries: Junior Stock Exchanges and Entrepreneurship." *Strategic Management Journal* 39 (10): 2643–65.

Eberhart, Robert N., Kathleen M. Eisenhardt, and Charles E. Eesley. 2014. "Institutional Change and Venture Exit: Implications for Policy." In *20 years of Entrepreneurship Research: From Small Business Dynamics to Entrepreneurial Growth and Societal Pros-*

perity, edited by Pontus Braunerhjelm, 128–38. Stockholm, Sweden: Swedish Entrepreneurship Forum.

Eberhart, Robert N., Charles E. Eesley, and Kathleen M. Eisenhardt. 2017. "Failure Is an Option: Institutional Change, Entrepreneurial Risk, and New Firm Growth." *Organization Science* 28 (1): 93–112.

Eesley, Charles E. 2016. "Institutional Barriers to Growth: Entrepreneurship, Human Capital and Institutional Change." *Organization Science* 27 (5): 1290–306.

Eesley, Charles E., and Yong Suk Lee. 2021. "Do University Entrepreneurship Programs Promote Entrepreneurship?" *Strategic Management Journal* 42 (4): 833–61.

Eesley, Charles E., and Yanbo Wang. 2017. "Social Influence in Career Choice: Evidence from a Randomized Field Experiment on Entrepreneurial Mentorship." *Research Policy* 46 (3): 636–50.

Eesley, Charles E., and William F. Miller. 2018. "Impact: Stanford University's Economic Impact via Innovation and Entrepreneurship." *Foundation and Trends in Entrepreneurship* 14 (2): 130–278.

Eesley, Charles E., David H. Hsu, and Edward B. Roberts. 2014. "The Contingent Effects of Top Management Teams on Venture Performance: Aligning Founding Team Composition with Innovation Strategy and Commercialization Environment." *Strategic Management Journal* 35 (12): 1798–817.

Eesley, Charles E., Jian Bai Li, and Delin Yang. 2016. "Does Institutional Change in Universities Influence High-Tech Entrepreneurship?: Evidence from China's Project 985." *Organization Science* 27 (2): 446–61.

Eesley, Charles E., Robert N. Eberhart, Bradley R. Skousen, and Joseph L. C. Cheng. 2018. "Institutions and Entrepreneurial Activity: The Interactive Influence of Misaligned Formal and Informal Institutions." *Strategy Science* 3 (2): 367–480.

Farrell, Michael P. 2001. *Collaborative Circles: Friendship Dynamics and Creative Work*. Chicago: University of Chicago Press.

FitzRoy, Felix R., and Kornelius Kraft. 1991. "Firm Size, Growth and Innovation: Some Evidence from West Germany." In *Innovation and Technological Change: An International Comparison*, edited by Z. Acs and D. B. Audretsch, 152–59. Ann Arbor, MI: University of Michigan Press.

Foster, Lucia, John Haltiwanger, and Chad Syverson. 2008. "Reallocation, Firm Turnover, and Efficiency: Selection on Productivity or Profitability?" *American Economic Review* 98 (1): 394–425.

Goolsbee, Austan. 1998. "Does Government R&D Policy Mainly Benefit Scientists and Engineers?" NBER Working Paper 6532, National Bureau of Economic Research, Cambridge, MA.

Haltiwanger, John, Ron S. Jarmin, and Javier Miranda. 2010. "Who Creates Jobs? Small vs. Large vs. Young." Paper No. CES-WP-10-17, US Census Bureau Center for Economic Studies, Washington, DC, August.

Holtz-Eakin, Douglas, David Joulfaian, and Harvey S. Rosen. 1994. "Entrepreneurial Decisions and Liquidity Constraints." *RAND Journal of Economics* 25 (2): 334–47.

Huergo, Elena, and Jordi Jaumandreu. 2003. "Firms' Age, Process Innovation and Productivity Growth." *International Journal of Industrial Organization* 22 (4): 541–59.

Hwang, Hokyu, and Walter W. Powell. 2009. "The Rationalization of Charity: The Influences of Professionalism in the Nonprofit Sector." *Administrative Science Quarterly* 54 (2): 268–98.

John-Steiner, Vera. 2000. *Creative Collaboration.* New York: Oxford University Press.

Klapper, Leora, Luc Laeven, and Raghuram Rajan. 2006. "Entry Regulation as a Barrier to Entrepreneurship." *Journal of Financial Economics* 82 (3): 591–629.

Lee, Yong Suk, and Charles E. Eesley. 2018. "The Persistence of Entrepreneurship and Innovative Immigrants." *Research Policy* 47 (6), 1032–44.

Lerner, Josh. 2009. *Boulevard of Broken Dreams: Why Public Efforts to Boost Entrepreneurship and Venture Capital Have Failed and What to Do About It.* Princeton, NJ: Princeton University Press.

Magaziner, Ira C., and Mark Patinkin. 1989. *The Silence War.* New York: Vintage Books.

McGill, Ian, and Anne Brockbank. 2003. *Action Learning Handbook.* London: Kogan Page.

Nee, Victor. 1996. "The Emergence of a Market Society: Changing Mechanisms of Stratification in China." *American Journal of Sociology* 101 (4): 908–49.

OECD (Organisation for Economic Co-operation and Development). 2000. *Knowledge Management in the Learning Society.* Paris: OECD Publications.

Oliner, Stephen D., and Daniel E. Sichel. 2000. "The Resurgence of Growth in the Late 1990s: Is Information Technology the Story?"

Finance and Economics Discussion Series 2000-20, Board of Governors of the Federal Reserve System (United States).

Pedler, Mike, ed. 2011. *Action Learning in Practice*. Surrey, England and Burlington, VT: Gower Publishing, Ltd.

Reedy, E. J., and Robert J. Strom. 2012. "Starting Smaller; Staying Smaller: America's Slow Leak in Job Creation." In *Small Businesses in the Aftermath of the Crisis*, edited by Giorgio Calcagnini and Ilario Favaretto, 71–85. Physica-Verlag Heidelberg.

Roberts, Edward B., and Charles E. Eesley. 2011. *Entrepreneurial Impact: The Role of MIT*. Hanover, MA and Delft, The Netherlands: Now Publishers Inc.

Sawyer, R. Keith. 2003. *Improvised Dialogues: Emergence and Creativity in Conversation*. Westport, CT: Greenwood Publishing Group.

———. 2006. "Educating for Innovation." *Thinking Skills and Creativity* 1 (1): 41–48.

Sawyer, R. Keith, and Sarah Berson. 2004. "Study Group Discourse: How External Representations Affect Collaborative Conversation." *Linguistics and Education* 15 (4): 387–412.

Saxenian, AnnaLee. 1994. *Regional Advantage: Culture and Competition in Silicon Valley and Route 128*. Cambridge, MA: Harvard University Press.

Shane, Scott. 2009. "Why Encouraging More People to Become Entrepreneurs Is Bad Public Policy." *Small Business Economics* 33 (2): 141–49.

Van Alstyne, William. 1971. "Tenure: A Summary Explanation, and Defense." *AAUP Bulletin* 57 (3): 328–33.

Wu, You (Willow), and Charles E. Eesley. 2021. "Regional Migration, Entrepreneurship and University Alumni." *Regional Studies*. Published ahead of print, August 5, 2021. https://doi.org/10.1080/00343404.2021.1934432

Wu, You (Willow), Charles E. Eesley, and Kathleen M. Eisenhardt. 2020. "Entrepreneurship in Dynamic Environments: A Comparison between the U.S. and China." *Quarterly Journal of Management* 5 (2): 1–17.

Wu, You (Willow), Charles E. Eesley, and Delin Yang. 2021. "Entrepreneurial Strategies during Institutional Changes: Evidence from China's Economic Transition." *Strategic Entrepreneurship Journal*. Published ahead of print, March 13, 2021. https://doi.org/10.1002/sej.1399

3 Entrepreneurial Scaling Strategy

Managerial and Policy Considerations

David H. Hsu

Beyond the start-up phase of venture development, an important practical aspect of the enterprise life cycle is the degree to which an organization is able to scale its operations. Such scaling is important for both private-sector firms as well as national governments, as most economically significant outcomes are associated with enterprises that successfully scale their operations (e.g., Chandler 1990). From the standpoint of private firms, successful scaling may be important to keep pace with shareholders' expectations (whether those equity owners are participants in the private or public markets). From the societal perspective, national competitiveness and economic outcomes such as employment growth and tax revenues can also be tied to successful venture scaling.

Perhaps less obvious from the policy perspective are a host of second-order effects that may be tied to very successful venture scaling. Not only is there a demonstration effect for participants in a given labor market, which can incentivize the next generation of entrepreneurs in an economy, but also successful scaling (particularly following an entrepreneurial liquidity event) can provide financial ("angel") capital and mentoring assistance to that next generation. Consider the case of ex-Google or ex-Facebook employees who, following successful initial public offerings, became angel investors and mentors to subsequent Silicon Valley start-ups. Venture scaling has been the subject of government discussion at both national and subnational levels, including in Singapore, the United Kingdom, and Israel. Known for its technology-intensive ventures, Israel has a reputation more as a "start-up nation" than as a "scale-up nation."

Venture scaling in the popular, lean start-up development framework involves seeking customer feedback based on a minimally viable product after identifying its market fit (e.g., Ries 2011). However, success in realizing this fit depends on a host of other decisions, some of which have not been fully appreciated in the literature. For example, early in the venture life cycle, entrepreneurs and managers may choose between different entry strategies. Two distinct examples are a cooperative, value-chain strategy (entailing working with existing participants in a given value chain, as is the case of Foxconn with Apple's iOS value chain), and a competitive, disruption strategy (competing against an industry incumbent's value chain, as is the case of Didi in the ride-sharing industry). Each of these entrepreneurial entry choices is associated with different aspirations for scaling direction. For a cooperative strategy, ventures are likely to scale on a specific segment of the value chain necessary to bring a product or service to market, whereas a competitive strategy likely entails scaling in a more full-spectrum manner. The entrepreneurial choice of entry strategies in turn is influenced by public policies (further discussed below), which help shape the economic environments in which ventures operate.

Thus, a possible revision to the view that a sufficient precondition to venture scaling is finding a fit between product attributes and marketplace needs is that such a choice also depends on the prior choice of entrepreneurial entry strategy. In turn, the venture entry strategy depends on the policy environment. Consequently, even though scaling decisions come at a particular juncture in venture development, I will be discussing decisions and influences at an earlier point of the venture life cycle, likely to influence the extent and direction of organizational scaling.

Entrepreneurial Entry Strategies

Even before we can discuss venture entry strategy, we need to recognize that policy may have a role in the initial financial capital necessary to get a venture off the ground in the first place. This is due to a number of factors: potentially high-growth ventures in particular rarely have a concentration of human and intellectual capital at the beginning, and what they have typically cannot be collateralized. Furthermore, high-growth ventures operate in a risky and long-term investment horizon environment. These challenges, in part, gave rise to the birth of the venture capital industry in the Boston area via the founding of the

American Research & Development Corporation in 1946 (Hsu and Kenney 2005). While this effort was through private means, government policies in both the United States and around the world have been important in developing financing schemes and institutions to meet the challenge of financing innovation (see Lerner [2009] for a discussion of ways some efforts have been misguided).

In the United States, the government established debt funding schemes (e.g., the Small Business Investment Companies program in 1958 through the U.S. Small Business Administration) and in 1982, the Small Business Innovative Research (SBIR) program was created. This required U.S. federal agencies to set aside a small part of their research and development budget to competitively award nondilutive capital to small businesses with the ultimate goal of furthering commercialization efforts. Similarly, in Israel, the Yozma program (established in 1993) matched private overseas funding with public funding to bolster the stock of enterprise development capital. While it is beyond the scope of my effort here to draw conclusions about the effectiveness of these specific government programs, the ex ante rationale for them is clear. A novel technology's path to market commercialization is uncertain and risky, yet there is potential for societal gain when such an effort is successful. I will not summarize the various attempts to evaluate the impact of government efforts to streamline the process (e.g., Howell 2017 and references therein). Also, I do not mean to suggest that financing is necessarily the linchpin of venture founding and entry. A host of policy levers may also shape the incentives for firm founding. Examples include the costs and administrative burden of business registration (e.g., Klapper, Laeven, and Rajan 2006), taxation policy, bankruptcy protection, and deregulation (e.g., in the banking sector). These domains are also beyond the scope of this chapter. Instead, I would like to move from the macro level of programs and policy to the micro: specifically, the managerial and entrepreneurial decision-making that may be influenced by alternative policy choices and economic environments.

Because the entry strategy a venture chooses can have a significant bearing on the scale-up choices it makes, I explore two types of entry strategies: cooperative (value chain) and competitive (disruption). Also, I discuss factors—including those tied to government policies—that can influence the choice of strategy. Why does the choice of a cooperative or competitive strategy matter for managers and for society? For managers of established firms, predictions associated with a venture entry strategy may shift investments as they prepare to work with or compete against new entrants. For society, the overall welfare effects of start-up strategy have not been settled in the literature. For example, while a competitive strategy avoids duplicative research and development and commercialization investments in a society, a competitive situation may spur innovation, which in turn would strengthen the economic impact.

Cooperative entry strategy

The literature has identified two factors that can shape the attractiveness of a cooperative entry strategy: (1) the intellectual property appropriability environment (Gans, Hsu, and Stern 2008), which is shaped by (among other things) intellectual property policy, and (2) the costs of assembling the organizational assets and resources necessary to bring the focal good to the marketplace (Gans, Hsu, and Stern 2002). The appropriability environment is relevant because the process of negotiating deal terms, including price, with any would-be partner involves disclosing in detail the innovation and/or the basis on which the venture competes. This information may otherwise be protected through other means, such as trade secrecy. If trade secrecy or formal intellectual property protection is relatively weak, the incentive for an entrepreneur to disclose innovation to the marketplace is weakened as a result of the enhanced risk of expropriation. Aside from the initial conditions associated with disclosure, the costs (and expectation of costs) of governing the ongoing cooperative relationship are also an important consideration. Some examples of these costs include dispute resolution and the management of the cooperative relationship, including more specific aspects such as tort laws, product liability, burden of proof, and the like. Different legal regimes will vary across dimensions of the contracting environment, which will be more or less hospitable to interorganizational cooperation.

A second lever that may affect the entrepreneurial choice to undertake a cooperative strategy is the cost of accessing or assembling the other relevant resources and assets necessary to enter the marketplace. Examples of these assets include the expertise necessary to obtain regulatory approval if the focal venture is operating in such a context, and the ability to organize the operations necessary to bring a good to market. If those costs are relatively low, then the venture may decide to forego a partnership commercialization model, particularly if there are high costs or frictions to contracting, as discussed in the preceding paragraph. As an example, consider the semiconductor industry. Without the presence of dedicated chip manufacturers such as Taiwan Semiconductor, stand-alone semiconductor chip design would not seem like a viable business model. Consequently, the preexisting economic ecosystem in a given geography, or access to such an ecosystem more generally, may also be an important driver of a cooperative strategy.

Government policy can play a role in shaping ecosystems. Government subsidy and tax policies, for example, play an important role in shaping the industrial composition of economies. While a full treatment is well beyond the scope of this chapter, one stream of the literature analyzes the desirability of specialized clusters of economic activity (e.g., Porter 1998). Related studies stress the economic benefits of clustering such as the orchestration of supply and demand, which in turn lowers the transaction costs of factor inputs such as capital and labor. Having sophisticated clusters of upstream suppliers, or having a concentration of demanding customers, will also shape entry costs (in the case of the suppliers) and the quality of competition and innovation (where customers are plentiful).[1] To the extent that there is a competitive upstream supplier base, and those suppliers are equally accessible to all entrepreneurs, those resources are "generic" (Teece 1986) and cannot be the basis for competitive differentiation, much like any undifferentiated input available on the open market. In the face of such a competitive upstream marketplace, there would seem to be two possible entrant strategies. The first would be to specialize in differentiation somewhere along the value chain, likely downstream of competitive supply, or bundle the offering in an effort to provide a superior

---

[1]   The geographic concentration of sophisticated customers is an interesting case. It might ease marketing or sales efforts, thereby lowering transaction costs. Yet it is not without downsides. These customers probably did not convene by accident. Their choice of location may be due to proximity to a key input or resource or because of experimentation in a given location over time. In both cases, producers find themselves in an extreme selection environment; inefficient or relatively less talented producers will likely exit the market rather quickly (or we would never observe entrants who are not of a sufficient quality). Porter (1998) and others have pointed out that sophisticated customers foster innovation, and of course link to scalability to the extent that economies producing more innovative products and services are more likely to see demand for scaled-up operations. However, compared with the competitiveness of supplier conditions (including access to the range of inputs necessary for market entry), the influence of concentrated demand conditions may be more complicated as they relate to venture entry strategy.

experience to the end consumer. The second would be to forego the cooperative strategy altogether in favor of a competitive strategy.

Competitive entry strategy

An entrepreneur's decision to take a competitive stance against the industry incumbent also relates to the appropriability regime and the costs of a firm's own entry, but in the opposite direction. A number of issues arise when deciding to compete. Competition can take place in the usual way of product or service differentiation, based on operational efficiency (lower costs, better access to customers, higher quality, and the like), but also based on a specific pattern, popularized by Christensen (1997). Though disruptive innovation was initially conceptualized from the perspective of incumbent firms guarding against being disrupted by entrants, I will discuss the concept mainly from the entrant's perspective.

In the Christensen framework, incumbents are sometimes surprised by new entrants and are disrupted due to two important elements. First, because the first generation of technical innovations typically performs poorly in key ways that matter to the incumbent's current customers, there is little motivation for the incumbent to want to invest in these innovations. Meanwhile, new entrants drive their development such that the rate of improvement exceeds that of the incumbent technology. If and when the performance of the new generation of technology eclipses the needs of current consumers, the incumbent is said to be disrupted.

Recall that "staying under the radar" is important for new ventures. As the Christensen framework points out, new innovations' initially poor ranking on key performance indicators is why incumbents are reluctant to invest. If incumbents were confident that a given technology would be disruptive, it is likely that they would invest; deterrents such as uncertainty and time horizon issues weaken the incumbents' incentive to invest. A host of policies provide some cover for new ventures. For example, in the United States, there is a veil of secrecy over the process of going public on the New York Stock Exchange (known as "regulation A+") that allows firms contemplating going public (and meeting certain requirements) to delay public disclosure of their offering memorandum by 21 days. This is one example of how, beyond the efforts available in the private sector, public policies may assist in helping a venture stay under the radar.

The second signature aspect of disruption is the ability to get on a performance trajectory that exceeds that of the industry incumbent (the new technology is able to break through the initial saturation levels of the prior technological trajectory). For a set of important technologies, this does not happen in a vacuum. In particular, government-funded initiatives such as global positioning system (GPS) technology or the advanced research projects agency network (ARPANET, the precursor to the internet), may be important in enabling faster trajectories of technological advance (and therefore consumer adoption). These basic and general-purpose technologies sometimes have as their precursor government-funded predevelopment.

While I have described the competitive entry strategy pathway as a disruptive strategy, there may be a different typology of competitive entry. While a disruptive strategy presumes that there is an existing incumbent that a new venture is disrupting, sometimes entrepreneurs enter a greenfield space that is essentially unoccupied. However, there is a common denominator here with disruptive dynamics—that is, that there are *latent* competitors. In the absence of substantial barriers to entry, incumbent firms or others could become fierce competitors. Therefore, new entrants would need to quickly scale in ways that keep ahead of would-be competitors in the greenfield space (Kim and Mauborgne 2015). In the many cases where there is no regulatory environment, significant efforts may be undertaken to shape it (e.g., Biber et al. 2017; Gao 2018).

To recap this section, I discussed two broad entrant strategies: cooperative (involving innovation in an existing value chain) and competitive (involving disruptive or greenfield entry). I discussed different forces that make each strategy more or less difficult, together with policy factors in the environment that affect those managerial choices. I will conclude this section by discussing how the choice of static cooperative or competitive venture entry is sometimes too simplistic.

Venture "switchback" strategies

Since venture scaling is a dynamic concept, it will be useful to discuss how venture strategies can shift over time, depending on the venture phase. For example, there could be circumstances in which a venture is initially blocked from undertaking its preferred steady-state strategy, and so may choose to temporarily follow a different strategy. I will discuss two "switchback" pathways of this type. While the most direct means of ascending a mountain is a straight path upwards, sometimes the more feasible strategy, albeit less efficient, is to take detours on the way up. New ventures often do this.

A cooperative strategy may be used temporarily even though the enterprise wishes to ultimately enter the product market by itself. A significant obstacle to immediate entry into the product market is the lack of a trusted organizational brand reputation. In such circumstances, temporarily cooperating with industry incumbents to conduct joint development or participate in various types of alliances, such as co-marketing, may accelerate the venture learning process, and enhance a firm's organizational capabilities. After a certain degree of learning takes place, the venture may decide to enter the product market by itself in the second stage of its development efforts. Asian original equipment manufacturer (OEM) and original design manufacturer (ODM) relationships in several electronics subsectors offer examples of such cooperation, before participating firms "graduated" to having their own brand. Another is Genentech's choice to license its first products to others in order to learn from their marketing efforts, before switching to full integration for its subsequent products (as quoted in Marx and Hsu 2015, 1816).

Are there policy aspects that affect the feasibility of this strategy? If the ultimate goal is to compete in the marketplace with one's own brand, noncompete clauses could come into play.

A second type of switchback pathway involves temporary competition. Here, the venture obstacle is a lack of credibility in the marketplace. In other words, as a result of an unverified value proposition, some ventures may have difficulty striking a cooperative deal, or one that is favorable enough from a bargaining power standpoint. With that backdrop, if the venture entered the product market and demonstrated its value proposition, the bargaining power would change. For example, Qualcomm vertically integrated into cellular communications equipment production (handsets and cell towers) in order to demonstrate the benefits of its new technology standard. It then divested those assets after the benefits of the standard had been proven in the marketplace (for more details, see Marx and Hsu 2015, 1821).

More generally, the switchback pathways described here reflect the broader point that organizational development and the associated bargaining power of a venture evolve over time. Amazon offers an example of such an evolution. In 2018 Amazon invited U.S. cities to compete to host its second headquarters location. Many offered significant tax and other concessions, with the hope that attracting Amazon would generate good prospects for future regional employment and economic growth. Amazon's bargaining power was enabled by its prominence at that juncture of its development path.

Venture Scaling

Background and dimensions of venture scaling

Now that we have considered how venture entry strategy can shape the nature, pace, and direction of venture scaling, we are ready to discuss this scaling itself. *Scaling,* a term often used in the popular press, has three key dimensions: vertical expansion (backward or forward linkages with other industry players), horizontal expansion (across industries), and geographic expansion (beyond the initial market). These categories are not mutually exclusive, of course. Furthermore, each of these dimensions of organizational expansion has been studied from a variety of perspectives, including from economics and management. I will not be offering a systematic review of those perspectives; rather, I will be discussing some aspects of these dimensions relevant to venture scaling.

TABLE 3.1 Venture scaling and entry strategy

Company	Founded	Vertical expansion		Horizontal expansion		Geographic expansion	
		Cooperative strategy					
Foxconn	1974	N/A		N/A		China	1988
						United States	2014*
		Competitive strategy					
Netflix	1997	Streaming	2007	N/A[†]		Latin America	2011
		Original content	2013			130 markets	2016
Amazon	1994	Marketplace	2000	AWS	2002	Europe	1998
		Kiva acquisition	2011[‡]	Kindle	2007	China	2004
		Drone delivery	?[§]	Prime video	2011	India	2013
Uber	2009	N/A[|]		EATS/courier	2014	Paris	2011
						Taiwan, South Africa	2013

NOTE: *Foxconn made an initial commitment to build a factory in the United States but has since wavered on its plans; [†]Possible expansion into gaming; [‡]Kiva developed robotics for shipping centers; [§]it remains unclear whether Amazon's drone delivery will ever come to fruition; [|]none to date, but there are strong indications that Uber will be moving into autonomous vehicles.
SOURCE: Author.

As previously noted, scaling pace can reflect the chosen entry strategy. Consider the scaling patterns of a notable cooperative entry strategist, Foxconn, a manufacturer and assembler of electronic devices such as the Apple iPhone and the Amazon Kindle. The company has no intention of trying to disrupt those industry incumbents, but rather competes against others for priority in supplying to them. Foxconn, founded in 1974, has arguably not undertaken horizontal or vertical expansion, as scaling in these dimensions might undermine its business model and make it less appealing to its value chain partners. Instead, the Taiwanese company expanded geographically into China 14 years after it started, probably for market and labor reasons.

In contrast, consider several companies undertaking a competitive strategy. Ventures choosing a disruptive or greenfield entry (both forms of competitive strategy), because of actual or latent competition, might find it quite important to scale up quickly. For example, Netflix and Uber needed to quickly outpace industry incumbents. As mentioned, in the classic Christensen (1997) framework, during a first phase in which a new entrant's technology offers worse customer value than that of incumbents, the entrant tries to improve this value in a manner that outpaces the incumbent's recognition and response.

For a greenfield technology, a slightly modified dynamic comes into play. Maybe an incumbent has not considered entering the new domain, or has delayed entry, such as hotel chains' slow response to Airbnb (in this case, they did not possess the distributed real estate assets needed to effectively respond to the entrant). In both the disruptive innovation and greenfield entry cases, rapid scaling at the appropriate time may be important for competitive positioning.

Also, from a temporal perspective, it could be important to strategically sequence the dimensions of scaling. For Amazon and Netflix, validating a core value proposition was at the heart of early organizational efforts, even while being cognizant of bottlenecks. For example, Amazon knew it had little bargaining power relative to providers of last-mile delivery services. Similarly, Netflix knew that while media content providers held substantial bargaining power, it could present itself as an alternative mode of downstream distribution. Having validated its core value proposition, the company then turned its attention to mitigating the upstream media content issue by (vertically) integrating into original content creation. This decision also affected the geographic expansion rate: having authority and control over its own content (as compared to negotiating rights by geography) allowed the company to self-determine where and when it could enter various geographic markets. As a consequence, the company entered some 130 additional markets in January 2016 (some 19 years after the company was founded). In summary, for Netflix, geographic scaling and expansion were enabled by backward vertical integration into content creation.

For Amazon, there were two important dimensions of scaling. Leveraging its capabilities in operations and data analytics, the company quickly expanded beyond its entry category (books) to horizontally enter the grocery, web services, and prescription drugs markets, among many others. This scope of horizontal expansion probably relates to the company's ongoing efforts to forward integrate into distribution (though, of course, enhanced bargaining power associated with greater scope likely translates into more favorable terms using the existing network of distributors).

Policy and scaling

A large number of policy aspects could affect the three dimensions of scaling (horizontal, vertical, and geographic). Aside from more general issues associated with antitrust and competition policy that have been discussed in the literature, in keeping with the more micro flavor of this chapter, I would like to discuss the role of institutions in fostering top management development and training. After all, it would be hard to imagine venture scaling without talented managers overseeing the efforts.[2] There are two parts to this discussion. The first regards the geographic distribution of managerial talent available for employment by ventures seeking to scale their enterprises. In areas of the world in which this labor market is not thick, there may be a public role in this regard. The second part of the discussion explores how organizational entities important to the scale-up phase of a venture, including venture capitalists, may be shaped by and help shape top managers and their composition in ventures.

Some regions of the world offer less opportunity for individuals to acquire managerial experience. This might be for a variety of reasons,

---

2   This theme relates to one debated in the literature about the role of venture founders. Top managers with a variety of experience may help ventures navigate the developmental life cycle (see, for example, DeSantola and Gulati 2017), though the countervailing force to such professionalization is the passion and incentive alignment typically found in founder-executives.

including long traditions of state-owned enterprises (as in China) and more generally an incentive environment less aligned with investment in managerial skills. Since skilled employees and executive talent are often required to effectively scale enterprises, and if such skills are specialized, the private investment required to train and educate is high and the payback to such private investment is uncertain, there could be a case made for societal investments. Schools as managerial training grounds may offer one solution, but the time required for high-quality institutions of higher education and training to enter may exceed that needed for the envisioned pace of economic development and opportunity in the focal country and region. Perhaps for this reason, there have been efforts at public-private business school partnerships in some countries such as Germany, Malaysia, and Singapore. Of course, while it is possible to import foreign-trained managers in an international labor market, additional frictions and costs may be associated with relying on expatriate managers, including lack of knowledge of local norms and culture. The dearth of specialized human capital may particularly be an issue in small countries such as Singapore; this has led that country to build schemes to subsidize and import high-potential individuals from neighboring countries to attract and retain home-grown talent. It will be interesting to observe how large countries such as China and India enact policy or develop schemes to cultivate their managerial ranks.

A second aspect to the role of managerial talent is that it can signal quality to would-be investors. Venture capitalists are involved in corporate governance and there has been documentation (e.g., Kaplan and Stromberg 2005) that top management team suitability and fit are key determinants of venture capital. It is also important to recognize that venture success is likely dictated not just by managerial talent (note that such talent can involve managerial judgement, as well as execution-oriented abilities), but also by the value proposition offered by the venture. At the same time, venture success is not entirely determined by the nature of the innovation, disembodied from the executives and managers associated with the enterprise. For example, one speculation about the U.S. government experience in financing innovation is that managerial and business development are underappreciated, often at the expense of prioritizing and rewarding technological development. As a consequence, we would expect investor involvement to be associated with founder-executive replacement, as well as enlargement of the executive team in the context of scaling an enterprise.

Summary

Venture scaling requires financial inputs to fund expansion, including for factors such as product or service development, operations, human capital, and other functions. Therefore, financial institutions and the business environment, as shaped by policy, affect the behavior of financial actors, and thus shape the desire and ability of entrepreneurial ventures to enter and scale their organizations.

More broadly, I argue in this chapter that the field should reconsider the idea that a sufficient precondition to venture scaling is finding a fit between product attributes and marketplace needs. I argue that venture scaling also depends on the choice of entrepreneurial entry strategy. Two policy implications emerge from this perspective. First, policymakers should be aware that there is no "one size fits all" way to undertake venture scaling—but rather the direction and pace of such scaling depends on prior entrepreneurial choices. Second, policymakers should nevertheless be cognizant that both financial and human capital can be significant bottlenecks to firms seeking to scale—and that there may be a compelling role of government in one or both of these arenas to help promote entrepreneurial development.

References

Biber, Eric, Sarah E. Light, J. B. Ruhl, and James Salzman. 2017. "Regulating Business Innovation as Policy Disruption: From the Model T to Airbnb." *Vanderbilt Law Review* 70 (5): 1561–626.

Chandler, Alfred Jr. 1990. *Scale and Scope: The Dynamics of Industrial Capitalism.* Cambridge, MA and London: Harvard University Press.

Christensen, Clayton M. 1997. *The Innovator's Dilemma: When New Technologies Cause Great Firms to Fail.* Boston, MA: Harvard Business School Press.

DeSantola, Alicia, and Ranjay Gulati. 2017. "Scaling: Organizing and Growth in Entrepreneurial Ventures." *Academy of Management Annals* 11 (2): 640–68.

Gans, Joshua S., David H. Hsu, and Scott Stern. 2002. "When Does Start-Up Innovation Spur the Gale of Creative Destruction?" *RAND Journal of Economics* 33 (4): 571–86.

————. 2008. "The Impact of Uncertain Intellectual Property Rights on the Market for Ideas: Evidence from Patent Grant Delays." *Management Science* 54 (5): 982–97.

Gao, Cheng. 2018. "Strategy in Nascent Industries: Navigating Regulatory Uncertainty in Personal Genomics." Working paper, University of Michigan.

Howell, Sabrina T. 2017. "Financing Innovation: Evidence from R&D Grants." *American Economic Review* 107 (4): 1136–64.

Hsu, David H., and Martin Kenney. 2005. "Organizing Venture Capital: The Rise and Demise of American Research & Development Corporation, 1946–1973." *Industrial and Corporate Change* 14 (4): 579–616.

Kaplan, Steven N., and Per Stromberg. 2005. "Characteristics, Contracts, and Actions: Evidence from Venture Capitalist Analyses." *Journal of Finance* 59 (5): 2177–210.

Kim, W. Chan, and Renée Mauborgne. 2015. *Blue Ocean Strategy: How to Create Uncontested Market Space and Make the Competition Irrelevant.* Boston, MA: Harvard Business School Press.

Klapper, Leora, Luc Laeven, and Raghuram Rajan. 2006. "Entry Regulation as a Barrier to Entrepreneurship." *Journal of Financial Economics* 82 (3): 591–629.

Lerner, Josh. 2009. *Boulevard of Broken Dreams: Why Public Efforts to Boost Entrepreneurship and Venture Capital Have Failed—And What to Do about It.* Princeton: Princeton University Press.

Marx, Matt, and David H. Hsu. 2015. "Strategic Switchbacks: Dynamic Commercialization Strategies for Technology Entrepreneurs." *Research Policy* 44 (10): 1815–26.

Porter, Michael E. 1998. "Clusters and the New Economics of Competition." *Harvard Business Review*, November–December.

Ries, Eric. 2011. *The Lean Startup.* New York: Crown Business.

Teece, David J. 1986. "Profiting from Technological Innovation: Implications for Integration, Collaboration, Licensing and Public Policy." *Research Policy* 15(6): 285–305.

II. Entrepreneurship Education

4 Innovation Policy and Star Scientists in Japan

Tatsuo Sasaki, Hiromi S. Nagane, Yuta
Fukudome, and Kanetaka M. Maki

Scientific research is the process of creating new knowledge. Transferring that resulting knowledge to industry can result in innovation, which is of great economic importance. Japan has the world's second-highest number of Nobel laureates in the natural sciences (MEXT 2018) and continues to maintain a strong global presence in scientific research. However, the number of Japanese scientific research publications and citations have declined over the past 10 years. Some have expressed concern that the weakening foundations of Japan's knowledge creation require attention.

One way to bolster these foundations is to support the country's star scientists. Star scientists (a phrase coined, for the field of biotechnology, by Zucker, Darby, and Brewer 1998) have outstanding achievements in terms of publications and research. Importantly, they contribute not only to academic circles but also to business performance by, for example, increasing the probability that start-up firms will launch products. In sum, a star scientist is involved in processes that create new scientific knowledge and achieve innovation by transferring it to industry (Zucker, Darby, and Armstrong 2002).

The Japanese government has a number of policies aimed at strengthening the development of young researchers who will be able to take global leadership positions (MEXT 2018), in order to bolster both scientific knowledge and innovation. To best design such policies

Acknowledgements: This research was supported by JST-RISTEX "Star Scientists and Innovation in Japan" & KAKENHI (18H00840). The authors thank research assistants Ryusei Ikezawa (Waseda University), Ryuichiro Akaho (Waseda University), and Miki Ishii (Waseda University).

in the Japanese context, it is essential to grasp the relationship between policy and scientific researchers' performance. Therefore, in this chapter, we investigate star scientists' performance under Japanese science and technology innovation policies that have been in place starting in 1995. In particular, we consider government efforts to promote the transfer of knowledge from academia to industry.

First, we summarize the current state of science, technology, and innovation policy in Japan. We then identify several star scientists and analyze their characteristics. We also examine how scientists engage with innovations, such as through patents, joint research, and start-ups. We then summarize our results and indicate directions for future research.

Science, Technology, and Innovation Policy in Japan

Innovation is achieved by transferring new knowledge born from research conducted in universities and public institutions to industry. Although the processes of both creating and transferring knowledge are expected to function well on their own, since scientific knowledge has the property of a public good, the investment of private companies will be less than the level required by society. Therefore, it is necessary to provide public support through policy (Steinmueller 2010). Economic growth will be achieved by advancing science and technology and realizing innovation in this way. The existence of scientists has a positive effect on regional economies (Horowitz 1966), as innovation in science-based electric products, the chemical industry, etc., improve the productivity of other industries (Pavitt 1984). In this section, we describe the policy and research environment surrounding Japanese star scientists.

After the World War II, Japan achieved high economic growth in the manufacturing sector, leveraging knowledge and technology developed abroad. However, in the 1980s, as competition in trade and technological innovation with the United States intensified, it became urgent for Japan to nurture homegrown, specialized human resources through advanced education in scientific research.

The Science and Technology Basic Law, introduced in 1995, ushered in major changes in how Japan addresses research and innovation. The Council for Science, Technology, and Innovation, chaired by the prime minister, was set up. Among its responsibilities was the formulation of a comprehensive innovation policy, outlined in a Science and Technology Basic Plan every five years. These five-year plans stipulate not only the promotion of fundamental research at universities but also policies that foster the application of this research-based knowledge to commercial products and services. In other words, in 1995, Japan started to develop consistent policies spanning all phases of the innovation process, from research and development (R&D) all the way to commercialization.

In 1998, the Act on the Promotion of Technology Transfer from Universities to Private Business Operators was enacted. Also known as the TLO law, this enabled the establishment of technology licensing organizations (TLOs). These are corporations that can obtain patents from the results of university research and are responsible for technology transfer to industry sectors. Full-time TLO staff encourage the utilization of patents and joint and contract research by matching technologies invented or improved at universities with the business needs of private companies. Importantly, this legislation made it possible for universities to acquire external funds beyond government budgets for innovation. The expectation was that both universities and private companies would gain economic benefits from collaborating with each other.

Subsequently, in 1999, the Industrial Technology Enhancement Act (commonly known as the Japanese version of the Bayh-Dole Act) was passed. Until then, rights to intellectual property gained as an outcome of government-funded R&D belonged to the government, and not to researchers. Under this model, researchers had to pay licensing fees to the Japanese government to implement the patents they had invented in government-funded R&D projects. Even if the government were to strengthen R&D investment, this would not provide sufficient incentives for innovators to boost private companies' growth. Recognizing this point, the Bayh-Dole Act, introduced in the United States in 1980, made it possible to attribute intellectual property rights born out of government-outsourced research to university researchers or trustees, including private companies. This legislation provides university researchers and private companies with an incentive to utilize their government-funded research. In a similar way, the Industrial Technology Enhancement Act promoted deregulation in Japan with the aim of encouraging private companies to utilize the knowledge generated by national universities and government funds.

To further ease the path to innovation, the Japanese government decided to support the establishment of start-ups. State-of-the-art knowledge derived from university-based research, which is tacit knowledge, may not be efficiently transferred to partner companies. Also, private companies may not be willing to invest in industry development if they cannot correctly evaluate the value of ingenious innovation. Therefore, it is expected that scientists who acquire tacit knowledge will become entrepreneurs, set up their own university start-ups, and innovate by themselves. In 2001, Takeo Hiranuma, then Japan's minister of economy, trade, and industry, proposed a plan to launch one thousand university-originated start-ups. In the proposal (known as the Hiranuma Plan), he set two goals: increase the number of patents issued by universities by tenfold over 10 years, and increase the number of university start-up companies to one thousand in three years. The Japanese government also provided support to start-ups in terms of founding, finance, and human resource development.

A law establishing the national university corporation as independent from civil administration governance was enacted in 2004. By establishing a national university corporation, it became possible to choose strategic personnel and allocate budgets without the direct management of the Japanese government and to incorporate a management method like that of private companies, under the leadership of a university president. As a result of the incorporation of national universities, each national university has been forced to hone its unique strengths in a competitive environment. Each university may procure external funds to attract better personnel and achieve superior research results. This can create a positive cycle in which talented people can generate the next innovation.

Before the mid-1990s, Japan's national universities had no juridical personality and thus could not possess intellectual property rights. Collaborative research between universities and companies was not undertaken formally via contracts, but instead informally at the discretion of university faculty, using scholarship donations as compensation (Zucker and Darby 2001). Once universities could incorporate, it became possible to formalize industry-academia collaborations. Now, when a university and a company collaborate, they must sign a contract, clarify research expenses, and attribute intellectual property. By giving scientists the right to obtain patents, regulations allow the transfer of knowledge—and facilitate it across a wide range of companies through TLOs.

With the advent of TLOs, the process of acquiring patents through university research has developed, and from 2005 to 2017, a steady stream of about seven thousand patents were filed (Japan Patent Office 2018). Although income from intellectual property rights exceeded about 3.5 billion yen in 2016 (MEXT 2016), their share of university budgets as a whole remains small. Research funds to universities from the private sector increased from 58.9 billion yen in 2011 to 84.7 billion yen in 2016 (MEXT 2016).

Since the launch of the Hiranuma Plan in 2001, the number of new start-ups has increased rapidly. Following the recession accompanying the global financial crisis in 2008, the number of new start-ups declined sharply but started to rise again around 2014, when university venture capital started to appear. In January 2014, the Industrial Competitiveness Enhancement Act made it possible for national universities to start venture capital funds. The legislation formed the basis for not only technical consultation and personnel but also the supporting environment for investment and management.

As we trace the trajectory of Japan's science and technology innovation policy from around 1995, it becomes evident that deregulation and structural reform have been promoted so that original and advanced knowledge generated by scientists is more likely to be applied to industry. In addition to collaborative research with companies, the system supports the acquisition of patents and the establishment of start-ups.

Star Scientists and Innovation

Scientists are key to innovation. When knowledge generated from scientific research is transferred to industry, new products and services based on market needs are realized. Meeting the needs of the market will ultimately lead to improvements in national welfare. In this sense, continuing to produce the results of cutting-edge scientific research is important for economic growth.

Previous studies have pointed out that scientists with an outstanding performance record have an impact on industry. Considering a sample of scientists who had discovered more than 40 genetic sequences, as reported in GenBank (1990),[1] Zucker, Darby, and Brewer (1998) analyzed the spatial relationship between such star scientists and start-ups in biotechnology. The authors pointed out that start-ups are located where star scientists conduct their research. Then, Zucker, Darby, and Armstrong (2002) focused on the United States and analyzed

---

[1] GenBank (https://www.ncbi.nlm.nih.gov/genbank/) is the National Institutes of Health genetic sequence database, an annotated collection of all publicly available DNA sequences.

relationships between the performance of start-ups and (1) star scientists, (2) top research universities, and (3) venture capital.

In conclusion, they suggested that coauthorship of academic articles with a star scientist is one of the most powerful factors influencing the performance of start-ups. Third, Zucker and Darby (2007) analyzed changes in the performance of star scientists in biotechnology who have relationships with start-ups (having academic papers coauthored with start-ups or having positions in start-ups). Star scientists who are committed to start-ups have larger numbers of academic papers and citations than do those who are not committed to start-ups. Furthermore, star scientists who not only have joint papers but also hold some position in a start-up have overwhelmingly larger numbers of citations than do star scientists who only have joint papers with start-ups. Therefore, Zucker and Darby (2007) suggested that there are "virtuous circles in science and commerce" by which scientists can improve research achievements and firms can improve corporate performance. Further, Zucker and Darby (2007) showed that 35 percent of star bioscientists were involved in firms commercializing their discoveries in the United States and Japan.

When focusing on the connection between the company and star scientist, it has been shown that university-industry partnerships in the 1980s made a big difference in the United States and Japan (Zucker and Darby 2001). The companies in which star scientists cooperated in the United States were mainly start-ups, whereas in Japan, they were large companies.

A series of studies by Zucker and Darby focus on this issue up to approximately the 1980s. Furthermore, most research focuses on the United States. Few studies (with the exception of Zucker and Darby [2001, 2007]) focus on star scientists in Japan, including in the years since the paradigm shift of 1995. To help fill this gap, we analyze the characteristics of star scientists in Japan using an original data set, and we analyze the relationship between star scientists and industry in the context of recent university innovation policy.

Basic Characteristics of Star Scientists in Japan

Our original data set encompasses about three thousand scientists with outstanding achievements in a variety of fields. Following the methodology of Highly Cited Researchers defined by Clarivate Analytics, we focus on the quality of publications, typically measured by the number of citations,[2] as a common criterion. Undoubtedly, the number of published papers or citations indicates only the academic value of research and does not necessarily forecast social and economic impacts.

We considered highly cited documents published in the years 2002–14 across 21 fields of the natural and social sciences. We collected information on the scientists' institutions, published papers, and patent acquisition status.[3] We then used this information to create panel data on 121 highly cited researchers whose careers span the years 1974–2015.

First, we consider the position of Japan's star scientists in the world. Figure 4.1 shows the distribution of star scientists by economy.[4] The overwhelming majority of star scientists are affiliated with research institutions in the United States. Japan has 121 star scientists, ranking the country in tenth place globally. Although omitted here, looking at the number of star scientists by country over the 2014–16 period, while the high rankings of the United States, United Kingdom, Germany, and China did not change, Japan fell from fifth to eighth and then to tenth place (Saito and Maki 2018).

Second, we show the distribution of star scientists by research field in the four top-ranking countries (United States, United Kingdom, Germany, and China), Japan, the Republic of Korea, Singapore, Taiwan, and other countries and economies.

The breakdown of the bar graph in figure 4.2 shows the number of star scientists by field. Japan, shown in solid black, produces a relatively large number of star scientists in animal and plant science, and immunology.

Third, we analyze patent applications as an aid to measuring star scientists' commitment to innovation. First, we show the number of patent applications filed by star scientists in Japan. Figure 4.3 depicts the distribution of Japan's star scientists by the cumulative number of

---

2   For this purpose, we use the Highly Cited Researchers (HCR) list published by Clarivate Analytics (http://hcr.stateofinnovation.com/), last accessed July 25, 2018.
3   For this purpose, we use the J-Global database of science and technology information in Japan: http://jglobal.jst.go.jp/en/ (last accessed July 25, 2018). J-Global provides basic information on researchers, major national scientific literature in Japan and abroad (about 20,000 foreign language journals and about 12,000 Japanese journals), and patent information gathered by Japanese patent offices.
4   Based on the 2016 HCR list.

FIGURE 4.1 Distribution of star scientists by economy, 2016

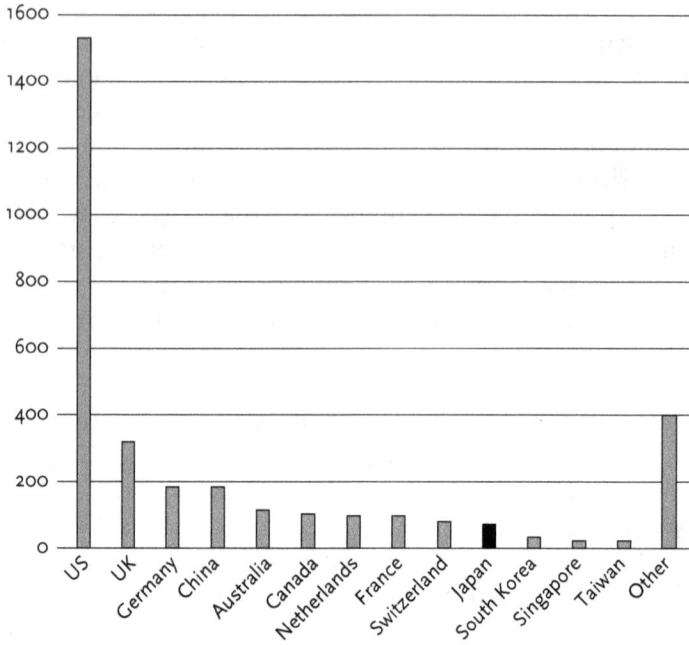

SOURCE: Highly Cited Researchers (HCR) list, published by Clarivate Analytics.

FIGURE 4.2 Distribution of star scientists by field, 2016

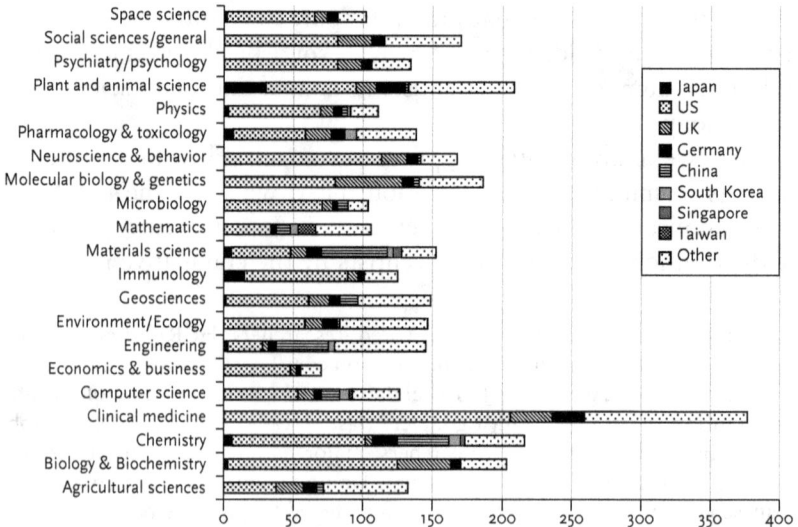

SOURCE: Highly Cited Researchers (HCR) list, published by Clarivate Analytics.

FIGURE 4.3 Distribution of Japan's star scientists by number of patent applications filed

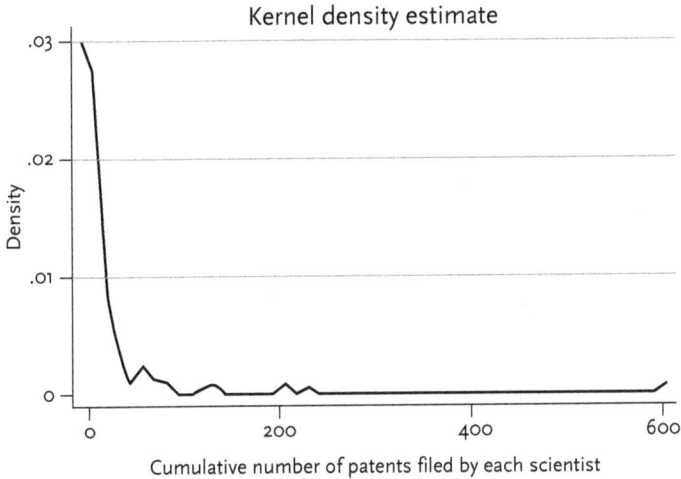

NOTE: This figure is based on the cumulative number of patents filed by each star scientist in Japan between 1974 and 2015; kernel = Epanechnikov; bandwidth = 3.8350.
SOURCE: J-Global database and Highly Cited Researchers (HCR) list published by Clarivate Analytics.

patents filed by each between 1974 and 2015, using kernel estimation. There is a concentration on the 0 value—32 star scientists filed no patent applications during the period. The star scientist with the most patent applications filed 601.

Surely, it is easier to file patent applications in some fields than others. Figure 4.4 shows the distribution by field. Scientists who have filed patents are indicated by the dark blocks, while star scientists who have never filed a patent application are indicated by the lighter blocks. Of the many star scientists in Japan in the fields of animal and plant science, and immunology, most are involved in patent applications. In some fields, such as material science and chemicals, all the star scientists are involved in patent applications. Patent applications are rare in the fields of space science, earth science, mathematics, and others.

Certainly, a patent application filed by a star scientist can signal a scientific contribution to an industry in the sense that scientific knowledge is connected to technology. However, knowledge transfer from star scientists to industry is not necessarily captured by patent applications

FIGURE 4.4 Japanese star scientists with and without patents, by number and field

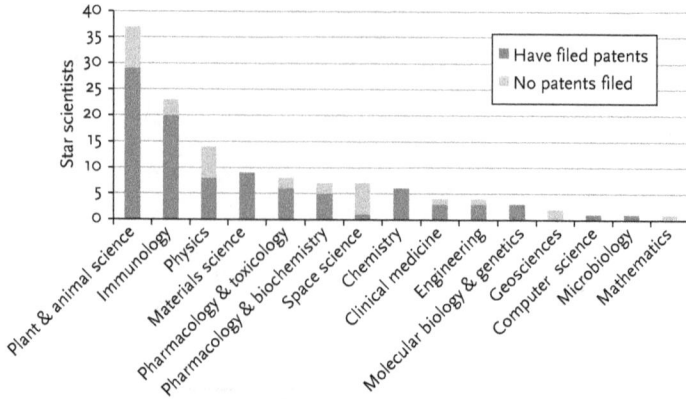

NOTE: Unit = person.
SOURCE: J-Global database and Highly Cited Researchers (HCR) list published by Clarivate Analytics.

alone. We should note that it is possible for scientific research to be transferred to the industrial side as implicit knowledge.

Japanese Star Scientists' Collaborative Research

For scientific knowledge to lead to innovation, a well-structured knowledge transfer mechanism from scientists to industry is important. Here we focus on collaborative research as a form of scientific knowledge transfer. Particularly for researchers belonging to companies, collaboration with star scientists ensures opportunities to absorb state-of-the-art scientific knowledge, which can lead to new technologies, products and services, and innovation.

Some previous studies focus on coauthorship and joint application relationships as an index to consider the connection between companies and scientists. Cockburn and Henderson (1997) focus on the coauthorship of papers and study how coauthorship between academic and corporate researchers affects drug discoveries and patent productivity. Saito and Sumikura (2010) focus on joint applications between universities and public research institutions and pharmaceutical companies, and specifically consider how much scientific knowledge companies absorb from universities and public research institutions.

TABLE 4.1 Number of collaborators with star scientists, by institutional affiliation

	Mean	Median	Min	Max
Total collaborators	63.05	39	1	230
National university	44.43	24	0	172
Special or independent administrative corporation	6.60	3	0	35
Private university	4.19	1	0	40
University interoperability organization	2.23	0	0	51
Company	1.83	0	0	18
Foreign university	1.21	0	0	20
Non-profit organization	1.20	0	0	13
Public university	1.14	0	0	9
National institute	1.03	0	0	19
Foreign institute	0.68	0	0	26
Local public entity	0.38	0	0	7
National college of technology	0.05	0	0	1
Foreign company	0.04	0	0	1
Public junior college	0.02	0	0	1
School corporation	0.02	0	0	1
Other	0.01	0	0	1
Foreign school	0.01	0	0	1
Private junior college	0.01	0	0	1
College (researchers with the same affiliation)	25.41	15	0	107

NOTE: We do not double count collaborators, even in cases of multiple-year collaborations. SOURCE: SPIAS, https://scirex.grips.ac.jp/topics/archive/160819_464.html (last accessed July 25, 2018).

The connection between a company and a researcher becomes obvious when it takes the form of an academic paper or patent application. On the other hand, joint research itself does not necessarily result in a thesis or patent, and so these measures in themselves cannot capture joint research connections.

We collected information on joint research funds that star scientists obtained as research representatives or shareholders.[5] Table 4.1 lists the number of collaborators of 111 star scientists, classified by type of institution.[6]

Most researchers who collaborate with star scientists belong to national universities. A cumulative average of 44.43 researchers belonging

---

5 Although we focus on research project representatives and assignees, some collaborators do not fit this description, as defined by the Japan Society for the Promotion of Science. Thus, participants in actual collaborative research are more varied and numerous than shown in our analysis (see JSPS 2017).

6 We used the data platform SPIAS, which includes information on collaborators (SciREX 2016). Because the database does not cover all the star scientists in our sample, we analyzed the collaborations of 111 star scientists in total.

to national universities collaborate with star scientists, followed by 6.6 researchers at special corporations and independent administrative corporations, 4.19 researchers at private universities, and 2.23 researchers at university interoperability organizations. On the other hand, a cumulative average of 1.83 researchers belong to companies. In many cases, star scientists collaborate with researchers at the same institution (an average of 25.41 people). The fact that many star scientists belong to national universities (Saito and Maki 2017) suggests that most of their collaborators are colleagues at the same universities.

Next, we review basic statistics of the institutions with which collaborators are affiliated. Since there are cases in which multiple collaborators belong to the same institution, the number of institutions with researchers is smaller than that with collaborators. On average, star scientists collaborate with researchers at 7.63 national universities. Table 4.2 suggests that star scientists tend to collaborate with researchers who belong to a national university even if it is not the same as theirs.

Our analysis then considers the network of star scientists' collaborators. Figure 4.5 depicts the connection between researchers who have participated in a joint research project with star scientists at least two or more times.

TABLE 4.2 Institutions with which star scientists collaborate

	Mean	Median	Min	Max
National university	7.63	6	0	25
Private university	2.38	1	0	18
Special or independent administrative corporation	1.86	1	0	9
Company	1.40	0	0	17
Public university	0.87	0	0	7
Foreign university	0.78	0	0	14
Non-profit organization	0.65	0	0	9
University interoperability organization	0.42	0	0	3
Foreign institute	0.33	0	0	4
Local public entity	0.32	0	0	4
National institute	0.28	0	0	4
National college of technology	0.05	0	0	1
Foreign company	0.04	0	0	1
Public junior college	0.02	0	0	1
School corporation	0.02	0	0	1
Other	0.01	0	0	1
Foreign school	0.01	0	0	1
Private junior college	0.01	0	0	1

SOURCE: SPIAS, https://scirex.grips.ac.jp/topics/archive/160819_464.html (last accessed July 25, 2018).

FIGURE 4.5 Network connections between star scientists and collaborators

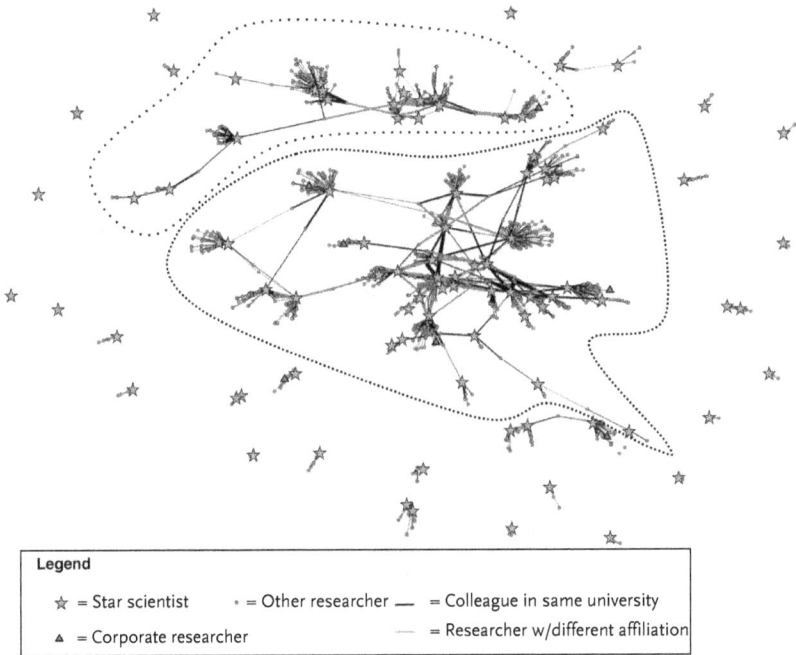

SOURCE: SPIAS, https://scirex.grips.ac.jp/topics/archive/160819_464.html (last accessed July 25, 2018).

In figure 4.5, stars represent star scientists, triangles corporate researchers, and circles any other type of researcher. We connect these nodes using solid lines when they involve at least two collaborations with star scientists. We focus on the relationship between star scientists and their collaborators and do not consider the relationship between non–star scientists who collaborate. The solid connecting lines become thicker according to the length of the collaborative research period. A solid black line shows collegial relations between collaborators affiliated with the same institution. A solid gray line denotes the lack of this mutual affiliation. From the large number of solid black lines in figure 4.5, we confirm that many star scientists collaborate with their colleagues. There is little collaborative research with companies. By connecting a solid line in this way, generally two large clusters can be seen. For the star scientists that make up the large upper cluster, there are 10 in physics, six in space science, and two in material science. For the

FIGURE 4.6 Star scientists and corporate researchers in collaboration, 1983–2016

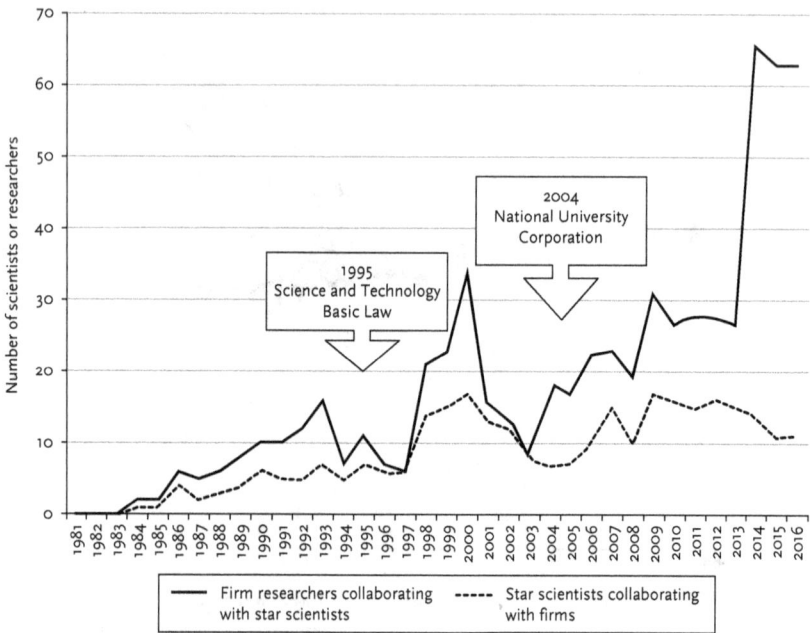

SOURCE: SPIAS: https://scirex.grips.ac.jp/topics/archive/160819_464.html (last accessed July 25, 2018).

large lower cluster, there are fourteen in immunology, fourteen in plant and animal science, five in biology and biochemistry, five in pharmacology and toxicology, four in clinical medicine, and one each in computer science, microbiology, and molecular biology and genetics. This cluster consists of star scientists in very different fields. Of course, these star scientists are not directly connected, but it may well be that any collaborators play the role of connecting researchers in different fields through the intervention of collaborators who connect them in some way.

Next, we show the changes over time in the number of star scientists and corporate researchers focusing on joint research (figure 4.6). The dotted line indicates star scientists collaborating with corporate researchers. The solid line indicates corporate researchers collaborating with star scientists. Of course, the movements of the former and latter interlock. The larger the difference between the dotted and solid lines, the greater is the increase in the number of corporate researchers cooperating per star scientist. The number of star scientists who

TABLE 4.3 Japanese star scientists' commitments to start-ups, 1996–2018

Scientist ID	Position	Field	Affiliation
A	Executive	Materials science	Yamagata University
A	Executive	Materials science	Yamagata University
A	Representative	Materials science	Yamagata University
A	Representative	Materials science	Yamagata University
B	Founder	Computer science	Keio University
B	Founder	Computer science	Keio University
B	Executive	Computer science	Keio University
C	Collaborator	Immunology	Osaka University
C	Executive	Immunology	Osaka University
D	Collaborator	Chemistry	Kyoto University
E	Collaborator	Materials science	University of Tokyo
F	Collaborator	Biology and biochemistry	Kyoto University
G	Collaborator	Pharmacology and toxicology	Tohoku University
H	Collaborator	Pharmacology and toxicology	University of Tokyo
I	Founder	Microbiology	University of Tokyo / University of Wisconsin–Madison

SOURCE: Database of university start-ups, http://univ-startups.go.jp/ (last accessed September 9, 2020); Entrepedia, http://entrepedia.jp/ (last accessed August 16, 2018); and Crunchbase, https://www.crunchbase.com (last accessed August 16, 2018).

collaborate with corporate researchers has grown to more than 10 researchers annually since around 1997; although it temporarily fell below 10 researchers around 2004, it remained over 10 after that. We find that, on average, there is an increasing number of star scientists who collaborate with corporate researchers. Additionally, almost all these corporate collaborators belong to large companies (a finding consistent with Zucker and Darby [2001]).

Further, in investigating the connections between star scientists and start-ups,[7] we find that nine of Japan's star scientists are committed to fifteen start-ups as a founder, a representative, an executive, or a collaborator. (One scientist in particular had committed to four.) Table 4.3 lists those star scientists with commitments to start-ups, along with their characteristics.

Figure 4.7 shows the trajectory of star scientists committed to start-ups after 1990.

---

7   We mainly used three databases: one devoted to university start-ups, http://univ-startups.go.jp/ (last accessed September 9, 2020); Entrepedia, http://entrepedia.jp/ (last accessed August 16, 2018); and Crunchbase, https://www.crunchbase.com (last accessed August 16, 2018).

FIGURE 4.7 Star scientists' commitments to start-ups, by number, 1996–2018

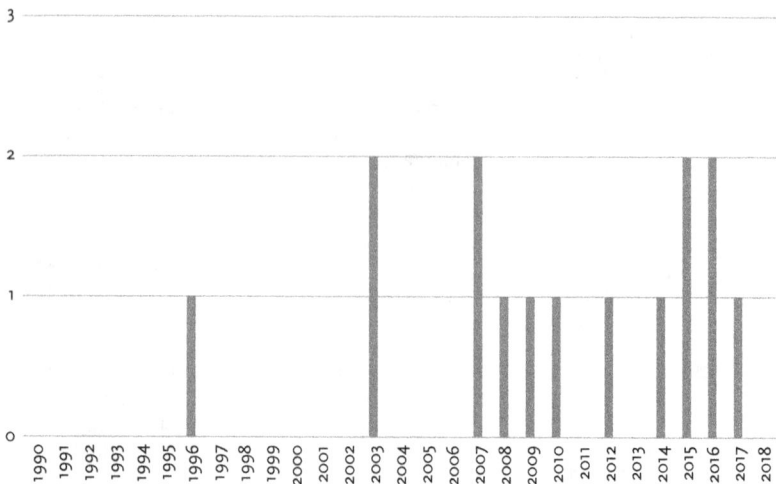

SOURCE: Database of university start-ups, http://univ-startups.go.jp/ (last accessed September 9, 2020); Entrepedia, http://entrepedia.jp/ (last accessed August 16, 2018); and Crunchbase, https://www.crunchbase.com (last accessed August 16, 2018).

The number of star scientists who commit to start-ups gradually rises after 2003. Almost every year after 2007, at least one star scientist committed to a start-up. This suggests that the incorporation of national universities in 2004 to some degree made it easier for faculty to serve in some capacity at private companies.

Conclusion

Our review of Japan's science, technology, and innovation policy since 1995 shows that deregulation and structural reforms have been implemented to facilitate the transfer of university-created knowledge to industry. Those policies were adopted to support university scientists' application for patents, joint research with private companies, and the establishment of university-originated start-ups.

The connection between the scientific output of star scientists and Japan's innovation policy is verifiable. We used scientific citations as the index of research performance and identified scientists with highly cited papers. Our investigation of the characteristics of star scientists in Japan confirmed that they not only publish academic papers but also acquire patents for their research outcomes. Although patent acquisitions differ across academic fields, 73 percent of the star scientists in our sample obtained their patents as inventors. Our interpretation of these results is that star scientists are aggressively striving to transfer the knowledge generated by their research to industry. Based on the number of collaborations we noted, it seems private companies acknowledge the value of collaborative research with star scientists, even as many of these scientists are committed to start-ups. In summary, the Japanese star scientists we chose for our analysis are fostering innovation, supported by the country's science and technology innovation policy.

In Japan, the number of academic papers published and the number of highly cited papers (in the global top 10) have declined, as well as the number of students entering doctoral courses (MEXT 2018). Furthermore, it has been reported that the number of star scientists in Japan declined from 2014 to 2016 (Saito and Maki 2018). Thus, training and supporting star scientists, and restoring the performance of the nation's scientific research, are immediate tasks.

In this study, we chose star scientists based on number of citations. However, as mentioned, their function is not limited to academic research, but also includes the strength of their contribution to industry. Evaluating this effect requires a large-scale data set that can account for not only papers but also patents and commitments to private companies, supported by thorough quantitative and qualitative analysis.

The distribution of star scientists in the world differs greatly from country to country depending on the scientific field (figure 4.1), as does their contributions to academia and industry. The trajectory of these influential researchers is influenced not only by national and regional policies but also by factors such as population dynamics, industrial structure, and cultural background. The research results obtained in one country cannot be directly applied to other countries. It is necessary to consider the context of the area and industry characteristics. In the future, it is expected that the theoretical understanding of star scientists will progress by aggregating the results by geographical areas and by performing meta-analysis.

References

Cockburn, Iain, and Rebecca Henderson. 1997. "Public-Private Interaction and the Productivity of Pharmaceutical Research." NBER

Working Paper 6018, National Bureau of Economic Research, Cambridge, MA. https://www.nber.org/papers/w6018.

Horowitz, Ira. 1966. "Some Aspects of the Effects of the Regional Distribution of Scientific Talent on Regional Economic Activity." *Management Science* 13 (3): 217–32. https://doi.org/10.1287/mnsc.13.3.217.

Japan Patent Office. 2018. *JPO Status Report 2018*. Tokyo: Japan Patent Office. Accessed July 24, 2018. https://www.jpo.go.jp/shiryou/toukei/status2018.htm.

JSPS (Japan Society for the Promotion of Science). 2017. *Handbook on the Grants-in-Aid for Scientific Research (KAKENHI) Program*. Accessed July 29, 2018. https://www.jsps.go.jp/j-grantsinaid/15_hand/data/h29/handbook_kenkyuusya.pdf.

MEXT (Ministry of Education, Culture, Sports, Science and Technology). 2016. "About the Implementation Status of Industry-Academia Collaboration, etc. at Universities in 2016." Accessed July 24, 2018. http://www.mext.go.jp/a_menu/shinkou/sangaku/1397873.htm

———. 2018. "White Paper on Science and Technology 2018." Accessed August 1, 2017. https://www.mext.go.jp/en/publication/whitepaper/title03/detail03/1420912.htm.

Pavitt, Keith. 1984. "Sectoral Patterns of Technical Change: Towards a Taxonomy and a Theory." *Research Policy* 13 (6): 343–73. https://doi.org/10.1016/0048-7333(84)90018-0.

Saito, Hiromi, and Kanetaka Maki. 2017. "Star Scientists: The Engine of Innovation in Japan." [In Japanese.] *Hitotsubashi Business Review* (Summer): 42–56.

———. 2018. "Japan's Innovation System and the Role of Star Scientists." [In Japanese.] SciREX Working Paper SciREX-WP-2018-#01, Science and Technology Innovation Policy Research Center, Tokyo.

Saito, Hiromi, and Koichi Sumikura. 2010. "An Empirical Analysis on Absorptive Capacity Based on Linkage with Academia." *International Journal of Innovation Management* 14 (3): 491–509. https://doi.org/10.1142/S1363919610002751.

SciREX. 2016. "SPIAS [SciREX Policy Formation Intelligent Support System] Alpha Version is Currently under Development." Accessed July 25, 2018. https://scirex.grips.ac.jp/topics/archive/160819_464.html.

Steinmueller, W. Edward. 2010. "Economics of Technology Policy." In *Handbook of the Economics of Innovation, Vol.2*, edited by Bronwyn H. Hall and Nathan Rosenberg, 1181–218. Amsterdam, The Netherlands: Elsevier.

Zucker, Lynne, and Michael Darby. 2001. "Capturing Technological Opportunity via Japan's Star Scientists: Evidence from Japanese Firms' Biotech Patents and Products." *The Journal of Technology Transfer* 26 (1–2): 37–58. .

———. 2007. "Virtuous Circles in Science and Commerce." *Papers in Regional Science* 86 (3): 445–70. https://doi.org/10.1111/j.1435 -5957.2007.00133.x.

Zucker, Lynne, Michael Darby, and Jeff Armstrong. 2002. "Commercializing Knowledge: University Science, Knowledge Capture, and Firm Performance in Biotechnology." *Management Science* 48 (1): 138–53. https://doi.org/10.3386/w8499.

Zucker, Lynne, Michael Darby, and Marilynn B. Brewer. 1998. "Intellectual Human Capital and the Birth of U.S. Biotechnology Enterprises." *The American Economics Review* 88 (1): 290–306.

5 The Creativity and Labor Market Performance of Korean College Graduates

Implications for Human Capital Policy

Jin-Yeong Kim

As of 2018, the Republic of Korea's per capita gross domestic product (GDP) surpassed $30,000, a remarkable achievement for a country whose per capita GDP was just over $80 in 1960. There are numerous studies on how Korea has achieved this incredible economic growth. Such factors as high savings and investment ratios, an export-oriented strategy, and a well-educated labor force have been widely cited.[1] As for Koreans themselves, human capital has always been thought to be the ultimate source of past economic growth.[2] Korea's achievement in human development, over a very short period, is indeed remarkable. In the twenty-first century, Korea records the highest college enrollment ratio among member countries of the Organisation for Economic Co-operation and Development (OECD 2020a).

Korea has a long tradition of regarding education and scholarship with the highest esteem, a regard that has come to encompass relatively modern professions such as scientists and technicians. Since the 1960s, demand for engineers and researchers has soared. By the 1980s, students with the highest scores on the national college entrance exam typically chose electronic engineering or physics as their major. With a resulting large pool of talented scientists and engineers, it is no wonder

---

1 For example, see the introduction in SaKong and Koh (2010).

2 The following sentence from SaKong and Koh (2010) reflects the general view of the Korean people on their education: "The successful expansion of education has been a key factor in Korea's industrialization and democratization during the last six decades. Without it, the 'Miracle on the Han' would have been impossible."

that Korea is at the frontier of the semiconductor, electronic device, and information and communication technology (ICT) fields.

But it should be admitted that, with few exceptions, Korea has been more a follower than a leader in research and development. Korea's human capital has specialized in narrowing the gap with the world's technological frontrunners at a high speed. Yet as this gap narrows, Korea needs more creators and innovators.

It is natural to ask why so many people in Korea, including policy-makers, CEOs, and students themselves, think that Korea's educational system fails to enhance creativity.[3] There are many reasons, both on the supply (or educational) and demand (or labor market) side. On the supply side, it could simply be that teachers have not been trained to be creative. In education colleges,[4] future teachers are trained in traditional ways, memorizing materials. Even the nation's highly competitive teacher examinations do not require much creativity. As for students, their creativity is not appreciated or even evaluated. It would take time and investment to change the status quo.

On the labor market side, there is little incentive to accumulate innovative human capital if the expected returns are not high. If, for any reason, creativity is not needed or sufficiently remunerated in the labor market, there would not be much incentive to spend time engaging in various activities that might foster creativity even if they are encouraged during school days. Especially in a strictly hierarchical workplace culture, where younger people should obey elders' orders, raising questions or expressing alternate viewpoints might be even harmful to an employee's future prospects. It is quite possible that those who have accumulated a high level of innovative human capital suffer from a high rate of depreciation.

In this chapter, we empirically explore the demand and supply of creative or innovative human capital in Korea.[5] More specifically, us-

---

3   This general perception was reflected in the Ministry of Education's slogan in the 2010s: "Education for creativity and upright character."

4   In Korea, elementary and secondary school teachers are trained separately. Teachers at elementary schools graduate from universities, most of which are public schools. Secondary school teachers are trained in specialized education colleges inside universities, both private and public.

5   There is no general consensus on the concept of innovative human capital. In fact, the term itself rarely shows up in the literature. For McGuirk, Lenihan, and Hart (2015), the concept encapsulates four elements: education, training, willingness to change in the workplace, and job satisfaction. In this work we take a dif-

ing an extensive data set derived from the Education–Labor Market Lifetime Path Survey, we will try to measure innovative human capital and estimate the pecuniary return to it in the Korean labor market. This data set contains information on the college and labor market experiences of three cohorts at 10-year intervals. The three cohorts are college graduates from the years 1982, 1992, and 2002. Through our analysis of the data, we try to get some idea of how Korea has evolved in terms of fostering innovative human capital, and better understand the incentives for and processes of accumulating it.

The rest of this chapter proceeds as follows. First, we briefly review the concept of creativity. We then introduce measures of two different types of human capital: "imitative" and "innovative." We then consider how different age cohorts perceive their ability to innovate, as well as the financial returns to this ability. The chapter concludes with policy recommendations.

The Concept and Pursuit of Creativity in Korean Education

Creativity has been a central issue in Korean education policy at least since the so-called 5.31 education reform in 1995.[6] Traditionally, creativity and an innovative mind were thought to be traits of only a few geniuses. Since 1995, building the creativity of each student has been a high priority. This shift in Korean education policy seems to reflect a similar paradigm shift in social and cultural understandings of creativity.

According to Glăveanu (2010), the concept of creativity has three paradigms: the He-paradigm, I-paradigm, and We-paradigm. The He-paradigm concentrates on the chosen few. In other words, creativity is something that only a few biological geniuses possess, and it is simply impossible to foster it through education. On the contrary, the I-paradigm, which emerged in the 1950s, focuses on individual creativity. According to this paradigm, everybody has the potential to be a creative person; proper education and a favorable environment can help one realize this potential. The third paradigm, the We-paradigm,

---

ferent approach to defining innovative human capital, which we measure based on survey respondents' self-reported ability to solve problems in new ways and ask new questions.

6   One of the major educational reforms in Korea to date, it is so named because the master plan of the reform was announced on May 31, 1995.

is a more recent one. Its basic premise is that every creative activity hinges upon existing knowledge, and is activated within and constantly affected by the social context. Thus, it is not individual cognitive skills but the sociocultural environment that fosters creativity. This paradigm shift makes it clear that both education and the social environment can play a key role in fostering creative minds.

Along with this conceptual change, very realistic concerns have been raised regarding education and human capital. Since the 1990s, Korea's fast pace of economic development has propelled it to the forefront of the world's technological frontier. There is wide consensus among economists and industrial leaders that if Korea really wants to obtain—and keep—the status of an advanced country, there should be more innovative human capital capable of making something new, as opposed to imitative human capital adopting and slightly modifying existing technology.

In the field of economics, Kim and Chung (2007) make it clear that Korea desperately needs creative human capital and educational reform to foster it. Considering the difference between imitative and innovative human capital, they argue that the future engine of growth will be creative human capital, which Korea has not so successfully accumulated. They propose several reform agendas. For example, they suggest that elementary and secondary schools should introduce research- and discussion-based curricula while emphasizing the importance of creativity and the futility of imitation, and that plagiarism should be punished in the classroom. Also, they propose that evaluations should be based on creative, open questions, and the college entrance system should be changed in accordance with the overall evaluation system.

In fact, it is not just a few economists who see the need for creativity in the classroom. Since the 1995 reform, there have been six presidents and at least three regime changes, but the emphasis on creativity in educational policy has continued, although there is still no consensus on how to best foster an innovative mindset.

One possibility is to provide students with more flexibility and opportunities for diverse activities. As is evident from the Programme for International Student Assessment (PISA) data, Korean students are spending more time studying than students from any other country (OECD 2020b). This shows in their impressive performance on international tests. Yet cramming for tests does not necessarily correlate with the critical and original thinking needed in an age of rapid technological change.

It has been proposed that, to foster creative mindsets, Korea needs a more flexible educational system. The 1995 reform set a comprehensive agenda, from elementary school to university. Its basic premise was that Korea needed to restructure its entire education system in preparation for a knowledge-based society. The goal was to create an open learning society. The proposal encompassed administrative deregulation, decentralization of the school system, curriculum reform, an increase in government education spending, and the use of ICT in schools. The creation of schools where greater autonomy is allowed in terms of student selection and curriculum choice was also proposed. The curriculum reforms focused on fostering the talents, aptitudes, and creativity of students to prepare them for a globalized and knowledge-based economy.

But educational reform was slow and people came to realize that education cannot be separated from other aspects of society. In particular, educational reform should be linked to changes in the labor market.

Measuring Innovative Human Capital

The main data in this study are from the Education–Labor Market Lifetime Path Survey. This unique data set was collected by the Korea Research Institute for Vocational Education and Training (KRIVET) from 2009 to 2011. It contains information on three cohorts of college graduates at 10-year intervals.[7] In the first year of the survey (2009), KRIVET collected yearbooks of 36 schools for the 1982 cohort, 41 schools for the 1992 cohort, and 53 schools for the 2002 cohort. Then it randomly selected 8,091 college graduates from these three cohorts. Questions on creativity were asked in the second year of the survey, and 5,031 of the first-year respondents participated. Besides the information on creativity, the data set contains detailed information about respondents' socioeconomic status (age, gender, family, education, etc.), monthly income, employment (industry, job function, primary job, secondary job, unemployment, etc.), as well as many other variables.

The most prominent difference across the three cohorts is the college entrance system they faced. The 1982 college graduate cohort had

---

7   Sharing the same graduation year does not imply that members of a cohort entered college in the same year. For example, male students might have taken from six months to three years off for military service. Thus, the same graduation cohort includes people who entered college in various years.

to take two examinations to enter their desired university: first, they had to take a nationwide exam to qualify to apply to any college; then they had to take individual university admission exams. The nationwide exam consisted of multiple-choice questions and the individual university exam usually consisted of challenging essay questions. The 1992 graduate cohort only had to take a nationwide exam consisting of multiple-choice questions. Depending on the college entrance year, those questions were drawn from textbooks on between 9 to 16 subjects. These changes in the college entrance system were made mainly to relieve the heavy burden on students, evident in the soaring costs of private tutoring.

Finally, the 2002 graduate cohort took an SAT-type nationwide exam on four to five subjects: language, English, mathematics, science, and social studies. This simplification also sought to relieve the burden on students, who had previously had to memorize the contents of a large number of textbooks to get a high score.

These very different experiences of Korea's college entrance system might have had a long-run effect on the cohorts' labor market performance. At the same time, each cohort's experience in the labor market was also different.

Since there is no widely accepted measure of creativity among individuals, we rely on a subjective measure based on self-evaluation. We asked respondents in each cohort to evaluate their abilities in: (1) memorizing, (2) solving problems using existing methods, (3) solving problems using new methods, and (4) raising new questions. We postulate that the former two are abilities related to imitative human capital while the latter two are related to innovative human capital. We asked respondents to grade themselves on each category of ability: (1) very low, (2) low, (3) average, (4) high, or (5) very high.

Another measure is a subjective creativity score. Respondents were asked to evaluate themselves on a scale of zero to 10, the higher number denoting higher creativity. There are, however, possibilities of measurement error as in any subjective measure, as well as the issue of reverse causation. Being aware of these issues, we will carefully discuss the possibility of reverse causation when we interpret our empirical results. For example, let us assume that we find a statistically positive correlation between creativity and wage. We can interpret this result as evidence that creativity is the cause of high wages. But it is also possible that higher wages make people think of themselves as more creative.

So, we need to keep in mind the possibility of this reverse causation when we interpret our empirical results.

There are two main sets of empirical questions regarding innovative human capital. One is about education. Such questions as "Does education contribute to fostering creativity among students?" and "Are younger cohorts more creative than older cohorts?" will be asked and answers sought in the next section. The other is about the labor market. Such questions as "Does it pay to be innovative?" or "Do the returns to innovative human capital increase over a lifetime?" will be asked in the section that follows.

College Graduates' Self-Evaluated Creativity

Before examining labor market performance, let us briefly review college graduates' self-evaluated creativity. We will focus on differences in responses across the three cohorts. Figure 5.1 summarizes self-evaluated creativity scores. Respondents in each cohort assign a high score to their creativity. The most frequent scores are 5, 7, and 8, which means they think of themselves as creative people. Around 30 percent of respondents marked themselves as below 5, and about 70 percent marked above 6. Many of them thought their creativity had undergone changes. They assign different creativity scores to their time in elementary school, middle and high school, college, and after college. This implies that many Korean college graduates think of creativity as something that can be changed during the course of one's life rather than as an innate trait that only a small number of people have. We can verify this fact by looking at the correlation coefficients of creativity scores at different points in time, as presented in table 5.1. The correlation coefficient of creativity scores between respondents' elementary school days and the present time is only 0.14. The correlation between college days and the present time is just over 0.3.

Meanwhile, differences among cohorts are evident, as shown in figure 5.1. The average creativity score is highest for the 1982 cohort. Both the 1982 and 1992 cohorts think that their creativity increased after college graduation, while the 2002 cohort thinks otherwise. One possible reason for this pessimistic view is that college graduates in the younger cohort did not have the opportunity to reveal their creativity in Korea's highly hierarchical workplace culture. In many cases, younger cohorts just follow the direction of their supervisors (who are

TABLE 5.1 Correlation coefficient of creativity score over time

	Elementary	Middle-High	College	Labor Market
Elementary	1	—	—	—
Middle-High	0.675	1	—	—
College	0.103	0.164	1	—
Labor market	0.138	0.399	0.301	1

SOURCE: Author.

FIGURE 5.1 Life-cycle changes in creativity

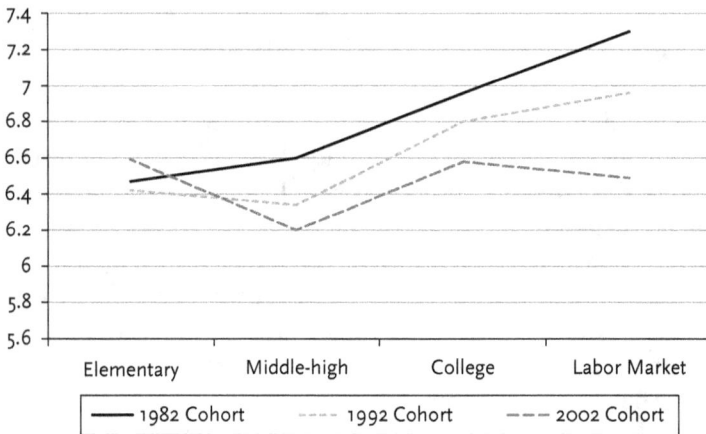

NOTE: This figure shows how each cohort of college graduates ranked their creativity at key points in their academic career and after.
SOURCE: Author.

usually older), and they do not have much room for proposing new ideas. Meanwhile, elder cohorts, as they are promoted to higher positions, have more opportunities to propose and carry out their ideas.

The 1992 and 2002 cohorts share the view that their creativity decreased during their middle and high school days. This is an indication that these cohorts did not appreciate secondary education, at least in terms of enhancing creativity, and perceived the college entry process as having an adverse effect on their creativity. It is not clear why the 1982 graduates did not share this view. Perhaps the college entrance system at the time provided them with a positive view of their creativity. At the time, less than 20 percent of high school graduates advanced to four-year colleges and to gain admission they had pass the difficult exams of individual universities.[8] It is possible that being part of this small college enrollment quota made them think of themselves as the "creative chosen few"; also, they probably thought they had increased their creativity by preparing for the difficult college entrance exam.

Whatever the reason, the younger generations' pessimistic views of their creativity cast some doubts on the quality of secondary education in Korea, which outside Korea receives high praise.

Now let us turn our attention to the different categories of ability. As mentioned above, we asked respondents to choose one of five scores: (1) very low, (2) low, (3) average, (4) high, and (5) very high. In the analysis below, we assign numbers 1 to 5 to these degrees, the higher number denoting higher ability.

As shown in table 5.1, a common feature of all cohorts is that they think their greatest ability is in solving problems using existing methods. This is followed by the ability to solve problems using new methods, and the ability to raise new questions, both of which were ranked at a similar level. The ability to memorize has the least positive evaluation.[9] This is not surprising, since problem-solving ability, along with memorization, has been consistently emphasized in Korean schools, at least up to the secondary level. This emphasis is reflected in the performance of Korean students on international tests such as PISA and Trends in International Mathematics and Science Study.

When we compare the three cohorts, the most notable finding is that the 1982 cohort evaluates its creativity more highly than do the younger cohorts. The proportion of people who think they have high or very high ability to solve problems and raise new questions is larger than in younger cohorts. This is a depressing finding, since creativity was emphasized in the education of the younger cohorts. As mentioned above, the college entrance system—namely, the difficulty of the examinations and the small size of the admissions quota—might be the cause

---

8   It is helpful to compare this number with other cohorts to understand how hard it was to enter college. In the case of the 1992 cohort, about 30 percent of high school graduates entered four-year colleges; in the case of the 2002 cohort, the number was about 70 percent.

9   This finding is interesting. It does not correspond with the fact that memorization is consistently emphasized in Korean schools. It is hard to give a clear explanation. Yet given the subjective nature of their evaluation, this does not seem to mean that they lacked memorization ability. It might be the case that respondents believe that their power of memorization was not strong enough to meet the high standard required during their time in school.

TABLE 5.2 Subjective evaluation of various abilities

		1982 Cohort		1992 Cohort		2002 Cohort	
		Ratio (%)	Freq	Ratio(%)	Freq	Ratio (%)	Freq
Memorizing	Very low	35	2.52	58	3.04	37	2.31
	Low	222	15.96	289	15.12	177	11.03
	Average	693	49.82	1,049	54.89	946	58.98
	High	357	25.66	428	22.4	390	24.31
	Very high	83	5.97	87	4.55	53	3.3
Problem	Very low	21	1.51	52	2.72	27	1.68
solving us-	Low	102	7.33	167	8.74	125	7.79
ing existing	Average	492	35.37	848	44.37	725	45.2
methods	High	619	44.5	728	38.1	618	38.53
	Very high	154	11.07	116	6.07	109	6.8
Problem solv-	Very low	22	1.58	36	1.88	18	1.12
ing using new	Low	131	9.42	208	10.88	169	10.54
methods	Average	558	40.12	854	44.69	797	49.69
	High	541	38.89	693	36.26	522	32.54
	Very high	137	9.85	120	6.28	97	6.05
Raising new	Very low	17	1.22	44	2.3	48	2.99
questions	Low	141	10.14	266	13.92	227	14.15
	Average	538	38.68	832	43.54	770	48
	High	553	39.76	639	33.44	464	28.93
	Very high	142	10.21	130	6.8	94	5.86

SOURCE: Author.

of the older cohort's positive view. But we should not neglect the possibility that their creativity could be enhanced after entry into the labor market. In figure 5.2, in which the average scores of self-perceived ability in different skills are presented, we can see that the 1982 cohort has the most positive view of their abilities overall, with the exception of memorization. This result corresponds well with what we have seen in the subjective creativity scores.

If we look at the correlation coefficient across different types of skills, and the subjective creativity index, as shown in table 5.3, we can presume that respondents consider the ability to solve problems in new ways and the ability to raise new questions to be more or less related to the concept of creativity. The correlation coefficients between the creativity score and self-perceived abilities increase, from lowest to highest, in the following order: memorizing, solving problems using existing methods, solving problems using new methods, and raising new questions. Among these, the correlation between solving problems in new ways and raising new questions is the strongest, with a correlation coefficient as high as 0.54. Respondents tend to think that

FIGURE 5.2 Scores of self-perceived ability, by type of skill and cohort

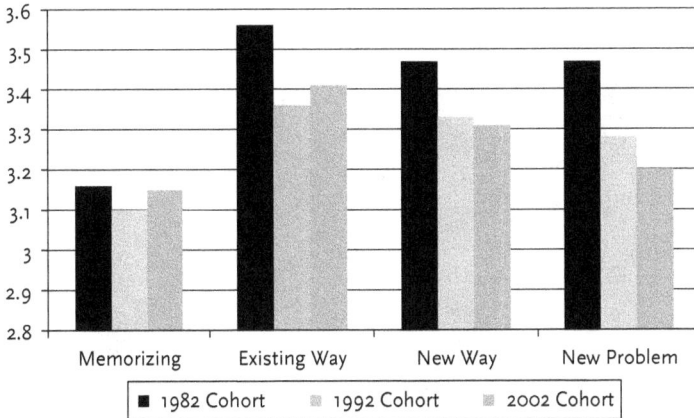

NOTE: "Existing way" is the ability to solve a problem using existing methods; "New way" is the ability to solve a problem using new methods; "New questions" is the ability to raise new questions.
SOURCE: Author.

TABLE 5.3 Correlation coefficient across different abilities

	Creativity index	Memorizing	Problem solving	Problem solving in new ways	Raising new questions
Creativity index	1	—	—	—	—
Memorizing	0.1818	1	—	—	—
Problem solving	0.1934	0.3085	1	—	—
New ways	0.3394	0.2073	0.3565	1	—
New questions	0.3905	0.2324	0.3203	0.5379	1

SOURCE: Author.

those two abilities are more related to creativity than the other two categories.

What we have seen so far is how college graduates self-evaluate their creativity, or the supply side of innovative human capital. To get some information on the demand side, we asked respondents if their jobs and duties require certain skills. More specifically, we asked if their jobs require memorizing, problem solving, or question raising. Figure 5.3 summarizes the responses. It turns out that each skill listed, including memorization, is required in the workplace. But the most needed, as perceived by all cohorts, is to solve problems in new ways. The ability to raise new questions is needed least.

FIGURE 5.3 Abilities necessary in the workplace, as ranked by three cohorts

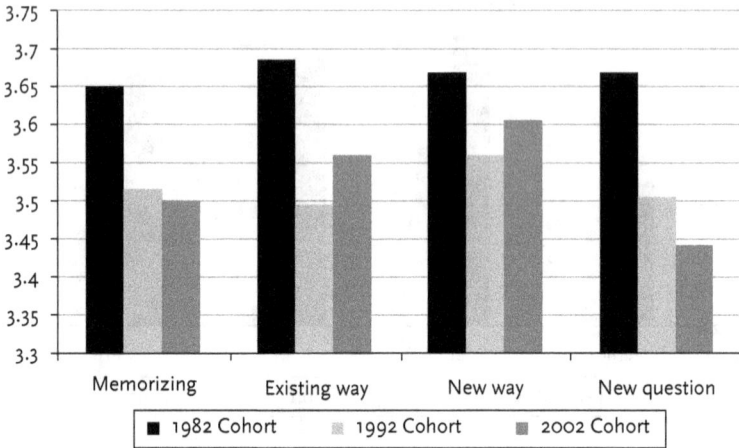

NOTE: See figure 5.2 for explanation of abilities.
SOURCE: Author.

The necessity of the skills is also ranked differently by cohort. This seems to reflect a combination of age- and job-specific effects. For example, for people in the oldest cohort, who might suffer from some loss of memory due to aging, the ability to memorize might be what they want most. In the case of the youngest cohort, it unlikely that they are assigned tasks that require raising new questions.

Now that we have considered both the supply and demand side of different skills, it is worth examining the gap between them. Figure 5.4 summarizes the results. It is interesting to note that the gap is largest for memorization. Skills related to innovative human capital show a smaller gap. One possible explanation is that innovative human capital can be accumulated after graduation. This hypothesis is supported by the fact that the demand and supply gap for innovative human capital tends to be smaller for the older cohort. By contrast, the ability to memorize can rarely be increased in old age. So this gap might be growing over time.

There is another piece of evidence that innovative human capital can be accumulated in the labor market. We asked respondents to evaluate the necessity of creativity on the job on a 10-point scale, from zero to 10. We then calculated the gap between the demand for creativity (necessity score) and the supply of creativity (self-evaluation score). As we can see in figure 5.5, for the 1992 and 2002 cohorts, this gap decreased

FIGURE 5.4 Supply and demand gaps, by skill and cohort

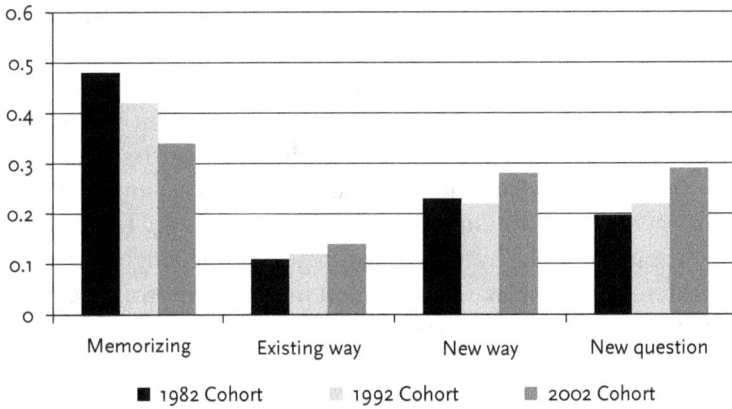

FIGURE 5.5 Evolution of the creativity gap over time, by cohort

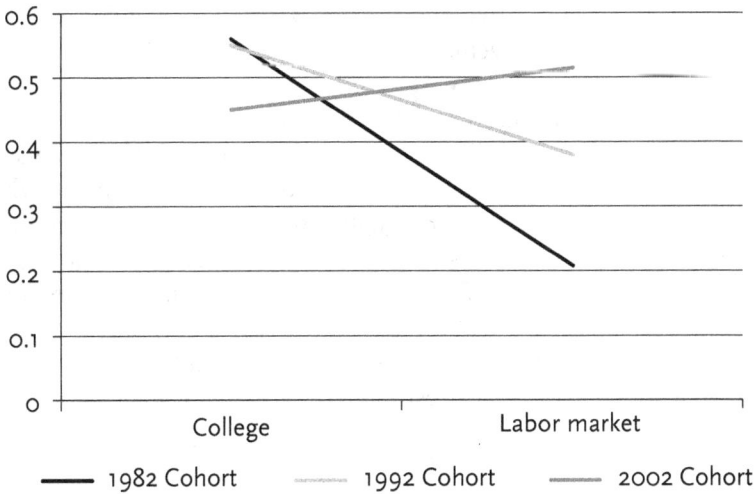

over time, from their college days to the present, mainly because their creativity score increased over time. But many members of the 2002 cohort, by contrast, believed that their creativity had decreased since graduation.

This gap analysis implies that we cannot attribute the accumulation of innovative human capital only to time in school. Our findings show that the workplace also plays an important role. By assigning proper roles to the younger generation, we can help them accumulate innovative human capital more rapidly and at a younger age. The pessimistic view of creativity held by the younger generation might reflect rigid and hierarchical workplace cultures that hinder them from seeking new approaches to old and new problems.

Innovative Human Capital and Labor Market Performance

Now, let us examine the returns to different skills in the Korean labor market. Before presenting and explaining regression results, it should be noted that all the relationships are not necessarily causal. For example, it is probable that people with higher wages tend to think of themselves as more creative and innovative than those who work for lower wages. But for convenience's sake, we will label the coefficient as return on human capital.

This section will proceed as follows: first we estimate the return on human capital using a small set of control variables, which do not seem to be correlated with ability. We then explore possible paths by which innovative human capital affects higher wages. Correlations between creativity and such factors as college choice, occupational choice, and firm size will be examined. Finally, through regressions with larger sets of control variables, we will see that creativity is correlated with unobservable personal traits that raise productivity and wages.

In what follows, we simply estimate the following wage equation:

$$\ln(\text{wage}) = \beta X + \gamma C + \varepsilon$$

Here, X represents variables including age and gender, and C is the measure of human capital. As noted above, there are two kinds of measures; one is the subjective creativity score, the other is a dummy variable indicating if the individual has certain categories of ability. Dummy variables include imitative human capital and creative human capital. They take a value of 1 if respondents think that they have ability in a certain type of skill to a high or a very high degree.

Current wage

The first set of regressions estimates the current wage with a small set of explanatory variables. Here, "current" means the year 2009, or the first year of the survey. Explanatory variables are age, age squared, a female dummy, and dummy variables indicating different types of human capital. As we have seen above, there are four different ability variables: memorizing, problem solving in existing ways, problem solving in new ways, and raising new questions. It should be noted that age and gender are exogenous, in the sense that they are determined at the time of birth, and cannot be changed by deliberate effort. We first estimate the wage equation for the full sample, then estimate it for each cohort.

In the full sample, each type of ability is positively correlated with wages, as we can clearly see in table 5.4. People who have the ability to memorize get 8 percent higher wages than those who do not, and those who have the ability to solve problems in existing ways get 9.2 percent higher wages than those who do not. The abilities to solve problems in new ways and to raise new questions are associated with 6.8 percent and 7.3 percent higher wages, respectively. The highest-paying ability is the

TABLE 5.4 Abilities and wages (full sample)

	(1)	(2)	(3)	(4)	(5)
Age	0.084	0.085	0.082	0.083	0.085
	(8.27)**	(8.37)**	(8.05)**	(8.13)**	(8.35)**
Age squared	–0.072	–0.074	–0.07	–0.071	–0.074
	(5.57)**	(5.70)**	(5.37)**	(5.47)**	(5.70)**
Male	0.359	0.362	0.36	0.357	0.356
	(19.32)**	(19.55)**	(19.39)**	(19.23)**	(19.22)**
Memorizing	0.08	—	—	—	0.05
	(4.86)**	—	—	—	(2.90)**
Problem solving	—	0.092	—	—	0.061
	—	(6.10)**	—	—	(3.67)**
New ways	—	—	0.068	—	0.021
	—	—	(4.50)**	—	(1.20)
New questions	—	—	—	0.073	0.037
	—	—	—	(4.80)**	(2.12)*
R²	0.29	0.29	0.29	0.29	0.3

NOTE: Number of observations is 4,089. Constants are not reported.
T-values are in parentheses. ** $p<0.01$, * $p<0.05$, + $p<0.10$.
SOURCE: Author.

TABLE 5.5 Abilities and wages (1982 cohort)

	(1)	(2)	(3)	(4)	(5)
Age	−0.039	−0.029	−0.021	−0.033	−0.024
	(0.37)	(0.28)	(0.21)	(0.32)	(0.23)
Age squared	0.022	0.014	0.006	0.017	0.009
	(0.22)	(0.14)	(0.06)	(0.17)	(0.08)
Male	0.395	0.394	0.396	0.397	0.394
	(9.68)**	(9.67)**	(9.73)**	(9.75)**	(9.66)**
Memorizing	0.04	—	—	—	0.02
	(1.35)	—	—	—	(0.66)
Problem solving	—	0.05	—	—	0.013
	—	(1.78)+	—	—	(0.43)
New ways	—	—	0.073	—	0.043
	—	—	(2.64)**	—	(1.33)
New questions	—	—	—	0.073	0.045
	—	—	—	(2.66)**	(1.43)
R^2	0.29	0.29	0.29	0.29	0.30

NOTE: Number of observations is 1,219. Constants are not reported.
T-values are in parentheses. ** $p<0.01$, * $p<0.05$, + $p<0.10$.
SOURCE: Author.

ability to solve problems in existing ways. When we include the four abilities in one wage equation, returns to innovative human capital are not statistically significant, whereas memorizing and problem solving pay off.

The results are different for different cohort samples. In the 1982 cohort sample, the return to the ability of memorizing is only about 4 percent and not statistically different from zero at the 10 percent significance level. The return to the ability to solve problems in existing ways is about 5 percent and not statistically different from zero at the 5 percent significance level. But returns on innovative human capital, namely on the abilities to solve problems in new ways and to raise new questions, are 7.3 percent and statistically different from zero at the 1 percent significance level. Innovative human capital pays for those who have been in the labor market for a long time, for example, more than 25 years. It could be the case that those who earn more are more likely to evaluate themselves as innovative. But the correlation itself is an important fact when we compare these results with younger cohorts.

As for the 1992 cohort, all four abilities pay off in the labor market. Solving problems in existing ways gets the highest returns. Those who think they have the ability to solve problems in existing ways get 10.6 percent higher wages than those who do not think so. The ability to solve problems in new ways also gets a high return, of 10 percent. The abilities to raise new questions and memorize also have good returns of

about 8.2 to 8.3 percent. In the equation with four ability dummy variables, only the dummy variable indicating the ability to solve problems
has a statistically significant coefficient. In general, imitative human
capital pays off more than innovative human capital in the 1992 cohort.

For the 2002 cohort, we get totally different results from the older
cohorts. The highest-paying ability is memorization. The next highest is
the ability to solve problems in existing ways. Innovative human capital does not pay much for this youngest cohort. The coefficients of the
dummy variables are not statistically different from zero.

To summarize, the longer people stay in the labor market, the more
innovative human capital pays. For example, consider the 2002 cohort.
Only seven years after their graduation, the ability to memorize remains
an important factor determining their labor market performance. They
might not get work assignments that require creative attitudes and innovative actions. As for the 1992 cohort, they have passed through the
stages that require simple memorization ability and now require the
ability to solve problems. For members of the oldest cohort, who have
spent more than 25 years in the labor market, the abilities to solve
problems in new ways and to propose new questions are highlighted.
This finding is likely more valid in the Korean labor market than in, for
example, the U.S. labor market. In the Korean labor market, where a
hierarchy by age or by date of joining the firm is often strictly enforced,

TABLE 5.6 Abilities and wages (1992 cohort)

	(1)	(2)	(3)	(4)	(5)
Age	0.229	0.215	0.234	0.201	0.253
	(1.18)	(1.11)	(1.21)	(1.04)	(1.31)
Age squared	−0.281	−0.264	−0.29	−0.248	−0.312
	(1.15)	(1.09)	(1.19)	(1.02)	(1.28)
Male	0.521	0.525	0.523	0.522	0.515
	(12.96)**	(13.13)**	(13.05)**	(13.00)**	(12.87)**
Memorizing	0.083	—	—	—	0.047
	(2.92)**	—	—	—	(1.61)
Problem solving	—	0.106	—	—	0.069
	—	(4.16)**	—	—	(2.47)*
New ways	—	—	0.099	—	0.05
	—	—	(3.87)**	—	(1.69)+
New questions	—	—	—	0.082	0.032
	—	—	—	(3.18)**	(1.12)
R^2	0.17	0.18	0.18	0.17	0.18

NOTE: Number of observations is 1,661. Constants are not reported.
T-values are in parentheses. ** $p<0.01$, * $p<0.05$, + $p<0.10$.
SOURCE: Author.

TABLE 5.7 Abilities and wages (2002 cohort)

	(1)	(2)	(3)	(4)	(5)
Age	0.187	0.14	0.15	0.141	0.165
	(0.68)	(0.5)	(0.54)	(0.51)	(0.6)
Age squared	−0.227	−0.15	−0.17	−0.153	−0.188
	(0.48)	(0.31)	(0.35)	(0.32)	(0.4)
Male	0.197	0.209	0.212	0.204	0.195
	(5.43)**	(5.77)**	(5.81)**	(5.59)**	(5.38)**
Memorizing	0.12	—	—	—	0.094
	(4.57)**	—	—	—	(3.37)**
Problem solving	—	0.097	—	—	0.074
	—	(4.13)**	—	—	(2.83)**
New ways	—	—	0.015	—	−0.041
	—	—	(0.64)	—	(1.5)
New questions	—	—	—	0.06	0.035
	—	—	—	(2.43)*	(1.27)
R^2	0.16	0.16	0.15	0.15	0.17

NOTE: Number of observations is 1,209. Constants are not reported.
T-values are in parentheses. ** $p<0.01$, * $p<0.05$, + $p<0.10$.
SOURCE: Author.

new entrants to a company cannot take risks and usually do routine jobs requiring little creativity.

Wages on the first job

In the previous section, we see that innovative human capital is paid more in the later stages of a professional career. This implies two possibilities. First, it could be the case that innovative human capital is accumulated according to the requirements of a job. Second, it is also possible that innovative human capital does not get much attention in the early stages of a professional career. Whatever the case, innovative human capital might not increase a person's wages at the time of labor market entrance. The Education–Labor Market Lifetime Path Survey asks respondents about their first wages upon college graduation. While not free from measurement error, the responses provide useful information. We will use this to examine the relationship between current ability and past wages.[10]

Table 5.8 presents the regression results, whose dependent variable is the wage at the time of labor market entry and explanatory variables

---

10   Past wages are changed into real terms (base year 2009) using a consumer price index.

TABLE 5.8 Abilities and wages on the first job (across all three age cohorts)

	(1)	(2)	(3)	(4)	(5)
Age	0.248	0.244	0.245	0.242	0.246
	(4.90)**	(4.83)**	(4.85)**	(4.79)**	(4.86)**
Age squared	−0.392	−0.385	−0.387	−0.382	−0.39
	(4.39)**	(4.32)**	(4.34)**	(4.29)**	(4.36)**
Male	−0.01	−0.007	−0.009	−0.009	−0.013
	(0.29)	(0.20)	(0.28)	(0.28)	(0.40)
Memorizing	0.037	—	—	—	0.032
	(1.28)	—	—	—	(1.06)
Problem solving	—	0.013	—	—	−0.007
	—	(0.50)	—	—	(0.25)
New ways	—	—	0.027	—	0.014
	—	—	(1.00)	—	(0.45)
New questions	—	—	—	0.034	0.025
	—	—	—	(1.27)	(0.82)
R^2	0.03	0.03	0.03	0.03	0.03

NOTE: Number of observations is 2,105. Constants are not reported.
T-values are in parentheses. ** $p<0.01$, * $p<0.05$, + $p<0.10$.
SOURCE: Author.

are self-evaluations of current abilities. The results clearly show that there is no statistically significant relationship between current ability and past wages. No coefficients of ability variables are significantly different from zero.

This lack of correlation is most evident for the 1982 cohort, as shown in table 5.9. No ability dummy variables have statistically significant coefficients in the regression. There could be measurement errors, since it has been more than 25 years since members of this cohort earned their first wages after graduation. But under the assumption that the measurement errors are not large, the result implies the following. If innovative human capital entails innate abilities, those innate abilities are not clearly revealed at the time of entry into the labor market, but are eventually noticed and remunerated. On the other hand, if innovative human capital is something that can be developed through the process of education and labor market experience, those who accumulate innovative human capital can enjoy pecuniary returns from it.

In the case of the 1992 cohort (table 5.10), the ability to raise new questions is positively related to wages at the time of labor market entry. It is interesting to note that the estimated value of the coefficient is even higher than what we get in the current wage regression. This is a unique phenomenon found only in the 1992 cohort. Other than this somewhat odd result, the result is basically the same as what we found

TABLE 5.9 Abilities and wages on the first job (1982 cohort)

	(1)	(2)	(3)	(4)	(5)
Age	0.273	0.276	0.274	0.269	0.272
	(3.24)**	(3.27)**	(3.25)**	(3.19)**	(3.21)**
Age squared	−0.374	−0.379	−0.376	−0.368	−0.374
	(2.59)**	(2.63)**	(2.61)**	(2.55)*	(2.58)*
Male	0.038	0.031	0.032	0.032	0.03
	(0.48)	(0.39)	(0.41)	(0.40)	(0.38)
Memorizing	−0.014	—	—	—	−0.039
	(0.25)	—	—	—	(0.64)
Problem solving	—	0.062	—	—	0.056
	—	(1.14)	—	—	(0.92)
New ways	—	—	0.053	—	0.032
	—	—	(0.98)	—	(0.52)
New questions	—	—	—	0.042	0.014
	—	—	—	(0.77)	(0.23)
R^2	0.09	0.09	0.09	0.09	0.09

NOTE: Number of observations is 570. Constants are not reported.
T-values are in parentheses. ** $p<0.01$, * $p<0.05$, + $p<0.10$.
SOURCE: Author.

TABLE 5.10 Abilities and wages on the first job (1992 cohort)

	(1)	(2)	(3)	(4)	(5)
Age	0.209	0.206	0.208	0.199	0.198
	(2.66)**	(2.64)**	(2.66)**	(2.55)*	(2.52)*
Age squared	−0.351	−0.348	−0.349	−0.334	−0.332
	(2.51)*	(2.49)*	(2.50)*	(2.40)*	(2.37)*
Male	0.097	0.097	0.09	0.092	0.093
	(2.04)*	(2.06)*	(1.91)+	(1.97)*	(1.95)+
Memorizing	0.007	—	—	—	−0.012
	(0.18)	—	—	—	(0.28)
Problem solving	—	0.021	—	—	−0.003
	—	(0.58)	—	—	(0.07)
New ways	—	—	0.047	—	0.011
	—	—	(1.27)	—	(0.25)
New questions	—	—	—	0.086**	0.084+
	—	—	—	(2.32)*	(1.97)*
R^2	0.03	0.03	0.03	0.04	0.04

NOTE: Number of observations is 879. Constants are not reported.
T-values are in parentheses. ** $p<0.01$, * $p<0.05$, + $p<0.10$.
SOURCE: Author.

in the 2002 cohort. Both imitative and innovative human capital were not remunerated at the time of their entry into the labor market.

The 2002 cohort shows quite different patterns in table 5.11. The most important ability factors that determine wages at entrance are memorization and solving problems in existing ways. Or, we can say

TABLE 5.11 Abilities and wages on the first job (2002 cohort)

	(1)	(2)	(3)	(4)	(5)
Age	0.186	0.149	0.137	0.131	0.191
	(1.19)	(0.95)	(0.87)	(0.84)	(1.22)
Age squared	−0.35	−0.283	−0.26	−0.251	−0.359
	(1.16)	(0.93)	(0.85)	(0.82)	(1.19)
Male	0.256	0.258	0.266	0.266	0.246
	(5.85)**	(5.86)**	(6.01)**	(6.01)**	(5.57)**
Memorizing	0.162	—	—	—	0.131
	(4.09)**	—	—	—	(3.10)**
Problem solving	—	0.114	—	—	0.065
	—	(3.19)**	—	—	(1.64)
New ways	—	—	0.058	—	0.012
	—	—	(1.58)	—	(0.30)
New questions	—	—	—	0.066+	0.014
	—	—	—	(1.77)	(0.35)
R^2	0.12	0.11	0.10	0.10	0.12

NOTE: Number of observations is 656. Constants are not reported.
T-values are in parentheses. ** $p<0.01$, * $p<0.05$, + $p<0.10$.
SOURCE: Author.

that imitative human capital is more important for the 2002 cohort at the time of labor market entry. It should be noted that it is only seven years since their entry into the labor market, so that the measurement error is smallest for this cohort. It is also worth noting that the returns to memorizing and problem-solving abilities are higher at the time of entry than in the year 2009. Those abilities are relatively easy to observe through the college name or test scores. It is possible that those observable characteristics of job applicants are correlated with memorizing and problem-solving abilities.

So far, we have examined the relationship between abilities and past and present wages. Implications from the regression analysis are quite consistent. In the Korean labor market, returns on innovative human capital rise as labor market experience is accumulated. For recent college graduates, the return on imitative human capital is higher than on innovative human capital. As a robustness check, let us look at the relationship between the self-reported creativity score and past and present wages.

We run sets of two regressions for each cohort. One looks at the relationship between the creativity index while in college and wages at the time of entry into the labor market, the other looks at the relationship between the current creativity index and present wages. The results are presented in table 5.12. As clearly shown in the table, there

TABLE 5.12 Creativity score and wages, by cohort

	1982 cohort		1992 cohort		2002 cohort	
	First job	2009	First job	2009	First job	2009
Age	0.273	−0.026	0.212	0.216	0.134	0.161
	(3.23)**	(0.25)	(2.71)**	(1.12)	(0.85)	(0.57)
Age squared	−0.373	0.01	−0.359	−0.267	−0.256	−0.188
	(2.59)**	(0.10)	(2.57)*	(1.09)	(0.84)	(0.39)
Male	0.039	0.395	0.097	0.519	0.274	0.21
	(0.49)	(9.69)**	(2.07)*	(12.8)**	(6.20)**	(5.76)**
Creativity index	0.006	0.016	−0.007	0.018	0.006	0.007
	(0.34)	(1.96)+	(0.65)	(2.50)*	(0.62)	(1.10)
Obs.	569	1,218	876	1,655	655	1,206
R^2	0.09	0.08	0.03	0.17	0.09	0.15

NOTE: Constants are not reported.
T-values are in parentheses. ** $p<0.01$, * $p<0.05$, + $p<0.10$.
SOURCE: Author.

is no relationship between creativity scores and wages on the first job. But in the case of present wages, high self-reported creativity scores are related to higher wages among the 1982 or 1992 cohorts. For the youngest 2002 cohort, there is no such relationship. Again, we can see that creativity does not pay at the time of labor market entry but pays off in the long run in the Korean labor market.

Creativity, college choice, and wages

Now it is time to examine the relationship between creativity and elite education. There is a widely acknowledged set of "top three" colleges in Korea: Seoul National University, Korea University, and Yonsei University. To gain admission to these elite colleges, a student needs to get through a very competitive individual university admission examination (1982 cohort), or score within the top 1 to 2 percent in a nationwide matriculation examination (1992 and 2002 cohorts). Our question is whether people with innovative human capital were more likely to enter elite colleges. We first set up a dummy variable that takes a value of 1 if the person graduated from one of the elite top three elite universities.

Table 5.13 shows the results of a probit analysis where the dependent variable is the elite college dummy. It is evident that the ability to solve problems in existing ways is the most prominent factor that raises the probability of entering an elite college. Marginal effects are about 4 to 6 percent. This is not surprising since, for any cohort in Korea, problem solving is the decisive factor determining college choice. We

TABLE 5.13 Top three universities and creativity scores (probit)

	Full sample	1982 cohort	1992 cohort	2002 cohort
Memorizing	-0.017	-0.1	-0.262	0.152
	(0.27)	(0.95)	(1.98)*	(1.54)
Problem solving	0.386	0.342	0.378	0.399
	(6.28)**	(3.12)**	(3.17)**	(4.00)**
New ways	0.076	0.155	-0.019	0.097
	(1.21)	(1.39)	(0.15)	(0.97)
New questions	-0.001	-0.076	0.156	-0.038
	(0.02)	(0.70)	(1.30)	(0.37)
Obs.	4,906	1,391	1,911	1,604

NOTE: Constants are not reported.
Z-values are in parentheses. ** $p<0.01$, * $p<0.05$, + $p<0.10$.
SOURCE: Author.

can consider that those who graduated from the top three universities in Korea belong to the top 2 percent performers in problem-solving ability, at least up to their time in high school. The data in table 5.13 are consistent with the fact that graduates of elite schools have been good at problem solving in existing ways.

It should be noted that creativity or innovation is not the reason for the wage premium of graduation from elite colleges. The average subjective creativity score of elite college graduates is lower than that of graduates from other colleges by 0.04. In addition, graduates of elite colleges think that their creativity has lessened compared to their college days. Graduates from other universities think the opposite is true. It is not clear why graduates from elite colleges enjoy an increasing wage premium despite their low self-evaluation on creativity; the elite college premium is not related to the innovative nature of its graduates.

Occupation type and creativity

Another factor that might be correlated with wages and creativity is a person's choice of occupation. We want to examine whether choosing or being employed in the public sector or in research or teaching jobs is related to creativity. These occupations have long been preferred by Korean college graduates. In the following analysis we categorize private, venture, and foreign companies as the private sector; government organizations, public enterprises, and government-funded institutes as the public sector; universities, and public and private research institutes as the research sector; and schools other than universities as the education sector. We will focus on the research, teaching, and public sectors.

TABLE 5.14 Occupation type and creativity (probit)

		Full Sample	1982 Cohort	1992 Cohort	2002 Cohort
Public sector	Memorizing	−0.098 (1.85)+	−0.002 (0.02)	−0.186 (2.22)*	−0.056 (0.59)
	Problem solving	−0.007 (0.13)	0.09 (0.89)	−0.094 (1.23)	0.057 (0.64)
	New ways	0.016 (0.30)	−0.075 (0.71)	0.153 (1.86)+	−0.111 (1.16)
	New questions	−0.042 (0.79)	0.189 (1.78)+	−0.113 (1.39)	−0.121 (1.24)
	Creativity score	−0.036 (2.80)**	−0.001 (0.05)	−0.049 (2.37)*	−0.041 (1.96)*
Research	Memorizing	0.056 (0.90)	0.027 (0.28)	0.127 (1.14)	0.06 (0.44)
	Problem solving	0.148 (2.37)*	0.148 (1.50)	0.186 (1.68)+	−0.034 (0.25)
	New ways	0.064 (0.96)	0.199 (1.91)+	−0.193 (1.63)	0.193 (1.40)
	New questions	0.186 (2.88)**	0.159 (1.57)	0.206 (1.79)+	0.037 (0.26)
	Creativity score	0.049 (2.86)**	0.003 (0.12)	0.076 (2.26)*	0.033 (1.01)
Education	Memorizing	0.109 (2.19)*	0.118 (1.48)	0.168 (1.84)+	0.057 (0.57)
	Problem solving	0.095 (1.97)*	−0.148 (1.86)+	0.168 (1.91)+	0.257 (2.64)**
	New ways	−0.175 (3.38)**	−0.212 (2.52)*	−0.167 (1.74)+	−0.137 (1.33)
	New questions	−0.015 (0.30)	−0.038 (0.45)	−0.049 (0.52)	−0.125 (1.20)
	Creativity score	0.034 (2.65)**	−0.011 (0.51)	0.006 (0.24)	0.048 (2.01)*
Obs.		4,895	1,390	1,905	1,600

NOTE: Dependent variables are dummy variables that take a value of 1 if the respondent is employed in the public, research, or educational sectors.
Constants are not reported. Z-values are in parentheses. ** $p<0.01$, * $p<0.05$, + $p<0.10$.
SOURCE: Author.

We create three dummy variables for these categories (again, for the private, public, research, and education sectors), then run a probit regression to examine if occupational choice is related to creativity. Table 5.14 presents the results. The most obvious finding is that the higher the self-reported creativity index, the lower the probability that one is hired in the public sector. This holds true across the full sample and also in the 1992 and 2002 cohort subsamples. The correlation seems to reflect causality in both directions. While there is a possibility that people with less self-perceived creativity prefer the public sector, it is also possible that public-sector jobs deprive employees of the opportunity to accumulate innovative human capital. We have good reason to believe that the latter is the more probable case, given the fact that many bright young people are in public-sector jobs in Korea.

Meanwhile, the probability of working in the research sector is higher for those with the self-perceived abilities to solve problems in existing ways and to raise new questions. A high creativity score is associated with a higher probability of working in the research sector. Teaching jobs also attract creative people. But it is also found that those with the self-perceived ability to solve problems in new ways have lower probability of working as teachers.

Higher degrees

It is possible that creative people seek higher degrees. We create two dummy variables for master's and doctorate degrees and run probit regressions. We find that the probability of getting a higher degree is

TABLE 5.15 Creativity and higher degrees

		Full sample	1982 cohort	1992 cohort	2002 cohort
Master's	Memorizing	0.023	0.064	−0.025	0.033
		(0.53)	(0.83)	(0.34)	(0.41)
	Problem solving	0.193	0.048	0.171	0.277
		(4.60)**	(0.63)	(2.47)*	(3.59)**
	New ways	0.044	0.048	0.056	0.05
		(0.97)	(0.59)	(0.75)	(0.62)
	New questions	0.211	0.237	0.204	0.11
		(4.78)**	(2.98)**	(2.79)**	(1.35)
	Creativity index	0.063	0.045	0.047	0.061
		(5.54)**	(2.04)*	(2.40)*	(3.19)**
Doctorate	Memorizing	0.096	−0.093	0.033	0.019
		(1.09)	(0.87)	(0.26)	(0.33)
	Problem solving	0.306	0.321	0.249	0.325
		(3.25)**	(3.11)**	(1.98)*	(5.50)**
	New ways	0.178	0.109	0.119	0.129
		(1.83)+	(1.00)	(0.92)	(2.10)*
	New questions	0.172	0.303	−0.055	0.2
		(1.80)+	(2.81)**	(0.43)	(3.30)**
	Creativity index	0.04	0.052	0.066	0.068
		(1.49)	(1.68)+	(2.04)*	(4.13)**

NOTE: Constants are not reported. Z-values are in parentheses. ** $p<0.01$, * $p<0.05$, + $p<0.10$.
SOURCE: Author.

greater for those who have the self-perceived abilities of problem solving and raising questions. Those who have a higher subjective creativity score are also more likely to have a higher degree. The results are similar for both master's and doctorate degrees. Again, dual causation seems to explain this correlation. It is natural to think that creative people want to seek higher degrees, but it is equally possible that graduate studies foster creativity.

Firm size

Finally, we consider the correlation between creativity and working in a large firm. In Korea, firm size is an important determinant of performance in the labor market. There is a large wage gap between large firms and small and medium ones, and there is strong competition among college graduates for getting jobs in large firms. We create a dummy variable for firms with more than 300 workers. Table 5.16 shows probit results for being employed in a large firm. There is no correlation between the subjective creativity score and the probability of working in a large firm. The ability to solve problems in existing ways is the only ability that is associated with a probability of working in a large firm. This finding corresponds well with previous analysis that shows that, among returns to different abilities, the return to the ability of solving problems in existing ways is the highest. It also corresponds with public belief that large firms prefer graduates from elite colleges and require high scores on various exams.

TABLE 5.16 Creativity and firm size

	Full sample	1982 cohort	1992 cohort	2002 cohort
Memorizing	−0.003	−0.038	0.034	−0.019
	(0.08)	(0.48)	(0.50)	(0.25)
Problem solving	0.133	0.150	0.078	0.221
	(3.28)**	(1.91)	(1.22)	(3.09)**
New ways	0.079	0.102	0.108	0.019
	(1.83)	(1.23)	(1.56)	(0.25)
New questions	−0.002	0.083	−0.060	0.022
	(0.04)	(1.01)	(0.87)	(0.29)
Creativity index	−0.013	0.022	−0.011	−0.022
	(1.19)	(0.98)	(0.64)	(1.30)

NOTE: Constants are not reported. Z-values are in parentheses. ** $p<0.01$, * $p<0.05$, + $p<0.10$
SOURCE: Author.

Creativity and wages: Including all the control variables

Now let us compare the results of regressions with minimum control and full control. In a regression of minimum control, only exogenous factors such as gender and age are included as explanatory variables. In the regressions with more control variables, dummies for occupation, elite college enrollment, higher degrees, and employment in a large firm are included as explanatory variables. If the subjective creativity score and variables related to innovative human capital are correlated with wages even after controlling for these variables, we can say that innovative human capital affects wages through the unobservable traits of creative people. Or we can say that people with innovative human capital earn higher wages compared to others with similar observable characteristics.

Table 5.17 shows the relationship between survey respondents' creativity score and wages.[11] We can see that the creativity score is positively correlated with the wage in the full-control regressions. It is true for the full sample and also true for the 1992 cohort and 2002 cohort subsamples.

From table 5.18 to table 5.21, we can see the returns to various abilities across the different cohorts. To sum up, innovative human capital generates higher returns for the older generation. In the 1982 and 1992 cohorts, the coefficients of the abilities to solve problems in new ways and to raise new questions are larger than those of the abilities to memorize or solve problems in existing ways. In the 2002 cohort sample, the result is just the opposite. It is also notable that coefficients of ability variables are smaller in fully controlled regressions than in regressions with minimum control. In particular, the coefficients of the ability to solve problems in existing ways are most affected by specification. This means that problem-solving ability is more strongly correlated with observable variables than other abilities. That is, this ability is related to graduating from a better college, and choosing a better occupation with a larger firm.

It is also interesting that in the 1992 cohort sample, the return to the ability of solving problems in existing ways is highest in the regression with minimum control, but in the full control regression, the returns to the abilities to solve problems in new ways and to raise new questions

---

11   To save space we do not report coefficients of control variables.

TABLE 5.17 Subject creativity index and wages

	Full sample	1982 cohort	1992 cohort	2002 cohort
Age	0.082	0.039	0.356	0.049
	(8.26)**	(0.39)	(1.89)	(0.19)
Age squared	−0.067	−0.042	−0.434	0.017
	(5.28)**	(0.43)	(1.83)	(0.04)
Male	0.294	0.306	0.440	0.147
	(15.88)**	(7.56)**	(10.94)**	(4.28)**
Creativity index	0.013	0.009	0.020	0.010
	(3.29)**	(1.19)	(2.84)**	(1.76)+
Top three	0.177	0.084	0.224	0.202
	(6.24)**	(1.71)+	(3.46)**	(5.52)**
Public	−0.171	−0.193	−0.104	−0.228
	(7.95)**	(4.02)**	(3.04)**	(7.21)**
Research	−0.234	−0.192	−0.196	−0.421
	(6.69)**	(3.40)**	(3.09)**	(6.78)**
Teaching	0.017	0.013	0.089	−0.010
	(0.79)	(0.36)	(2.03)*	(0.26)
Master's	0.039	0.040	0.047	0.002
	(2.17)*	(1.29)	(1.47)	(0.09)
Doctorate	0.091	0.083	0.081	−0.101
	(2.71)**	(1.64)+	(1.33)	(1.37)
Large firm	0.297	0.369	0.298	0.227
	(17.44)**	(10.16)**	(10.72)**	(9.32)**
Obs.	4079	1218	1655	1206
R^2	0.35	0.17	0.24	0.28

NOTE: Constants are not reported. T-values are in parentheses. ** $p<0.01$, * $p<0.05$, + $p<0.10$.
SOURCE: Author.

TABLE 5.18 Abilities and wages (full sample)

		(1)	(2)	(3)	(4)	(5)
Minimum control	Memorizing	0.080				0.050
		(4.86)**				(2.90)**
	Problem solving		0.092			0.061
			(6.10)**			(3.67)**
	New ways			0.068		0.021
				(4.50)**		(1.20)
	New questions				0.073	0.037
					(4.80)**	(2.12)*
	R^2	0.29	0.29	0.29	0.29	0.30
Full control	Memorizing	0.070				0.048
		(4.40)**				(2.93)**
	Problem solving		0.062			0.034
			(4.25)**			(2.10)*
	New ways			0.067		0.013
				(4.58)**		(0.77)
	New questions				0.052	0.044
					(3.53)**	(2.63)**
	R^2	0.36	0.36	0.36	0.36	0.38

NOTE: Number of observations is 4,089.
Constants are not reported. Z-values are in parentheses. ** $p<0.01$, * $p<0.05$, + $p<0.10$.
SOURCE: Author.

TABLE 5.19 Ability and wages (1982 cohort)

		(1)	(2)	(3)	(4)	(5)
Minimum control	Memorizing	0.040 (1.35)				0.020 (0.66)
	Problem solving		0.050 (1.78)+			0.013 (0.43)
	New ways			0.073 (2.64)**		0.043 (1.33)
	New questions				0.073 (2.66)**	0.045 (1.43)
	R^2	0.07	0.08	0.08	0.08	0.08
Full control	Memorizing	0.036 (1.29)				0.025 (0.85)
	Problem solving		0.027 (1.03)			-0.003 (0.09)
	New ways			0.058 (2.18)*		0.030 (0.96)
	New questions				0.052 (1.96)+	0.041 (1.36)
	R^2	0.17	0.17	0.17	0.17	0.18

NOTE: Number of observations is 1,219.
Constants are not reported. Z-values are in parentheses. ** $p<0.01$, * $p<0.05$, + $p<0.10$.
SOURCE: Author.

TABLE 5.20 Ability and wages (1992 cohort)

		(1)	(2)	(3)	(4)	(5)
Minimum control	Memorizing	0.083 (2.92)**				0.047 (1.61)
	Problem solving		0.106 (4.16)**			0.069 (2.47)*
	New ways			0.099 (3.87)**		0.050 (1.69)+
	New questions				0.082 (3.18)**	0.032 (1.12)
	R^2	0.17	0.18	0.18	0.17	0.18
Full control	Memorizing	0.077 (2.80)**				0.047 (1.64)
	Problem solving		0.080 (3.21)**			0.043 (1.60)
	New ways			0.083 (3.30)**		0.045 (1.57)
	New questions				0.088 (3.55)**	0.043 (1.53)
	R^2	0.24	0.24	0.24	0.24	0.24

NOTE: Number of observations is 1,661.
Constants are not reported. Z-values are in parentheses. ** $p<0.01$, * $p<0.05$, + $p<0.10$.
SOURCE: Author.

TABLE 5.21 Ability and wages (2002 cohort)

		(1)	(2)	(3)	(4)	(5)
Minimum control	Memorizing	0.120 (4.57)**				0.094 (3.37)**
	Problem solving		0.097 (4.13)**			0.074 (2.83)**
	New ways			0.015 (0.64)		−0.041 (1.50)
	New questions				0.060 (2.43)*	0.035 (1.27)
	R^2	0.16	0.16	0.15	0.15	0.17
Full control	Memorizing	0.108 (4.43)**				0.091 (3.51)**
	Problem solving		0.070 (3.15)**			0.046 (1.87)+
	New ways			0.058 (2.52)*		−0.041 (1.63)
	New questions				0.006 (0.27)	0.043 (1.67)+
	R^2	0.29	0.28	0.28	0.28	0.29

NOTE: Number of observations is 1,209.
Constants are not reported. Z-values are in parentheses. ** $p<0.01$, * $p<0.05$, + $p<0.10$.
SOURCE: Author.

are higher. This is another piece of evidence that problem-solving ability served as an important screening device for entry into the Korean labor market. Problem-solving ability is the most respected among the abilities considered, and helps college graduates in Korea to get better jobs. Yet it should be emphasized that innovative human capital—as measured by the self-evaluated abilities to find new ways of solving problems and to raise new questions—is an important factor determining productivity and pays off in the long run. Its monetary value becomes more evident as one spends more time in the labor market.

Conclusion and Policy Implications

The basic premise of this chapter is that reforms in education alone cannot make a society take actions to foster innovative human capital. We must also consider the labor market and see if it pays to be creative and innovative. As we have seen above, innovative human capital, such as the ability to solve problems in new ways or to raise new questions, does not pay much for the young college graduate just entering the labor market, but as time goes by, its value (in terms of higher wages) increases. Even if creativity was not emphasized in their education, workers in their forties and fifties have accumulated innovative human capital in the labor market. The analysis shows that creativity is needed more in the labor market than in college, and that it pays to be innovative.

The accumulation of human capital is a lifelong process. Especially in an era of fast technological changes, the accumulation of human capital after graduation will be of more and more importance. Educational reform cannot be completed within the education sector alone. To facilitate the process of accumulating innovative human capital, we need to give opportunities to young workers to reveal their innovative ability. In some sense, we seek a fundamental change from the labor market. This could be called a "backward induction" approach. Changes in the labor market will change the ways colleges train students, and in turn college education will change secondary education. Most of all, the labor market must be more competitive, less discriminative, and freer from rent-seeking behaviors.

Also, it must be noted that the most important place for the accumulation of human capital is the school, and more specifically, the classroom. We need to enhance diversity through decentralization and make schools more competitive by granting them greater autonomy and holding them accountable for results. Teachers have a key role to play. Engaging students in the asking of questions with many possible answers, and facilitating learning by doing, might be an effective way to the construction of innovative human capital.

Finally, we cannot overemphasize the importance of cultural aspects. Think about the U.S. case. It is well known that the average PISA score of U.S. students is only mediocre, and adults in the United States likewise get below-average scores for numerical competency as measured by the Programme for the International Assessment of Adult Competencies. Yet the United States is maintaining one of the most innovative economies in the world. There must be many reasons, but one that cannot be ignored is the cultural aspect. Along with labor market efficiency, U.S. attitudes toward risk and failure constitute an important factor behind the innovation of the U.S. economy. These kinds of attitudes can hardly be found in Korea, even among young people. Workers in Korea fear failure, since they think it is hard to overcome. To change this attitude, Korean educators and employers need to foster a culture that encourages challenges and risk-taking behaviors, with more lenient attitudes toward unintentional mistakes. Top-down command

and control inside firms and organizations is another hindrance that makes it hard to utilize innovative human capital in Korea.

In some sense, Korea is at risk of becoming a victim of its previous economic success. That success might not have been a result of a top-down organizational culture but came along with it. Because that kind of top-down approach worked, or is thought to have worked in the past, organizations, wary of failure, are reticent to change. But Koreans need to understand that innovation is a process involving a series of failures and uncertain prospects; if Korean culture cannot accept failure as a part of that process, it will be hard to accumulate innovative human capital in Korea.

References

Kim, Se-Jik, and Unchan Chung. 2007. "The Creative Human Capital as a Future Engine of Growth and Educational Reform." *Korean Economic Journal* 46 (4): 187–214.

Glăveanu, Vlad Petre. 2010. "Paradigms in the Study of Creativity: Introducing the Perspective of Cultural Psychology." *New Ideas in Psychology* 28 (1): 79–93.

McGuirk, Helen, Helena Lenihan, and Mark Hart. 2015. "Measuring the Impact of Innovative Human Capital on Small Firms' Propensity to Innovate." *Research Policy* 44 (4): 965–76.

OECD (Organisation for Economic Co-operation and Development). 2020a. "Enrolment Rate in Secondary and Tertiary Education." https://data.oecd.org/students/enrolment-rate-in-secondary-and-tertiary-education.htm.

———. 2020b. *PISA 2018 Results (Volume V): Effective Policies, Successful Schools.* Paris: PISA, OECD Publishing. https://www.oecd.org/publications/pisa-2018-results-volume-v-ca768d40-en.htm.

SaKong, Il, and Youngsun Koh. 2010. *The Korean Economy Six Decades of Growth and Development.* Seoul: Korea Development Institute.

6 The Rise of Tsinghua University as an Entrepreneurial University

Organizational and Educational Development

Zhou Zhong, Fei Yan, Chao Zhang, and Jizhen Li

This chapter aims to describe and explain the rise of Tsinghua University as an entrepreneurial university over the past three decades, since the 1980s. We first discuss the concept of the entrepreneurial university and the popularization of entrepreneurship education in the international context. We then adopt a modified six-element analytical framework to examine the development of Tsinghua as an entrepreneurial university. The elements we discuss are divided into three groups of culture, academic, and administrative characteristics; periphery interface and funding base; and entrepreneurship education. In particular, this chapter analyzes the structure and processes of Tsinghua's entrepreneurship education system, which both derives from and drives the larger entrepreneurial dynamism of the whole university. We argue that such dynamism arises from the university's relational, networking, and collaborative approaches to talent and knowledge development through resource orchestration and circulation within the university and at the level of university-industry-government interaction. Such dynamism drives the university to become more open, more integrated, and also more focused in terms of carrying on its educational, academic, and service missions.

The English word "university" entails a basic concept of making the multitudes into one encompassing whole, of developing an equilibrium between one and many. The term evolved from the medieval Latin word "universitas," with the root "uni-" meaning the one and "vert-" meaning turning, converting, or transforming. The university originally referred to both an integrated community of scholars and students and an integrated space of teaching, learning, scholarship, and service to the communities where it is located or to which it belongs. The idea of a unified university implies a boundary-spanning quality that enables it to hybridize through connection and coordination across boundaries.

The word "multiversity" encapsulates a contemporary large research university as "a city of intellect" with, as Kerr (2001, 1) describes , "a whole series of communities and activities held together by a common name, a common governing board, and related purposes." He continues to say, however, that with such a plurality of meanings and individuals, "it must, of necessity, be partially at war with itself" (Kerr 2001, 7). Clark (1998) observed that the multiversity was besieged by "demands on universities [that] outrun their capacity to respond." He argues that the rise of the entrepreneurial model helped a multiversity to overcome demand overload by aligning five elements: an integrated entrepreneurial culture, a strengthened steering core, a stimulated academic heartland, an expanded developmental periphery, and a diversified funding base (Clark 1998). Such overall alignment creates a fusion of academic values, administrative capability, and outreach proactiveness, so that the university can regain focus, autonomy, and efficiency, and carefully achieve measured expansion in scale and scope with intensified industry and social engagement.

Instead of a coping strategy, Etzkowitz argues for the rise of the entrepreneurial university as a proactive act. Based on the cases of Stanford and MIT, he explains that such an act was driven by a university's aspiration to make practical contribution to the economy, its academic capacity to connect basic science and advanced technology, and its administrative capacity in creative and careful resource orchestration to enable technology transfer, support venture capital, and create spin-offs (Etzkowitz 1988, 2013a). As science has become a vital engine of economic growth, the university as knowledge institution has become an economic actor in its own right. Hence the university has become an ever-more encompassing enterprise with educational, sociocultural, and also economic roles. The transition into the entrepreneurial model is marked by the university developing an integrated strategic framework to interact "a reverse linear dynamic moving from problems in industry and society and seeking solutions in academia" with "the classic forward linear model producing serendipitous innovations from the meandering stream of basic research" (Etzkowitz 2017). At the core of this model are the university's entrepreneurial scientists, who are able to "interface basic knowledge with the innovation goal"

(Etzkowitz 1983). To support entrepreneurial scientists, the university "has to have a considerable degree of independence from the state and industry, but also a high degree of interaction with these institutional spheres" (Etzkowitz 2013b), so that the scientists can combine multiple purposes and sources of funding to generate polyvalent knowledge that is simultaneously theoretical and practical across academic disciplines and social sectors in the university-industry-government triple helix (Etzkowitz 2010).

Moreover, the global spread of economic and social entrepreneurship since the 2010s has spurred an alternative model of the teaching-focused entrepreneurial university. With students as their core "deliverable," universities have come to foster and "graduate" students and spin-offs together, often in interaction with each other. No longer specialized education for business specialists, entrepreneurship education has become a generic competence for all. Many universities have incorporated entrepreneurship education to enhance basic competencies and graduate employability, through efforts often underpinned by international and national educational policies (Manimala and Thomas 2017; Reilly 2018). Moreover, many studies have shown that entrepreneurship education is effective in the promotion of student and graduate entrepreneurship as well as in the augmentation of transformative competencies such as creativity, exploration, and social responsibility (Jansen et al., 2015; Zhang, Zhong, and Li 2018; Berglund and Verduyn 2018; Martínez-Gregorio, Badenes-Ribera, and Oliver 2021).

The goal of entrepreneurship education is to develop not only the knowledge and skills for starting up new enterprises, but also to foster a general enterprising mindset. The United Nations (2015) articulated a landmark global commitment to this end in the fourth of its Sustainable Development Goals (SDGs) on quality education. SDG 4.4 endeavors to "by 2030, substantially increase the number of youth and adults who have relevant skills, including technical and vocational skills, for employment, decent jobs and entrepreneurship." In this respect, entrepreneurship education has been absorbed into the global movement of Education for Sustainable Development (ESD), hence creating an entrepreneurship education imperative for all schools, especially for research universities at the apex of the education system. Furthermore, as SDGs and ESD are themselves ambitious and ambiguous, they stimulate and also rely on educational actors for diverse interpretations of both sustainability and entrepreneurship.

Entrepreneurial Culture, Academic Heartland, and a Steering Core

Tsinghua University's development as an entrepreneurial university is embedded in institutional aspirations and characteristics, Chinese higher education reforms, and the rise of entrepreneurship in China. Tsinghua has integrated entrepreneurship into its world-class university (WCU) vision. Tsinghua's academic entrepreneurship began around 1985, the same period when the university set an aim to build itself into a WCU in the twenty-first century (Tsinghua University 2017). This goal itself was entrepreneurial, because lacked an agreed-upon definition or clear path. Tsinghua interpreted a WCU as one that is open, hence a socially and internationally engaged university, and recognized entrepreneurship as indispensable to the WCU vision (Tsinghua University 1996). China adopted a national WCU strategy in 1998 (MOE 1998) and has committed to it until 2050 at least (State Council 2015a). University entrepreneurship has been recognized as an indispensable task in this national strategy. Tsinghua's efforts at building a WCU, including its entrepreneurship development, amount to a new model of university development in China.

Tsinghua's entrepreneurship constitutes a crucial part of China's entrepreneurship. China adopted system-wide institutional reforms in order to reinvigorate its economy, education, and science and technology (S&T) sectors in 1984–85. In particular, education and S&T reform granted the universities more autonomy, including the freedom to develop joint ventures with external entities in technology transfer (CPCCC 1985a, 1985b). The university in this respect stood at the frontier of reform in developing new industries, new technologies, and new organizational forms in China. Tsinghua founded Tsinghua Technology Service as China's first university S&T spin-off company in 1980, then founded Tsinghua University S&T Development Corporation in 1988. In the intervening years, Tsinghua cooperated with neighboring universities and research institutes and their spin-offs and municipal and national governments to develop its surrounding area, Zhongguancun, from paddy fields into China's Silicon Valley. The area, which became China's first National High-Tech Zone in 1988, was renamed as Zhongguancun Science Park in 1999 and also became China's first National Innovation Demonstration Zone in 2009 (China Daily 2013).

Zhongguancun is China's most important higher education, research, and science and technology hub. In this approximately 200-square-kilometer area, Tsinghua neighbors with about 50 universities; 200 research institutes of the Chinese Academy of Sciences and Chinese Academy of Engineering; 120 National Key Laboratories, National Engineering Research Centers and National Engineering Technology Research Centers; 170 entrepreneurship parks, such as university science parks, incubation centers, acceleration centers, parks for Chinese academic returnees from overseas, etc.; and 11,000 high-tech enterprises (China Daily 2020). As of 2020, Tsinghua has 80 academic schools and departments, 53,300 students and 15,800 staff (Tsinghua University 2021a). Tsinghua and its surrounding area, Zhongguancun, has developed a symbiotic relationship in entrepreneurial development, with spin-offs serving as nexuses in the university-industry-government triple helix (see table 6.1).

Tsinghua's entrepreneurial culture is a result of its institutional history and characteristics. Tsinghua was founded in 1911 as a modern school aiming to cultivate China's leaders in modernization, and became a full-fledged university in 1928. The university has, since its establishment, championed holistic talent development with hands-on learning and practical wisdom as indispensable components of university education. In 1943, Tsinghua president Yiqi Mei and Provost Guangdan Pan advocated for the development of both technological and technological management education with an entrepreneurial spirit in order to cultivate talent for the nation's industrialization (Mei and Pan 1943 [2015]). This idea—that innovative and entrepreneurial thinking stand alongside broad and solid knowledge, a global mindset, and social responsibility as core attributes of Tsinghua students—still resonates today in the Tsinghua University charter (Tsinghua University 2014). Tsinghua became a polytechnical institution when China adopted the Soviet command economy model and restructured its entire higher education system in 1952–53. It was not until the late 1970s when Tsinghua began to gradually restore and expand its arts and sciences departments. Tsinghua today is a large comprehensive university with a leading role in most subfields of engineering. Its strong engineering culture champions creative and pragmatic problem-solving as well as self-discipline, collectivism, and strong social commitment.

TABLE 6.1 Landmarks in Tsinghua University spin-off history

Year	Spin-off founded	Notes
2013	MOOC-CN Education Co., Ltd.	A subsidiary of Tsinghua Holdings Co Ltd., specializing in online education and venture capital in education, and operating the largest Chinese massive open online course platform, xuetangx.com.
2013	Tsinghua Holdings Habitat Development Group	A subsidiary of Tsinghua Holdings Co Ltd., with two national professional qualifications and 142 professional institutions.
2012	Tsinghua Asset Management	A subsidiary of Tsinghua Holdings Co., Ltd. specialized in operating and managing financial assets and businesses.
2004	Tus-Holdings Co., Ltd.	Renamed TusPark Construction Holdings Co., Ltd.
2003	Tsinghua Holdings Co., Ltd.	Incorporated all of Tsinghua's affiliated enterprises into a solely state-owned limited liability corporation.
2000	TusPark Construction Holdings Co., Ltd.	Incorporated TusPark Development Center. Launched the construction of TusPark's main campus, adjacent to the Tsinghua campus.
1997	Tsinghua Tongfang Co., Ltd.	The first Tsinghua spin-off listed on the stock exchange.
1995	Tsinghua University Enterprise Group Co., Ltd.	A new phase of coordinated management of Tsinghua spin-offs.
1994	TusPark Development Center	China's first university science park and national demonstration enterprise in modern service industry. Launched the building site of TusPark.
1993	Tsinghua Unigroup	Tsinghua's first group company.
1988	Tsinghua Technology Development Corporation	Tsinghua's first comprehensive high-tech company.
1980	Tsinghua Technology Service	China's first university technology spin-off.

SOURCE: Tsinghua Holdings 2021a.

Enterprising academic and administrative development

Tsinghua's long-term WCU pursuit has been steered by strong leaders who are also well versed in entrepreneurship. Over the past two decades, Tsinghua has been expanding its academic scope and scale toward a more comprehensive university while maintaining a core strength in engineering+. That is, engineering in dynamic "orchestration" with sciences, arts, and other mutually reinforcing disciplines and fields for a synergy of interdisciplinary, inter-departmental, and university-industry development.

Two of Tsinghua's recent presidents are good examples of this synergy. Yong Qiu and Dazhong Wang are Tsinghua graduates and professors and both have achieved major scientific breakthroughs and strategically important technology transfers. Current president Yong Qiu, before taking office in 2015, led the Tsinghua Organic Light Emitting Display (OLED) research team for two decades and won China's National Technological Invention Award in 2011. He also founded Visionox in 2001, a Tsinghua spin-off that became China's first OLED industry provider in 2008 with independent intellectual property (IP) ownership. Visionox was the world's second-largest producer of passive matrix OLED in 2011 and was ranked among China's 500 most valuable private companies in 2019, with a market value of ¥22.5 billion (Hurun 2020).

Dazhong Wang served as Tsinghua's president from 1994 to 2003 and won China's most prestigious national award in science and technology in 2020. Wang led a joint industry-university research team in the advancement of China's capabilities in the process of high-temperature gas-cooled reactor technology (MSC 2021).

Another example of this synergy is Tsinghua's green university plan, which exemplifies academic leadership and entrepreneurship in the emerging field of environmental studies. Tsinghua developed China's first bachelor degree program in environmental engineering in 1977; China's first interdisciplinary environmental engineering institute in 1981 (by incorporating Tsinghua's strengths in environmental science, chemistry, chemical engineering, nuclear technology, thermal energy, hydraulic engineering, engineering physics, and motor vehicles); and China's first doctoral program in environmental engineering in 1988, a field that was also one of the nation's first "national key disciplines" (Tsinghua University 2021b). Then, inspired by the Talloires Declaration in 1990 and the United Nations Conference on Environment and Development in 1992, Tsinghua initiated China's first green university plan in 1992, aimed at incorporating the principles of sustainable development and environment protection into all of Tsinghua's activities and processes. Tsinghua incorporated this plan into its WCU strategy in 1998, and set up its Green University Office, led by a vice president for coordinated development in green education, green research, and green campus.

The goal of green education is to cultivate competence in sustainability in university talent so that they can become seeds in promoting green development in service of the nation and the world. From 1998 to 2019 Tsinghua developed an expansive network of related learning resources for all Tsinghua students, including about 240 courses and 200 other green-development learning activities each year. The green research goal aims to make all Tsinghua research environmentally sound, and to achieve academic breakthroughs in environmental protection and sustainable development. As of 2019, Tsinghua had developed 55 interdisciplinary research centers and had undertaken around 3,000 research projects in environmental protection and sustainable development.

Finally, the green campus goal aims at building an ecologically friendly campus distinguished in energy and water efficiency, natural and cultural environment protection, and social and cultural equity. Tsinghua has played a key role in developing China's National Green Campus Evaluation Standard in 2013 and its revision in 2019 (MHURD 2019). In 2013 the university founded a new spin-off, Tsinghua Holdings Habitat Development Group, which endeavors to offer systematic solutions for new-type urbanization in China by drawing upon Tsinghua architect Dr. Liangyong Wu's theory of human settlement science, to integrate big science, culture, and art, and to also draw upon the combined strengths of the university's schools of architecture, environment, arts and design, and engineering.

The above examples demonstrate a symbiosis in academic and entrepreneurial development in science and engineering at Tsinghua. Together they have fused into a vibrant power in advancing China's high-tech industry. However, all these would not be possible without a strong administrative backbone. Tsinghua has a tradition of faculty holding both short-term and long-term joint posts as administrators. A substantial proportion of Tsinghua faculty and administrators have been Tsinghua graduates, although over the past two decades the percentage has declined as the university expands into new disciplines and fields. This helps the Tsinghua community maintain a unified identity with a mutual understanding of the university's needs, and aids with efficiency in communicating and acting.

Enterprising Frontiers as Service Interface and Funding Base

An expanded developmental periphery

As a major nexus in Tsinghua's entrepreneurship ecosystem, Tsinghua's technology transfer system has developed in the context of its rise as a research university increasingly opening up to Chinese society and the world. Rapid growth in both research funding and research output propelled Tsinghua to develop a highly complex, professionally managed technology transfer system. The current system encompasses the entire chain of university technology transfer, ranging from university-industry collaboration, IP and technology transfer, university spin-off incubation, and technology-capital connection service. This system is led by the Tsinghua University IP Leading Group and is mainly operated by the Office of Technology Transfer, established in 2014.

In 2015 China amended the 1996 Law on the Promotion of Application of Scientific and Technological Achievements in order to deepen university-industry collaboration and tackle bottlenecks in knowledge transfers. Tsinghua then, from 2015 to 2017, put forward a series of new policies to provide incentives, raise efficiency, and build service capacities in IP management and technology transfer. For example, in 2015 the university settled the distribution of IP rights at 70 percent for the researcher or the research team, 15 percent for the researcher's academic department/school, and 15 percent for the university. Individual departments or schools may elaborate their IP policies, such as specifying that certain proportion of IP benefits will be transferred back to the researcher or research team (Tsinghua University 2016a). The combined new policy measures have helped to clarify IP ownership and ensure substantial benefits for researchers. As a result, Tsinghua's knowledge transfer income rose from less than ¥100 million ($15.6 million) in 2014 to over ¥700 million ($109 million) in 2018 (Wang, Zhang, and Wang 2018).

Tsinghua has two main models of technology transfer. The first model is the triple helix university-industry-government collaboration. Tsinghua set up its technology development office in 1983 to manage industrial and regional collaborations and related technological service contracts and IP rights. When Tsinghua adopted the WCU strategy in 1985, it regarded it imperative to develop direct links with industry in order to maximize knowledge transfer. Tsinghua set up the University-Industry Cooperation Committee (UICC) in 1995 as a unified platform to manage the university's industrial cooperation and facilitate technology transfer. The rapid development of Tsinghua Automotive Dynamics & Control Group demonstrates the dynamic dual processes of reciprocal learning between the university and the auto industry through academic entrepreneurs (Meng, Li, and Rong 2019).

In 2021, UICC provided services for over 150 Chinese enterprises and 40 multinational enterprises (Tsinghua University 2021c). Since

2003 Tsinghua has set up regional liaison offices as a university interface with the science and technology sections of regional and municipal governments across China to explore technology transfer opportunities. These offices organize meetings for university and regional representatives to exchange information about research development and market needs, facilitate negotiations about specific projects, and conduct policy consultations (Tsinghua University 2021d).

The second model is technology transfer through IP rights and university spin-offs. In general, the process is like this: when a frontier academic team achieves a new research breakthrough, the Office of Technology Transfer provides IP rights protection, commercial evaluation, and recommendations for investment and market needs, such as through industry or regional liaison offices; then, either an established enterprise take-over or spin-off is created and incubated to put the IP into practical use. Often Tsinghua alumni join the spin-offs as co-founders.

Looking ahead, two challenges to Tsinghua's technology transfer are the need to strengthen IP rights protection and application and to optimize technology transfer channels. Main measures to address these two issues involve capacity building in IP rights and technology transfer decision-making, and process management at the levels of both central administration and individual scholars and students, as well as capacity building in university-industry cooperation and university-region engagement.

A diversified funding base

Tsinghua has developed an increasingly diversified portfolio of income streams to augment its total resources through proactive outreach engagement. With such growing scale and scope of resources, Tsinghua has strengthened its financial discretion and hence institutional independence. Two of Tsinghua's most important non-government funding bases are Tsinghua Holdings Co., Ltd. and Tsinghua University Education Foundation. As a "carrier" of many Tsinghua spin-offs, Tsinghua Holdings is positioned as a unified vehicle to commercialize Tsinghua's major scientific and technological breakthroughs. Its star projects include the world's first high-temperature gas cooled reactor nuclear power plant (developed by Dazhong Wang), a freight container inspection system that has the largest global market share, China's first public safety and emergency response system with complete and independent

IP rights, and the world's first gene test chip for hereditary deafness. Based on a registered capital of ¥2.5 billion ($395 million) in 2003, Tsinghua Holdings achieved total assets of ¥100 billion ($15.6 billion) with revenue of ¥60 billion ($9.4 billion) in 2014, and ranked the 137th in China's Top 500 enterprises by revenue and third by R&D efforts in 2018 (Tsinghua Holdings 2021b). Moreover, it has also applied for 18,000 patents in China and overseas and developed seven joint research institutes with Tsinghua University by 2019 (Tsinghua Holdings 2021b).

As a key affiliate of Tsinghua Holdings, Tsinghua Science Park (TusPark) serves as a special funding base for Tsinghua University. TusPark was founded in 1994 as China's first national university science park (NUSP) in 2001. The company became Tus-Holdings Co., Ltd. in 2000 as the builder and operator of TusPark, and has been a subsidy of Tsinghua Holdings Co., Ltd. since 2004. TusPark has developed a strong brand as a host of R&D headquarters of multi-national corporations, Chinese high-tech enterprise headquarters, and of innovative startups. Since 2001, TusPark has been the largest and the best performing NUSP among the 141 currently in China (as of 2021). In 2021, TusPark hosted over 1,500 tenant companies in science parks with a total area of 770,000 square meters, and has developed a global innovation service network with more than 300 incubators, science parks, and science zones in over 80 cities in China and overseas (Tsinghua Holdings 2021c). It also served as the shareholder of over 800 listed and non-listed enterprises and managed total assets of about ¥200 billion ($31 billion) (Tsinghua Holdings 2021c).

Tsinghua founded the Tsinghua University Education Foundation (TUEF) in 1994 as China's first university education foundation since the founding of the People's Republic of China in 1949. Since then, TUEF has performed as one of the most successful non-public foundations in China, with the largest sum of donations received among Chinese universities. When Tsinghua reached a total budget of ¥29.7 billion ($4.6 billion) in 2019, TUEF raised ¥1.7 billion ($274 million) in donations and expended ¥1.2 billion ($184 million) in public benefits in the same year (TUEF 2021a). The university also established Tsinghua Education Foundation (North America), Inc. in 1998 and Tsinghua University Education Foundation (Hong Kong SAR) Limited in 2003. TUEF has raised funds for Tsinghua both to cope with emergencies and to seize new opportunities for strategic development. When the COVID-19 pandemic broke out globally, the foundation raised a

¥150 million ($23.4 million) emergency research fund in March 2020 from Tsinghua alumna to support research in combating the pandemic, and secured a donation of ¥200 million ($31 million) to open the Tsinghua University Vanke School of Public Health in April 2020 (Tsinghua University 2020). TUEF over the years has set up a series of funds to support Tsinghua in climate change and green development, including the new fund for the Tsinghua Institute for Carbon Neutrality, opened in September 2021 (TUEF 2021b).

While TUEF has endeavored to enable a virtuous cycle between the university and the wider society to support educational and academic causes, Tsinghua Holdings has tried to do the same among technology, finance, and science park space, through incubating and serving enterprises in order to connect the university with industry and government. However, Tsinghua Holdings is not without frequent market disturbances. Such challenges are also shared by universities and their spin-offs across China. With this issue in mind, Tsinghua has actively promoted the creation of institutional and national policies and regulations that enable clear legal and financial separation between universities and their spin-offs. In general, both TUEF and Tsinghua Holdings help to ensure Tsinghua's financial discretion, and hence strengthen the university's autonomy, integration, and resilience in face of market and governmental financial uncertainties, and among increasingly intensive domestic and international higher education competition.

Entrepreneurship Education as an Ecotone

Above we have examined how Clark's five aspects of the entrepreneurial university apply to Tsinghua University's development and characteristics. While Clark's late 1990s model still remains generally applicable today, it does not take into account the increasingly important role of entrepreneurship education. The case of Tsinghua illustrates entrepreneurship education as both a driver and an outcome of entrepreneurial university development and of local, national, and international development at large. Entrepreneurship education interconnects with all other five elements in the Clark model through dynamic resource orchestration in service of fostering the value, knowledge, skills, and actions of entrepreneurship.

The dynamic development of entrepreneurship education at Tsinghua reflected the dynamics at the national level. The rise of entrepreneurship in China's economy beginning in the late 1990s stimulated a national movement to promote entrepreneurship education for all. China's tenth (2001–05), eleventh (2006–10) and twelfth (2011–15) Five-Year Plans in National Education Development all stated a goal of raising entrepreneurship awareness in students. Entrepreneurship education was made compulsory for all college students in 2014 (MOHRSS 2014), and then in 2015 the State Council issued a policy to promote mass entrepreneurship as a means to advance employment, economic dynamism, and social mobility and equity (State Council 2015b). China's Thirteenth Five-Year-Plan in National Education Development devoted a special section to elaborate its goals of developing students' entrepreneurial mindsets and competencies, and also laid out various measures aimed at fostering student entrepreneurship actions through connecting the links among education, research, and industry (State Council 2017).

Tsinghua has a rich, long culture of encouraging creative solutions to real-world problems. One study shows that long before Tsinghua adopted a formal policy of promoting entrepreneurship education, it was already fostering an enterprising spirit in its institutional culture, especially through the exemplary effects of the Tsinghua faculty and through students' innovative activities in science and technology (Zhang, Zhong, and Wang 2021). Tsinghua formally became one of the first educational institutions to be named a National Experiment Institution for Entrepreneurship Education in 2002. In 2009, Tsinghua set a goal to integrate creativity, innovation, and entrepreneurship education throughout its system (Tsinghua University 2018). The university became one of China's first demonstration universities in entrepreneurship education in 2014, and since 2014 has marked the last Saturday of every November as Tsinghua Makers Day to promote entrepreneurial ethos.

In 2016 Tsinghua put forward four strategies to accelerate entrepreneurship education (Tsinghua University 2016b): (1) Setting up an entrepreneurship education committee led by the Tsinghua president to coordinate activities across the university; (2) integrating entrepreneurship education into Tsinghua's education system, and coordinating all relevant curricular, co-curricular, and extracurricular activities; (3) creating interdisciplinary double degree and minor-degree programs in innovation and entrepreneurship, and integrating entrepreneurship education into all academic degree programs; (4) promoting international exchange and collaboration in entrepreneurship education; (5) sharing entrepreneurship education resources with the wider society to support mass entrepreneurship.

The classroom learning space

Tsinghua's entrepreneurship education system consists of three interconnected spaces: the classroom, the campus, and the community. There are five key players in the classroom space in the Tsinghua entrepreneurship education system. All of them are centers of excellence in entrepreneurship scholarship, entrepreneurship education, and entrepreneurship practices. They all share the characteristics of strong interdisciplinary, international, and industrial engagement.

The School of Economics and Management (SEM), founded in 1984, is a leading business school and a global center of excellence in entrepreneurship studies. One of its core strengths lies in technological economics and entrepreneurship. Tsinghua's Fundamental Industry Training Center, known as iCenter, was opened in 2014 as a 15,000-square-meter technopreneurship maker space. The center's opening marked a century of providing hands-on training at Tsinghua. The Academy of Arts and Design (AAD) was originally founded in 1956 as the Central Academy of Arts and Design, China's first design school, and merged with Tsinghua in 1999. The Graduate School of Finance (GSF) was jointly founded by Tsinghua and the People's Bank of China in 2012, on the foundation of the Graduate School of the People's Bank of China, founded in 1981. Tsinghua Shenzhen International Graduate School (SIGS) opened in 2019 on the basis of Tsinghua Shenzhen Graduate School, which was opened in 2000 in the southern seaport city of Shenzhen at Tsinghua's branch campus. In the past thirty years Shenzhen has grown into an international hub of manufacturing, high technology, and finance.

All these players have developed new entrepreneurship education program series since 2015, often in collaboration with one another.[1] Moreover, many Tsinghua departments have also set up their in-house

---

1   Some examples: SEM offers undergraduate minor programs in innovation and entrepreneurship leadership; GSF does the same with internet finance and entrepreneurship; AAD, SEM, and iCenter jointly offer an undergraduate minor in technopreneurship; SIGS and SEM jointly offer a certificate program in entrepreneurship; master's programs in sci-tech and finance are offered jointly by GSF, Tsinghua's Office of Technology Transfer, and Beijing Tsinghua Industry R&D In-

entrepreneurship centers in collaboration with their industry partners and alumni associations. By 2017, Tsinghua developed 157 courses in entrepreneurship, with over 70 percent of these having faculty and students with interdisciplinary backgrounds.[2]

The campus learning space

The annual culmination of Tsinghua's campus entrepreneurship education space is the Tsinghua Entrepreneurship Competition, which began in 1998. The competition itself was an entrepreneurial act by a group of Tsinghua students who were inspired by the original MIT $50K Entrepreneurship Competition. The first Tsinghua Entrepreneurship Competition attracted 16,000 participants in 1998. Then China's National Entrepreneurship Competition began in 1999, modeled after the Tsinghua one.

There are three key pillars that support Tsinghua's entrepreneurship education campus space. The first is the Entrepreneurship Development Center, opened in 2011 by the Tsinghua Office of Student Affairs, which provides support to student clubs and groups for entrepreneurship training, internships, work space, seed funding, mentoring, and network opportunities, etc. The second pillar is the aforementioned iCenter, which not only runs formal courses in fundamental industry training but also fosters and hosts many student research teams, maker groups, and entrepreneurship clubs. In 2018, the iCenter provided industry training for over Tsinghua 4,500 students; courses for degree and certificate programs; support for student research projects, and technology design competitions for over 7,500 students; professional development programs for over 2,000 teachers in vocational education; and industry internships for over 1,500 students across China. Moreover, iCenter also conducts research in science and technology education and technopreneurship education, and serves as an open laboratory for technology transfer projects.

The third pillar is the x-lab, co-launched in 2013 by SEM, 15 Tsinghua academic departments/schools, Tsinghua TusPark, Tsinghua

---

stitute; and SEM, AAD, and Sotheby's Institute of Art jointly offer the Tsinghua-Sotheby's master's in art business.

2   For example, the course "Introduction to Entrepreneurship: Meeting the Entrepreneurs" enrolled over 700 Tsinghua students annually, and attracted over 350,000 social learners the course became available online in 2017.

Holdings, Tsinghua Entrepreneur and Executive Club, and several other Tsinghua spin-offs. x-lab offers a comprehensive set of training and services to support entrepreneurship from idea to action, encompassing resources and support, raising capital and expert mentoring, legal consultation, design consultation, and company registration. Over six years, x-lab as an open and free charity platform has served over 30,000 students; has produced 1,500 entrepreneurship projects run by Tsinghua students and alumni; and has hosted over 50 in-residence industry mentors and investors and over a hundred enterprises as venture capital partners (x-lab 2021). The startups incubated by x-lab have created employment for over 8,000 people and raised a total funding of ¥3 billion ($469 million) (x-lab 2021). In particular, Tsinghua Holdings and its affiliates provided x-lab with ¥30 million ($4.7 million) as "DNA" seed funding in 2013. This funding achieved a nine-fold return by 2017, and Tsinghua Holdings then donated ¥1million ($156,000) back to the university to support entrepreneurship education (Zhang, Zhong, and Wang 2021).

The community learning space

The community space of entrepreneurship education can be seen as a set of concentric areas surrounding Tsinghua campus. Tsinghua has proactively shaped its adjacent and extended surrounding areas in realestate development and entrepreneurship service provision. TusPark plays a unique role in the university through the co-location and creative combination of space, capital, technology, policy, service, and knowledge. TusPark commercializes the university's research through technology transfer, and also provides timely and continuous feedback to the university about the latest needs for top-notch technology and high-caliber talent from the market. Such a feedback loop helps the university to see further into the future and prepare for that future through fostering new academic disciplines and fields.

For example, the founder of TusPark, Meng Mei, is a Tsinghua alumna and former professor of automation at the university. She has taught elective courses on entrepreneurship at Tsinghua since 2003.[3] Alumni like Mei have brought entrepreneurs, investors, and marketing

---

3   These courses include "Theory and Practice of Science and Technology Entrepreneurship," "Starting a New Company," and "Sensing and Seizing Entrepreneurial Opportunities and Business Planning."

and training specialists into the classroom, so that high-performing students are not only rewarded with academic credit but also mentoring, investment, and incubation services.

In turn, TusPark as a Tsinghua spin-off and an ideal startup launching pad supports these courses and other Tsinghua entrepreneurial education activities with such benefits as a free company registration service for Tsinghua students and alumni; a cluster of R&D centers, incubators, intermediate services; and also a cluster of Tsinghua spin-offs with associated core technologies and social networks.

Another example is MOOC-CN, a Tsinghua spin-off that has developed an integrated community of frontier education technology through the co-location of education, research, and industry in one organization and in one e-learning platform, XuetangX.com. XuetangX is a lifelong learning provider that operates the largest Chinese massive open online course platform, with over 3,000 courses taught by Chinese and overseas universities, and other organizations. The China Institute of Entrepreneurship is a special XuetangX sub-platform, with open and free entrepreneurship education provided by Tsinghua University. XuetangX also provides products and services for hybrid digital learning environments mainly based on technologies transferred from Tsinghua University. XuetangX has a role in research through its hosting of the Ministry of Education Research Center for Online Education and is active in providing venture capital in education technology.

Tsinghua University has also cooperated with local and municipal governments in Beijing and other cities to jointly provide work space, seed funding, mentoring, and incubation services for various types of entrepreneurship, including social entrepreneurship and creative culture.

Discussion and Conclusion

Tsinghua presents two forms of entrepreneurship education. The first is a model of specialization. The university creates a streamlined learning progress in which learners move through the chain of design thinking, from creativity to innovation and then to entrepreneurship. During this process, the learners "flow" through learning spaces, from the classroom to the campus and then the community, and along the way receive differentiated and specialized support. In this model, each learning space fulfills a specialized role. The three spaces are closely interconnected and well coordinated, but may not be well integrated. The division of spaces and of labor buffers the participants from potential conflicts of interest between the educational and the commercial.

The second is a model of integration. It creates a pebble-in-the-pond learning process taking place in concentric spaces. It helps to drive the learners' ideas as inspirations to ripple through the entrepreneurship education ecology to reach more resources along the way in order to transform ideas into value. The learning spaces merge into a holistic network through co-location, for example, in a course, a competition, a campaign, or a student club activity. The classroom may not necessarily be the starting point of the learning process. Any node may stimulate an inspiration, then resources can be pooled in along the network links to drive the interaction among creativity, innovation, and entrepreneurship. As in the case of the Tsinghua course "Starting a New Company," students can only win a seat in a course by having already created or operated an entrepreneurship plan. Hence, the relationship among creativity, innovation, and entrepreneurship may not be linear or sequential. In this model, learning may either be pre-defined as in the case of a normal course, or it could also be as dynamic as just-in-time learning by individual demand, as in the case of a campus competition.

The second model functions as an ecotone, that is, a boundary environment that connects two adjoining ecosystems. Boundaries of each learning space become more porous as conducive interfaces to facilitate communication among learners, faculty, staff, and industry mentors. The learning spaces fuse into a network dependent on resources from each participant as suppliers of ideas, knowledge, funds, and other services from both inside and outside the boundaries of the university. Hence the co-location of the three learning spaces reduces the degree of mutual outsidership of different parties to each other—the educational, research, and commercial—reducing both physical and psychic distance among them. In this context of entrepreneurial learning by doing, the student's performance is dependent upon making full use of the interconnected relationships in the networked learning space. Learning becomes a function of sensing and seizing opportunities that emerge in the ongoing interactions in one or more relationships. In the meanwhile, faculty, staff, or firm mentors as learning organizers or co-organizers are required to coordinate the learning network development with simultaneous educational and commercial goals. Mutual trust and commitment to entrepreneurship learning grows with good level of student performance and satisfaction, especially with the successful incubation of student startups.

Both forms of entrepreneurship education enable learning-driven entrepreneurship, which drives a value-creating process to transform learners' ideas into intellectual properties in critical technologies. Such ideas not only come from students' academic knowledge, but also their interests, experiences, and personalities. Hence such entrepreneurship education promotes entrepreneurial pedagogies that highlight a design-thinking mindset, fostering a creative fusion of students' academic knowledge but also their lived experiences, and using a wide range of teaching and learning methods beyond conventional lectures and seminars. At Tsinghua many courses adopt entrepreneurial pedagogies to foster general entrepreneurial ethos. This entrepreneurial orientation is encapsulated in the remarks of Tsinghua provost Bin Yang (2015), a professor of strategic management: "University entrepreneurship education should focus not on setting up new enterprises, but on cultivating the entrepreneurial attributes, such as daring to do it first, and creative and critical problem-solving."

A dialogue with the Etzkowitz model

In addition to the Clark model, the case study of Tsinghua can also help to update other entrepreneurial university models by adding the educational dimension and fusing it with elements. For example, Etzkowitz (2017) presents a model of the entrepreneurial university based on five elements that primarily revolve around "research," but we can supplement this descriptive model by adding in educational elements (our additions to Etzkowitz are in italics):

(1) The organization of group research and *entrepreneurship education*;
(2) the creation of a research and *educational* base with commercial potential;
(3) the development of organizational mechanisms to move research out of the university as protected IP, *meanwhile bringing into the university entrepreneurial resources to enrich education both on and off campus*;
(4) the capacity to organize firms within the university and "graduate" them, including using *entrepreneurship education spaces as startup incubators*;
(5) integration of academic and business elements into new formats such as university–industry research centers and *educational activities in entrepreneurship education*.

Etzkowitz (2013b) posits that the entrepreneurial university "can be expressed in . . . four propositions": interaction, independence, hybridization, and reciprocity. Based on the discussion above, we can elaborate on this model:

(1) The university has a goal to maintain autonomy, relative **independence**, in terms of being relatively self-defining, self-regulating, and self-financing.

(2) The university can achieve this goal by creating **hybridization** in its organizational format to enable good coordination among the three dimensions of its academic units, administrative units, and service units, and support their ability to liaise internally and externally.

(3) In this way the university achieves dynamic **reciprocity** in value creation in terms of producing polyvalent knowledge that is simultaneously educational, academic, practical, and informs policy, and also in terms of relationship building, to enable collaboration among the multiple stakeholders of learners, instructors, researchers, investors, and other service providers.

(4) Such reciprocity takes place through **interaction** among the various stakeholders both within the university and beyond in the university–industry–government interfaces.

Based on the application and modification of Clark's and Etzkowitz's theories, the development of Tsinghua as an entrepreneurial university can be understood as the university's embrace of beliefs and ideas that enable its proactive transformation into a world-class university. Tsinghua has built this vision on a set of the university's dynamic capacities: cultivating strong-minded change agents in its top leadership as well as at other levels of administration; sustaining and strengthening a unifying institutional identity as an open, comprehensive, and research-intensive university during the changes; embracing a fusion of new managerial and service-oriented values with traditional academic values; forming an integrated attitude and capacity in entrepreneurship across its widely divergent disciplines and fields; building agile institutional structures and diversified functions that support processes of change, in particular, building a matrix structure of discipline-based academic departments supplemented by flexibly organized, carefully monitored, and strategically positioned service units; and expanding and diversifying institution-wide resources.

The case of Tsinghua also demonstrates that entrepreneurship education can effect a parallel process of knowledge translation outside the standard offices for technology transfer. The spaces for entrepreneurship education form a varied array of problem-based and project-based multifunctional interfaces that enable reciprocal connections among its participants between the university and the outside world. While those participants are committed to entrepreneurial learning by doing, they engage in a dynamic and iterative process of synthesis, dissemination, exchange, and ethically sound application of knowledge to move individual ideas, classroom knowledge, and research findings into the hands of people and organizations who can put them to practical use, with direct economic and social benefits.

The dynamism of entrepreneurship education

To a large extent, the dynamism in Tsinghua's entrepreneurship education reflects that of Tsinghua's general entrepreneurship ecosystem. It lies in the creative tensions between the ambidexterity and co-specialization of the university's core resources, that is, the learners, researchers, investors, and other service providers from both inside and outside the university. In terms of ambidexterity, university entrepreneurship grows with versatile entrepreneurial scientists and students who grow to be not only IP creators and holders but also entrepreneurs themselves as focal points of entrepreneurial undertaking. They create polyvalent knowledge that is simultaneously academic, educational, and practical for real-world problem-solving. With regard to co-specialization, on the other hand, there is a clearer division of labor in the entrepreneurship undertaking. In this aspect, scholars and students who are not themselves interested or skilled in entrepreneurship can conveniently find support from the university's enriched entrepreneurial ecosystem. In general, a resource is specialized when it cannot be put to alternative use without a substantial loss in value, and resources are co-specialized when the value of each resource is a positive function of its use in conjunction with the other resources (Teece 2018).

Both ambidexterity and co-specialization make a university more interconnected and more focused on serving its missions. The creative tensions both result in and from the university forming complex organizational and inter-organizational architecture as multi-hub, multi-lateral, and multi-directional networks committed to university entrepreneurship. Each hub in such networks, such as a learning space or a research space, has both mutuality and heterogeneity. "Mutuality" means serving the educational, academic, and service missions of the university simultaneously. "Heterogeneity" means each hub has a different formula in combining the educational, academic, and service aspects of the university.

The increasing level of interconnectivity and complexity in university architecture creates growing challenges for communication pathways, power dynamics, and assertions of identity in the university community (Li, Li, and Gao 2020). The entrepreneurial university then makes it desirable or even imperative for its members to hone relational, network, and collaborative abilities in order to forge positive and productive connections among individuals and groups in tackling common problems. These include the abilities to listen, identify others' interests and concerns, search for mutual interests, open to differences, respect pluralism and diversity, and develop measures to build confidence that foster trust and commitment. Many such abilities are important for the university to maintain autonomy and responsibility through deliberation and cooperation within its own community and across the communities in society. Moreover, such deliberation and cooperation foster entrepreneurial orientation and opportunities for creating an integrative multilateral agreement: All parties collaborate to tackle common challenges and contribute toward outcomes that are better for the whole than if these tasks were split among individual entities; that is, the whole is greater than the sum of the parts. For the university, entrepreneurship registers not only a response to social demand overload, but also a proactive engagement in the form of a new social contract between the university and the society. Hence the entrepreneurial university continues to uphold the original idea of the university, transforming the many into the one, the common good for the larger whole.

References

Berglund, Karin, and Karen Verduyn. 2018. *Revitalizing Entrepreneurship Education: Adopting a Critical Approach in the Classroom.* London: Springer.

China Daily. 2013. "Introduction to Zhongguancun Science Park." *China Daily*, December 4, 2013. http://regional.chinadaily.com.cn/bjzpark/2013-12/04/c_441685.htm.

———. 2020. "Introduction to Haidian Subpark of Zhongguancun Science Park." *China Daily*, March 10, 2020. http://regional.chinadaily.com.cn/bjzpark/2020-03/10/c_444697.htm.

Clark, Burton R. 1998. "The Entrepreneurial University: Demand and Response." *Tertiary Education and Management* 4 (1): 5–16.

CPCCC (Communist Party of China Central Committee). 1985a. *Decision of the CPC Central Committee on the Reform of the Educational System*. Beijing: CPCCC, May 27, 1985.

———. 1985b. *Decision of the CPC Central Committee on the Reform of the Science and Technology System*. Beijing: CPCCC, March 13, 1985.

Etzkowitz, Henry. 1983. "Entrepreneurial Scientists and Entrepreneurial Universities in American Academic Science." *Minerva* 21 (2/3): 198–233.

———. 1988. "The Making of an Entrepreneurial University: The Traffic among MIT, Industry, and the Military, 1860–1960." In *Science, Technology and the Military*, edited by Everett Mendelsohn, M. R. Smith, and Peter Weingart, 515–539. Dordrecht, Holland: Reidel.

———. 2010. "Polyvalent Knowledge and the Entrepreneurial University: A Third Academic Revolution?" *Critical Sociology* 36 (4): 595–609.

———. 2013a. "StartX and the 'Paradox of Success': Filling the Gap in Stanford's Entrepreneurial Culture." *Social Science Information* 52 (4): 605–27.

———. 2013b. "Anatomy of the Entrepreneurial University." *Social Science Information* 52 (3): 486–511.

———. 2017. "Innovation Lodestar: The Entrepreneurial University in a Stellar Knowledge Firmament." *Technological Forecasting & Social Change* 123: 122–29.

Hurun Research Institute. 2020. "2019 Hurun China Top 500 Private Enterprises." January 11, 2020. http://money.163.com/special/hrmy500/.

Jansen, Slinger, Tommy van de Zande, Sjaak Brinkkempera, Erik Stam, and Vasudeva Varma. 2015. "How Education, Stimulation, and Incubation Encourage Student Entrepreneurship: Observations from MIT, IIIT, and Utrecht University." *The International Journal of Management Education* 13 (2): 170–181.

Kerr, Clark. 2001. *The Uses of the University*. Cambridge, MA: Harvard University Press.

Li, Xiaohua, Jizhen Li, and Xiaodong Gao. 2020. "The Third Mission of the University: Transform from Research University to

Entrepreneurial University." [In Chinese.] *Studies in Science of Science* 38 (12): 2131–139.

Manimala, Mathew J., and Princy Thomas. 2017. "Entrepreneurship Education: Innovations and Best Practices." In *Entrepreneurship Education, Experiments with Curriculum, Pedagogy and Target Groups*, edited by Mathew J. Manimala and Princy Thomas, 3–53. London: Springer.

Martínez-Gregorio, S., L. Badenes-Ribera, and A. Oliver. 2021. "Effect of Entrepreneurship Education on Entrepreneurship Intention and Related Outcomes in Educational Contexts: A Meta-analysis." *The International Journal of Management Education* 19 (3): 1–15.

Mei, Yiqi, and Guangdan Pan. (1943) 2015. "Industrial Education and Industrial Talents." [In Chinese.] In *Anthology of Pan Guangdan*, edited by Wenhao Lü, 496–504. Beijing: China Renmin University Press.

Meng, Donghui, Xianjun Li, and Ke Rong. 2019. "Industry-to-university Knowledge Transfer in Ecosystem-based Academic Entrepreneurship: Case Study of Automotive Dynamics & Control Group in Tsinghua University." *Technological Forecasting and Social Change* 141: 249–262.

MOE (Ministry of Education of China). 1998. *Action Plan for the Revitalization of Education in the 21st Century*. December 24, 1998. Beijing: Ministry of Education of the People's Republic of China.

MHURD (Ministry of Housing and Urban-Rural Development of China). 2019. *Green Campus Evaluation Standard of China* (GB/T51356-2019). https://www.mohurd.gov.cn/gongkai/fdzdgknr/tzgg/201909/20190911_241758.html.

MOHRSS (Ministry of Human Resources and Social Security). 2014. "Notice of the Ministry of Human Resources and Social Security and Other Eight Departments on Implementing the Entrepreneurship Guidance Plan for College Students." [In Chinese.] May 22, 2014. http://www.mohrss.gov.cn/SYrlzyhshbzb/ldbk/jiuye/gaoxiaobiyesheng/201405/t20140530_131188.htm.

MSC (Ministry of Science and Technology of China). 2021. "Dazhong Wang, Winner of the 2021 National Award in Science and Technology." [In Chinese.] http://www.most.gov.cn/ztzl/kjrw/202111/t20211103_177779.html.

Reilly, John E. 2018. "Education Policy Perspective on Entrepreneurship." In *The Palgrave Handbook of Multidisciplinary Perspectives* on *Entrepreneurship*, edited by Romeo V. Turcan and Norman M. Fraser, 293–314. London: Palgrave Macmillan.

State Council of China. 2015a. "Overall Plan for Promoting the Construction of World-class Universities and World-class Disciplines." [In Chinese.] November 5, 2015. http://www.gov.cn/zhengce/content/2015-11/05/content_10269.htm.

———. 2015b. "Opinions on Several Policies and Measures to Vigorously Promote Mass Entrepreneurship and Innovation." [In Chinese.] June 16, 2015. http://www.gov.cn/xinwen/2015-06/16/content_2879971.htm.

———. 2017. "China's 13th Five-Year Plan in National Education Development (2016–2020)." January 19, 2017.

Teece, David J. 2018. "Co-specialization." In *The Palgrave Encyclopedia of Strategic Management*, edited by Mie Augier and David J. Teece. London: Palgrave Macmillan.

Tsinghua Holdings. 2021a. "Development Path of Tsinghua Holdings Co., Ltd." https://www.thholding.com.cn/news/index/catid/7.html.

———. 2021b. "About Tsinghua Holdings Co., Ltd." http://en.thholding.com.cn/2016-07/23/c_53617.htm

———. 2021c. "About TusPark." http://en.tusholdings.com/h/tuspark/

Tsinghua University. 1996. "Tsinghua University Nineth Five-Year Plan (1996–2000)." [In Chinese.]

———. 2014. "Tsinghua University Charter." [In Chinese.] https://www.tsinghua.edu.cn/publish/newthu/openness/jbxx/qhdczc.html.

———. 2016a. "Measures for the Evaluation, Disposal and Benefit Distribution of Scientific and Technological Achievements." [In Chinese.]

———. 2016b. "Implementation Plan of Tsinghua University on Deepening Innovation and Entrepreneurship Education Reform." [In Chinese.]

———. 2017. "Tsinghua University Double World-class University Strategy." Beijing: Tsinghua University. [In Chinese.] December 28, 2017.

———. 2018. "The Development of Tsinghua University Creativity-Innovation-Entrepreneurship Education System: A Report for the 2018 National Education Excellence Award." [In Chinese.] http://qiyuan.tsinghua.edu.cn/intro/info_award_2018.jsp

———. 2020. "Tsinghua Launched Vanke School of Public Health." [In Chinese.] https://www.tsinghua.edu.cn/thu109/info/1039/1056.htm.

————. 2021a. "Tsinghua University Facts and Figures in December 2020." https://www.tsinghua.edu.cn/en/About/Facts_and_Figures .htm.

————. 2021b. "History of the School of Environment at Tsinghua University." https://www.tsinghua.edu.cn/enven/About/History.htm.

————. 2021c. "University-industry Collaboration." [In Chinese.] https://www.tsinghua.edu.cn/kxyj/kyhz/qyhz.htm.

————. 2021d. "University-region Collaboration." [In Chinese.] https://www.tsinghua.edu.cn/kxyj/kyhz/dfhz.htm.

TUEF (Tsinghua University Education Foundation). 2021a. "TUEF Annual Work Report for 2019." [In Chinese.] http://www.tuef .tsinghua.edu.cn/sites/pdf/infomation/2019gzbg.pdf.

————. 2021b. "Mr. Gao Yingshi Donated to Support the Tsinghua University Carbon Neutralization Fund." [In Chinese.] http://www .tuef.tsinghua.edu.cn/info/xwdt/4663.

United Nations. 2015. *Transforming Our World: The 2030 Agenda for Sustainable Development.* Paris: UNESCO.

Wang, Yuzhu, Yousheng Zhang, and Yan Wang. 2018. "Tsinghua University Technology Transfer and IP Management." [In Chinese.] *Beijing Education* 5: 80–82.

x-lab. 2021. "About x-lab." http://www.x-lab.tsinghua.edu.cn/about .html#xlabjj.

Yang, Bin. 2015. "Entrepreneurship Education as Strategy for Holistic Talent Development and Nation Building." *China Daily*, May 5, 2015.

Zhang, Chao, Zhou Zhong, and Jizhen Li. 2018. "University Imprint: Education Reflection from the Perspective of Alumni Entrepreneurs: An Example of Tsinghua University." [In Chinese.] *Research in Higher Education of Engineering* 4: 168–74.

Zhang, Chao, Zhou Zhong, and Sunyu Wang. 2021. *Research on Entrepreneurship Education in Entrepreneurial Universities.* [In Chinese.] Beijing: Social Sciences Academic Press.

7 Education and Human Capital for Innovation in India's Service Sector

Rafiq Dossani

Services account for the major share of the economy in most countries. More-developed economies typically record larger shares of services in the labor force and in gross domestic product (GDP) than do less-developed economies. The service sector has also been a focal point for innovation in recent decades, particularly in the information technology (IT) service subsector, led by firms such as Google and Microsoft.

Given the experience of developed countries, many developing countries have looked to their service sector to drive economic growth through innovation. While service-sector growth and innovation have been studied in developed countries, not much is known about the critical factors that shape service-sector growth in developing countries. Certain factors that have been documented as critical in developed countries may seem to be as critical in developing countries, such as the quality of human capital.

This chapter discusses the role of services in India's economy, with a focus on understanding the critical factors that shaped India's experience, particularly the impact on innovation in services. Through this case study of India, we hope to draw wider lessons about the importance of services for driving growth, particularly innovation-led growth, in developing economies.

India is an important country in which to study the potential for service-led growth and innovation. Like most developing countries in the postcolonial period, Indian growth policies favored industrialization for the domestic market. Protectionist policies supported domestic industry. With the benefit of hindsight, we know that these policies failed almost everywhere they were tried. India was no exception.

By contrast, some East and Southeast Asian countries, starting with Japan in the 1950s, favored a combination of protection for domestic industry with openness to trade. This strategy succeeded and was imitated by Hong Kong, Korea, Singapore, and Taiwan in the 1960s and 1970s, also with success. Several Southeast Asian countries that had earlier tried the same approach as India switched to the Japanese model from the 1970s onward and experienced success. China also underwent a similar shift in the 1980s, with great success.

Despite their different experiences, a common feature was a slow development of the service sector in all these countries relative to the rate of development in countries that did not adopt protectionist policies.

India was a latecomer to the trade-led manufacturing model. It was only in the 1990s that India shifted away from protectionism. However, unlike the other Asian economies, which still protect domestic industry, India did not do so, and opened all its sectors to foreign investment. While manufacturing did not particularly benefit from this openness, in part due to its latecomer status, services, which remained protected in the rest of Asia, offered India an opportunity. Particularly in the IT service subsector, the combination of skills, low cost, and openness to foreign investment provided India with advantages that it could exploit to develop its service sector. Interestingly, China also shifted to a more open stance toward foreign investment during this period, particularly after it joined the World Trade Organization in 2001.

The findings of this chapter show that, despite a nearly unique, open stance to foreign investment and trade in services among developing countries, and despite the progress of certain service subsectors, notably those related to IT, the Indian service sector remains low value-added. This is an interesting finding because it suggests that openness to trade and improved education are not sufficient to develop a sector to global levels.

To explain this apparent anomaly, we inquire how services relate to a sector in which, as we have noted above, India was left behind, i.e., the manufacturing sector. Through global comparisons, we argue that the growth and innovativeness of the service sector usually depend on the progress of the manufacturing sector. This means that services, at least initially, play a complementary rather than a substitutive role in relation to manufacturing.

In India's case, the inadequate manufacturing base meant that services grew independently of manufacturing. This was possible in some sectors, notably the IT sector, in which services' growth catered to the export economy. However, other services, such as logistics and banking, were unable to grow in sophistication in a manufacturing vacuum, and remained low value-added and lacking in innovation.

This suggests that Indian policymakers need to take a fresh look at their growth policies, particularly at ways to better integrate services' growth with manufacturing. China offers an interesting case study in this regard.

The chapter proceeds as follows. I first provide data on the growth of human capital in India and relate it to the growth of the service sector. The main finding is the strong link between human capital formation and the sector's growth. A second important finding is that the stock of human capital in India has outperformed global averages in recent years. Next, I seek to understand why the service sector is important for growth and innovation. I discuss the changing role of services in relation to growth and establish that different sources of GDP growth, such as the growth of business services, have different associations with manufacturing. Through examining the experience of several countries, including China, I show that, in the cases discussed, manufacturing growth was critical for service growth. In the next section, I take up the Indian case. I first discuss the lessons for India from China and other countries and then explore how public policy led to a different Indian experience. In particular, it led to a focus on a particular kind of manufacturing that restricted the contribution of services to growth and innovation. I then discuss the role of the service sector in India's growth, including a subsector in which India has developed global competence, IT services, and explore whether that success offers a suitable approach for developing an innovative service sector in India more generally. As I then examine the types of services that compose India's service sector, I find that they are characterized by a generally low level of professionalization, an apparent anomaly between the growth of human capital stock in India and its deployment. I discuss whether this anomaly can be explained by the country's shortfalls in manufacturing. Finally, I discuss policy options.

The Growth of Human Capital
and the Service Sector

In the postcolonial period, there has been a steady rise in global living standards. This has been accompanied by a rise in educational attainment, and a rise in the share of services in GDP (see figure 7.1).

As figure 7.1 shows, world GDP per capita has risen over time. The average annual growth in world GDP per capita is 3.2 percent over the 1995–2016 period. During this time, gross enrollment in tertiary education (TGER) rose from 15.6 percent to 36.1 percent, for an average annual growth of 4 percent per year. During this same time, the share of services in GDP rose from 58 percent to 69 percent, i.e., an average annual growth of 0.9 percent. The foregoing implies that, on average, a 1.0 percent rise in TGER was associated with a 0.8 percent rise in per capita GDP. To the extent that there is a causal relationship between human capital growth and economic growth, as is widely believed (de Meulemeester and Rochat 1995; Stevens, Kurlaender, and Grosz 2015; Jepsen, Troske, and Coomes 2014), it took a 1.25 percent increase in TGER to achieve a 1.00 percent increase in per capita GDP. Interestingly, if there is a causal relationship for services as well, which is also widely believed (Oliner and Sichel 2000; Calderon 2003; Dritsakis 2004),[1] a 1.0 percent rise in the share of services in GDP has a stronger leveraging effect, as it is associated with a 3.5 percent rise in per capita GDP. Further, the graph shows that the growth of per capita GDP over the period was accompanied by steady declines in the share of manufacturing and agriculture. While the share of services grew 0.9 percent annually on average, the share of manufacturing declined by 1.7 percent annually and that of agriculture declined by 1.3 percent annually. For India, as figure 7.2 shows, the TGER rose from 5.6 percent to 26.9 percent over the 1995–2017 period, for a rise of 7.8 percent annually, on average. During the same period, the share of services rose from 40.1 percent to 53.8 percent, for an average annual rise of 1.4 percent. During this time, per capita GDP rose by 7.6 percent annually, on average. Every 1.0 percent rise in TGER thus is associated with a 0.97 percent rise in per capita GDP, somewhat more than the global impact. A

---

[1]   The causal relationship between services and economic growth has been demonstrated for some key service sectors.

FIGURE 7.1 World growth in GDP per capita, GDP components, and human capital, 1995–2016

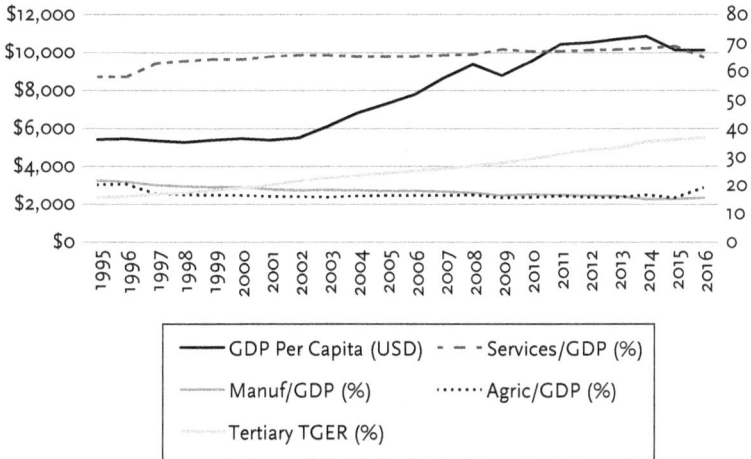

SOURCE: World Bank, https://data.worldbank.org/.

FIGURE 7.2 India's growth in GDP per capita, GDP components, and human capital, 1995–2017

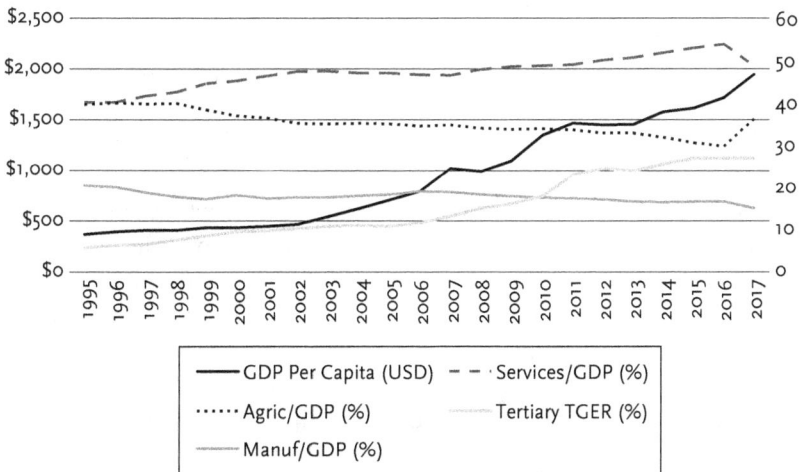

SOURCE: World Bank, https://data.worldbank.org.

FIGURE 7.3 Undergraduate gross enrollment ratio, 1970–2014, across three countries

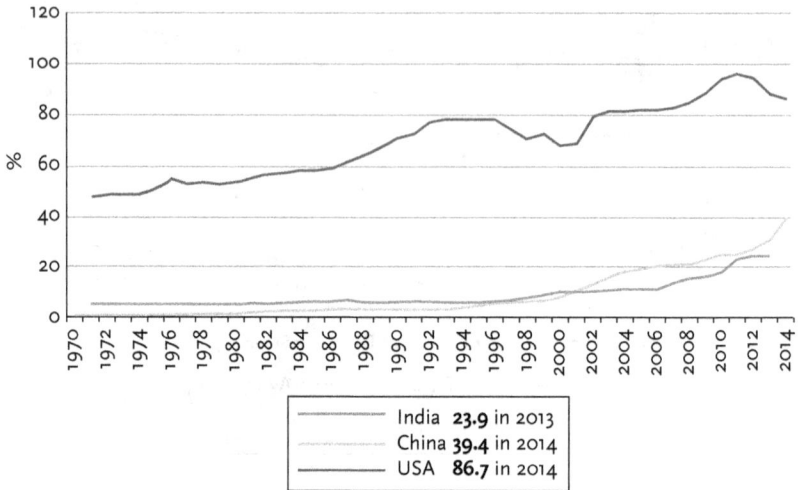

SOURCE: "Gross Enrolment Ratio in Tertiary Education," Knoema, https://www.knoema .com.

1.0 percent rise in the share of services has thus been associated with a 5.5 percent rise in per capita GDP, which is greater than that of the relationship with world GDP.[2]

Further, during this period, as figure 7.2 shows, the share of manufacturing and agriculture in India's GDP each declined by about 1 percent annually, on average.

Put in a comparative context, as figure 7.3 shows, India's progress in educational attainment is impressive, though it was a late starter.

India has also made impressive progress in doctoral programs, as table 7.1 shows. Partly as a result of its large commitment to doctoral programs, India has become a significant producer of academic research, especially in science, technology, engineering, and mathematics (STEM), as table 7.2 shows.

The association between educational attainment, services, and GDP growth has not gone unnoticed. Quite the contrary, it has led to a

2   As the R^2 (coefficient of determination) indicates, 80 percent of the rise in per capita GDP can be "explained" by services growth. By comparison, the coefficient of determination between the corresponding global data is 54 percent.

TABLE 7.1 State of doctoral education in India, China, and the United States

Country	PhD enrollment	PhD graduates	Average years to degree (post-baccalaureate)	Graduation rate (%)
China (2017)	361,997	58,032	5	N/A
India (2016)	126,451	24,171	5	92
United States (2015)	775,000	55,006	8.2	76

SOURCE: MOE 2017; MHRD 2016; Lederman 2016; NSF 2017; Okahana and Zhou 2017; National Science Board 2018.

TABLE 7.2 Science and engineering publications of selected regions and countries, by field, 2017 (percentage)

Field	World	United States	European Union	China	Japan	India
Engineering	18.4	12.3	14.6	28.9	17.1	24.2
Astronomy	0.6	0.8	0.9	0.3	0.5	0.4
Chemistry	7.9	5.1	6.7	12.3	9.1	10.1
Physics	8.7	6.7	8.3	9.9	12.4	9.0
Geosciences	5.7	5.0	5.5	7.1	3.8	4.9
Mathematics	2.3	2.0	2.6	2.0	1.7	1.9
Computer sciences	8.3	6.4	8.6	8.7	8.1	14.1
Agricultural sciences	2.2	1.2	2.0	2.2	1.5	2.6
Biological sciences	15.3	17.9	15.0	14.0	15.2	14.5
Medical sciences	22.1	29.3	24.4	13.3	27.9	15.3
Other life sciences	1.2	2.4	1.3	0.2	0.4	0.4
Psychology	1.7	3.5	2.1	0.3	0.6	0.2
Social sciences	5.3	7.2	8.0	1.0	1.5	2.4
All articles (number)	2,295,608	408,985	613,774	426,165	96,536	110,320

SOURCE: https://nces.ed.gov/programs/coe/indicator_chb.asp; data from Scopus.

widespread belief both in India and globally that the modern paradigm of growth is to raise spending on education, especially higher education, and to support service-sector growth. In fact, this paradigm is seen as critical for offsetting inevitable declines in manufacturing and agriculture. For example, a 2009 Asian Development Bank report on the service sector notes that:

> The service sector is an important component of any country's economy. It makes a direct and significant contribution to GDP and job creation,

and provides crucial inputs for the rest of the economy. In the process, services exert significant effects on economy-wide performance and on the overall investment climate. (Sauvé 2009, 4)

In India, a similar belief in "knowledge-based services as the engine of growth" has been enthusiastically championed by the government's policymakers. The service subsectors that are usually associated with high GDP growth are the sophisticated ones, such as IT, banking, tourism, and supply-chain management, rather than more traditional services, such as trucking, real estate, and domestic work (Singh 2016).

I have discussed the importance of education in India's economic growth and shown how the rising and high share of services in economic growth suggests that productivity and innovation in India will be driven by a rising share of human capital in the Indian service sector. I have also shown the rising stock of human capital in India, as seen by educational attainment data. This raises the following question. How is this stock being deployed? I turn to this topic next.

The Importance of Services for Growth and Innovation

I shall, in this section, progress as follows. First, I will analyze in more detail how services contribute to economic growth and innovation. This will lead to a typology of services, consisting of different types of business and consumer services. Second, I will consider the experiences of several different countries.

The first consideration I offer is that the contribution of services to economic growth is not automatic, and needs careful analysis. The positive association of services with economic growth in the postcolonial era does not necessarily mean that services drive higher economic growth.

There are several possible reasons for this. First, manufacturing may be the real driver of growth, and service growth may be largely dependent on manufacturing. Some services, such as banking and logistics, may grow by playing a supporting role, while some services may grow by playing a complementary role (such as design services). As manufacturing becomes more sophisticated, it might be expected that there will be greater demand for more sophisticated services, be they supporting services (e.g., technology-enabled freight) or complementary services (e.g., technology-enabled design). The share of services in GDP relative to manufacturing would then depend on where value is added. If manufacturing technology remains stable while service technology becomes more sophisticated, we might expect to see a growing share of services in GDP.

This "story" is typical of how economies with open domestic markets for labor and capital develop. If this is the case for India, it has important policy implications, such as for where public money should be spent. For instance, if public spending on computer science education primarily helps services to grow, while public spending on vocational training primarily helps manufacturing to grow, the above story should alert policymakers to the importance of dedicating resources to both kinds of human capital improvement.

In several countries that have successfully transitioned their economies to a higher income status, such as China and Korea, there is indeed a balance of public money spent on the manufacturing and service sectors. Such money typically supports education and training, as well as physical infrastructure improvements directed toward improving both services and manufacturing, such as industrial parks and tax incentives for exports. One highly developed country, Germany, not only followed such a balanced strategy during its transition to high-income status, but continues to do so.

The second possibility is that services on their own drive economic growth, independent of manufacturing. For example, the growth in India's software industry, which is largely export oriented and serves industries overseas, is an example of the service sector contributing to a country's growth on its own. The policy implication is that policy priorities and resources should largely support business services exports.

However, it should be noted that there may be limits to such growth. Only a few small economies, such as Hong Kong and Singapore, have successfully transitioned to a largely business-services-driven economy. In Hong Kong's case, services accounted for 92 percent of GDP in 2016. Hong Kong's ability to make this transition was due to its role relative to China's economy, as an exporter of business services to support China's industrial growth. However, for a large country such as India, reliance on business services exports as an engine of long-term economic growth would be much more difficult to achieve.

A third, and separate, possibility is that domestically provided personal services, such as retail and consumer banking, drive economic growth, independent of manufacturing. The spending power of the consumer on these services, in this case, may be generated from such services as well—as in the case of a barber paying for a shoeshine with a haircut. These are typically less-developed economies, stuck in a low-income self-sufficiency trap. There are no examples of such economies transitioning out of this low-income status through reliance on domestic personal services.

Interestingly, two successful East Asian economies, Japan and Korea, derive substantial growth from domestically provided personal services. For example, Japanese banks and retailers (rather than multinationals) dominate consumer spending on such services in Japan. However, the difference from the earlier case is that exports of manufactured goods generate the spending power for the consumer to spend on domestic personal services. This suggests that the driver of economic growth is export-oriented manufacturing rather than personal services.

Another class of economies in which personal services rise with growth is those with poor access to sophisticated human capital. Consider, for example, an economy in which only a small proportion of the population is well educated and has access to physical capital. If such an economy restricts the transition of labor from low- to higher-quality human capital, perhaps because of inequitable access to education and, possibly, labor laws, it is likely that the elite will invest their capital in automated means of production. In such an economy, it is likely that the gains from growth will largely be captured by the elite, while the mass of the population remains in capital-starved informal services, such as small retail and domestic work. National-level data would show a significant share of services in GDP. But GDP growth rates would be low and largely driven by population increases.

Several postcolonial developing countries (including India up to the 1980s) that followed import substitution policies are examples of this type of growth.

The rise of sophisticated consumer (and mixed business-consumer) services in recent years, such as search engines and social media sites, raises the possibility that such services might power growth. The establishment of Google and Facebook are examples of the impact of consumer services on the U.S. (and global) economy.[3] While evidence of the potential of such services to power economic growth on their own is still limited, reliance on such services to power growth could work if

---

3   Google and Facebook's annual revenue together is equal to over two-thirds of India's total software exports.

TABLE 7.3 Sources of GDP growth

Source of GDP growth	Service sector of primary importance	Primary driver of economic growth
Type 1: Balance between services and manufacturing	Business services	Manufacturing
Type 2: Export-oriented business services	Business services	Services
Type 3: Domestic consumer services	Consumer services	Services
Type 4: Capital-intensive manufacturing	Consumer services	Manufacturing
Type 5: Global consumer services	Consumer services	Services

SOURCE: World Bank Database: https://data.worldbank.org/.

they can be exported and/or the domestic manufacturing base to generate consumer spending power remains intact.

I summarize the different roles of services in table 7.3.

As the above analysis indicates, a variety of situations is possible, with different implications for growth and policymaking. The above is intended to provide a framework for assessing the past trajectory of services in India and for making useful recommendations for future policies.

A closer look at China

China's rise has been widely documented as based on the growth of its manufacturing sector from 1980 to the present time (Kroeber 2016; Borensztein and Ostry 1996). Yet, as figure 7.4 shows, the association between services and the rise in GDP per capita appears to be as strong in China as it was in India during the 1991–2016 period.

Further, as the figure indicates, the relationship between services and growth started to become significant only from around 1990 onwards, i.e., a decade after manufacturing started to grow. However, even during the first decade of China's high-growth period, 1980–90, services' share of GDP grew from 22.3 percent to 35.3 percent.[4]

China offers an interesting comparison to India, which started reforming its economy from the early 1990s. At that time, the two countries' per capita income was similar (see table 7.4). Yet China was able to increase its GDP at a much faster rate thereafter.

---

4 The R^2 between GDP per capita and the share of services in economic growth during the period 1960–90 was just 3.8 percent. For the period 1991–2017, it rose to 82.7 percent.

FIGURE 7.4 Growth of GDP per capita and GDP components, China, 1966–2016

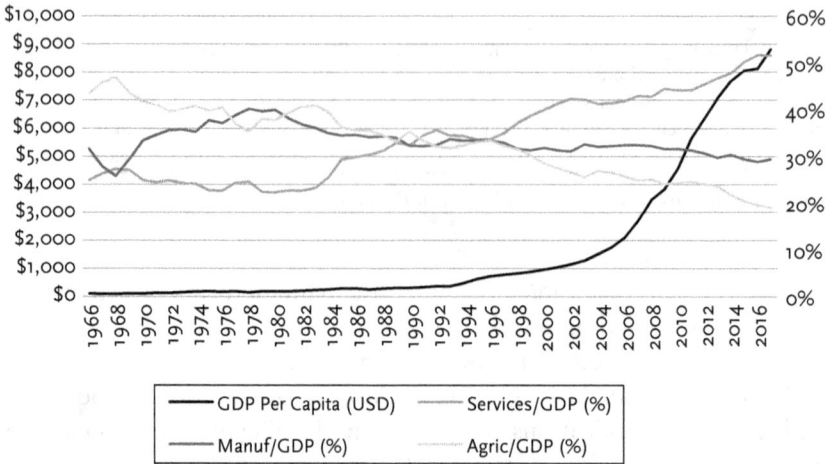

SOURCE: World Bank, https://data.worldbank.org.

TABLE 7.4 Growth of GDP per capita,
China and India (USD)

	1990	2017
China	$318	$8,827
India	$364	$1,942

SOURCE: World Bank Database: https://data
.worldbank.org/.

We know, from several studies, that in India manufacturing has not been a driver of economic growth from independence up to the present time (Arnold et al. 2016). This raises the question: how did China accomplish growth through manufacturing without a strong contribution from the service sector till 1990, and why did the relationship change thereafter?

The data suggest that China best fits the description of a Type 1 economy, as outlined in table 7.3. In the initial years, the policy focus was on manufacturing. Yet, to support the rise in manufacturing, there needed to be a growth of supporting business services such as banking and logistics. In the absence of manufacturing growth, there would have been little demand for business services. At the very least, there should have been an accompanying rise in supporting business services even before 1990.

Since the China story is so well documented, we know that its growth in manufacturing was largely oriented toward the export market in the early years. The exporting businesses usually originated from somewhere in East or Southeast Asia—usually Hong Kong or Taiwan, though Korea, Singapore, and Japan were strong contributors as well. That is, firms in, say, Hong Kong, set up operations to manufacture goods in China, which were then exported to developed countries.

In this situation, the supporting business services were provided by foreign investors and importers. For example, trade finance and other trade facilitation services such as logistics were provided by importers and foreign direct investors in the initial years.

Why did this situation not continue? China, after 1990, increasingly developed the service infrastructure to support export-oriented manufacturing. In some cases, this was because of improved physical infrastructure. For instance, prior to 1990, Hong Kong was the main transshipment point for goods made in China. Goods manufactured in China would arrive into Hong Kong, where they were put through quality control and repackaged before being shipped to buyers in developed countries.

The development of a sophisticated ports and banking infrastructure in China in the 1990s, along with a capable labor force, meant that foreign investors found it cheaper to organize the shipment of goods directly from China. Thus, over a period of time, quality control and packaging moved to China along with direct shipment. While Hong Kong paid the price by losing its premier status as China's main transshipment port, this loss was more than fully offset by the gains from moving away from quality control and packaging services toward handling only the most sophisticated cargo, often by air, as well as offering complementary services, such as design and currency risk management.

More recently, since the start of this century, China has shown an ever-increasing ability to provide more sophisticated services (and manufacturing). This can come back to hurt its client firms. For example, the Asian bicycle exporting industry was, for many decades, controlled by Taiwanese firms. Through the 1970s, bicycles were made in Taiwan and exported to developed countries. The designs for the bicycles were provided by developed-country buyers. With China's opening up, Taiwanese firms shifted manufacturing to China and focused on marketing and, later, design and development. By about 2000, this move was largely accomplished. Foreign buyers increasingly relied on Taiwanese firms for design specifications and quality control. However, as China-based operators (often owned by Taiwanese interests) moved into design and quality control, Taiwanese firms have been affected by the inability to move even further upstream in recent years. This threat, witnessed in other countries as well, such as Korea and Japan, has come to be termed as the threat of the "red supply chain."

However, since there seems to be no limit on how sophisticated services can become, more nimble locations, such as Hong Kong and Singapore, have managed to move into ever more sophisticated services. China's less agile partners—Korea, Japan, and Taiwan—seem to have been less able to move into higher-end services, and have suffered through lower growth in consequence. We now turn to the Indian case.

The Case of India

In this section, I first discuss the lessons for India from China and other countries, and explore how public policy led to a focus on a particular kind of manufacturing that restricted the contribution of services to growth and innovation. I then discuss the success of India's IT sector, and the types of services that comprise India's service sector.

Lessons from China

The China experience offers lessons that may be worth considering for India. As has been discussed, in the early days of its industrialization in the 1980s, China focused on export-oriented manufacturing and did not provide business services. Foreign direct investors provided supporting business services from their home bases, typically from East Asia or Southeast Asia.

This situation arose because the skills to provide business services from China, such as transport services and financial services, were relatively scarce. This, in turn, was due to a weak base of service infrastructure, such as commercial banking services. In short, China lacked the skills to provide business services. Foreign direct investors filled this gap.

However, China was able to quickly move into services after 1990. This was in part because of the development of a sophisticated ports and banking infrastructure in China in the 1990s, along with a rising quality of human capital. Foreign firms quickly took advantage of these opportunities to shift services to China. They did this because of the close relationship its firms had with their buyers. The typical manufacturing firm in China was usually co-owned or fully owned by some Asian firm that was the Chinese firm's client. This allowed for a relatively free flow of business knowledge from the Asian firm to the Chinese firm. The Asian firms needed to do this for competitive reasons. Chinese policymakers welcomed this shift due to the higher value addition that resulted within China. As discussed in the earlier section, while foreign firms benefited from this shift in the short term, in the longer term, the continued shift of ever more sophisticated services to China from other parts of Asia has adversely affected the ability of the other countries to compete with China. This effect is less noticed in the more "agile" locations of Asia, such as Hong Kong and Singapore, and more in Korea, Japan, and Taiwan.

India should not seek to replicate the Chinese model, since the domestic and global environments are different. For instance, India, relative to its stage of industrialization, has an IT sector that is more sophisticated than China's. It should seek to leverage these advantages.

But there are still important lessons to learn from the Chinese experience. The first is the recognition of the role of export-oriented manufacturing in providing the base for a service sector. China's business service sector developed, with a lag, from its export-oriented manufacturing sector. To create this sector, China opened its manufacturing economy to foreign investment through reducing barriers to trade and foreign direct investment.

While India has come a long way since its 1991 reforms in reducing tariffs and allowing foreign direct investment, high nontariff and investment barriers still impede trade and foreign direct investment (US Department of Commerce n.d.). These barriers usually arise from local businesses seeking to exclude foreign competition. Nontariff barriers such as local content rules or inspection regimes are very hard to circumvent through normal competition rules, due to domestic business and labor interests.

In China's case, this was not an issue, since foreign firms were the main manufacturers and labor policy was subsumed by the importance of manufacturing. In India, however, it will be more difficult due to the presence of established domestic firms. It will require considerable political will to overcome these barriers in India.

A second lesson concerns labor force capability and physical infrastructure. Given the competitive environment in Asian supply chains, it is likely that the richer countries of Asia would have moved services work even earlier than 1990 to China, provided its labor force was capable and the matching infrastructure, particularly physical connectivity, basic utilities, and trading systems, was in place.

For India, this appears to be a crucial lesson. Again, while India has come a long way since it began its reforms in 1991, both labor force capability and physical infrastructure have been inadequate (World Bank 2014; UNDP n.d.).[5]

Policymaking in India

It is worth asking why such obvious lessons were not learned and put into practice. Even today, India is in a situation where the service sector and, to a lesser extent, manufacturing, are seen as independent engines of growth. The linkages between them are not recognized and addressed.

This may be because it is a complex task. Given the mixed experience with services, it is worth asking what the role of services should be relative to manufacturing and the economy as a whole, and where policymakers' efforts should be focused.

This is a task to which, until recently, inadequate attention has been paid in India. Indian planners until the turn of this century were emphasizing the incremental capital-output ratio as the key variable to assess the economy's efficiency and growth potential. This reflected their view that tangible assets (i.e., capital goods) rather than intangible assets (such as a well-trained work force) were the drivers of growth. Their standard was the Harrod-Domar model, which was based on capital accumulation, as explained below.

In this view, though they were behind the times, they were grounded in earlier scholarly work. Until the 1960s, economists globally tended to regard the service economy as a distraction. Most growth theories of the time, such as the Harrod-Domar and Baumol models, were built around capital accumulation and its relationship to output (Baumol 1967; Solow 1956). Baumol's growth model divided the economy into two sectors: a productive sector, consisting of manufacturing and agriculture, and one unproductive sector (services).

---

5   For example, electricity consumption per capita in India was just a fifth of China's. Gender inequality is significant in India. The Human Development Index ratio for females relative to males was 0.84 in India in 2017, compared to 0.95 in China.

The Harrod-Domar growth model, for example, is represented as follows:

$Q = f(K)$

Where:

- Q is output
- K is the supply of capital
- dQ/dK represents the marginal product of capital (or, the inverse of the incremental capital-output ratio) and is a constant
- $f(0)=0$ indicates the capital necessary for output

Under this model, the only way to increase output per capita is to make more capital available. This was seen as a suitable model for developing countries, where the supply of labor was plentiful, but capital was scarce.

Much less emphasis was put on how to improve labor productivity through investments in education. A well-known economist of the time (incidentally, a favorite teacher of the former prime minister Manmohan Singh), Nicholas Kaldor, diagnosed the slow growth of the British economy as an outcome of the excessive growth of the service sector, which, he argued, retained labor when it was in short supply (Kaldor 1966).

For India, a focus on models like Harrod-Domar led policymakers to prioritize improving the capital stock through imports of capital goods and investments to support the productivity of capital (such as through building physical infrastructure). Fiscal policy was focused on improving public savings through high taxes, and the channeling of those savings into publicly funded infrastructure. Inadequate emphasis was put on education, training, healthcare, and other ways to improve the productivity of labor. The idea that services could contribute to economic growth remained neglected.

The historian C. H. Lee (1984) notes that the government of the United Kingdom in the 1960s even introduced a selective employment tax that was designed with the specific intention of "shaking excess labor out of services by levying a charge on employment in that sector while the creation of manufacturing employment was rewarded with subsidies." The rationale was that services were unproductive. Lee cites Bacon and Eltis, who argued that Britain's slow growth at the time was because of the size of the public sector (which was entirely in services), which absorbed workers who would have been better employed in manufacturing (Bacon and Eltis 1976).

This view of services as being low-end, labor-consuming activities without producing anything of value reflected the reality of the day, perhaps grounded in Adam Smith's definition of services as activities whose results "generally perish in the very instance of their performance and seldom leave any trace or value behind them for which an equal quality of service could afterwards be procured" (Smith and McCulloch 1838). Most of these services were low-end ones. For example, in Britain, in the nineteenth century, the single largest category of service employment was domestic service, reflecting both economic growth and the inequitable distribution of income and wealth. Even as of 1950, there were as many as half a million domestic servants employed in Britain (Lee 1984).

The Nobel Prize–winning economist Simon Kuznets (1957) emphasized the shift from agriculture to manufacturing in the course of economic growth, concluding that the share of services in economic growth did not change with economic growth. Such analyses reinforced the view among many economists of the time that many low-end services would not be able to compete with automation and would decline as a result.

This view of services as a useless appendage started changing as economies integrated within, moving from isolated "town and village economies" to national markets. This created a large demand for transport, distribution, and financial services, which grew at the expense of government services and personal services.

A still more positive global view of services started emerging from the 1970s, driven in large part by the rise in international trade. Large multinational service companies, particularly in the financial sector, found that rising international trade of manufactured goods sparked a large increase in demand for sophisticated services within the private sector. Many such services, such as currency hedging, reinsurance, and offshore finance, had largely been the domain of government until the Bretton Woods system collapsed in 1971. With the freeing up of capital controls, the risk of currency fluctuations shifted in large part to the private sector, leading to the rise in demand for financial services within richer countries that were unlinked to the state of manufacturing internally. Even today, developed economies account for 74 percent of global services trade (UNCTAD n.d.). But the trend in the rise of services in international trade is widespread, and, as of 2017, accounted for a quarter of total trade (Loungani et al. 2017).

Later models sought to address the limitations of these capital-oriented growth models by emphasizing the importance of labor supply, particularly its productivity as influenced by labor-improving investments and technological change. The Solow-Swan model is one example of such a growth model, which was derived from the firm-specific production function of Cobb-Douglas.

Under the Solow-Swan model:

$Q(L,K) = (AL)^\beta K^\alpha$

Where:

- Q is output
- L is the supply of labor
- K is the supply of capital
- A is a constant, representing the improvement in labor productivity contributed by both labor-improving investments and new technology (together, AL represents "effective labor")
- α is a constant between 0 and 1 measuring the marginal product of capital
- β is a constant between 0 and 1 measuring the marginal product of effective labor
- The model is consistent with decreasing, constant, or increasing returns to scale ($\alpha + \beta <,=,$ or > 1, respectively)

The key changes from the earlier Harrod-Domar model are, first, that labor is no longer seen as in plentiful supply. Even in highly populated and poor economies like India, recognizing that AL, or effective labor supply, can be as important a contributor to growth as capital, allows policymakers to focus on ways to improve output through augmenting the quality of labor through labor-improving investments and technological progress.

Even as global recognition of the importance of labor has risen, macroeconomic trends have led to a sharp decline in capital costs. In some countries, such as Japan, borrowing costs are near zero, and savers may even receive negative interest on their savings.

In such a condition, the marginal product of capital is near zero. Perhaps it is time for a revised Harrod-Domar model, which would replace capital with labor as the sole variable in the output equation. In such a model, the driver of growth is the marginal product of labor, and the model recognizes that labor is necessary for output.

While a recognition of the importance of labor productivity had become established globally from the 1970s onwards, the importance of services was seen in its changing role as an ancillary to manufacturing. Eichengreen and Gupta (2013) argue that a key change occurred around 1990, when "traditional services that once dominated—lodging, meal service, housecleaning, beauty, and barber shops—[were] supplemented by modern banking, insurance, computing, communication and business services." They show that this change cut across low- and high-income economies, although it was more predominant in high-income economies. They believe that the change was enabled and accelerated by the application of information and communications technology to the production of services, enabling services that once had to be produced locally to be sourced from long distances and traded across borders. This brought down the cost of providing services, which had earlier been thought to necessarily rise faster than that of manufacturing as an economy grows.

Understanding the service sector's role in India's growth

From the above discussion, it appears evident that services should not necessarily be considered as an independent set of activities whose increase is desirable for economic well-being. We have discussed earlier the case (Type 1 of table 7.3) in which manufacturing is the driver of growth, while services grow to support manufacturing and would not survive independent of the growth of manufacturing. However, India's subpar performance in manufacturing, while at the same time witnessing a large rise in the service sector, suggests that this is not the right explanation for services' growth in India.

The phenomenal success of selected service subsectors that are usually considered high end might suggest that India's growth may be explained by such sectors. The growth in software services,[6] telecommunications, and banking in India, starting in the 1970s and accelerating in the mid-1990s, has been argued to be an important driver of India's capability to provide business (Karnik 2015).[7]

What sparked this change, and does it have the capacity to benefit the whole economy, i.e., could India be a Type 2 economy, as defined in table 7.3? One view is that opening up exports through liberalizing foreign direct investment and lowering import barriers was the

---

6 Note that the primary buyers of software services from India are manufacturing firms or other business services.

7 Together, these three sectors earn about $300 billion in gross revenue a year.

driver of growth in sophisticated services (IBEF n.d.; Sunkara 2016). Arnold et al. (2016), however, argue against conventional explanations for India's post-1991 growth that focus on industrial delicensing and trade liberalization. They argue that reforms in services, particularly in banking, telecommunications, insurance, and transportation had significantly positive effects on the productivity of manufacturing firms.

This explanation reinforces the view that manufacturing drives growth, but that the size, quality, and perhaps even sustainability of growth improve when complementary services develop. However, the low rate of manufacturing growth and its relatively low sophistication suggest that either manufacturing is intrinsically unable to drive growth, or that the services needed to support or be complements to manufacturing have not yet adequately developed.

This still leaves unanswered the question as to why India, given the low sophistication of manufacturing and its low contribution to GDP, has witnessed a continued rise in services. It suggests that services' growth has been, to a significant extent, independent of manufacturing, i.e., the rise in services is not complementary to that in manufacturing.

Two possible explanations suggest themselves. The first is that global services (such as software exports) have driven services' growth and economic growth (Type 2 growth). The second is that services' growth over the period continues to be driven by personal (including government-provided) services (Type 3 growth).

Note that, by itself, understanding which types of services are driving growth does not tell us much about the sophistication of these services. Personal services of the traditional kind, such as domestic services, tend to be of low sophistication and have low educational requirements. On the other hand, nontraditional personal services such as the use of the smartphone for social media require sophisticated skills. Government services can similarly be low end (manual street cleaning) or high end (public tertiary healthcare). Even globally traded services can be low end (call center salespersons, migrant worker remittances) or high end (software application developers, currency swaps).

To understand the potential for Type 2 (global service–led growth), we take up the case of the software industry in India. The Indian software services industry consists primarily of two kinds of services. The first is software development, such as applications development, and related services, such as system integration and engineering services. The second is IT-enabled services, such as online accounting. India's software services are provided almost entirely for business clients, both

TABLE 7.5 Growth of the Indian software sector

Software services (A)	2000–01 ($ bn) (B)	2017–18 ($ bn) (C)	Annual growth (%) (D)	Growth relative to global/ national growth (%) (E)
Export revenue	6.54	126	19.0	4.8x
Domestic revenue	2.18	41	18.9	2.1x

NOTE: Column (D) is average annual growth between 2016–17 and 2000–01; Column (E) is annual growth relative to world GDP per capita annual growth (4.0%) for the row "export revenue" and relative to Indian GDP per capita growth (9.1%) for the row "domestic revenue."
SOURCE: nasscom.in; NASSCOM (2018); Indian IT Center Statistics; Centre for Development Informatics, University of Manchester, UK, http://www.cdi.manchester.ac.uk.

in India and overseas, although a domestic consumer software industry has also developed in recent years. While exports of these services are significant and account for over 5 percent of GDP, the domestic output of software services has not kept pace, as table 7.5 indicates.

Table 7.5 shows that exports of software services not only exceeded the growth of domestic software services, but grew at nearly five times the rate of growth of world GDP per capita. By contrast, domestic software services grew at 2.1 times the rate of growth of India's GDP per capita.

This illustrates both the capacity of software service exports to drive economic growth and their limitations. The sector can continue to contribute to economic growth if it is able to find markets and the labor to provide services. There is clearly considerable scope for providing more software services. The Indian software industry is still small relative to the world's software industry, which generated revenue of about $1.4 trillion in 2016 (Statista n.d.). Hence, the potential for continued export growth is significant. In addition, the relatively small contribution of domestic software services to per capita GDP implies that Indian industry is still in the early stages of using technology. This suggests that the potential to increase the use of technology in domestic manufacturing is high.

The limitations are of two kinds. First, it is unrealistic to expect a sector that contributes about 5 percent of GDP to be an engine of growth.[8] Second, even if the potential of the sector could be raised,

---

8 While the IT sector's revenue exceeds 5 percent of GDP, its value addition will be lower.

perhaps through intensive government programs to increase the IT intensity of manufacturing, the labor force to provide such services needs to be available.

We now turn to the second possibility, that services' growth over the period continues to be driven by personal (including government-provided) services (Type 3 growth). Nayyar (2012) has studied the composition of the service sector in India in 1983–84 and 2004–05. This was a period of reforms in significant service subsectors with the potential to generate high-end services, as argued by Arnold et al. (2016). Nayyar finds that the productivity of services rose relative to industry. As seen in table 7.6, during the period 1983–84 and 2004–05, industry's share of total employment rose from 13.8 percent to 18.8 percent, while service employment rose from 17.6 percent to 24.8 percent. During this period, industry's share of GDP changed from 19 percent to 18 percent, while services' share changed from 35.1 percent to 47.4 percent. This indicates that services generated more GDP per capita than manufacturing. Each percentage point of service employment accounted for about 2 percent of GDP per capita, while for manufacturing, the corresponding ratio was 1.4 in 1983–84 and 0.95 in 2003–04. This implies that not only does service employment steadily drive more GDP than industry, but that the contribution of employment in industry to GDP has declined over the period.

Nayyar's findings on employment imply a certain level of independence of services' growth from industrial growth. This suggests that personal, government, and global services have driven growth.

Our significant discursion into the service sector has allowed us to establish that manufacturing-led business services are going to be the key driver of growth and innovation in India. Focusing policy attention on other kinds of services should at best be seen as providing supplements to growth. These are important, but, by themselves, unlikely to address the role of services as a platform for high-end human capital and innovation (Rao and Varghese 2009).

TABLE 7.6 Comparing the contribution to growth of manufacturing and services

Sector	(A) Share of GDP per capita (%)		(B) Share of employment (%)		Contribution to growth (A)/(B)	
	1983–84	2004–05	1983–84	2004–05	1983–84	2004–05
Manufacturing	19.0	18.0	13.8	18.8	1.4x	0.9x
Services	35.1	47.4	17.6	24.8	2x	1.9x

SOURCE: Nayyar (2012) and World Bank Database: https://data.worldbank.org/.

The deployment of human capital

We now turn to the deployment of services. I consider this by examining the composition of employment in the service sector, using data provided by Nayyar (2012). Table 7.7 shows the composition.

The second and third columns of table 7.7 indicate that services that might be considered traditional, such as wholesale and retail trade, hotels and restaurants, transport, public administration and defense, and education and health accounted for about 80 percent of total employment in services in both periods. This suggests that personal and government services continued to drive growth.

The fourth and fifth columns of table 7.7 show the composition of the workforce in each sector. The fourth column indicates professional workers. These include professional, technical, administrative, executive, and managerial workers. The fifth column (nonprofessional workers) includes clerical, sales, and service staff. The data are for 2004–05.

The data show that, with the exception of business services, education, and health services, professional workers make up a small share of total employees. Further, in both education and health, wages are significantly below wages of those in industrial sectors. As Nayyar (2012) notes, "This is plausible as a majority of teachers and health professionals are employed in public institutions which pay relatively low salaries."

TABLE 7.7 Composition of employment in India's service sector

Service sector	1993–94*	2004–05*	Professional workers	Nonprofessional workers
Wholesale and retail trade	35.0	37.0	9.4	90.6
Hotels and restaurants	3.8	5.0	20.1	79.9
Transport	11.4	13.0	10.5	89.5
Communications	0.8	2.0	24.6	75.4
Financial services	3.0	2.0	21.9	78.1
Real estate (including rentals)	0.4	0.5	42.3	57.7
Business services	1.5	2.0	55.0	45.0
Public administration and defense	17.0	11.0	17.6	82.4
Education	9.5	11.0	87.1	12.9
Health	3.0	3.0	72.9	27.1
Other	14.0	11.0	16.9	83.1
Total	100	100		

NOTE: *Percent of total service sector employment.
SOURCE: Nayyar 2012.

The picture that emerges of India's service sector is that of a continued growth in services' employment and contribution to GDP that is significant, but independent of the industrial sector and, instead, concentrated in traditional, low-end personal and government services. Thus, there are elements of a Type 3 economy (see table 7.3). However, the manufacturing sector also exists and independently contributes to growth, albeit less so than services. The manufacturing sector relies on low-end business services. Other studies have shown a high capital intensity of Indian manufacturing (Hasan, Mitra, and Sundaram 2013). This suggests that part of India's growth can also partly be explained by such manufacturing, marking the economy as a Type 4 economy.

THE CRISIS IN INDIAN HIGHER EDUCATION

The inability to use human capital effectively is a puzzle when compared to the rising stock of human capital, as measured by tertiary enrollment (see table 7.1), albeit that tertiary enrollment remains low compared to world standards and China (World Bank 2017). Part of the reason is that the quality of education is poor (Carnoy et al. 2013).

The rest may have to do with how education was managed. Under India's federalist constitution, education is a "concurrent" subject. This means that both the state (provinces) and the national government share responsibility for the country's education system. In practice, there is a division of responsibility, with the states being responsible for service delivery and the national government being responsible for funding and quality control. As part of its quality mandate, the national government also delivers education selectively through high-end institutions, such as the Indian Institutes of Technology. However, most education at the primary, secondary, and tertiary levels is delivered by the states.

After India gained its independence in 1947, the national government declared an intention to shape education to support industrialization. This became very quickly an area of disagreement between the national government and the states, with debates focused on what to teach in higher-education institutions. States preferred to focus on delivering general, nontechnical education, while the national government favored technical education.

There were sound political reasons for the states' preference for general education. The pace of industrialization was too low (a situation that has remained a constant) to generate jobs for the masses.

There were some unexpected, if perfectly logical, outcomes from this disagreement between the national government and the states. First, the national government, in pursuance of industrialization, set up high-quality institutions to provide technical education, such as the well-known Indian Institutes of Technology. These were relatively costly initiatives and were subsidized heavily, leaving little by way of resources for the states to spend on education. Due to their limited scale, these institutions catered largely to the elite, who were thus able to access a high-quality education at a subsidized rate. Meanwhile, the masses were excluded from such education. Given the depressed state of industrialization at the time, there were, in any case, few technical jobs available.

The states would have liked to promote widespread general education. However, they lacked the resources to do so. The states would have turned to the private sector, but private institutions were only willing to provide education in return for profit. This faced a legal hurdle: according to the Indian Constitution, educational provision must be conducted as a not-for-profit activity. Through the 1990s, this rule was strictly enforced by the courts, with the result that private provision remained a small component of total educational provision.

In the 1990s, the interpretation of "not-for-profit" by the courts changed to allow private providers to generate surpluses, provided those surpluses were fully retained within their institutions and used to improve the institutions. This new interpretation allowed the states to charter private providers to create institutions that rewarded them well, provided they were in executive roles. In all but name, these became for-profit institutions. This led to a surge in private provision. Concurrently, by the early 1990s, a shortage of labor in technical fields had developed. The private providers, therefore, specialized in engineering provision and other technical fields.

Quality was a casualty of this shift. The poor quality arose from the inability of private providers to recruit high-quality faculty at a reasonable cost, and from the poor quality of incoming students—in turn due to the low quality of K–12 education.

By the early 2000s, there was an oversupply of profit-seeking private institutions relative to job demands. While the supply of faculty has remained steady to the present time, the quality of the faculty remains poor, and the quality of graduates is, on average, below job market needs.[9]

---

9   According to a leading private firm that tests graduates for job suitability, over 95 percent of engineering graduates were unable to code correctly.

India, as of 2019, has a bimodal higher-education system. A small proportion of students, less than 5 percent, study at elite, subsidized public institutions run by the national government. The remainder are about equally divided between publicly owned, state-level institutions providing a general education and privately owned institutions with state charters providing technical education. The average quality of both types of state-level institutions is significantly below that of the public, national institutions and below the level needed for the job market.

The above assessment of the deployment of human capital shows that India's rising stock of human capital, in both quantity and quality, was not, up to the recent past, effectively deployed. This may indicate a lack of opportunity for qualified workers due to the low-tech nature of the industry and service sectors. It also indicates, as we have discussed above, that the quality of the capital stock remains poor, something that has been documented by other studies. Both findings suggest some important lessons for policymakers. We turn to this next.

Options for Policymakers

For policymakers, the goal seems clear: to use policy to support the transition of the Indian service sector away from its current status as a hybrid of Types 3 and 4 to an economy that moves in a higher value-added, more innovative direction. This implies the following options. One is to support the transition of capital-intensive manufacturing to manufacturing that can be supported and made more productive through business services (in a shift from a Type 4 to a Type 1 economy). Under such policies, the focus would be on manufacturing, letting it "drag along" the service sector. A second option is to support the service sector, and to rely on the growth of sophisticated personal services to propel economic growth (a Type 5 economy). To support the movement from a Type 4 to a Type 1 economy, there would need to be a greater emphasis on vocational training, basic education, and healthcare services. But, to be effective, equal attention needs to be paid to improving the infrastructure for manufacturing, such as ports, roads, and other infrastructure that improves industrial connectivity. The latter option, moving to a Type 5 economy, would suggest focusing more on human capital improvements through tertiary education, especially graduate STEM education. Physical infrastructure would still be important, but there would be an emphasis on different kinds of physical infrastructure, such as data bandwidth and intraurban connectivity.

To discuss this further, we shall create a classification of services that is useful for policymakers. We have already seen a classification of services between traditional and modern services. However, it should be clear from the above discussion that many traditional services, such as transport services, need to be supported by sophisticated, modern services, such as IT-enabled logistics, to make them useful for manufacturing.

We will separate services into four categories: Category 1, services that support manufacturing, such as freight services and business banking, and grow in some proportion to the output of manufactured goods. This category also includes business services provided by the government, such as regulations and compliance measures; Category 2, complementary services that add value to manufacturing, such as business process improvements, inventions, and design services; Category 3, intermediate personal services that support citizens' productivity but are not themselves productive, such as personal banking, healthcare, and government services; and Category 4, end-user personal services that are themselves end-user items desired by consumers, such as haircuts and social media. Table 7.8 maps the categories of services that will support the development of different economy types.

How can the policymaker's objective of moving away from the current state of the Indian economy (a hybrid of Types 3 and 4) to a more sustainable and higher phase of growth be achieved? The desired stages should most likely include a Type 1 economy, at least. However, given the advanced stage of several service sectors in India, policy support to achieve a Type 2 economy should also be considered. At a later stage, facilitating the transition to a Type 5 economy could be supported.

To move to a Type 1 economy, it is likely not just that new kinds of services as indicated in table 7.8 will have to be developed, but that ways to enable labor to move away from Categories 3 and 4 (personal services) toward business services will be required. Policymakers could, for example, prioritize two key sectors, trade and transport, that together employ about half of all service workers and in which over 90 percent of the workforce is nonprofessional. The strategies to be employed could include simplification of business rules, support for digitization of business processes, and support for vocational training. The first two are components of supporting business services

TABLE 7.8 Mapping economy and service types

Source of GDP growth	Policymaker priority	Service category	Human capital strategy
Type 1: Balance between services and manufacturing	Business services	Category 1: Support services Category 2: Complementary services	Vocational training, in both services and manufacturing
Type 2: Export-oriented business services	Business services	Category 2: Complementary services	Tertiary education, with a focus on STEM
Type 3: Domestic consumer services	Consumer services	Category 4: End-user personal services	Tertiary education
Type 4: Capital-intensive manufacturing	Consumer services	Category 3: Intermediate personal services	Vocational training, with a focus on manufacturing
Type 5: Global consumer services	Consumer services	Category 4: End-user personal services	Tertiary education, with a focus on graduate training

SOURCE: Author.

(Category 1) and the last named is part of intermediate personal services (Category 3). A sometimes unrecognized but important input is healthcare. While there are no studies we are aware of that document the relationship between healthcare provision and worker productivity of low-end services in India, studies in other countries show a definite and positive link (Erdil and Yetkiner 2009). Low income is connected to life expectancy globally (Donkin, Goldblatt, and Lynch 2002) and low worker productivity is likely partly due to shortfalls in calorific consumption, but also due to inadequate or unaffordable healthcare.

As the manufacturing sector's productivity rises in response to the improvement in service sector productivity, less factory labor will be needed to supply the same output. The reduced labor costs will, in turn, enable manufacturing to invest in purchasing both support and complementary services that are high value-added, such as business banking, telecommunications, and software services, in which India already has established skills.

To move to a Type 2 economy, there should be a focus on complementary services with high value-added. While it seems that Indian industry is well prepared to move into this area, judging by the success of India's software, banking, and telecommunications sectors, policymakers should analyze why only software has been exportable, that too at the low end (Dossani 2007). Certain factors that may come into play here include the quality of professionals, the environment for innovative work, and the role of government as a first-mover client for sophisticated services. Policymakers may need to support all these aspects in order to stimulate value-added complementary services.

The growth of high-end end-user personal services in recent years offers an opportunity for the Indian economy to incorporate elements of a Type 5 economy powered by global consumer services. At the present time, this has emerged as an exciting area of growth in developed countries, sparked by the smartphone and social media. Personal end-user services at the high end are exciting because of their customer-centric approach. The smartphone succeeded despite initially having fewer applications than so-called feature phones, in part, because it fit in with lifestyle changes of using the web for applications that were already under way. The smartphone added mobility to activities such as search, and thus succeeded. These applications then seamlessly found their way to the business world.

Such services can thrive largely independently of manufacturing. However, they require many of the same skills as value-added business services, such as design skills, to be successful. Often high-end personal services are reinvented as business services, such as the use of virtual reality, initially developed for gaming, in commercial fields such as architecture. These factors suggest that entering into a Type 5 economy will be subsequent to India developing a Type 1 economy and need not be a high policy priority. However, policymakers should enable the growth of this sector by supporting tertiary education, especially at the graduate levels. This raises the question as to whether the significant investment that India is making in graduate education, particularly in STEM-related fields, is an appropriate use of public money.

Conclusion

This chapter began with showing the relationship between GDP growth and its components, including human capital. It was shown that there is a strongly positive relation between GDP and human capital, and that the dominant role of services in GDP warranted particular attention to the role of human capital in service sector growth and innovation.

We discovered that the underlying causes of service-sector growth and innovation are complex. This is because the positive relationship between the service sector and GDP could be driven by manufacturing, by the openness of the economy, and by the share of trained persons in the workforce, among other factors. I identified five sources of GDP growth and related each source to the corresponding service category, and provided global examples of each type, including a detailed case study of China and its learnings for India. The lessons included the importance of labor force capability, but within contexts of a strong manufacturing base, openness to overseas service providers, and physical infrastructure.

I then turned to the case of India. In India, until recent times, the service sector was neglected. This was an outcome of policy models that premiated capital over labor, on the assumption that labor supply was plentiful. This overlooked the important role that productive labor could play in growth. Instead, it led to a focus on a particular kind of manufacturing that restricted the contribution of services to growth and innovation.

During the 1990s, the growth of software exports and of sophisticated service subsectors such as banking and telecommunications—each of which contribute significantly to India's GDP—brought attention for the first time to the importance of services and to the importance of sophisticated human capital. However, the services that dominate GDP are low-end personal services provided by a workforce that is overwhelmingly not professionally trained.

I then turned to how policymakers can support a transition to a high value-added, innovative economy consisting of both high value-added services and manufacturing. I argued that, to improve manufacturing, policymakers' support should consist of providing basic intermediate personal services well, such as basic education and healthcare, while fostering the digitization of businesses and the more efficient provision of government services to businesses, such as regulations and compliance measures. To improve services, I discussed the importance of improving the quality of professional and technical education, the environment for innovative work, and the role of government as a first-mover client for sophisticated services.

Finally, I discussed the potential for India to move into high-end global consumer services. Such services (such as digitized taxi hailing) already exist. They are mostly patterned on service types that originated elsewhere, and they remain a tiny segment of the economy. I argued that a significant contribution of such services to the overall economy would happen only after India developed a manufacturing base. This raises the question as to whether the significant investment that India is making in graduate education, particularly in STEM-related fields, is an appropriate use of public money. While more study is required before making definite conclusions, it appears that there is a case for a more balanced approach to human capital, focusing on vocational training and undergraduate education as priorities.

I conclude by noting that the contribution of human capital to India's past growth and innovation was constrained by public policy that favored a low value-added manufacturing economy. The education sector responded to this situation by producing graduates suited to work that was low-end and not innovative. A transition to a higher-growth, innovative economy will require attention to both services and manufacturing, and a matching human capital policy that emphasizes vocational training and undergraduate education.

References

Arnold, Jens Matthias, Beata Javorcik, Molly Lipscomb, and Aaditya Mattoo. 2016. "Services Reform and Manufacturing Performance: Evidence from India." *Economic Journal* 126 (590): 1–39. doi: 10.1111/ecoj.12206.

Bacon, Robert, and Walter Eltis. 1976. *Britain's Economic Problem: Too Few Producers*. London: Macmillan.

Baumol, William J. 1967. "Macroeconomics of Unbalanced Growth: The Anatomy of Urban Crisis." *American Economic Review* 57 (3): 415–26.

Borensztein, Eduardo, and Jonathan D. Ostry. 1996. "Accounting for China's Growth Performance." *American Economic Review* 86 (2): 224–28.

Calderon, Cesar. 2003. "The Direction of Causality between Financial Development and Economic Growth." *Journal of Development Economics* 72 (1): 321–44.

Carnoy, Martin, Prashant Loyalka, Maria Dobryakova, Rafiq Dossani, Isak Froumin, Katherine Kuhns, Jandhyala B. G. Tilak, and Rong Wang. 2013. *University Expansion in a Changing Global Economy: Triumph of the BRICs?* Stanford, CA: Stanford University Press.

de Meulemeester, Jean-Luc, and Denis Rochat. 1995. "A Causality Analysis of the Link Between Higher Education and Economic Development." *Economics of Education Review* 14 (4): 351–61

Donkin, Angela, Peter Goldblatt, and Kevin Lynch. 2002. "Inequalities in Life Expectancy by Social Class, 1972–1999." *Health Statistics Quarterly* 15: 5–15.

Dossani, Rafiq. 2007. "Entrepreneurship: The True Story behind Indian IT." In *Making IT: The Rise of Asia in High Tech*, edited by Marguerite Gong Hancock, 221–66. Stanford, CA: Stanford University Press.

Dritsakis, Nikolaos. 2004. "Tourism as a Long-Run Economic Growth Factor: An Empirical Investigation for Greece Using Causality Analysis." *Tourism Economics* 10 (3): 305–16.

Eichengreen, Barry, and Poonam Gupta. 2013. "The Two Waves of Service-Sector Growth." *Oxford Economic Papers* 65 (1): 96–123.

Erdil, Erkan, and I. Hakan Yetkiner. 2009. "The Granger-Causality between Health Care Expenditure and Output: A Panel Data Approach." *Applied Economics* 41 (4): 511–18.

Hasan, Rana, Devashish Mitra, and Asha Sundaram. 2013. "What Explains the High Capital Intensity of Indian Manufacturing?" *Indian Growth and Development Review* 6 (2): 212–41.

IBEF (India Brand Equity Foundation). N.d. "Telecom Industry in India." Accessed on September 15, 2020. https://www.ibef.org/industry/telecommunications.aspx.

Jepsen, Christopher, Kenneth Troske, and Paul Coomes. 2014. "The Labor-Market Returns to Community College Degrees, Diplomas, and Certificates." *Journal of Labor Economics* 32 (1): 95–121.

Kaldor, Nicholas. 1966. *Causes of the Slow Rate of Economic Growth in the United Kingdom*. London: Cambridge University Press.

Karnik, Madhura. 2015. "India's Banking Sector in Five Charts." Quartz India. https://qz.com/india/580667/indias-banking-sector-in-five-charts/.

Kroeber, Arthur R. 2016. *China's Economy: What Everyone Needs to Know?* 1st ed. New York: Oxford University Press.

Kuznets, Simon. 1957. "Quantitative Aspects of the Economic Growth of Nations: II. Industrial Distribution of National Product and Labor Force." *Economic Development and Cultural Change* 5 (4): 1–111.

Lee, C. H. 1984. "The Service Sector, Regional Specialization, and Economic Growth in the Victorian Economy." *Journal of Historical Geography* 10 (2): 139–55.

Lederman, Doug. 2016. "The New Ph.D.s: New Federal Data Show American Universities Awarded a Record Number of Ph.D.s in 2015." Inside Higher Ed, December 9, 2016. https://www.inside

highered.com/news/2016/12/09/phd-recipients-increase-number
-job-prospects-vary-new-us-data-show.

Loungani, Prakash, Saurabh Mishra, Chris Papageorgiou, and Ke
Wang. 2017. "World Trade in Services: Evidence from a New
Dataset." International Monetary Fund working paper WP/17/77.

MHRD (Ministry of Human Resource Development). 2016. *All
India Survey on Higher Education, 2015-2016*. New Delhi, India:
MHRD. https://www.education.gov.in/sites/upload_files/mhrd/files/
statistics-new/AISHE2015-16.pdf.

MOE (Ministry of Education, China). 2017. "Educational Statistics
in 2017: Number of Students of Formal Education by Type and
Level." http://en.moe.gov.cn/documents/statistics/2017/national/
201808/t20180808_344698.html.

NASSCOM. 2018. *The IT-BPM Sector in India: Strategic Review
2018*. Noida, India: NASSCOM. https://nasscom.in/sites/default/
files/uploads/temp/Strategic_Review_2018_Final_13032018.pdf.

National Science Board. 2018. "Academic Research and Development." In *Science & Engineering Indicators 2018*. Alexandria, VA:
NSF. https://www.nsf.gov/statistics/2018/nsb20181/assets/968/
academic-research-and-development.pdf.

Nayyar, Gaurav. 2012. "The Quality of Employment in India's Services Sector: Exploring the Heterogeneity." *Applied Economics* 44
(36): 4701–19.

NSF (National Science Foundation), National Center for Science
and Engineering Statistics. 2017. *2015 Doctorate Recipients from
U.S. Universities*. Special Report NSF 17-306. Arlington, VA:
NSF. https://www.nsf.gov/statistics/2017/nsf17306/static/report/
nsf17306.pdf.

Okahana, Hironao, and Enyu Zhou. 2017. *Graduate Enrollment and
Degrees: 2006 to 2016*. Washington, DC: Council of Graduate
Schools. https://cgsnet.org/ckfinder/userfiles/files/CGS_GED16_
Report_Final.pdf.

Oliner, Stephen D., and Daniel E. Sichel. 2000. "The Resurgence of
Growth in the Late 1990s: Is Information Technology the Story?"
Journal of Economic Perspectives 14 (4): 3–22. doi: 10.1257/
jep.14.4.3.

Rao, T. V., and Sumeet Varghese. 2009. "Trends and Challenges of Developing Human Capital in India." *Human Resource Development
International* 12 (1): 15–34. doi: 10.1080/13678860802638800.

Singh, Anushree. 2016. "How the Services Sector Is the Key Growth Engine for India." Business Insider India, February 26, 2016. http://www.businessinsider.in/Howthe-services-sector-is-the-key-growth-engine-for-India/articleshow/51156624.cms.

Smith, Adam, and John Ramsay McCulloch. 1838. *An Inquiry into the Nature and Causes of the Wealth of Nations*. Edinburgh: Thomas Nelson.

Solow, Robert M. 1956. "A Contribution to the Theory of Economic Growth." *Quarterly Journal of Economics* 70 (1): 65–94.

Statista. N.d. "Revenue from Information Technology (IT) Services and Software Worldwide from 2005 to 2016." https://www.statista.com/statistics/268632/worldwide-revenue-from-software-and-it-services-since-2005/.

Stevens, Ann, Michal Kurlaender, and Michel Grosz. 2015. "Career Technical Education and Labor Market Outcomes: Evidence from California Community Colleges." Working paper, National Bureau of Economic Research, Inc., Cambridge, MA.

Suavé, Pierre. 2009. *Trade and Investment in Services: An ADB-ITD Training Module for the Greater Mekong Subregion*. Manila, Phillippines: Asian Development Bank.

Sunkara, Keshav. 2016. "In Charts: How India's Software Services Exports Grew in Recent Years." VCCircle. https://www.vccircle.com/charts-how-india-s-software-services-exports-grew-recent-years/.

UNCTAD (United Nations Conference on Trade and Development). N.d. "Global Transport Cost Dataset." https://unctadstat.unctad.org/EN/.

UNDP (United Nations Development Programme). N.d. "Human Development Reports: Gender Development Index." http://hdr.undp.org/en/indicators/137906.

US Department of Commerce, International Trade Administration. N.d. "India Commercial Guide." https://www.trade.gov/knowledge-product/exporting-india-market-overview?section-nav=3095.

World Bank. 2014. "Electric Power Comsumption." Accessed September 15, 2020. https://data.worldbank.org/indicator/EG.USE.ELEC.KH.PC.

———. 2017. "School Enrollment, Tertiary (% gross)." Accessed September 15, 2020. https://data.worldbank.org/indicator/SE.TER.ENRR.

8 The Implications of AI for Business and Education, and Singapore's Policy Response

Mohan Kankanhalli and Bernard Yeung

Computing, communication, sensor, and data storage technologies have rapidly developed in parallel over the past few decades and often feed into one another's further development. Significant advancements have been made in sensor technologies that provide critical, often real-time, data and enable the Internet of Things. These quantum leaps in technological capabilities empower progress in manufacturing and engineering (e.g., additive manufacturing), health and biomedical sciences (e.g., digital genome), and urban solutions and sustainability (e.g., digitized logistics management), and also create new spaces in the service and digital economy (e.g., driverless cars, automated customs entry, robotic advisory services, Uber, Grab, Dadi, crowd-funding, etc.). Data analytics, machine learning, and thus artificial intelligence (AI) offer interesting new approaches, adopted as fintech, reg-tech, marketing-tech, legal-tech, and the like, redefining business and industry landscapes. The results imply rapid changes in our lives and societies, business models, international economic and political relations, security, public services and governments, and so on.

These changes create both new opportunities and heightened anxiety. The intertwined phenomena of the internet, cloud computing, and commerce dramatically reduce the hurdles to innovations and entice entrepreneurship. Innovators can strike gold quickly (e.g., Carousell, Flipkart, PatSnap, and Grab). Entrepreneurial endeavors have spread into many industries and business functions. Asia, in particular, is well suited to embrace these innovations as they allow for leapfrogging developments without the legacy of brick and mortar, bypassing layers of intermediation and raising transaction efficiency.

Behind this excitement, however, is economic anxiety as innovations disrupt business models and heighten competition. Even innovative companies are not immune, as can be seen in the ongoing competition between Intel and NVidia or Uber and Grab. Economic anxiety, however, expands beyond the threats of firm survival. As machine labor substitution morphs into machine human capital substitution, even the well educated worry about their job security and their skill sets becoming obsolete. Corporations, educators, and governments are all busily reflecting and plotting how to embrace the future economy propelled by the Fourth Industrial Revolution.

In this chapter, we share our thinking on embracing innovations from a management, education, and government policy perspective. As the scope of such discussion can easily become excessively broad and unwieldy, we choose to focus on how corporations and educators may face a critical development, AI, which is attracting widespread attention in many countries. AI is an umbrella term that covers a confluence of multiple technologies such as machine learning (which includes deep learning based on neural networks), cognitive computing, natural language processing, and recommendation systems. It is driving the broad-based automation and robotics industry, and transforming healthcare, manufacturing, transportation, retailing, and financial services, among others. AI has the potential to enable significant cost savings, improve work processes, and enhance optimization. In the following, we first offer a short summary of what AI is about and propose four corporate responses, then suggest several educational responses. Finally, we discuss Singapore's government policy trends as it prepares to face the future.

What Is Artificial Intelligence?

AI refers to the theory and development of computer systems able to perform tasks normally requiring human intelligence, such as visual perception, speech recognition, decision-making, and translation between languages. These "machine-based but human-like" functions are possible because we now have the technological ability to employ data analytics, machine learning, computer vision, and natural language processing in a machine. These technologies allow "machines" to carry out human capabilities, sometimes better than human beings themselves; AI can partially mimic a superhuman, as in science fiction.

There are many fascinating applications of AI. In medicine, AI helps in deciphering scans and x-ray images to improve the reading of a patient's physiological condition. In airports, facial recognition is used to speed passengers through boarding pass and luggage tag checks. Police forces use the same to identify criminals. In agriculture, farmers are using drones equipped with AI to count plants and allow sharp and reliable predictions of yields. In finance, some financial institutions are using intelligent robots to help serve customers, while others are using machine learning to identify trustworthy borrowers or worthy investment prospects. In construction, AI helps in surveying, railroad construction, and maintenance. In city planning, AI coordinates traffic lights to improve traffic flows and to guide emergency vehicles in efficient routes to their destination.

AI does more than carry out individualized and self-contained tasks. Because machines can speedily acquire and process a huge amount of information on a real-time basis, they help companies to sharpen their understanding of customers and employees, and thus improve forecasting, optimize processes, offer new services, and in the end better serve all stakeholders. AI also streamlines consumer search and user feedback processes, and increases the efficiency of transactions between buyers and sellers. AI thus enhances firm-level efficiency and market competition in a wholesale manner, with impacts on all business functions.

In the AI era, machines are doing some human jobs better than human beings can: machines have an advantage over humans in analytical skills and in carrying out nonemotional cognitive functions. However, human beings have a great advantage over machines in their creativity and inquisitiveness. Thus, machines and human beings will be complementary coworkers in organizations. This leads to two natural questions: (1) How do entrepreneurs create AI applications, that is, how do they move toward machine and human collaboration?[1] (2) How should we prepare for the AI age, when intelligent machines will work alongside intelligent people? We provide our speculations regarding question (1) here, then devote the remaining part of the chapter to addressing question (2).

Entrepreneurial discovery is usually based on constructive dissatisfaction—one finds a constructive solution for something one is dissatisfied with. For example, humans invented telephones because they were

---

[1] Entrepreneurship usually refers to the creation of new businesses based on new products or new production processes. There is a huge literature on this subject. To adopt a workable focus here, we overlook issues like personality, and institutional and social climate, to focus on entrepreneurial discovery.

not happy with slow and geographically confined communication. This kind of entrepreneurial discovery is based on finding solutions to problems. The other kind of entrepreneurial discovery is about connecting the dots—finding problems to which a solution applies. Both are important. The impact of AI on entrepreneurial discovery lends greater currency to the second approach. The applied and translational potential of AI is awaiting entrepreneurial discovery. This type of entrepreneurial discovery relies on familiarity with the technology and exposure to demonstrative anecdotes.[2] We speculate that young people brought up in the digital era may have an advantage because they are familiar with the technology and in imagining what can be done with it. We further speculate that those who indulge in creative pursuits such as reading science fiction may also have an edge in coming up with new ideas.

In the business world, there is a sense of inevitability regarding the arrival of AI. A survey conducted about five years ago (Ransbotham et al. 2017) found that across the board in telecommunications, consumer and financial services, healthcare, industry, energy, and the public sector, 65 percent of the executives surveyed expected the impact of AI to be very large within five years (while only 15 percent thought AI's effect was large at the time).

At the corporate level, AI will heighten competition as leading companies improve their efficiency and offer valuable new products and services. Laggards will not survive. Corporate leaders who appreciate digital technology—how it functions and the required working ingredients—may be at an advantage. At the individual level, as thinking machines work alongside people, the nature of jobs and the design of work processes have to change. Workers failing to adapt to changes will be displaced. At the national level, governments may have to provide policy initiatives to nurture peoples' inclination and ability to benefit from and indeed to lead the movement rather than to fall behind. Yet, we are at a confusing stage because there are no historical patterns to guide us in how to be smart leaders rather than laggards in this fast-moving new world.

---

2   Learning happens in two ways: via principles and rules or via mimicking. For example, adults learn a language in the first way, by learning the rules of grammar. Infants, on the other hand, learn a language just by mimicking the sounds and speech patterns they hear (McAfee and Brynjolfsson 2017). Not discounting the importance of the first type of learning, the second type of learning is instrumental in inducing entrepreneurial discovery of AI applications.

Four Vital Corporate Responses

Executives have to make complex and holistic changes quickly with no clear road map. It is hard to talk about lessons as the rules of the game are yet to emerge. Nevertheless, the following generic points ought to be useful.

Start from the top

Corporations are hierarchical in nature, no matter how flat their organizations are (Coase 1937). Senior leaders' appreciation of AI matters greatly: they have to develop a feel for how AI functions in serving customers, staff, and investors.

The starting point is to deepen their understanding of their customers' desires and journeys as well as the work processes that will meet these.

Uber highlights how machines can link customers with services. Someone needs a ride within a reasonably predictable time frame. A driver wants to pick up a rider at a convenient time and location in a predictable way. Two-way feedback (rating customers and drivers) allows Uber to generate trust—customers will still pay a sum of money if they cancel, drivers with good customer feedback get bonuses, and their ratings are known to ordering customers. This simple example illustrates the importance of understanding customers and providers, and how machines can replace humans to efficiently facilitate their meeting. Smart taxi companies that knew AI well could have potentially modified their business models before an outside player, Uber, was born. Luckily for Uber, no such taxi companies existed before its creation.

The next step is that senior leaders need a firm grasp on how AI offers powerful outcome predictors and optimizers to improve efficiency, to reduce costs, and to better serve customers. The core of the current AI revolution is mostly data driven. However, it is not a given that the right type of data is being collected and fed into AI systems. It is very important for business leaders to think hard about what data to collect and how to use them. Not all data have the same value; an AI system will follow the garbage-in, garbage-out principle. Moreover, unsavvy use wastes good resources. Collecting the right data and using them intelligently is the driver of competitive advantage.

Develop a collective AI culture

Leaders can, and should, try to think critically about what data to collect and how to use them. Intelligent data collection and utilization are grounded in a deep collective appreciation of the customer journey and relevant work processes. They call for collaboration between thoughtful and knowledgeable leadership and internal crowd sourcing. Business leaders need to develop a flat organization where they themselves, AI/data scientists, and other employees work together. In particular, senior executives need to foster a holistic view among employees of a firm's services, both for customers and suppliers. They need to encourage employees to take a proactive stance and a cross-unit collaborative spirit in using smart machines and applications to improve the company's overall service and performance. The big picture needs to be internalized by the entire organization. We call this a collective AI culture.

The March 8, 2018, issue of the *Economist* looked at DBS, Singapore's largest bank, highlighting its digitalization efforts. DBS collected data about its various types of customers—both those who access services digitally and those who do not—and what they each want, including across a variety of products. DBS digitized and integrated its customer data across multiple departments as well as regions and developed numerous applications for cross-referencing and marketing. The result was the provision of better, more, and less-costly services to more customers using fewer employees. DBS's share value soared.

The article illustrates that AI functions well with good integrated data, digitalization, and smart, effective apps. Data scientists and employees need to jointly examine work processes, be conscious of data collection and integration, and develop smooth and connected digital pathways that are conducive to good data analytics and machine learning that enhance performance. Good interfaces (including apps) ensure that clients and coworkers have a positive journey. For example, they provide more suitable choices and services, and create timely, appropriate, and customer-oriented unbundling and rebundling of products and services. Clumsy interfaces, conversely, drive users away.

Some companies' business rests on providing a platform and many other businesses and customers benefit from their interfaces. There exists a deep relationship between the interface, the platform, and design. Platform capabilities allow for the design of interfaces to help provide needed services. Businesses and their customers (whether other businesses or individual consumers) interact via these interfaces on platforms. These interactions drive future services as well as future design. They can even open up possibilities for totally new services. Keen attention therefore needs to be paid to these delicate interrelations. Companies offering platforms might be first in line to observe the functions and dynamics between the interface, the platform, and design. However, only keen observers see relevant and useful patterns.

Risking belaboring the obvious, we reiterate that senior executives will not have the detailed information needed to direct the collection, integration, and use of data. They will not have firsthand observations of the dynamic developments at hand. Employees will. Yet, the work requires the whole team: smart data scientists are indispensable and senior executives' support is instrumental. Deep strategic thinking about the core business is required of leadership. Very often, there will be resistance as employees are too busy dealing with their daily tasks. Some employees may not appreciate AI and lack a sense of urgency in finding ways to apply it. Others may know, deep down, that their importance inside the company could be at risk. They will want to overcome obstacles in data collection, integration, and redesigning workflows.

Hence, developing a collective AI culture involves educating as well as motivating employees to develop capabilities complementary to smart machines: to use human cognitive functionality (learning, perceiving, understanding context, and using common sense to make decisions based on incomplete information) as well as powerful machine learning (using continuously updated learning from data) to create and pursue opportunities.

Invest in human resources

Ironically, companies that are investing in human capital substitution also need to raise their investment in human capital. There are two parts to the process.

First, senior executives obviously need to recruit the right talent in data science, machine learning, and software, which is still in short supply.

Second, they need to recognize that the process is not just about getting talent, but getting the *right* talent. They need to find people who will understand the firm, existing staff members, and work processes, and who have an inclination toward constructive dissatisfaction—seeing what *can* done but has not been done yet— and the ability to build firm capabilities and convince members to make changes. All this is easier said than done. This involves more than hiring smart data scientists with a head for business; training them alongside existing employees so that they gel enough to generate collective thinking is the hard part.

Meanwhile, the AI revolution is progressing at a dizzying pace. Models and algorithms are being improved almost on a monthly basis. So, there is a need to foster a "research culture" in companies along two fronts. First, many corporate data scientists need to attend academic conferences to catch up on to the latest trends in research.

Second, in the dynamic competitive world, senior executives, data scientists, and staff have to engage in a continuous research dialogue questioning the efficacy of their data collection, data management, and utilization of AI capabilities. In this fast-moving world, they need to continually improve their joint delivery of company objectives, to better serve customers, suppliers, and employees. Indeed, it is well known that data can have biases, variables can lose their representativeness, prediction models can have missing variables and thus become biased, and feedback effects can inadvertently erode a previously powerful model's predictive capability. These risks are exacerbated by the fact that some of the best-performing AI models are black-box models. For example, a deep learning model is often a network with hundreds of thousands of hyper-parameters. When the deep network makes a prediction, the values at the intermediate nodes are not meaningful. It is not clear what aspects of the training data have led to a particular prediction. Hence, explainability becomes critical—and this is an area of active research.

In a world of dynamic competition, change is the only constant. Companies need senior executives, data scientists, and employees with up-to-date human capital. Continuous investment in human resources, training, and customized executive education programs becomes a competitive necessity. Companies need to continuously keep their employees engaged in the latest thinking and collectively update their deployment of appropriate technology to serve their clients.

Inculcation of value

The above builds on familiar concepts: leading from the top, cross-unit cooperation, embracing change, collective understanding of the customer journey, and practicing continuous critical thinking and learning, among others. These are hallmarks of a strong company culture that strives for excellence, teamwork, innovation, and a devotion to serve. Thus, the fundamental focus is on building the right corporate culture.

A point worth emphasizing is the value of service. AI disruptions are characterized by a frenzy of new business arrangements. Yet, fundamentally, arrangements that better serve the world prevail. However, in the fast-paced pursuit of bottom-line efficiency, a company's AI practice may inadvertently lead to ethical issues. Recently, unauthorized use of information without originators' consent has made headlines (e.g., Cambridge Analytica). Respecting customers' and business partners' privacy will become increasingly critical. New regulatory regimes related to data ownership, provenance, sharing, and protection are being enacted. Furthermore, algorithmic fairness is becoming a big issue—if biased data are collected, the AI system will make biased decisions. Even without biased data, an AI system can be prone to statistical discrimination when a company is overly focused on the bottom line.

Safeguard measures go beyond just setting up guidelines and regulations. We believe that the key is in inculcating good, intrinsic values as a part of the corporate culture. Human beings pursue transactional and intrinsic value; the first is economically driven while the second involves a purely internal reward for doing the right thing. The two are interrelated. Individuals who pursue only transactional value do not have any second thoughts about making profits from products that harm consumers, for example, narcotics. Individuals who act according to intrinsic value would be willing to sacrifice some profits for others' well-being. This consideration is very important for organizations. The more employees pay attention to intrinsic value, the less likely it is that a company will make inadvertent mistakes.

This point is worth elaborating further: the collective consciousness of intrinsic value can bring value to an organization. As a company busily pursues efficiency in the fast-moving world of data analytics, it may inadvertently step into "social mistakes," for example, inappropriate use of data and statistical discrimination. These can result in ex post negative judgments that damage a company's reputation, demoralize employees, and might even lead to sizeable fines. A company is less likely to make these mistakes if its employees and management regularly reflect on whether the company is respecting its constituents' rights and well-being.

Business Education Responses

AI is affecting higher-learning institutions' research, teaching, and administration. In economics and business-related areas, many research papers now utilize techniques like data crawling, big data analysis, machine learning, and so on. It is a similar story in case writing. AI will ultimately make administration more efficient. It will also have considerable impact on teaching over time. Some faculty members are already using machine learning to analyze discussions and classwork to improve teaching efficiency. They may even use chatbots to conduct simulations. Predictive analytics are beginning to be used to improve the student experience by suggesting which courses to take or even alerting professors about students who may need extra help. Generally, younger faculty members embrace the technology while older faculty members are doing what they are good at.

Thinking of the longer term is more interesting. Let us ask, in the next five to ten years, what kind of graduates do we need?

The future will be a world of smart people working with intelligent machines that can learn, forecast, and optimize. Graduates and these intelligent machines need to complement each other and work interactively.[3] We would like to make a few points based on the literature regarding developing student skills complementary to those of thinking and learning machines.

We will start with a given: students cannot function in the future world without data literacy and technology literacy.

Second, we need to strengthen students' learning literacy. Machines are still not good at unsupervised learning; humans have an advantage. A two-year-old toddler takes less than a minute and a bite to learn what a hot dog is. She will carry forward the experience as she learns about other edibles and non-edibles. Machines require hundreds of thousands or more pictures to learn to identify a hot dog. Educators will give students an advantage if they train students to be lifelong unsupervised learners who can find ways to improve their work with intelligent machines. That means inspiring the development of curiosity

---

3   There are some very stimulating books on these topics, for example, *Robot-Proof: Higher Education in the Age of Artificial Intelligence*, by Joseph E Aoun, and *Machine, Platform, Crowd: Harnessing our Digital Future*, by Andrew McAfee and Erik Brynjolfsson.

and providing a solid foundation for the use of scientific principles in self-motivated learning. Indeed, that is how doctoral students are trained to be lifelong learners.

Third, to train our students to complement intelligent machines, we need to be aware of the current bugs in machine thinking and train human brains to see pitfalls in intelligent machines' predictions and optimization. Fundamentally, the current machine understanding of the world is shallow and fragmented. A model trained to visually recognize hot dogs and bananas would not know that they are linked (as food for humans). Humans understand the world in a seamless, connected manner in which each concept is linked to the other in some form of a causal or associative relation.

There are abundant examples of the brittleness and narrow constraints of machine intelligence. Our machines' intelligence is often limited by the set of data we feed into them. Machines do not see biases, missing variables, overfitting, and out-of-sample human behavior. Such factors allegedly cost Hillary Clinton her election. So, we need to firm up our training in critical thinking: train students to be curious, inquisitive, and rigorous logic auditors (to challenge assumptions, and differentiate endogenous correlations from causal correlations). These students will recognize pitfalls in AI systems and find ways to address them.

Furthermore, machines cannot connect the dots based on human context and experiences; that is, machines are not able to make judgements based on common sense. The machine may say that our blood pressure is fine, but this may be in a moment of off-work calm. It fails to see that our blood pressure can surge under stress. Likewise, machines face challenges understanding metaphors, idioms, and homonyms. Machines still cannot motivate human passions and the development of social skills—for example, they cannot coach a team to work together, to break through a pain threshold, or to take pride in losing a game honorably. Students need to continue to develop humanistic literacy.

Machines cannot be entrepreneurs: they are good at convergent thinking but have yet to demonstrate divergent thinking; that is, machines are not able to see additional worthy applications of their algorithms. Human entrepreneurs do the bridging. Good entrepreneurs are those who see dissatisfaction and find (or borrow) a constructive solution. Thus, students need to develop entrepreneurial leadership with a caring heart.

In summary, to train students to be contributors in the future human-AI world, schools need to emphasize literacy in moral principles, data management, technological innovation, and humanism. They also need to step up efforts in developing students' curiosity, critical thinking, creativity, entrepreneurial thinking, and leadership.

Public Policy to Encourage Innovations in the AI Era

In the current era of rapid technological advancement and mushrooming innovations, many governments take a proactive stance in promoting innovation. The Singapore government is no exception, and indeed has always been proactive. Its policies involve multiple parts: (1) direct investment in building a foundation, (2) a "pull" strategy to bring industries and academics to work together, and (3) a "push" strategy to develop data banks and capabilities to induce innovative practices based on modern analytics. The objectives underlying these strategies are to utilize market incentives and to build the right institutions and ecology for advancement. Finally, the government has been mindful of the larger and longer-run purpose of preparing the nation in its continuous endeavors to be a global leader. Together these factors have contributed to making Singapore an innovative economy. Indeed, in 2018, the Bloomberg Innovation Index ranked Singapore as the third-most innovative economy in the world.

Building a foundation for innovation

Investment in human capital and in research and development is necessary for advancing innovation. Singapore has a strong primary and secondary education system; its students regularly rank among the highest in standardized math and science tests. In recent years, its leading universities, like the National University of Singapore (NUS) and Nanyang Technology University, are among the most highly ranked in Asia and globally. Its Agency for Science, Technology and Research (A*STAR) conducts advanced research in science and technology and serves as a catalyst and facilitator of significant research initiatives in Singapore and around the globe.

Singapore has increased its investment in research. From 2016 to 2020, it planned to invest more than S$19 billion on basic and translational research in advanced manufacturing, health and biomedical sciences, urban solutions and sustainability, and the digital economy, part of which was administered by the National Research

Foundation.[4] In 2015, the government established the Social Science and Humanity Research Council to fund social science research. Government agencies, including the monetary authority, also invest much in supporting forums and conferences that breed intellectual intensity.

Industry-academia partnerships

Singapore adopts an outcome-oriented style in applying government resources to support research and development and innovations. For example, both seed money grants and larger grants may be released only if preset targets are met. Also, the government often asks for explicit commitment and partnership among recipients of public money. For example, it gave seed money to multiple units of NUS and a corporation to set up a Business Analytics Centre for research and graduate degree program training. Conditions had to be met within a given time period for the partnership to utilize the grants. Requirements related to proof of concept, multiple industry participants, and up-front investment commitments ("skin" in the game) are the norm.

Academic-industry partnerships are thriving, subsidized by the government or not. Beyond joint research, these partnerships can be classified by their focus: (1) the development of human capital for innovation and entrepreneurship and (2) translational research.

Developing students' innovation and entrepreneurship

Over the years, Singapore's higher education institutions have increasingly emphasized practicality and relevancy. They leverage business partnerships. For example, in the NUS Business School, doing a real-life business project is a graduation requirement at both the undergraduate and graduate levels. The NUS School of Computing requires a compulsory internship for all of its students. The Master of Science in Business Analytics Programme (a joint venture of the Business School and the School of Computing) has a capstone course in which students have to do real-life business analytics projects with domestic or overseas companies. This practice stimulates students' curiosity since they

---

4 Singapore's GDP in 2017 was S$324 billion. Hence, the sum is about 5 percent of the 2017 GDP, which means on average about an additional 1 percent of GDP per year for five years.

need to ask questions and apply their academic training in practice; it possibly stimulates the faculty's research too. Importantly, the practice inculcates among students innovation and entrepreneurial spirit and leads them to develop capabilities relevant to lifelong learning.

Furthermore, NUS has a cross-disciplinary division, bringing together schools and faculty to develop students' entrepreneurship—the NUS Enterprise. The division aims to "stoke the fires of those born with the entrepreneurial spirit and spark the flames of entrepreneurial passion in others," as stated on its website. It has an incubator that offers immersion programs and a range of avenues and support to students to materialize their entrepreneurial dreams. This is internationalizing, including through expansion into China and members of the Association of Southeast Asian Nations. Also, an overseas college program provides a unique immersion experience for students seeking to gain entrepreneurial exposure: participating students undertake full-time internship programs with overseas start-up companies while concurrently attending entrepreneurship-related courses in highly reputable partnership universities, including Stanford and Berkeley, in the United States.

Beyond the NUS Enterprise, the university also works with leading corporations to enrich training in entrepreneurship. For example, students in the aforementioned master's program in business analytics have internship and mentoring opportunities in Alibaba Cloud. These students have access to a handsome collection of venture capital specialists to help them foster innovative ideas that use data, data science, AI, business acumen, and the understanding of people to solve problems.

Translational research

Individual schools and faculty members in Singapore's universities actively promote translational research. For example, NUS's Yong Loo Lin School of Medicine, School of Computing, Business School, and Faculty of Engineering all have translational research units. More recently, the university has explicitly coupled translational research with graduate education in the Office of the Provost to encourage DeepTech start-ups and technology licensing. All these represent a wholesale effort to transform NUS's scientific research into practice.

The Singapore government often works directly with higher-learning institutions to enhance Singapore's technological innovation and development of relevant human capital. For example, the Government

Technology Agency of Singapore (GovTech) collaborates with NUS in developing data science training for civil servants and in developing solutions in cyber security, AI, and data science, and meaningful cross-unit internships.

A government push

The Singapore government also engages in a "push strategy," that is, the government provides direct leadership to push for development. An example of this strategy in the area of digitalization—and a critical step that raises innovative practices in the era of data analytics and AI—is the setting up of a countrywide data bank. The government is also innovating its services through digitalization. For example, it has established the Smart Nation and Digital Government Group to support agencies by laying out overall blueprints, building common platforms and systems, and setting and enforcing information and communications technology standards. The Singapore Government Technology Stack aims to provide a collection of common digital services and infrastructure available to all government agencies to build their digital applications. The work involves building a data hub (data centers) and application infrastructure. It will set data standards and develop the data architecture to ensure the usability of data across government digital platforms and services. These developments, if done right, should immensely help existing businesses as well as future entrepreneurs.

Institutional environment, market, and cultural diversity induce innovation

The success of both the push and pull strategies depend on being able to attract talent to Singapore and providing that talent with an environment that fosters innovation. A large literature supports the strong relations between innovation and an economy's institutional environment; Fogel et al. (2006) provide a summary and supportive regression results.

The literature also suggests that entrepreneurial supply is related to the following institutional factors: well-defined rules and regulations that govern transactional behavior but are not burdensome for business, an uncorrupt government that respects property rights, and an efficient and effective judicial system. Also, entrepreneurial supply is related to financial and economic stability and a functioning financial market in which entrepreneurial ideas can get financed while risk can be distributed. Since the establishment of statehood, Singapore's government has consciously built and maintained such an institutional environment.

Singapore has thus emerged as a financial center and a regional hub for multinationals. An implication is that Singapore has a rich mixture of a variety of corporate practices, leading to a high degree of market diversity. Moreover, Singapore has attracted a considerable pool of talent because of its safe social environment, first-class accommodations, efficient road system, and a very good international school education system that appeals to non-Singaporeans from other parts of Asia and Western countries. With an already heterogeneous mix of local citizens with ancestral roots in Southeast Asia, India, China, and other parts of Asia, Singapore has become a compact society with a high degree of cultural diversity.

Its market and cultural diversity adds to Singapore's attractiveness as a fertile ground for innovations that can be fruitfully spread across the region. In the first place, diversity breeds innovation, as Fogel et al. (2006) and many others have shown. Furthermore, innovations in Singapore can be tested across multiple ethnicities and corporate cultures as well as practices. These can lead to meaningful adjustments and help to adopt the innovations outside Singapore. Also, innovations from outside of Singapore can be further tested in Singapore, utilizing its rich environment and diverse talents in basic and applied sciences, with social scientists, lawyers, and business leaders clustered in a compact environment. In sum, Singapore is a focal point for the development of innovations that can spread across the region. Singapore has positioned itself as a living lab for innovations—be they in fintech, in autonomous taxis and buses, or in smart road pricing.

Policies for structural change

Building the foundation for innovation, and applying results-oriented push and pull strategies grounded in a receptive environment, the government has strived to make Singapore a leader in innovation (according to Bloomberg Innovation Index 2018) (Straits Times 2018). Yet, there is a broader challenge in the era of rapid technological innovation: changing peoples' mindsets so that they will collectively embrace changes and thrive during them.

Human beings do not naturally embrace change. At the beginning of the nineteenth century, Luddites protested against capital labor substitution as they feared that their investment in learning the skills of their craft would lose value. Fast forward, deep learning neural networks and artificial super intelligence prompted prominent scientists like Stephen Hawking to warn against machines controlling humans (BBC News 2014) and industry leaders like Bill Gates to express similar concerns (Fox News 2016). The fear is that technology may vastly disrupt human lives, potentially enabling excess citizen surveillance and eroding our free choice, for example.

Beyond such worries is economic anxiety harbored even by well-trained professionals in the face of possible machine–human capital substitutions. Indeed, graphically the function of earnings and human capital has become more convex than ever. In the 1960s, a high school diploma and a job in a factory might mean a ticket to middle-class America. In the seventies, it took a good skill-based university degree. Now, perhaps a postgraduate degree is the new requirement. While the required investment in human capital has expanded, technological disruption erodes job safety. The outcome is high economic anxiety.

Fear and anxiety naturally breed aversion and resistance to change. They are likely the basis for the rise in populism and protectionism in some large, advanced economies. This is neither desirable nor viable for Singapore.

The Singapore government chooses to inculcate in its residents the willingness to accept changes, indeed, to take advantage of them. Our observation is that relevant policy in this direction will proceed in multiple stages stretching over almost a decade.

In 2009, the Singapore government's Economic Strategies Committee's report (2010) started a drive to stimulate the development of human capital and firm-level productivity, including limiting the importation of foreign labor. This prompted Singaporean companies to innovate and to embrace change to raise their productivity, instead of relying on old modes of operations and technology, and a continuous supply of overseas labor to maintain livelihoods. In 2013 the country launched its "Skills Future" program, a national movement to provide Singaporeans opportunities to develop their fullest potential throughout life. In 2015, the government set up the Future Economy Council to develop strategies to build a vibrant and resilient economy that creates opportunities for all. It strategizes and creates synergies across many programs and agencies to efficiently and effectively enhance the competitiveness of Singapore's various industries so as to embrace the fast-changing and globalizing business world.

To illustrate, the Singapore government offers a moderate subsidy (less than S$5,000) for each of its citizens to enroll in qualified skill training programs. There are now many such programs for people to acquire training in data analytics, finance, tech-enabled services, digital media, cyber security, entrepreneurship, urban solutions (e.g., systems engineering), and advanced manufacturing. Universities have gotten into gear by offering lifelong learning and continuous education courses. Since 2018, graduates may go back to NUS for free to learn new skills. For those interested to learn more, they can enroll in fee-based programs (supported by some government subsidies) or even to take up a new degree. Then there are many government supported or even explicitly sponsored industry- or community-level workshops to raise awareness and develop approaches to self-enhancement. Government agencies focused on entrepreneurship, and small and medium enterprises and their internationalization are now combined to provide coordinated synergistic approaches in attaining their missions.

The long-term effort goes beyond Singapore residents' embrace of change. It entails fostering an innovation culture. Earlier in this section, we briefly discussed efforts at the university level, for example, the National University of Singapore's effort via NUS Enterprise. The equilibrium of innovation supply and demand, however, is vitally affected by culture. To foster an innovation culture, a holistic effort has to be initiated.

The education system plays a critically important role. Singapore faces transition. The education system has for long emphasized technical competence and conformity, which have served Singapore well. In the future of work, Singapore needs to also develop a strong innovation spirit, a point that the government and the Ministry of Education in particular have repeatedly emphasized. The *Report of the Committee on the Future Economy* (February 2017), in its "Exchange of Letters with the Prime Minister," states that "Our vision is for us to be pioneers of the next generation." The government has been advocating multiple channels to success. For example, in 2018 the Ministry of Education issued a press release that stated,

> In line with the Ministry of Education (MOE)'s continuing efforts to develop future generations of resilient, innovative and curious lifelong learners who are empowered to chart their own paths of success, and rooted in sound values and a shared Singapore identity, MOE will: (A) Nurture innovation through Applied Learning [and] (B) Refresh our approach to National Education. . . . Experienced educators will spear-

head pedagogical innovation within the teaching fraternity, to support their peers in guiding discussions in the classroom. (MOE 2018)

The Committee on the Future Economy points in the right direction, and the Ministry of Education suggests how to get there, indicating the need to change students' attitudes toward learning early in their childhood, which is fundamental for Singapore to become innovative. The challenge is that student behavior is influenced by parents, higher-education institutions' admission offices, and future employers' selection processes. Teachers' approaches also affect student attitudes. Hypothetically, if teachers were evaluated by students' test results, university admissions were mainly based on test scores, and employers' hiring decisions were heavily weighted toward grades, students would train themselves to be exam takers, not joyful and innovative learners. Singapore is fully aware of the challenge in changing the social equilibrium, as is seen in other societies, for example, China.

There are three basic elements in these continuous decade-long efforts to develop an innovation culture. First, in helping Singaporeans to prepare for change, it is important to induce a forward-looking culture in Singapore. Second, these efforts cultivate a drive toward continuous learning, to actively prepare for the fast-changing future. They thus change people's mindsets from resisting to embracing changes. Third, they go beyond transactional value to promote self-motivated learning. Weighing costs and returns to investing in human capital, the costs appear weightier since technological progress and disruption make the returns to humans more convex and riskier than ever. However, the joy of learning can be intrinsic, something that we humans recognize if we experience it. As the government works to adjust its policy approach to education, from kindergarten to the university level, it seeks to induce a holistic change in the social environment with an emphasis on looking forward into the future, and embracing change and the joy of learning, which are the critical ingredients of a vibrant and innovative society.

Conclusion

The world is mesmerized by the frantic pace of technological progress in the AI era. Many expect disruptions on all fronts, leading to positive changes in our lives and also challenges. Some harbor the anxiety that machines will trump human skills and take away our jobs. At the extreme end, some worry about machines becoming our masters.

The reality is that humans create machines. In all kinds of technological evolution, humans work alongside machines to produce meaningful results. Steam engines, railways, cars, planes, and rockets are functional because humans visualize their transportation trails. Machines spin fabrics but humans design inspiring fashion. In every wave of innovation, humans adapt and create further innovations in the way we organize organization, society, and our own lives.

In this era of AI revolution, the adjustment will be significant, which is understandable given the potential. AI brings to us a hitherto unimaginable ability to collect and process information, and tremendous improvement in the quality of services. It offers the potential for machines to anticipate and provide for many human needs. The needed adjustments are uncertain as further innovations continue to evolve; it is an iterative process. The key is to identify the gist of the adjustment needs so that intelligent people, organizations, and society can coevolve with intelligent machines to raise the quality of life.

We analyze the issues accordingly and advance the following suggestions. For the private sector, we advocate (1) enhancing leaders' understanding and appreciation of AI and the basics of how it can serve a company; (2) raising the consciousness of employees, data scientists, and senior executives regarding how AI can assist customer journeys and support processes; (3) continuously investing in human capital and nurturing a companywide "continuous learning" and "reflection" mindset; and (4) staying focused the corporation's purposes and value in serving its constituents. For the education sector, we emphasize the need to get students ready to be contributors in future human-AI collaborations. Following the literature, we advocate fostering literacy in moral principles, data literacy, technology, and humanism, while nurturing curiosity, critical thinking, entrepreneurship, and leadership. For government policymakers, using Singapore as an example, we reiterate the usual: push and pull strategies as well as the need to develop the right institutional ecology to attract collective talent. A central point is that the government must take the lead to nurture the development of the mindset and attitudes needed to embrace changes and to develop innovations.

The central focus of our recommendations is that intelligent humans and machines can and need to work together to generate welfare-improving AI revolutions. Our thoughts can be summarized in the following three points.

First, there is a knowledge paradox: a machine's intelligence comes from human inputs and when a human stops feeding intelligence into the machine, the machine should have no intelligence. Blind faith in a machine's intelligence without continuous human inputs will result in pseudo optimization, which deviates over time from the true optimum. A machine, no matter how smart, cannot be intelligent without human input. While this principle may possibly change over time as deep machine learning may create a new reality, until that day arrives machines need humans to maintain and increase their intelligence. Thus, there is a need to establish human consciousness of the drivers of good AI performance: human wisdom, knowledge, and intelligence are needed in the development of machine intelligence.

Second, meaningful, continuous human inputs and adjustments are based on clear goals, aligned incentives, and a caring attitude. A smart car can approach a destination effectively and efficiently. In between, it makes judgments to avoid hitting a puppy or a child according to human values incorporated in its algorithms. In other words, humans decide on the destination and the parameters in charting the optimal path. Thus, the human beings generating the direction and the parameters have to know the serving purposes and to have their constituents' well-being in mind in a comprehensive manner. It takes collective and conscious human efforts, exercising our values and humanistic empathy to do this right—to allow humans to stay in control of powerful machines and get them to work according to social values and principles. We note that this is grounded on a set of ethical principles about what is right, which can change over time. Yet, that is precisely the point: we need continuous human evaluation of outcomes based on current social values and ethics.

Third, the collaboration between intelligent machines and humans is based on wise and evolving complementarity. Humans have valuable capabilities in asking questions and connecting the dots while machines have the superior ability to collect and use data, manage information, and make reliable judgments in a focused manner. This complementarity is not a constant. As machine capabilities expand, including into machine learning, humans need to explore new arenas of collaboration. There is no rule book for how this is done. But history shows that curious humans who embrace changes prevail; corporate leaders, educators, and government all can contribute significantly in nurturing the development of this spirit.

References

Aoun, Joseph E. 2017. *Robot-Proof: Higher Education in the Age of Artificial Intelligence*. Cambridge, MA: MIT Press.

BBC News. 2014. "Stephen Hawking Warns Artificial Intelligence Could End Mankind." BBC News, December 2, 2014.

Coase, Ronald, H. 1937. "The Nature of the Firm." *Economica* 4 (16): 386–405.

Committee on the Future Economy. 2017. "Exchange of Letters with the Prime Minister." In *Report of the Committee on the Future Economy*. https://www.mti.gov.sg/-/media/MTI/Resources/ Publications/Report-of-the-Committee-on-the-Future-Economy/ CFE_Full-Report.pdf.

Economic Strategies Committee, Singapore. 2010. *Report of the Economic Strategies Committee: High Skilled People, Innovative Economy, Distinctive Global City*. February 2010. https://www.mti.gov .sg/-/media/MTI/Resources/Publications/Report-of-the-Economic -Strategies-Committee/Full-ESC-Report---Ministry-of-Finance.pdf.

Fogel, Kathy, Ashton Hawk, Randall Morck, and Bernard Yeung. 2006. "Institutional Obstacles to Entrepreneurship." In *Oxford Handbook of Entrepreneurship*, edited by Mark Casson, Bernard Yeung, Anuradha Basu, and Nigel Wadeson, 540–79. New York: Oxford University Press.

Fox News. 2016. "One-on-One with Bill Gates." Fox Business, January 22, 2016. https://www.youtube.com/watch?v=EmfrMKLwr3k.

McAfee, Andrew, and Erik Brynjolfsson. 2017. *Machine, Platform, Crowd: Harnessing Our Digital Future*. New York: W. W. Norton & Company.

MOE (Ministry of Education, Singapore). 2018. "Many Paths, New Possibilities—Ready for a New World Together: Empowering Individuals, Nurturing Joy of Learning." Press release, March 5, 2018. https://www.moe.gov.sg/news/press-releases/20180305-many -paths-new-possibilities-ready-for-a-new-world-together-empower ing-individuals-nurturing-joy-of-learning.

Ransbotham, Sam, David Kiron, Philipp Gerbert, and Martin Reeves. 2017. *Reshaping Business with Artificial Intelligence*. Research report, Fall 2017, 1–17. Cambridge, MA: MIT Press.

Straits Times. 2018. "Singapore Soars to Third Place in Global Innovation Ranking." January 23, 2018.

III. Financing Entrepreneurs and Innovation

9 Financing Innovation in Japan

Challenges and Recent Progress

Takeo Hoshi and Kenji E. Kushida

Many Asian economies have experienced rapid economic growth and by now have achieved the status of developed economies. Of these, Japan was the first to grow rapidly and catch up with the advanced economies of North America and Europe by the 1980s. Then, Korea, Singapore, Taiwan, and Hong Kong followed. In the current century, China and India have grown rapidly, and China has become the second-largest economy in the world, surpassing Japan.

When an economy finishes the catch-up phase of economic growth and tries to continue growing as a developed economy, innovation becomes an essential source of economic growth. During the catch-up phase, an economy can rely on imported technologies and domestic capital accumulation. As a developed economy, however, it has to come up with indigenous technological progress for sustained growth.

In this transition from being a catch-up economy to a mature-growth economy, there are often serious challenges to face, since the economic institutions that were suitable for the catch-up phase are not necessarily so for sustained growth based on technological progress. As Hoshi and Kashyap (2011) argue, Japan ran into this problem of upgrading economic institutions after its catch-up phase, failed to do so effectively, and experienced a couple of decades of economic stagnation.

The challenges are especially acute in the financial system because financing innovation is very different from financing traditional manufacturing companies or retailers. The outcomes of innovation are highly uncertain, and the problem of asymmetric information between financiers and entrepreneurs is particularly acute. Japan's bank-led financial system, which supported rapid economic growth very well, turned out to be not suitable for innovation. Looking for a model of an economic system to back innovation-based growth, Japanese policymakers (like policymakers in other countries) were drawn to the ecosystem in Silicon Valley, especially its financial system, wherein venture capital (VC) firms play essential roles.

This chapter studies Japan's attempt to transform its financial system from a bank-dominant one to a system that promotes innovation. Here our focus is on radical innovations that we observe in many high-tech industries of today and are often associated with the Silicon Valley ecosystem, rather than marginal and incremental innovations. After many policy attempts to encourage VC firms in Japan, with little result, the Japanese system for financing innovation seems finally to be taking off.

The rest of the chapter is organized as follows. The next section briefly traces the development of VC firms in Silicon Valley and discusses how their financing mechanisms are suitable for generating innovation. The section that follows examines Japan's traditional, bank-dominant financial system and the challenges such a system faces in promoting innovation. The final section outlines Japan's recent attempts to promote VC firms. While slow to develop, the VC industry may be finally establishing itself.

Venture Capital in Silicon Valley

Venture capital is at the core of the Silicon Valley financial system. Metrick and Yasuda (2011) define a VC firm by five defining characteristics. According to them, such a firm:

- Is a financial intermediary
- Invests in private companies
- Takes an active role in monitoring and helping portfolio companies
- Has a primary goal of maximizing its financial return by exiting investments
- Funds the internal growth of companies

First, a VC firm is a financial intermediary that collects funds from investors and invests in a portfolio of companies. At this level, it is not different from any other financial intermediary such as a commercial bank that accepts deposits and makes loans. Yet a VC firm is different from other financial intermediaries in terms of both its funding mechanism and investment scheme. On the funding side, a VC firm is typically organized as a limited partnership. A VC company starts a fund as the general partner (GP) and solicits other investors to become limited partners (LPs). LPs are typically large pension funds and corporations. The contract between the GP and LP is written to give an appropriate incentive for the GP to monitor the companies that the fund invests in. On the investment side, a VC firm typically receives convertible preferred shares in the portfolio companies.

A convertible preferred share before the conversion is somewhat like a bank loan: predetermined dividends accrue to what the company owes to the investors. This feature gives a VC fund limited protection from downside risk. If the start-up turns out to be only a little profitable, the value of equity may be close to zero, but the VC firm can receive accrued dividends. If the start-up turns out to be completely unprofitable, which happens very often, the VC firm does not get anything, so VC funding is still a lot riskier than bank loans. If the start-up turns out to be very successful, the VC firm can convert the preferred shares into common shares and exit through an initial public offering (IPO) or sales to other companies. In this case, venture capitalists can enjoy substantial capital gains. This potential gain from upside risk separates VC funding from traditional bank loans. The use of convertible preferred shares allows VC funds to gain from upside risk while providing some protection from downside risk.

Second, a VC firm invests only in private companies. This makes venture capital a type of private equity. Unlike public companies, which have securities valued in formal markets, the information on private companies is not easily available. This means that the growth potential of private companies is not known to general investors. This is another difference between venture capitalists and banks, wherein venture capitalists derive great upside value (Kenney and Florida 2000).

Even for VC firms, however, it is difficult to obtain full information about private companies. This leads to the third defining characteristic of a VC firm: it not only provides money but actively monitors and helps start-ups. Venture capitalists often obtain representation on a start-up's board, sometimes even occupying the chair's position. Through active monitoring, venture capitalists reduce the problem of information asymmetry between them and their portfolio companies. It is no coincidence that many VC firms were started by successful entrepreneurs themselves and focus on particular industries where they have expertise and are able to perform as competent monitors.

Another mechanism to mitigate the information problem is to make funding contingent on achieving well-defined benchmarks (such as successful demonstration of a prototype). These benchmarks create a series of financing "rounds": the first round (also called Series A) is when a company initially receives the fund, which is followed by second round (Series B), third round (Series C), and so on. The financing rounds are different from "stages" of start-up companies, which are discussed later.

Fourth, a venture capitalist's goal is the maximization of financial returns. A VC firm tries to achieve this by exiting investments. VC exits come in the form of sales or IPOs. GPs have to realize gains to distribute them to the LPs (Kenney and Florida 2000). The compensation of GPs comes in two forms. First, a GP receives a fraction of committed capital (the amount of capital the venture capitalist collected from partners) as a management fee every year as long as the VC fund exists. The management fee typically starts at 2% but declines to lower levels in later years (Metrick and Yasuda 2011). Second, a GP receives a constant percentage of returns from the investment (exit proceeds minus the committed capital). This is called the carried interest and is typically 20% of the returns. The rest of the returns are distributed to LPs. Over a VC fund's typical life span (10 years), the total amount of carried interest exceeds the total management fees if the 10-year rate of return on investment exceeds 100% (a little more than 7% per year), assuming a 2% management fee, 20% carried interest, and no discount. Indeed, Metrick and Yasuda (2011) find that the largest proportion of GP compensation comes in the form of carried interest in the United States. This structure allows GPs to maximize the financial returns on investment.

Finally, the proceeds a portfolio company receives from venture capitalists are used to expand their business, not to acquire other companies. This distinguishes venture capital from other types of private equity, such as buyout funds and distress funds.

Venture capital in Silicon Valley emerged as a distinct and prominent investment mechanism in the 1970s, growing rapidly following American regulatory shifts. Relaxation of U.S. Labor Department restrictions in 1979 enabled pension funds to invest into VC funds. Just around then, capital gains taxes—the maximum personal tax rate on capital gains—decreased from 3.5% in 1977 over a few years to 2.8% in 1980, and 2% in 1982, making the payoff from VC investments more attractive. The combination of these two regulatory shifts helped fuel a sudden, massive rise in VC financing. The net new commitments to VC firms rose from $133 million in 1973 to $4.6 billion by 1984 (Poterba 1989).

The Silicon Valley VC industry grew symbiotically with U.S. postwar electronics and computer industries. In contrast with traditional industrial patterns of growth characterized by short bursts of invention and innovation, followed by long periods of incremental innovation, the electronics industry experienced continuous bursts of new firms ushering in new design paradigms. Waves of new technologies led to new firms becoming dominant, to be quickly superseded by new technologies and business models that disrupted the incumbents before stable sets of firms experienced long periods of stable growth. Venture capital both drove and benefited from this pattern of rapid and continual disruption in the electronics, computer, and to a lesser degree the biopharmaceutical industry (Kenney and Florida 2000).

Major early VC-backed start-ups in Silicon Valley that IPO'd on the Nasdaq exchange and transformed industries, growing into large companies—though many were later disrupted themselves—included Intel (IPO in 1971), AMD (IPO 1978), Apple (IPO 1980), 3Com (IPO 1984), Sun Microsystems (IPO 1986), and numerous others.

Globally by size, the United States has continually been the center of VC fundraising, investment, and deal flows. In 2004, the United States was host to 77% of global fundraising by dollar amount, and in 2019, this share was 67%. Also in 2004, the United States accounted for 85% of deal flows by dollars, a share that fell to 52% in 2019. Even as deals outside the United States increased, the United States still accounted for just over half of the global total. Of VC exits by dollar amount, the United States was host to 77% in 2004 and 78% in 2019 (NVCA 2020).

Japan's Postwar Model of Finance

The Japanese postwar financial system was centered on banks. Until financial reforms that started in the late 1970s, Japan's system was largely closed off from international markets, corporate finance was dominated by bank loans, and household savings flew to the banking sector rather than the bond or equity markets. Banks were the primary financial intermediaries that collected household savings and used them to provide industrial and commercial loans.

Japan's postwar industrial structure revolved around a few large banks that would extend loans to, exercise power as one of the largest shareholders of, and take seats on the boards of borrower companies. The main banks also monitored the firms to which they extended loans: bankers would step in and take over the management of firms that were performing badly. These banks also decreased the economic cost of the customers' financial distress (Aoki and Patrick 1994; Hoshi 1994).

Overall, the bank-dominated financial system served the Japanese economy well during the catch-up phase of its economic growth. Bank financing, however, was not ideal for start-ups that invest in potentially very profitable but highly uncertain innovative projects. If a project fails, the start-up cannot pay back the loan, and the bank loses money. With an established company that has physical assets in place, the bank may be able to take those assets as collateral, which the bank can seize when the company fails to pay back the loan, but start-ups usually do not have collateralizable assets. If a project succeeds, that may bring huge profits to the company, but the gain for the bank is limited: all it gets is the bank loan fully paid back with interest. This limited gain from upside risk makes banks reluctant to lend to high-risk/high-return start-ups.

In the Japanese system, the main banks are also the largest share-holders of the corporations that borrow from them. This means that they can gain from the upside risk that the borrowers may face. The po-tential gain from shareholding, however, is usually much smaller than banks' profits from loans. A bank's shareholding is strictly limited by law (typically under 5 percent of the total number of shares issued by the company). Moreover, realizing capital gains from these sharehold-ings is difficult, because maintaining a relationship with corporations is the most important rationale for cross shareholding. Selling the cus-tomers' shares to realize capital gains would jeopardize the future of the relationship.

Japan's Venture Capital

Given Japan's historically bank-centered financial system, it is perhaps unsurprising that Japan's "VC industry" originated with consortia of investment companies that used loans as their primary financial tool. Japan's first VC firm was established in Kyoto. Japanese executives of a regional business association in Kyoto, the Kyoto Keizai Doyukai, traveled to Boston in 1971 and visited the American Research and Development Corporation (ARDC). ARDC, a pioneering VC firm established in 1946, had become famous for investing in the Digital

Equipment Corporation and then enjoying a vast return upon its IPO. Inspired by this trip, Kyoto-based firms including Tateishi Denki (now Omron), Kyoto Bank, and others created Kyoto Enterprise Development (KED).[1]

Other VC companies were set up soon thereafter by consortia of financial institutions and industrial groups. Nippon Enterprise Development (NED) was created by 39 companies led by the Long-term Credit Bank, Fuji Bank, Daiwa Securities, and Itochu Corporation. Nippon Venture Capital Co., Ltd. (NVCC) was formed by 15 companies in the Sumitomo group. Japan Associated Finance Co., Ltd. (JAFCO) was a product of Nomura Securities, Sanwa Bank, and Nippon Life Insurance.

These early Japanese "venture capital" firms were very different from the VC firms in Silicon Valley in a couple of important ways.[2] First, early VC firms in Japan were not partnerships but general joint-stock companies funded by the parent corporations. They did not accept funds from investors other than the founders and used their own accounts for investing in portfolio companies. Gradually, some of them started to form investment partnerships, but the concept of limited partnership was absent in Japanese law, which meant all the partners had unlimited liability. Only after the introduction of the Limited Partnership Act for Investment in 1998 and its substantial revision in 2004 did Japanese VC firms started to finance companies through VC funds.

Second, early VC firms in Japan used not only equities or equity-like securities (such as convertible bonds and warrant attached bonds) but also loans. In fact, lending was the dominant form of financing for a long time.

The early VC firms generally invested a small amount of their own funds (typically less than $1 million) in companies that were almost ready for an IPO. Their primary focus was not on capital gains but rather fee revenues from arranging the companies' IPOs. Given the prominence of securities houses as important founders of these VC firms, this bias toward fee revenues is understandable. The start-ups that these firms invested in were generally not technology-based or R&D-intensive companies. They were in established sectors such as

---

1 The description of the early history of Japanese VC companies in this and the next two paragraphs depends heavily on Hata, Ando, and Ishii (2007, 151–78).

2 Kenney, Han, and Tanaka (2004, 70–72) provide a concise summary of the operational characteristics of early VC firms in Japan.

TABLE 9.1 Japan's venture capital funding by type (billions yen)

	1985	1990	1995
Loan	154	1,007	420
Own fund	100	385	588
VC fund	52	142	266
Total	306	1,534	1,273

SOURCE: Sako and Kotosaka (2012), based on data from the Venture Enterprise Center, Japan.

retail, wholesale trade, and restaurant chains. The recession following the oil shock in the late 1970s led to a rapid decline of IPOs, from 66 in 1973 to between 20 and 30 by the late 1970s. VC funds curtailed their activities, and the pioneering KED was liquidated in 1980.

JAFCO, set up in 1982, was the first VC fund in Japan that was structured as a partnership investment fund and thus able to take funds from outside investors. Japan's VC industry, however, did not take off. Table 9.1 shows the composition of funding by venture capitalists in Japan in 1985, 1990, and 1995. The table shows that they continued using loans to fund portfolio companies well into the 1990s. As late as 1995, 33 percent of total VC funding was in the form of loans. The table also shows that the Japanese venture capitalists invested predominantly out of their own accounts. The amount that went through investment funds established by them was small. In 1995, just 21 percent of total VC funding was by investment funds.

The environment for financing start-ups in Japan started to improve somewhat in the mid-1990s as the Ministry of International Trade and Industry (MITI) spearheaded a number of efforts to support Japan's start-up ecosystem. Table 9.2 lists major policy actions that MITI took to promote the VC industry in Japan in the 1990s and the 2000s. In 1994, MITI created a division to support start-ups. The same year, the government amended its antimonopoly guidelines to enable VC firms to send executives to the companies into which they invested. This opened the way for venture capitalists to actively monitor their portfolio companies if they wished.

In 1995, the implementation of "Temporary Measures to Facilitate Specific New Businesses" allowed companies to use stock options albeit at a limited scale. Stock options were further liberalized as the Commercial Code was revised in 1997 and again in 2001.

In 1998, the Limited Partnership Act for Investment made it possible to form limited partnership funds with limited liability for investors,

TABLE 9.2 Policies of the Ministry of International Trade and Industries (MITI) to promote venture capital companies in Japan

Year	Policy
1994	MITI creates new division to support the venture capital (VC) industry.
	The guidelines of the Act of Prohibition of Private Monopolization and Maintenance of Fair Trade were revised, lifting the ban on the dispatching of executives by VC firms to portfolio companies, allowing VC firms to provide hands-on support to such companies.
1995	SME (Small and Medium Enterprises) Creative Business Promotion Law enacted.
	The Law on Temporary Measures to Facilitate Specific New Businesses was revised, introducing a limited stock options scheme.
1997	Generalization of stock options by Commercial Code.
1998	Enactment of the Limited Partnership Act for Venture Capital Investment. This measure established a scheme for limited partnership funds with an explicit limited liability for fund investors through the legal status of limited partner.
1999	Establishment of Mothers (Market of the High-growth and Emerging Stocks) by the Tokyo Stock Exchange.
	Amendment of the Small and Medium Enterprise Basic Law.
2000	Establishment of NASDAQ Japan by the Osaka Stock Exchange and NASDAQ.
2001	Expansion of stock options and other revisions of the Commercial Code.
2002	Introduction of a substantial preferred stock scheme by the Commercial Code.
2013	The Industrial Competitiveness Enhancement Act. Support and incentives to promote investments into venture businesses; national universities allowed to invest in venture funds (METI, n.d.).

SOURCE: Adapted from Hata, Ando, and Ishii (2007).

paving the way for larger investments into VC funds (Hata, Ando, and Ishii 2007).

Gradual financial deregulation that started in the late 1970s continued into the 1990s and the 2000s. A noteworthy development for financing start-ups was the formation of small capitalization markets. In late 1999, Mothers (Market of the High-growth and Emerging Stocks) was created by the Tokyo Stock Exchange (TSE) as a market for young companies that would not satisfy the regular listing standards of the Tokyo Stock Exchange. Similarly, the Osaka Stock Exchange established Nasdaq Japan as a partnership with the U.S. Nasdaq and Softbank. These two exchanges provided Japan's start-ups with new opportunities to seek IPOs without satisfying stringent conditions to become listed companies on the Tokyo Stock Exchange or the Osaka Stock Exchange. Nasdaq Japan changed its name to Hercules when the U.S. Nasdaq and Softbank pulled out of the business in 2002. In

2010, Hercules merged with Jasdaq and NEO (other small exchanges for emerging companies) and became the New Jasdaq. After the merger between the Tokyo Stock Exchange and the Osaka Stock Exchange in 2013, the administration of the New Jasdaq was transferred to the Tokyo Stock Exchange. Thus, both stock exchanges for emerging companies (Mothers and the New Jasdaq) are now run by the Tokyo Stock Exchange.

In the late 1990s, as numerous start-ups got listed in Japan's new small-cap markets, some VC funds enjoyed substantial returns on their investments. A group of notable entrepreneurs also amassed significant personal wealth, and their success became a focal point of the start-up ecosystem. Some companies grew to be established companies, including the e-commerce portal Rakuten (listed on Mothers in 2000), online advertising company Cyber Agent (listed on Jasdaq in 2000), and the software firm Cybozu (listed on Mothers in 2000). Many more companies, however, failed to grow after IPOs. It is symbolic that the first two companies that were successfully listed on Mothers, Liquid Audio Japan and Internet Research Institute, experienced numerous managerial scandals and turnovers, business changes, and name changes, and were eventually delisted. Another infamous company listed on Mothers is Livedoor. Livedoor was a fast-growing company but its management was found guilty of falsifying accounting information and it got delisted in 2006. Institutional investors shunned these small-cap markets as places for venture company founders and venture capitalists to make quick money at the expense of retail investors.

Some legitimate VC firms were established in the late 1990s and demonstrated promise to be important financiers of innovation. For example, Globis Capital Partners (GCP, or Globis) began with a small fund of just over $5 million in 1996. The first fund eventually yielded around 8 times the investment with 6 of the 13 firms listed through IPOs. In 1999, it partnered with British private equity firm Apex Partners to create a much bigger, $200 million fund, investing in 47 companies, of which 8 were IPO'd. A third fund of $180 million was formed by Globis alone. As of March 2018, 14 of 44 portfolio companies had already been listed through IPOs. A fourth fund of $115 million in 2013 and a fifth fund of $160 million in 2016 followed. Both of these were formed by Globis alone (Globis Capital Partners n.d.).

After the Silicon Valley–centered dot-com bubble burst, VC funding in Japan took a downturn as well. Yet, the recovery in total amount of funding was relatively rapid. More important than the recovery of the amount, however, was a shift in the forms of capital disbursement. As figure 9.1 shows, loans that dominated VC funding well into the 1990s were replaced by funding through VC funds. In as late as 1998, loans comprised 17% of total VC funding, but the share of loans dropped to 1.8% by 2001. The importance of disbursement using the VCs firms' own accounts also declined. By 2011, more than 75% of VC funding was done by VC funds.

The composition of VC types also changed. Corporate venture funds, which were large players in funding venture companies in Japan, were reduced in importance, while independent VC funds became more important sources of funds. A general critique of corporate venture funds is that they tend to pull out quickly and discontinue their funds when a company's overall performance dips. From the standpoint of a start-up ecosystem, this is unconstructive because the large corporate ventures are not seen as being fully committed to the start-ups. Japan's shift toward independent VC funds rather than corporate venture funds was driven by this exact dynamic of large corporations pulling out, thereby confirming the general suspicion.

The increase of VC funding in Japan following the favorable regulatory developments, however, did not last long. Figure 9.2 shows the

FIGURE 9.1 Venture capital funding in Japan by type, 1985–2011

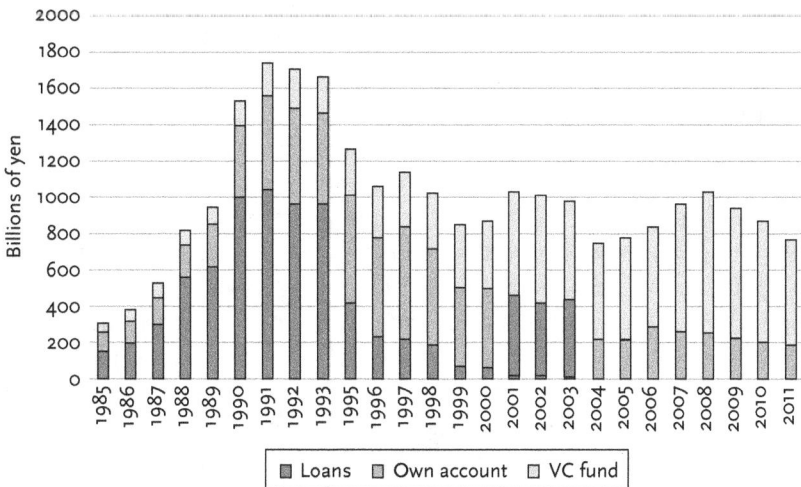

SOURCE: Sako and Kotosaka (2012), based on data from the Venture Enterprise Center, Japan.

FIGURE 9.2 Investment by venture capital firms in Japan, FY1999–2019

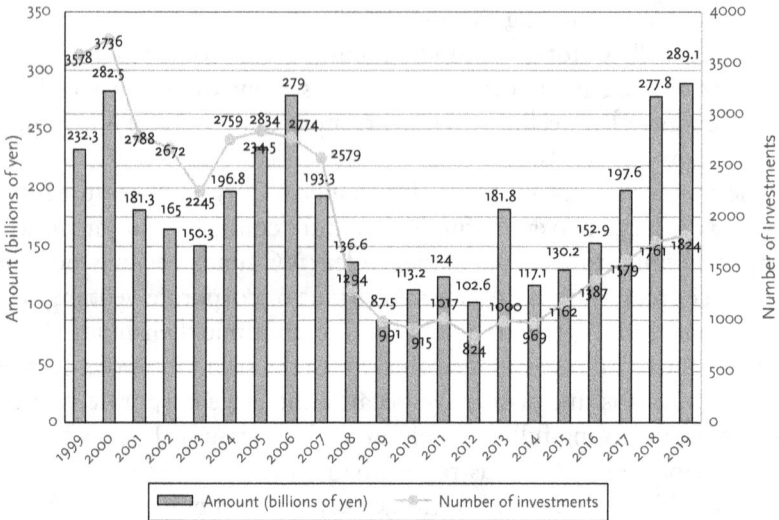

SOURCE: Venture Enterprise Center, Japan (2019).

number of investment deals and the total amount of investment by Japan's VC firms for each fiscal year from 1999 to 2019. Japan's level of VC investment rose and decreased in tandem with the dot-com boom in the United States. It began to rise again in the mid-2000s, only to fall sharply in 2007. The timing coincides with the delisting of Livedoor. The accounting fraud case of Livedoor was widely reported and its delisting had a huge chilling effect on IPOs and venture companies in general. Since then, Japan's VC investment levels have grown steadily, and in 2019 reached levels slightly exceeding those seen in 2006.

The size of Japan's VC industry is a tiny fraction of that of Silicon Valley's, although Japan is not unique in this comparison, since every other VC industry is far smaller than that of Silicon Valley as well. As table 9.3 shows, even after more than doubling from 2010 to 2018, Japan's VC investment was about 5 percent that of Silicon Valley and slightly more than 2 percent that of the United States in 2018. There are some emerging signs, however, that suggest Japan's VC industry is finally becoming a reliable and effective source of financing for innovative companies.

First, the independent venture capitalists, which are not affiliated with banks, securities houses, other financial institutions, or non-financial corporations, are becoming dominant. To the extent that

TABLE 9.3 Venture capital investment amounts (billions USD)

FY	2010	2015	2018
Japan*	1.04	1.19	2.55
U.S. total	27.45	66.69	109.31
Silicon Valley	10.68	29.41	52.14

NOTE: *Calculated at 2019 average JPY/USD exchange rate of 109.
SOURCE: Silicon Valley Institute for Regional Studies (n.d.); Venture Enterprise Center, Japan (2014, 2019).

independent VCs do not have the problems associated with the affiliated VCs, the increased share of independent VCs will help grow funding for innovative companies.

Second, university-based venture capitalists are rapidly increasing in importance. These may have better access to the newest scientific knowledge and also have a greater ability to evaluate technical innovations. Although it is too early to evaluate their contributions to innovation in Japan, it seems clear that Japanese researchers today are more aware of the ways they can commercialize scientific findings thanks to the activities of these funds.

Third, the stock markets for emerging companies such as Mothers continue to recover. Although the markets still suffer from the reputational damages sustained in the 2000s and have not succeeded in attracting (especially foreign) institutional investors, there is now an established pathway for legitimate start-ups to advance to the First Section of the Tokyo Stock Exchange.

In the rest of this section, we take up each of these three developments in more detail.

Rise of independent venture capitalists

Table 9.4 shows the amount of VC investment by VC type. From 2010 onward, the investment by independent VCs exceeded that of all other types of VCs, including those related to financial firms. As a proportion of total VC investment, the investment by independent VCs was 21% in 2008, but grew to 30% by 2017. The percentage of companies supported by independent VCs, however, did not change very much from 2008 to 2017, as table 9.5 shows. This implies that independent VCs have increased the size of each investment over time.

The rise of independent VCs is clear from other measures as well. In 2015, independent funds raised 35% of total funds raised by VCs.

Corporate venture capital was second, raising 28%, followed by financial institution venture capital (18%). In 2008, the number of independent firms was 37 out of 134 VC firms (28%), but it grew to 69 out of 219 (32%) by 2017.

The increasing share of independent VC firms suggests that Japan's VC industry is getting better at financing innovation projects that have high expected returns but also high risks. The VC firms owned by or affiliated with financial institutions were reluctant to finance such high-risk/high return projects. Many bank-run VC firms acted more like bankers than venture capitalists, concerned with minimizing failures rather than searching for fast-growing but risky "home run" start-ups. Many employees at such firms (often dispatched by the founder banks) lacked the ability to provide other value-added roles of venture capitalists such as interpersonal networks and business advice. The rise of independent VC firms, whose employees benefit from the upside risk of start-ups, is beneficial to the start-up ecosystem in Japan. Further experience in growing large numbers of companies and building interpersonal networks would help independent VC firms continue to dominate the industry.

Who are these independent venture capitalists? Some major funds include World Innovation Lab (WiL), Globis Capital Partners, B Dash Ventures, and others. In 2016, half of the funding raised by such firms were by JAFCO and WiL, totaling almost 10 billion yen (around $90 million). JAFCO remains the largest Japanese VC firm, while some

TABLE 9.4 Amount of venture capital investment by type, 2008–17 (billions of yen)

	2008	2009	2010	2011	2012	2013	2014	2015	2016	2017
Independent	7	4.9	8.3	19.7	7.2	23.6	28.9	24.3	33.2	34.4
Finance-related	13.2	9.5	6.5	7.2	3.5	7.5	11.7	16.1	33.8	25.3
Government*	4.7	0.2	7.3	2.8	4.0	11.6	13.9	11.1	12.8	22.1
Foreign	4.6	1.3	2.7	2.7	1.0	5.5	9.1	11.2	17.8	14.1
Corporate	1.7	2.1	4.3	2.2	3.2	5.6	7.6	10.2	11.9	9.5
University	1.0	0.9	0.6	0	0.3	0.8	2.4	3.7	4.9	4.4
Hybrid	0.6	0.4	0.7	0.8	0.4	0.5	0.1	0.6	3.2	3.3
Other	1.1	0.1	2.8	10.0	2.0	0	0.6	0.9	0.3	1.6
Total	33.8	19.5	33.2	45.4	21.7	55.1	74.4	78.2	117.7	114.7

NOTE: *Includes local government.
SOURCE: Data from Entrepedia (2018).

TABLE 9.5 Number of companies invested in by type of venture capitalist,
2008–17

	2008	2009	2010	2011	2012	2013	2014	2015	2016	2017
Independent	82	64	81	114	118	181	233	234	280	274
Finance-related	92	54	44	61	53	76	111	124	238	208
Government*	123	11	10	11	15	29	38	33	33	40
Foreign	8	9	11	8	17	24	36	50	60	57
Corporate	33	35	15	55	64	83	89	126	127	138
Other[†]	23	19	17	19	14	14	24	43	76	94
Total	361	192	178	281	281	407	531	610	814	811

NOTE: *Includes local government; [†]"Other" includes university-based, hybrid, and unknown types of venture capital firms.
SOURCE: Data from Entrepedia (2018).

newcomers, in particular WiL, also have raised large funds (by Japanese standards).

JAFCO launched its first partnership fund in 1982 and began operations in Silicon Valley in 1984. Listed on the TSE's First Section in
2001, JAFCO has established over a hundred investment funds with investors that include financial institutions, pension funds, and large corporations. It had managed over 980 billion yen ($8.8 billion at 2018
exchange rate) by 2018, when it had approximately 350 billion yen
($3 billion) under management. By that year, it had invested in almost
4,000 companies total, with around 3,150 in Japan and 850 elsewhere,
taking over 1,000 of them to IPOs. Its notable recent Japanese portfolio companies include Money Forward, Cookbiz (an online recipe
platform), and Cyberdyne. It also had small stakes in successful Silicon
Valley companies such as Twitter and Nvidia (JAFCO n.d.).

WiL started in 2013 with a first fund of $300 million from large
Japanese corporate investors including Nissan, Sony, ANA, Mizuho
Bank, Daiwa Financial Group, Seven Bank, Hakuhodo, JVC Kenwood,
and others. Headquartered in Palo Alto with offices in Tokyo, WiL focuses on efforts toward innovation within its large company investments as well as investment in start-ups. In 2018, it raised a second
fund of just over $400 million. Its exits as of 2018 included the IPO of
Mercari in 2018 (the largest IPO on Mothers by far) and the merger
and acquisition of Soracom (one of the largest acquisitions of a start-up
by a large company to date).

Some JAFCO alumni have spun out to create their own independent
VC funds. GMO Venture Partners was founded in 2005 by a former
fund manager of JAFCO who was in charge of its U.S.-based portfolio

companies. By mid-2018, GMO Venture Partners established five funds and had around 10 billion yen under management. It had taken 13 out of its 55 portfolio companies public as of mid-2018, including Money Forward, Mercari, and Rakusul. It also invested internationally, mostly in Asia with notable investments including Qihoo 360 technology, China's fourth-largest internet company, which had a billion-dollar IPO on the New York Stock Exchange in 2011. GMO has raised funds from a variety of large corporate LPs including Sumitomo Mitsui Financial Group, as well as Japan's Small and Medium Enterprise Promotion Agency, and other GMO group companies.

Another independent VC firm is Globis Capital Partners, which we touched upon above. GCP raised five funds by mid-2018, with over 60 billion yen under management, and invested in around 150 companies, with over 40 exits. Some notable portfolio companies include Mercari, Mobile SNS and gaming platform Gree, smartphone news app SmartNews, online asset management service Money Design, and drone-as-a-service company Sensyn Robotics.

University-based venture capital funds

Another notable development in the Japanese VC industry is the growth of university-based venture capitalists. These show potential to increase funding for innovations based on new scientific discoveries that often occur in academic research institutions.

The top public universities, such as the University of Tokyo, Kyoto University, Osaka University, Tohoku University, and Tokyo Institute of Technology, all have affiliated VC funds. Private universities Keio, Waseda, and Tokyo University of Science also have closely affiliated VC funds. Table 9.6 lists some of the prominent university VC firms.

The oldest and most successful Japanese university-affiliated VC is the University of Tokyo Edge Capital (UTEC). Established in 2004, UTEC raised three funds by mid-2018, completing its first one, which raised 8.3 billion yen, invested in 34 companies, and exited 31 of them, including 9 IPOs and 7 acquisitions. Notable IPOs include tella, a research and development company for cancer treatments; Morpho, a start-up founded by University of Tokyo researchers that engages in the research, development, and licensing of image processing technologies; and PeptiDream, a biopharmaceutical company that focuses on the research and development of non-standard peptide therapeutics. Several of its companies were also acquired by larger companies: Phyzios, a

TABLE 9.6 University venture capital funds

Name	Affiliated university	Year*	Funds†	Investment areas	Start-ups‡	Exits§
Keio Innovation Initiative	Keio University	2015	4.5	Information technology (IT), digital health, bio informatics, medicine/regenerative medicine	11	
Tokyo University of Science Investment Management	Tokyo University of Science	2014	4	Energy, HRtech, software, energy	10	
University of Tokyo Edge Capital	University of Tokyo	2004	54.3	Life science and healthcare, IT, physical science and engineering	90	19
UTokyo Innovation Platform Co.	University of Tokyo	2016	25	Internet of Things (IoT)/wearables, biotech	3	
Kyoto University Innovation Capital Co.	Kyoto University	2014	16	Biotech, information and communications technology (ICT)/Artificial Intelligence (AI)/IoT, energy	18	2
Osaka University Venture Capital	Osaka University	2014	12.5	Life (regenerative medicine, vaccination, nursing, preventative treatments, medicine), Green (energy, environment, smart community), Platforms (robotics/AI, smart devices, nanotech, security, ICT/Big Data)	15	1
Tohoku University Venture Partners Co.	Tohoku University	2015	9.6	Energy, sensors, medicine, biotech, health tech	11	1
Innovations and Future Creation Inc. (MIRAI SOUZOU)	Tokyo Institute of Technology	2014	3.34	Software, sensors, communication/networking, cloud services, edtech, healthcare	9	

NOTE: *Year of founding; †funds raised in billion yen; ‡number of start-ups invested; §exits to date.
SOURCE: Adapted from Nikkei (2018).

software company applying physics simulation technologies to entertainment, was acquired by Google; popIn, an information integration service that assists Internet users in browsing websites, by Baidu; Cirius Technologies, a mobile advertising company that develops location-based self-serve ad platform, by Yahoo!Japan; and medical treatment statistics data service provider, Japan Medical Data Center, by Olympus.

UTEC's second fund, which began in 2009, raised 7.15 billion yen, invested in 13 companies, and had one exit, Naked Technology, acquired by social networking service company mixi. Its third fund, founded in 2013, raised 14.5 billion yen and invested in 29 companies.

Mothers to the Tokyo Stock Exchange

The markets for emerging stocks in Japan such as Mothers continue to be small. Although Mothers may be recovering from the shocks in the mid-2000s (first the "Livedoor shock" and then the "Lehman shock"), it has not recovered to its peak level seen around 2000. The observation made by Sako and Kotosaka (2012) that "the layering of new stock exchanges onto the existing stock exchanges has not taken off and remains thin" still rings true in 2020. They also pointed out that Japan's small-cap markets are three-fourths domestic individual investors rather than the TSE's First Section, which includes a large proportion of foreign investors.

In the last several years, however, an important role of Mothers complementary to rather than competing with more established markets of the TSE has emerged. This role is as a pathway to the established sections of the TSE. It is increasingly common for start-ups to first list on Mothers, then eventually list on the First Section of the TSE. From the inception of Mothers in 1999 to the end of 2016, 484 firms were listed on the exchange. Of these, 25%, or 119 companies, moved up to the TSE's First Section eventually, while 10% (50 companies) moved to the TSE's Second Section; 54% (262 firms) remained on Mothers, and the rest were delisted. Of the 119 companies that moved to the TSE's First Section, half of them (60) moved within a year of IPOs on Mothers (IBER-Kotosaka Seminar 2017).[3] Thus, the fast-growth companies

---

3   More recent data from the Tokyo Stock Exchange (n.d.) confirm the continued role of Mothers as a pathway to the First Section. In the two years of 2017 to 2018, a total of 114 companies were newly listed on Mothers. Of these, 31 (27%) moved up to the First Section by mid-2020.

that listed on Mothers continued to grow and were able to qualify for the more stringent listing requirements of TSE's First Section.

Thus, Mothers seems to be becoming an entry point for Japan's start-ups that aspire to grow and become established companies in the First Section of the TSE. Some start-ups inevitably fail to grow and get delisted eventually, but others succeed and graduate to the TSE. The low cost of listing on Mothers is another attraction for start-ups as well as venture capitalists that invest in those companies. For venture capitalists, Mothers also provides an environment for a relatively more predictable exit strategy, as Riney (2016) points out.

One potential drawback of having an easy market for IPOs is that it may hinder truly large high-growth firms from emerging. Once firms are listed at a smaller scale, they tend to become more risk averse and pursue stable rather than exponential growth. An established pathway to become larger and be listed in the First Section of the TSE may further help by giving incentives for start-ups listed on Mothers to continue growing.

The issue is related to another characteristic of Japanese start-ups that is often pointed out: lack of "unicorns." So far, Japan has produced only two unicorns defined as pre-IPO start-up companies valued at over $1 billion. Since companies can IPO on Mothers at a small scale, venture capitalists are more interested in small IPO exits rather than in growing companies to become large. The implication is that Japanese start-ups are therefore pushed into business models and business strategies that do not entail high-risk, high-return growth, but are rather aimed at lower risk and lower return.

While this might be fine for the domestic Japanese market, the argument is that it can put Japanese start-ups at a global disadvantage if they are unable to grow rapidly to become large in their home market. On the other hand, given that start-ups having a way to receive VC funding and IPO is a relatively recent development, one could view the low listing requirements as an important development in Japan's start-up ecosystem that enables venture capitalists to face a more predictable exit strategy environment. A large number of entrepreneurs experiencing exits, while on a smaller scale than in the United States, may also help create a group of Japanese serial entrepreneurs and investors who have some individual wealth—of the sort that cannot be accumulated by being a salaried worker at an elite Japanese firm in a long-term employment structure.

Conclusion

This chapter examined the funding environment for start-ups in Japan. The traditional bank-centered financial system was not ideal for financing potentially high-return but high-risk start-ups. After the catch-up phase of economic growth ended by the 1980s, Japanese policymakers realized the importance of promoting drastic innovations in high-tech industries to sustain economic growth. VC firms, which have played prominent roles in financing many successful start-ups in Silicon Valley, have been slow in developing in Japan.

Japanese VCs were very different from the VCs in the United States. Many of them were subsidiaries of large financial firms, provided loans to their portfolio companies rather than equities, and used their own balance sheets rather than forming investment funds. In fact, it was legally impossible for Japanese venture capitalists to form limited liability investment partnerships similar to VC funds in the United States. Only in the mid-2000s did Japanese venture capitalists stop advancing loans to their portfolio companies and start to form limited liability investment funds (which was legally permitted in 1998).

The growth of the Japanese VC industry is still slow and its size is tiny compared with the United States. There are, however, some recent developments that may turn out to be the beginning of a lively VC industry in Japan. The VC firms owned by or affiliated with large financial firms and/or large nonfinancial companies have reduced in importance, and independent VCs are becoming dominant players. Some university-based VCs are rising especially in fields that require scientific and technical expertise. Mothers, a market for emerging companies, is growing steadily. Though the market is often criticized for its generous standards that incentivize start-ups (and VCs) to IPO prematurely, the market seems to have established itself as a pathway to the First Section of the TSE, which has more stringent standards.

References

Aoki, Masahiko, and Hugh T. Patrick. 1994. *The Japanese Main Bank System: Its Relevance for Developing and Transforming Economies*. Oxford; New York: Oxford University Press.

Entrepedia. 2018. *Japan Startup Finance 2017*. https://initial.inc/enterprise/report/jsf2017/.

Globis Capital Partners. N.d. "History: Pioneering Venture Capital in Japan." Accessed August 18, 2018. http://www.globiscapital.co.jp/en/about/history/.

Hata, Nobuyuki, Haruhiko Ando, and Yoshiaki Ishii. 2007. "Venture Capital and Its Governance: The Emergence of Equity Financing Conduits in Japan." In *Corporate Governance in Japan: Institutional Change and Organizational Diversity*, edited by Masahiko Aoki, Gregory Jackson, and Hideaki Miyajima, 151–78. New York: Oxford University Press.

Hoshi, Takeo. 1994. "The Economic Role of Corporate Grouping and the Main Bank System." In *The Japanese Firm: The Sources of Competitive Strength*, edited by Masahiko Aoki and Ronald Dore, 285–309. Oxford: Oxford University Press.

Hoshi, Takeo, and Anil Kashyap. 2011. *Why Did Japan Stop Growing?* NIRA Report. Tokyo: Nippon Institute for Research Advancement. https://www.nira.or.jp/pdf/1002english_report.pdf.

IBER-Kotosaka Seminar. 2017. "Tosho Mothers kara Tosho Ichibu ni shijyo-henko wo shita kigyo data" [Corporate data that changed the market from TSE Mothers to TSE First Section]. *International Business and Entrepreneurship Research-Kotosaka*, November 6. http://iber.sfc.keio.ac.jp/?p=10251.

JAFCO (Japan Associated Finance Co., Ltd). N.d. "JAFCO Website." Accessed August 6, 2020. http://www.jafco.co.jp.

Kenney, Martin, and Richard Florida. 2000. "Venture Capital in Silicon Valley: Fueling New Firm Formation." In *Understanding Silicon Valley: The Anatomy of an Entrepreneurial Region*, edited by Martin Kenney, 98–123. Stanford, CA: Stanford University Press.

Kenney, Martin, Kyonghee Han, and Shoko Tanaka. 2004. "The Globalization of Venture Capital: The Cases of Taiwan and Japan." In *Financial Systems, Corporate Investment in Innovation, and Venture Capital*, edited by Anthony Bartzokas and Sunil Mani, 52–84. Northampton, MA: Edward Elgar Publishing.

Metrick, Andrew, and Ayako Yasuda. 2011. "Venture Capital and Other Private Equity: A Survey." *European Financial Management* 17 (4): 619–54.

METI (Ministry of Economy, Trade and Industry). N.d. "Industrial Competitiveness Enhancement Act." Accessed August 6, 2020. http://www.meti.go.jp/english/policy/economy/industrial_competitiveness_act/index.html.

Nikkei. 2018. "Daigaku VC Sei-ei OB ga Hitohada" [Talented Alumni Pitch in for University VCs]. Nikkei, May 16, 2018. https://www.nikkei.com/article/DGKKZO30563440V10C18A5TCN000/.

NVCA (National Venture Capital Association). 2020. *National Venture Capital Association 2020 Yearbook*. Washington, DC: NVCA.

Poterba, James M. 1989. "Venture Capital and Capital Gains Taxation." NBER Working Paper 2832, National Bureau of Economic Research, Cambridge, MA.

Riney, James. 2016. "7 Things Investors & Founders Need to Know about the Japan Startup Ecosystem." 500 Startups, May 19, 2016. Accessed June 1, 2016. http://500.co/japan-startup-ecosystem-founders-investors/.

Sako, Mari, and Masahiro Kotosaka. 2012. "Continuity and Change in the Japanese Economy: Evidence of Institutional Interactions between Financial and Labour Markets." In *East Asian Capitalism: Diversity, Continuity, and Change*, edited by Andrew Walter and Xiaoke Zhang, 132–57. Oxford, UK: Oxford University Press.

Silicon Valley Institute for Regional Studies. N.d. "Venture Capital Investment—Silicon Valley and San Francisco." Accessed August 6, 2020. https://siliconvalleyindicators.org/data/economy/innovation-entrepreneurship/private-equity/venture-capital-investment/.

Tokyo Stock Exchange (Japan Exchange Group). N.d. "New Listings/Transfers/Delistings." Accessed August 6, 2020. https://www.jpx.co.jp/english/listing/stocks/index.html.

Venture Enterprise Center, Japan. 2014. *2014 VEC Yearbook*. Tokyo: Venture Enterprise Center.

Venture Enterprise Center, Japan. 2019. *2019 VEC Yearbook*. Tokyo: Venture Enterprise Center, Japan.

10 Promoting Entrepreneurship under the Shadow of Big Business in Korea

The Role of the Government

Hicheon Kim, Dohyeon Kim, and He Soung Ahn

The Republic of Korea (Korea hereafter) represents an unprecedented case of economic development. In 1961 its gross domestic product (GDP) per capita was less than $100; in 2018 this exceeded $30,000. In 1996 Korea joined the Organisation for Economic Co-operation and Development (OECD), a club of the developed countries, becoming the second Asian country after Japan to do so. Korea has emerged as a global leader in many industries, including semiconductors, LCD displays, mobile phones, steel, and automobiles. In recent years, Korean cultural products such as K-pop, drama, and movies have also gained popularity around the world. At the heart of Korea's rapid and successful industrial transformation have been the family-controlled, diversified business groups known as the *chaebol*, which have at times been praised and at other times criticized.

Any account of Korea's economic rise over the past 60 years should revolve around the central role played by the chaebol. At the start of the country's industrialization process, the government channeled scarce financial capital to a small group of entrepreneurs who were selected to be partners in the government's national development projects. As they demonstrated their entrepreneurial capabilities and succeeded in the export market, they became qualified for continued funding and for other national development projects that were more challenging and attractive. This focused, conditional support from the government led to the rise of the chaebol, which in turn drove rapid industrialization. Tight family control has enabled the chaebol to make long-term investments, for example, in research and development (R&D), and to take large risks as necessary. They have transformed themselves from being exporters of cheap products to being major global players in scale-sensitive, high-tech sectors.

However, some observers have long claimed that the unique chaebol model is running out of steam. When Korea was hit by the Asian financial crisis in late 1997, the chaebol and their viability came to be strongly challenged. Of the 30 largest chaebols in 1996, about half went through bankruptcy proceedings or bank-sponsored restructuring programs (Kim et al. 2004). They were accused of being excessively diversified, globally noncompetitive, and poorly managed. The Korean economy was described as being stuck "in the nutcracker"—lagging behind advanced countries such as Japan, while being chased closely by emerging countries such as China. The government therefore initiated reforms to make the chaebol more disciplined, competitive, and transparent on the one hand, and to foster start-ups and entrepreneurship to reinvigorate the Korean economy on the other. Start-ups were hailed as a new source of growth that would take the Korean economy to the next level.

The government introduced a series of initiatives to promote start-ups and entrepreneurship and to jump-start the venture capital (VC) industry. It infused public funds directly into the domestic VC market via the Small and Medium Business Fund (SMBF), which was under the Small and Medium Business Administration (SMBA). The SMBF established Dasan Venture as a government-funded VC firm to directly invest in start-ups in 2001, and also invested in a range of limited partner funds to channel capital to particular sectors. In addition, the government provided guarantees on equity investments and loans. For instance, the Technology Credit Guarantee Fund provided 70–100 percent guarantees on equity investments and full guarantees on loans to high-tech start-ups. These efforts led to the rapid growth of the domestic VC market, with VC investments increasing fourfold from 1998 to 2000 to reach ₩2 trillion (0.63 percent of GDP).

Despite this, the start-up boom did not last long, globally and domestically. As capital markets collapsed, enthusiasm about and investments in start-ups waned accordingly. In addition, the recession caused by the financial crisis did not last long; the economy quickly rebounded and Korea's GDP came to surpass its 1996 level by 2002. Many chaebol reemerged as stronger global players and regained their reputation, partly due to their painful restructuring efforts (Kim et al. 2004). Furthermore, the dominance of the chaebol in the economy turned out to be a major hindrance to the formation and growth of start-ups. Since they had the advantages of financial resources, access to distribution channels, service networks, and complementary technologies, the chaebol were often better positioned to commercialize and profit from innovation (Kim 2010). Only a few start-ups founded in this period grew enough to make it to the list of the top 100 Korean companies by market value in 2018 (e.g., Naver, Kakao, Netmarble Games, NCSoft, and Celltrion), which clearly indicates the lingering dominance of the chaebol (see appendix A, table A.1).

Enthusiasm over start-ups was reignited when the Park Geun-hye administration announced a plan to move the country toward a "creative economy" in 2013. The plan recognized that the catch-up strategy of the past had reached its limits and called for a new growth model based on innovation and entrepreneurship. The existence of abundant vibrant high-tech start-ups came to be seen as a crucial indicator of a creative economy, and therefore constituted the focus of the government's policy. Once again, the government set out to promote start-ups and entrepreneurship throughout the country, using measures similar to those used in their previous attempt, often on a larger scale. These ranged from granting financial support and tax incentives to opening innovation hubs through the country to promoting entrepreneurship in universities. The Moon Jae-in administration (inaugurated in 2017) continued, and even furthered, this support for start-ups and entrepreneurship. No country in the world can match the Korean government's efforts, not to mention its determination, to promote start-ups. In fact, per capita, the country has the highest government backing of start-ups (Guttman 2018).

This chapter introduces and critically reviews the government's recent initiatives to finance and promote start-ups in Korea as well as the challenges it faces, the most notable of which is the dominance of the chaebol in the Korean economy. Recent promotional endeavors face the same challenges that made the government's efforts unsuccessful in previous attempts. The chaebol's sheer size, vertical integration, and diversified business portfolios serve as a hindrance to the formation of start-ups and a discouragement to entrepreneurship. For instance, large companies accounted for around three-fourths of private R&D investments, crowding out small- and medium-sized enterprises (SMEs). In addition, start-ups and SMEs have difficulties attracting talent. Graduates in Korea have traditionally been quite risk averse, preferring to work for big companies such as Samsung, LG, or Hyundai. Thus, it is quite challenging to promote start-ups under the shadow of big business.

We start with a brief overview of the government's programs to promote entrepreneurship, and then look at the roles played by the Korean government in financing start-ups via government venture capital and debt guarantee programs. Next, we turn to the capital markets and large corporations, which present opportunities for start-ups to exit or sell their equity to investors or another company. Finally, we conclude with an evaluation of the government's initiatives and public policy suggestions.

Overview of the Government's Programs for Entrepreneurship

Experts in Korea often jokingly say that initiating a new government program for entrepreneurship in Korea is impossible. The Korean government's entrepreneurship policies and programs have expanded considerably over the past two decades by benchmarking best practices from various countries (sometimes without evaluating and testing applicability). The number of entrepreneurship programs in Korea—both financial and nonfinancial—are estimated to be more than 180, and include almost every type of entrepreneurship policy and program designed by leading countries (Yang 2017). Indeed, entrepreneurs often struggle to choose the most appropriate program. The OECD has even pointed out the presence of "policy activism" in Korean innovation and entrepreneurship policy (OECD 2014).

The Korean government's steadfast support for entrepreneurship stems from its recognition that high-growth entrepreneurial firms are the driving force of economic growth, especially in employment. For example, according to the Job-to-Job Flows survey by Statistics Korea (2020), large corporations (employing 300 or more employees) cut 150,000 jobs in 2019, while small businesses (with fewer than 50 employees) created 2,510,000 jobs. Thus, although their slogans have varied slightly, all recent administrations have made the creation of start-ups a policy priority.

Within the government, the Ministry of SMEs and Start-ups (MSS), upgraded from the SMBA in 2017, bears primary responsibility for developing and implementing entrepreneurship policy. It supports the creation of start-ups, provides R&D support for SMEs, and plays a major role in financing entrepreneurial firms. It runs the Korea Fund of Funds (KFoF), the key financier of most Korean VC firms and various loan programs for SMEs. However, the Park Geun-hye administration's introduction of the so-called creative economy in 2013 changed this situation. Government departments other than the MSS also started developing their own entrepreneurial policies and programs in accordance with the "creative economy" initiative. For example, the Ministry of Science, Information, Communication, and Technology (MSIT) operates support programs for start-ups related to information and communication technology; the Ministry of Culture, Sports, and Tourism incubates and funds culture- or tourism-related start-ups; and the Ministry of Agriculture, Food, and Rural Affairs and the Korean Intellectual Property Office have similar industry-focused programs. The Ministry of Education (MoE) has also increased its budget for entrepreneurship education in schools, attempting to extend it to all students. Local governments have also become more active in developing regional entrepreneurship programs: 17 local governments spent ₩68.8 billion on such programs in 2017 (Park 2017).

Financial support for start-ups comes in three forms: subsidies,[1] loans, and credit guarantees. Korean start-ups received an estimated ₩750 billion in governmental subsidies in 2017. Government investment in the KFoF was around ₩300 billion, while government-issued direct loans reached ₩1,800 billion. Counting the nearly ₩21 trillion in government credit guarantees, the government's total entrepreneurship budget climbed as high as ₩24 trillion in 2017 (see table 10.1).

Many government departments utilize public agencies for policy implementation. For example, the MSS has 12 public agencies[2] and the Ministry of Agriculture, Food, and Rural Affairs (despite its small budget) has six agencies commissioned to run their entrepreneurship programs. Local governments are no exception to this trend: Daegu metropolitan city, for example, has five agencies that help local entrepreneurs. An estimated 75 such agencies operate in Korea. In addition to pointing out their lack of expertise, critics often highlight the

---

1   Subsidies can largely be categorized as venture creation grants, R&D subsidies, incubation subsidies, free education, and so on.
2   The largest is the Korean Institute of Start-up and Entrepreneurship Development.

TABLE 10.1 Government spending on entrepreneurship programs in 2017
(100 millions of Korean won)

	Subsidies	Loans	Investments	Total
Ministry of SMEs and Start-ups	5,484	17,500	2,650	25,634
Ministry of Science and ICT	676	400	—	1,076
Ministry of Education	301	—	120	421
Ministry of Culture, Sports and Tourism	72	—	—	72
Ministry of Agriculture, Food and Rural Affairs	17	—	120	137
Ministry of Employment and Labor	150	—	—	150
Korean Intellectual Property Office	82	—	—	82
Subtotal	6,782	17,900	2,890	27,572
Local government	688.5	—	—	688.5
Total	7,470.5	17,900	2,890	28,260.5

SOURCE: Ministry of SMEs and Start-ups (MSS) K-Startup website, www.k-startup.go.kr.

fragmentation of these agencies and programs as a source of redundancy and inefficiency. One recent report by the Board of Audit and Inspection of Korea (2017) illustrates that quite a few companies get support from different government agencies that offer very similar programs for start-ups. In particular, the MSIT and MSS offer a substantial number of duplicate programs. The audit report also pointed out that the output and outcomes of these programs are not systematically collected and analyzed, and are often exaggerated or erroneous.

Korean lawmakers have actively legislated entrepreneurship policies. Table 10.2 summarizes the related laws and relevant government departments. The "Act on Special Measures for the Promotion of Venture Businesses," established in 1997 in an attempt to cope with the Asian financial crisis of the late 1990s, provided an overarching framework for government policies and programs promoting start-ups and entrepreneurship. It provides a legal basis for promoting venture capital in the country and enables government funds to contribute to VC funds. The act also provides fast tracks for start-ups (called "venture businesses" in the act) in establishment, stock issue, and mergers. The act's most prominent benefit is tax reduction and exemption—along with the Restriction of Special Taxation Act, it reduces income and corporate tax for start-ups. Investors in start-ups and VC funds also get generous tax credits. The act also supports the employment of talented people in start-ups, such as university faculty and public researchers. Some employees are even exempt from mandatory military service, a perk that has been a strong magnet drawing young Korean males to start-ups.

TABLE 10.2 Key government acts related to entrepreneurship policy (by ministry)

Act	Focus
Ministry of SMEs and Start-ups	
Support for Small and Medium Enterprise Establishment Act (1986)	Nascent start-ups and small- and medium-sized enterprises (SMEs)
Act on Special Measures for the Promotion of Venture Businesses (1997)	
Act on Support for Female-owned Businesses (1999)	
Special Act on Support for Human Resources of Small and Medium Enterprises (2003)	
Act on the Facilitation of Entrepreneurial Activities of Persons with Disabilities (2005)	
Act on the Fostering of Self-employed Creative Enterprises (2011)	
Ministry of Trade, Industry, and Energy	
Industrial Technology Innovation Promotion Act (1995)	Technology transfer to start-ups
Technology Transfer and Commercialization Promotion Act (2000)	
Industrial Convergence Promotion Act (2011)	
Ministry of Science and ICT	
Software Industry Promotion Act (1988)	Research and development support for high-tech start-ups
Framework Act on Science and Technology (2001)	
Special Act on Support of Scientists and Engineers for Strengthening National Science and Technology Competitiveness (2004)	
Special Act on Promotion of Special Research and Development Zones (2005)	
Special Act on Promotion of Information and Communications (2013)	
Ministry of Education	
Industrial Education Enhancement and Industry-Academia-Research Cooperation Promotion Act (1963)	Education for entrepreneurs
Ministry of Strategy and Finance	
Restriction of Special Taxation Act (2006)	Tax benefits for investors and start-ups

SOURCE: Park 2017, revised.

Equity Financing and Government Venture Capital

Korean media and policymakers often lament the difficulties entrepreneurs face in acquiring equity financing, and petition for improvements. However, though Korean start-ups are heavily dependent on
debt financing, this should be interpreted as an indicator of the ease

FIGURE 10.1   Venture capital investments as percentage of GDP, 2017

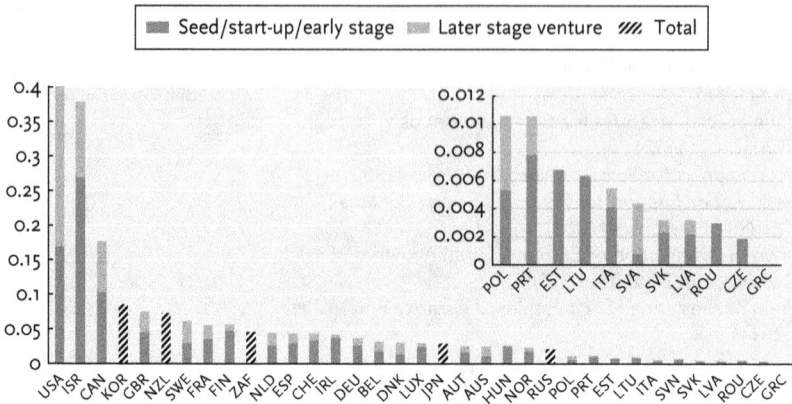

NOTE: Percentage in 2017 or latest available year.
SOURCE: OECD 2018a.

with which they can access debt financing rather than a symptom of an underdeveloped equity financing market. In fact, Korea actually ranks among the countries with the highest volume of VC investment per GDP (see figure 10.1).

The market failure rationale has made government support of venture capital a common phenomenon in many countries. To be more specific, three basic presumptions justify government support for entrepreneurship: (1) the existence of significant market failure in the innovation process leads to insufficient innovation; (2) innovators are capital constrained and would innovate more if they could access more financing; and (3) providing support to venture capitalists is an effective method of increasing innovation financing (Brander, Du, and Hellmann 2015). Korean policymakers generally agree with these presumptions, and the government has therefore played a crucial role in providing entrepreneurs with equity financing.

As early as in the mid-1970s, the Korean government started to establish government VC institutions: the Korean Technology Advancement Corporation in 1974, the Korea Technology Development Corporation in 1982, the Korea Development Investment Corporation in 1982, and the Korea Technology Finance Corporation in 1984. In establishing these institutions (with their confusingly similar names), the government aimed to promote the commercialization of technology

developed in government research organizations such as the Korea Institute of Science and Technology. They were thus dubbed "technology
finance" institutions rather than venture capital institutions, although
they provided venture capital for technology entrepreneurs.

Two laws enacted in 1986 facilitated the rise of private VC firms
in Korea: the Small and Medium-Size Enterprise Start-up Support
(SMESS) Act and the New Technology Enterprise Financial Support
(NTEFS) Act. They provided the legal basis for the establishment and
operation of VC firms, and five years after their enactment, the number
of VC firms reached 50. However, most VC firms at that time were not
very active in equity financing, and preferred safe loans to start-ups
over equity investment. Not until the enactment of the Act on Special
Measures for the Promotion of Venture Businesses in 1997, which included various tax benefits for VC investors, did VC firms begin actively investing in start-ups. The KOSDAQ market (the Korean version
of the NASDAQ) opened that same year and the government continued introducing strong policies to support VC firms, including pension
fund investment in private VC funds and direct government investment
in VC funds. All these efforts led to Korea's first VC boom. In early
2000, Korea was home to more than 160 VC firms, with investments
exceeding ₩2 trillion. However, the so-called IT bubble soon ended
the boom; in 2004, after the bubble burst, only about 90 VC firms remained with total investments of less than ₩600 billion.

The year 2005 witnessed substantial changes in policy-level support
for venture capitalists, which aimed not only at boosting the feeble VC
industry but also at dramatically improving the efficiency of government investment. The government also launched the KFoF, which integrated all government VC assets as well as assets invested in private VC
funds. Figure 10.2 illustrates the structure of the KFoF.

Government departments are the main investors in the KFoF—depending on their policy goals, they commit certain portions of their
budgets to it. For example, the MOE committed ₩12 billion in 2017
to support its mission of university entrepreneurship (the committed
money is called an "account"). The Korea Venture Investment Corporation (KVIC), a public investment company, manages the KFoF as the
general partner. Since the KFoF is a fund of funds, the KVIC needs to
select funds to invest in. Rather than investing in established funds, the
KVIC usually invests in new VC funds that follow a certain investment
policy as suggested by the KVIC. In most cases, therefore, VC firms
submit investment proposals to the KVIC that fit the policy goals of

FIGURE 10.2 Organization and operation of the Korean Fund of Funds (KFoF)

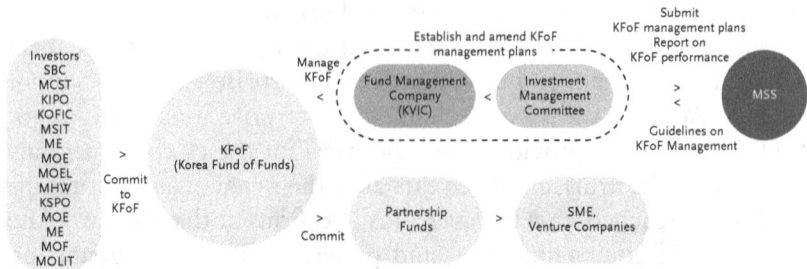

NOTE: KIPO = Korean Intellectual Property Office; KOFIC = Korean Film Council; KSPO = Korea Sports Promotion Foundation; MCST = Ministry of Culture, Sports, and Tourism; ME = Ministry of Environment; MHW = Ministry of Health and Welfare; MOE = Ministry of Education; MOEL = Ministry of Employment and Labor; MOF = Ministry of Finance; MOLIT = Ministry of Land, Infrastructure and Transport; MSIT = Ministry of Science, Information, Communication, and Technology; MSS = Ministry of SMEs and Startups; SBC = Small & Medium Business Corporation; SME = small- and medium-sized enterprise. SOURCE: Korea Venture Investment Corporation (KVIC) website.

each account. For example, the KVIC has selected three VC firms to manage partnership funds investing in university entrepreneurship and committed the MOE account (₩12 billion) to these funds. The KFoF's assets under management reached an estimated ₩4 trillion in 2018.

Almost all Korean VC firms rely heavily on public money for fundraising, which could be interpreted both as a policy success and as a manifestation of the lack of private funding in the VC market. The public funding to VC funds is over 40 percent[3]—two-thirds is contributed by the KFoF,[4] while the Korean Development Bank and the Growth Ladder Fund are other key sources. As of May 2018, Korea was home to 120 VC firms with 737 VC funds, having an estimated ₩21 trillion of total assets under management. VC fundraising has grown by ₩1 trillion each year (₩2.6 trillion in 2015, ₩3.5 trillion in 2016, and ₩4.5 trillion in 2017). This high growth of VC funds has driven recent active investment (as figure 10.3 shows), which exceeded ₩4 trillion in 2019.

---

3   Public funding to VC funds was 46 percent in 2015, and 43 percent in 2016 (Asan Nanum Foundation 2017).

4   KFoF contribution was 30 percent in 2015 and 31 percent in 2016 (Korean Venture Capital Association 2017b).

FIGURE 10.3 Venture capital investment, 2014–19

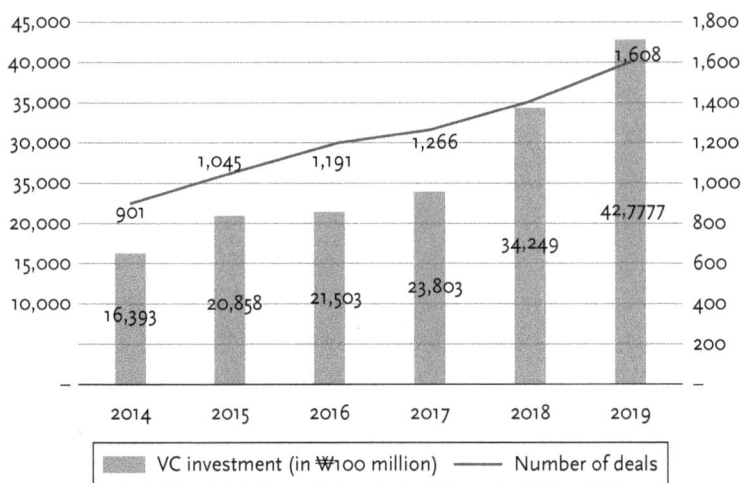

SOURCE: Korean Venture Capital Association 2020.

TABLE 10.3 Top five start-up investment deals in 2019

	Start-up	Type	Funding raised (billions won)	Investor type
1	Wemakeprice	E-commerce	470	Mixed: Corporate (Nexon), venture capital (IMM)
2	Yanolja	Accommodation online-to-offline (O2O)	213	Mixed: Singaporean sovereign wealth fund (GIC), corporation (Booking Holdings)
3	Musinsa	E-commerce	200	Foreign venture capital (Sequoia Capital)
4	Carplat	Car sharing/rental	200	Mixed: Corporate (Humax), private equity (Stic investment)
5	Zigbang	Real estate	160	Mixed: Financial investor (Goldman Sachs PIA), private equity (Stonebridge, DS, etc.)

SOURCE: Venture Square 2020, revised.

However, these VC statistics do not capture the full complexity of the current entrepreneurial equity market. Various types of investors have started participating in start-up investment, with the largest deals being led by non-VC investors. The top five deals in 2019 were led by private equity firms, tech giants, and foreign investors (see table 10.3). This is part of a global phenomenon: as the size of start-up investment

FIGURE 10.4 Growth of angel funds, 2009–18 (billions of Korean won, accumulated)

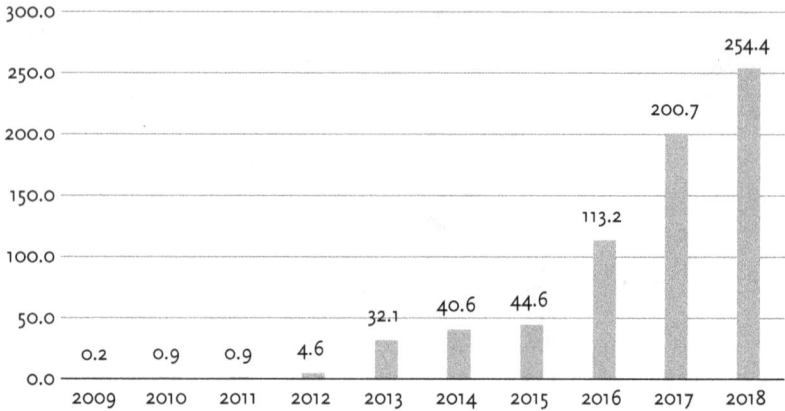

SOURCE: Korean Venture Capital Association 2019.

grows,[5] private equity firms and tech giants often lead the deals while VC firms increase their fund sizes as well. As is often pointed out, however, there are few non-VC investors.

A weak point of entrepreneurial finance in Korea is its lack of informal investors, such as angel investors. These play an important role in seed and very-early-stage equity financing, since overly small deals are not profitable for VC firms that must follow a formal process (with costs). Before 2012, there were almost no informal investors in Korea. The government therefore increased the income deduction for angel investment from 10 percent in 2010 to 50 percent in 2014, and also introduced the angel matching fund (a passive matching fund for angel investors) in 2013.[6] As a result, the accumulated size of angel funds rose to over ₩250 billion in 2018 (see figure 10.4).

---

5   The mean size of a deal doubles every five years in the United States: $7 million (2013) to $14 million (2017) for series B; $12 million (2013) to $22 million (2017) for series D (KPMG Enterprise 2018).
6   Since the angel matching fund provides a call option to angel investors, the return of angel investors may substantially increase.

Debt Financing and Government Loan Guarantees

SMEs in Korea depend heavily on debt financing. Total borrowing of SMEs from banks increased, although slowly, to over ₩650 trillion as of May 2018. Meanwhile, despite a recent spurt in growth, equity financing of SMEs was only about ₩3.2 trillion in 2017. Although high leveraged growth, a recipe once adopted by Korean conglomerates, was found to be very risky during the Asian financial crisis of the late 1990s, many Korean SMEs still rely heavily on debt financing. This is often explained by the relatively inefficient equity market and the strong government policy of fueling loans to SMEs.

As shown in figure 10.5, the volume of direct loans from government agencies is around ₩10 trillion each year, and is mostly directed toward small SMEs and early-stage start-ups. The two key government agencies responsible for this are the Korea SMEs and Startups Agency and the Korean Development Bank.

However, one of the government's major policies has been the adoption of loan guarantee programs to finance start-ups and SMEs. A

FIGURE 10.5 Policy direct loans, 2011–17 (in trillions of Korean won)

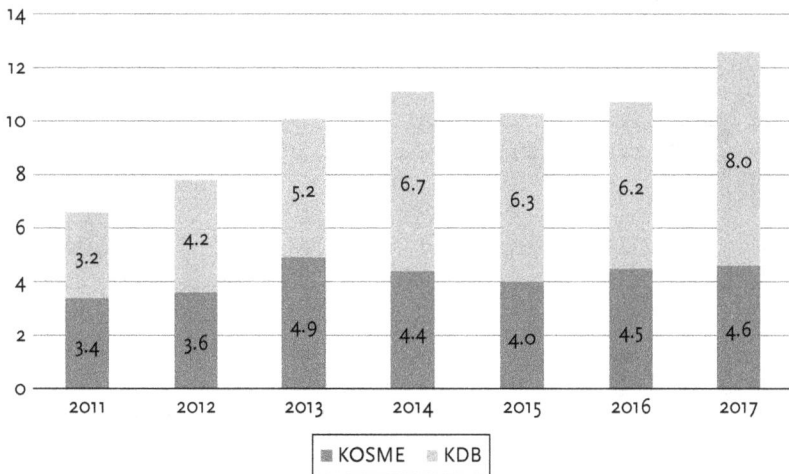

NOTE: KOSME = Korea SMEs and Startups Agency; KDB = Korean Development Bank.
SOURCE: KOSME and KDB websites.

recent OECD report (2018a) ranked Korea as providing the second-largest (as a percentage of GDP) loan guarantees for SMEs, second only to Japan (see figure 10.6). However, the report did not include the credit guarantees provided by local governments. If this is counted, Korea could well be regarded as the most generous country in terms of guaranteeing loans for SMEs (see figure 10.7).

There are three major loan guarantee agencies in Korea: the Korea Credit Guarantee Fund (KODIT), which provides loan guarantees to banks for SMEs with high credit yet insufficient collateral; the Korea Technology Finance Corporation (KOTEC), which guarantees loans to SMEs with high technology potential; and local credit guarantee foundations (LCGFs), which provide guarantees for local SMEs. However, their programs have become increasingly similar, calling into question their proprietary roles.

The credit guarantee and loan process is illustrated in figure 10.8. The particular case shown is that of KODIT, but the same process applies to the other agencies. It is possible for banks to reject a guarantee or require further collateral from a debtor, since a government loan guarantee does not necessarily cover 100 percent of the loan. However, the government has strongly advised banks against doing this.

FIGURE 10.6 Government loan guarantees for SMEs in selected countries, as percentage of GDP, 2016

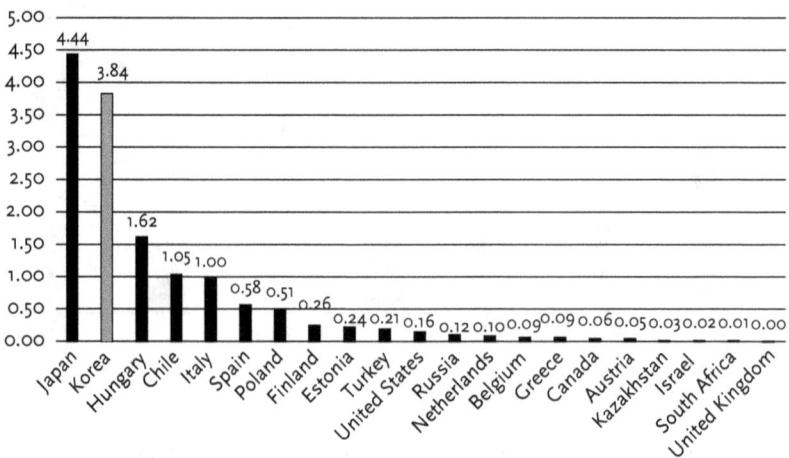

SOURCE: OECD 2018b.

FIGURE 10.7 Loan guarantees by government agencies, 2008–17 (trillions of Korean won)

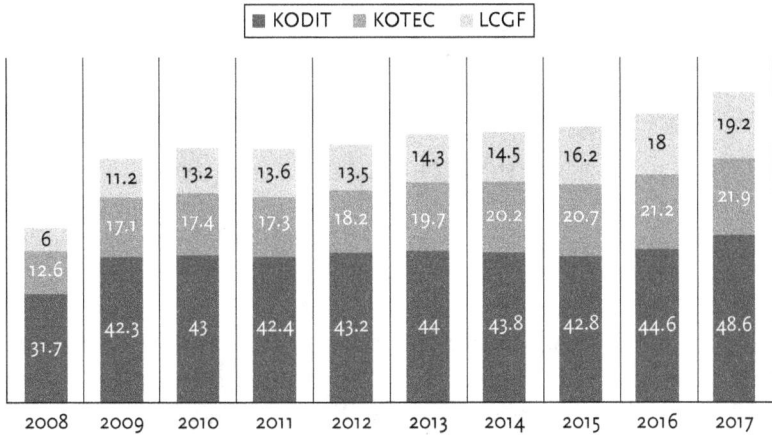

NOTE: KODIT = Korea Credit Guarantee Fund; KOTEC = Korea Technology Finance Corporation; LCGF = local credit guarantee foundation.
SOURCE: e-Nara Index website.

FIGURE 10.8 Credit guarantee process

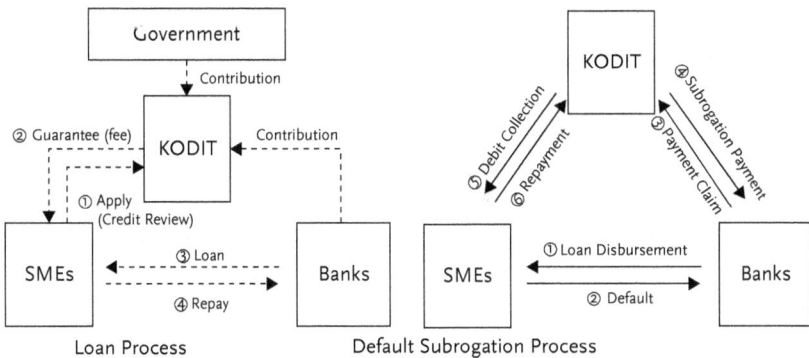

NOTE: KODIT = Korea Credit Guarantee Fund; SMEs = small- and medium-sized enterprises.
SOURCE: KODIT website.

This abundant supply of credit guarantees for SMEs and start-ups, and easy accessibility and availability of loans, has been criticized as a source of financial market distortion that weakens the equity finance market. In light of this criticism, the two credit agencies, KODIT and KOTEC, have recently started to invest in the start-ups that they guarantee.[7]

Capital Markets for Start-ups

One of the biggest problems that persists in the Korean start-up ecosystem is the lack of attractive exit options. Although a successful exit allows entrepreneurs and investors (e.g., venture capitalists) to "harvest" the value that has been created and foster a culture that rewards risk taking, the reality is that very few Korean start-ups are able to exit through initial public offerings (IPOs) or mergers and acquisitions (M&As). According to the Korean Venture Capital Association (2017b), only 3.1 percent of VC-backed start-ups exited through acquisitions in 2016. Others state that "hardly any Korean start-up" exits through an M&A (McKinsey & Company 2015, 14) compared with the United States, where the proportion is as high as 86 percent. As a result, Korean start-ups rely heavily on IPOs rather than M&As as an exit option, even though an IPO itself is not an easily accessible exit strategy.

Although more than half of the firms that are able to go public are in fact VC backed (see table 10.4), it takes an average of 13.3 years to reach an IPO in Korea compared with only 6.8 years in the United States (McKinsey & Company 2015, 14). This is not surprising given that start-ups often have difficulty satisfying KOSDAQ's tight listing requirements (viewed as excessive and detrimental to the growth of start-ups), even though the secondary market was created in 1996 in order to support financing for SMEs and start-ups. In particular, the requirement of continuous profitability is considered a major hindrance for start-ups looking to go public (see table 10.5). If a company is certified by the Korea Venture Business Association as a "venture company" the requirements are lowered, but the burden of presenting proof of profitability remains the same. Thus, the irony is that while government policy has helped boost VC investments in start-ups, venture capitalists

---

7   This is referred to as a guarantee-linked investment.

TABLE 10.4 KOSDAQ listing status, 2010–19

	Total listed firms	New listings	VC-backed firms (among new listings)
2010	1,029	50	32 (64.00%)
2011	1,031	55	37 (67.27%)
2012	1,005	20	14 (70.00%)
2013	1,009	34	26 (76.47%)
2014	1,061	40	26 (65.00%)
2015	1,152	57	46 (80.70%)
2016	1,209	48	33 (68.75%)
2017	1,267	78	40 (51.28%)
2018	1,323	90	47 (52.22%)
2019	1,405	97	53 (54.64%)

NOTE: Excludes re-listings and special-purpose acquisition companies (SPACs). Years 2017–19 include all IPO firms. IPO =initial public offering; VC = venture capital.
SOURCE: Korea Venture Capital Association 2014, 2017a, 2020.

TABLE 10.5 KOSDAQ listing requirements for continuous profitability

	General company	Venture company[a]
1. Return on equity	Higher than 10 percent	Higher than 5 percent
2. Net income	Greater than ₩2 billion	Greater than ₩1 billion
3. Sales amount and total market capitalization	Sales amount: greater than ₩10 billion Total market capitalization:[b] greater than ₩30 billion	Sales amount: greater than ₩5 billion Total market capitalization:[b] greater than ₩30 billion
4. Sales growth (for sales greater than ₩5 billion)	Higher than 20 percent	

NOTE: Companies must be able to satisfy one of the above four criteria.
[a]Companies that are certified by the Korean Venture Capital Association.
[b]Total market capitalization = price for public offering-number of stocks to be listed.
SOURCE: Global KRX (global.krx.co.kr) website.

are often unable to obtain returns on their investments through profitable exits.

Recognizing that in the initial stages of development it is difficult for start-ups to generate profits, the Korean government has been trying to foster a more active IPO market by curtailing regulatory barriers for early-stage start-ups. The aim of financial authorities is to lower the bar for start-ups that are looking to raise funds through capital markets, even if they are not yet profitable. Since 2005, a fast-track program allows firms that pass technology capability assessments conducted by multiple professional appraisal agencies to be listed in the KOSDAQ market as "growth technology companies." By the end of November 2018, 61 firms had been listed through this program, 51 of which were

FIGURE 10.9 Number of IPOs in the KOSDAQ market through the Technology Evaluation Fast-Track Program, 2005–19

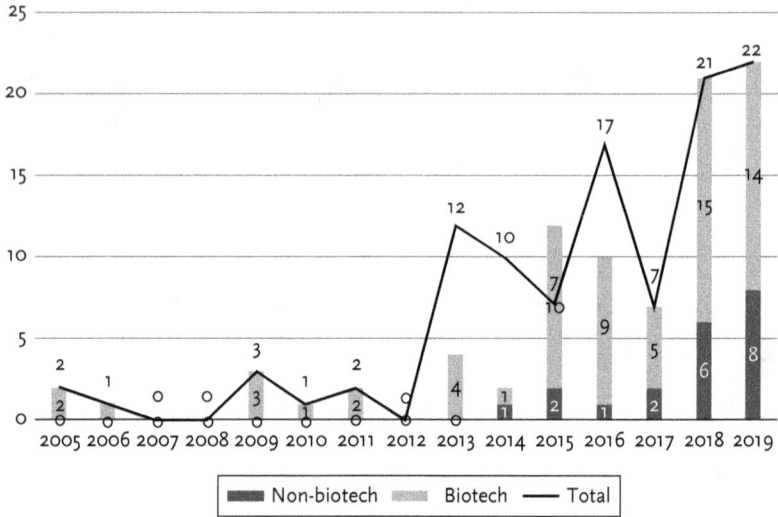

SOURCE: Kim 2020.

biopharmaceutical firms (see figure 10.9). This program has been especially popular among biotech firms because the industry requires a long-term perspective when making R&D investments. However, this is raising concerns regarding excessive valuations in the biopharmaceutical industry (Song 2017). For instance, in 2017, 70.7 percent of all listed biopharmaceutical firms enjoyed a growth in stock prices (Nam 2018), and the Korea Exchange's Health Care Index and the KOSDAQ Pharmaceuticals Index jumped by 96.5 percent and 123.3 percent, respectively (Han and Han 2018). Considering that this phenomenon in the biopharmaceutical industry is not globally ubiquitous,[8] there are serious concerns that this stock price growth may be indicative of a bubble due to overvaluations (Choi 2018). Such concerns may be reasonable given that, while regular firms listed on KOSDAQ are forced to be delisted from the market if they are unprofitable for five consecutive years, firms listed through the technology evaluation fast-track program receive an exemption.

---

8   The Nasdaq Biotechnology Index increased only by 8.8 percent during 2017.

In response to the criticism that innovative start-ups may have diffi-culty passing the technology evaluations and yet still have high growth potential, the government has recently introduced an additional policy to facilitate new listings on KOSDAQ. The initial fast-track program required firms to receive one grade higher than A and one higher than BBB from two technology assessment institutions, which was consid-ered to be an excessively tough requirement. In 2016, the Financial Services Commission announced plans to lower KOSDAQ's listing requirements. Under the new so-called Tesla standard, tech start-ups that are not yet profitable are able to raise capital via the KOSDAQ market to fund their future growth without having to pass any tech-nology evaluation processes. Start-ups that are recommended by in-vestment banks for securities firms will be evaluated in terms of their growth potential and IPO advisors must grant a "put-back option" to protect general investors, who can exercise the option within three months of the IPO date.[9] The initiative was implemented in January 2017 and the first firm to go public under this special policy did so in February 2018.[10]

Moreover, a third stock exchange called the Korea New Exchange (KONEX) opened on July 1, 2013, as part of a government initiative to facilitate IPOs of young start-ups not yet mature enough to be listed on either the main market or the secondary KOSDAQ market.[11] Num-bers show that the KONEX market seems to have helped ease financ-

---

9   The exercise of the put-back option requires the underwriter to purchase stocks from investors if the stock price of firms that went public under the "Tesla stan-dard" falls below 90 percent of the IPO price. In January 2018, the government an-nounced that underwriters will receive exemptions from the put-back option either if (1) the underwriter has previous experience in such listings where the listed firm has not experienced a share price decline below 90 percent of its IPO price within the first three months following its listing, or (2) the listed firm has transferred from the third-tier KONEX market.

10   In February 2018, Cafe24 became the first company to be listed on KOSDAQ despite not meeting the profitability requirement. Founded in 1999, Cafe24 had posted operating losses between 2012 and 2016. To be listed on KOSDAQ, com-panies were required to meet either one of the following requirements for profit-ability: (1) an annual net profit above ₩2 billion, or (2) a return on equity (ROE) above 10 percent.

11   As a result, there are currently four markets that are governed by the Korea Exchange: Korea Composite Stock Price Index (KOSPI), KOSDAQ, KONEX, and the derivatives market.

ing difficulties for early-stage start-ups. Its market capitalization grew from ₩558 billion in July 2013 to ₩6.23 trillion in December 2018. By the end of 2018, a total of 153 firms were listed on the KONEX market and 44 firms had obtained funds successfully and "graduated" by transferring to the KOSDAQ market.[12] On average, it took 1.8 years to transfer to the KOSDAQ market.

The Role of Large Corporations

Until recently, large corporations have played a relatively minor role in the newly emerging start-up ecosystem—they have been inactive in acquiring start-ups and making corporate VC investments. Large corporations in Korea are among the most vertically integrated in the world as they have traditionally been reluctant to absorb knowledge, ideas, and technologies from the outside. Yet, the reason behind their lack of participation in the current start-up ecosystem is more complex. While some argue that large corporations have a responsibility to repay society for the privileges that they have received by making active investments, others are more skeptical and perceive that their concentrated economic power could stifle entrepreneurship in the country (OECD 2018b). Large corporations fear that unfavorable public sentiment has also led to the risk of M&As being viewed as predatory and infringing on the rights of the target firms (Kim 2017). The weakly developed M&A exit market can also be partially attributed to their lack of participation.

In fact, government regulations have traditionally aimed to ensure that large corporations do not hinder fair and free competition and to rein in chaebol dominance over the Korean economy. As a result, government regulations play a role in obstructing large corporations' role in the start-up ecosystem. For example, the principle of separation of banking and commerce, espoused in the Monopoly Regulation and Fair Trade Act, currently dictates that a large corporation, if it is structured in the form of a holding company, cannot operate a corporate VC firm as an affiliated company under its corporate umbrella. Since the current law recognizes a corporate VC firm as a financial company,

---

12 Firms listed on the KONEX market can transfer to the KOSDAQ market through the following four paths: (1) the special provision for "technology growth companies," (2) fast track, (3) ordinary listing, and (4) special purpose acquisition company (SPAC) merger.

large corporations are banned from operating corporate VC firms to invest in innovative start-ups.

Nevertheless, large corporations have begun engaging more in the start-up ecosystem. First, they are now starting to acquire domestic start-ups, whereas in earlier years they had largely focused on high-potential foreign start-ups. In November 2017, Samsung Electronics made its first acquisition within the domestic start-up ecosystem. Fluenty, the first Korean start-up to be acquired by the largest electronics maker in the country, was founded in 2015 and was a participant in Samsung's start-up incubation program. Other acquisitions have mostly been executed by IT firms (e.g., Kakao, Naver) founded during the start-up boom of the late 1990s and the early 2000s. For now, there still seems to be a long way to go before the chaebol can be considered active participants in the M&A market for start-ups.

Second, large corporations are becoming more active in corporate VC activities, establishing their own incubation programs for nurturing their employees' ideas in order to support their commercialization and eventually to create independent start-ups through spin-offs. Examples include Venture Plaza, launched by the Hyundai Motor Group in 2000;[13] Creative Square, run by Samsung Electronics' mobile communication division since 2016;[14] and more recently, SK Hynix's HiGarage, which started in 2018. Since 2012, Samsung Electronics has also been running an in-house start-up incubator program called Creative Labs (C-Lab) in which its employees are encouraged to develop their own ideas.[15] At the same time, large corporations are slowly becoming more open to—and recognizing the value of—seeking outside knowledge residing in start-ups. Companies are establishing open innovation programs in which they are not only investing directly in start-ups but also actively engaging in collaborative projects. For instance, Hyundai Cradle (formerly, Hyundai Ventures), located in Silicon Valley, is the corporate VC and open innovation business of the Hyundai Motor Group, and SK Telecom established True Innovation in 2017. These changes in the relationship between the traditional chaebol and the

---

13   As of May 2020, it was running 53 in-house start-ups and had successfully created 16 spin-off start-ups.

14   By July 2018, 25 start-ups in the mobile communications industry had been launched.

15   A spin-off initiative for projects with high commercialization potential was added in August 2015. As of May 2020, 45 start-ups had been created through C-Lab.

start-ups are raising hopes for synergies that will benefit the whole ecosystem.

Discussion and Conclusions

Start-ups in Korea have been very actively supported by various government programs. Strong government intervention in entrepreneurship may be traced back to the successful industrial policies of the high-growth era. The founders of the chaebol were serial entrepreneurs who recognized new opportunities and mobilized resources, in collaboration with the government and also on their own. The early success of industrialization and the rise of the chaebol could be attributed, to a large degree, to the entrepreneurship of both the businesspeople involved and the government. Government intervention and support are necessary to overcome the market failures associated with the formation and growth of start-ups, just as they were required to address the problems of underdeveloped capital, labor, and product markets at the beginning of industrialization in Korea. Amsden (1997) therefore refers to the Korean economy as one of "state entrepreneurial capitalism," as compared to the personal capitalism of Britain, the competitive managerial capitalism of the United States, or the cooperative managerial capitalism of Germany.

To create jobs and rejuvenate the economy, long dominated by the chaebol, the government has been aggressive in promoting start-ups and entrepreneurship through many public entities and programs. This has made the start-up ecosystem bigger and better: in 2018, VC investment hit a record high of ₩3.4 trillion, surging 43.9 percent from that of 2017 (Kim 2019). There are around 140 accelerators, 60 percent of which were launched in 2018 partly due to government initiatives. All these efforts have produced some promising outcomes. In 2018, the amount of VC exits reached another record high of ₩2.6 trillion, a 49.1 percent increase from the previous year. Now Korea is a home to several unicorns: Woowa Brothers, Crafton (formerly Bluehole), Yello Mobile, L&P Cosmetic, Big Hit Entertainment, Viva Republica, and Coupang, with more unicorns on the way.[16]

---

16 Woowa Brothers operates the mobile delivery service app Baedal Minjok; Crafton is the developer of the survival game Battlegrounds; Yello Mobile is a mobile business platform operating in shopping, media content, travel, marketing and advertising, and O2O business; L&P Cosmetic is a maker of beauty products; Big

Nonetheless, the government's efforts have been subject to some criticism. To start with, there are an excessive number of public entities (77 agencies) with many fragmented and sometimes duplicated programs (over 180). In addition to inefficiencies and redundancies, too many government initiatives and subsidies might distort and even crowd out private incentives for and investments in start-ups and entrepreneurship. It might allow uncompetitive start-ups to survive, hindering the growth of prominent start-ups. These marginal start-ups might be more interested in securing additional subsidies than developing innovative products, services, and business models. Some of the incubators, accelerators, or advisory services that are being fed by governmental subsidies have not been serious in attracting, nurturing, and profiting from client start-ups. While acknowledging the importance of government intervention for catalyzing the virtuous circle for start-ups and entrepreneurship, the question of how the role of government should evolve as the roles of the private sector expand should be revisited.

Observers have repeatedly pointed out that the amount of the government's credit guarantee is too large, and has even increased slightly in recent years. At the beginning of the industrialization process, the government controlled the banks and tunneled bank loans to select entrepreneurs to finance national development projects. The government now appears to be employing a similar approach to nurture start-ups. Political pressure has also been a factor, with every presidential candidate promising to increase government support to SMEs. The easy credit guarantee, however, may lead to a moral hazard problem for Korean banks, as they have little incentive to deepen their credit assessment and risk management capabilities. This problem was predicted by contract theory (Chiappori and Salanié 2000) and has been empirically tested in the Japanese context (Saito and Daisuke 2014). A recent empirical study (Liang et al. 2017) found potential traces of moral hazard among Korean banks with government-guaranteed loans. Since it is very easy to get loans, start-ups are often highly leveraged rather than invested in, hindering the start-up investment community and increasing the personal credit risk for entrepreneurs. Under the strict bankruptcy laws in Korea, entrepreneurs still have to repay the amount owed to credit agencies after the banks get paid by the agencies, which is why it is hard for them to recover from failures and move on to

---

Hit Entertainment is the agency behind the boy band BTS; Viva Republica operates the money transfer service "Toss"; and Coupang is an e-commerce platform.

other ventures. The transition from debt financing to equity financing has been a primary focus of the entrepreneurship policy, but has not actively gone forward.

It is undeniable that the KFoF has played a key role in providing equity finance for start-ups, especially during the stagnant period (2005–12) of VC investment. However, there is growing criticism of its rigid operation. First, there are doubts about whether the KFoF can balance policy goals and market situations. The KFoF generally seeks to contribute to the funds that fit into policy goals. Since it is exceedingly difficult to satisfy given policy goals and investment returns at the same time, private investors avoid participation in VC funds. The so-called *bottom-up* contribution may be one solution to this problem. For instance, instead of leading fundraising, the KFoF can only act as a passive limited partner to the VC funds designed to meet the market situation.

Second, experts believe that heavy reliance on the KFoF weakens the competitiveness of the Korean VC industry. Since it has been the easiest source of money for the industry, the KFoF's internal guidelines on fee structure and fund duration have become de facto standards in Korean VC funds, thereby homogenizing them. However, in recent years purely private VC funds have been formed, without the participation of the KFoF. This change has been led by leading venture capitalists with successful track records and a few foreign venture capitalists.

Many observers claim that government regulations are often too stringent, to the extent that entrepreneurship is actually discouraged and rendered less viable. The regulations render many innovative ideas and business models illegal or place them in gray areas. A study by McKinsey Korea suggests that approximately 40 percent of the top 100 global start-ups cannot operate in Korea, because they would be deemed illegal under the current regulatory framework (Asan Nanum Foundation 2017); another 30 percent would only be able to operate in the country on conditional terms. For example, Uber launched its operations in Korea in June 2013, but in March 2015 the government suspended its ride-sharing service, UberX. In April 2017, the court ruled that Uber Korea illegally used private vehicles for commercial purposes and issued a fine of ₩10 million ($8,800) for violating the Passenger Transport Service Act. The globally successful peer-to-peer holiday rentals service Airbnb is also restricted from operating in Korea due to the country's tough regulations, namely the Korean Lodging Act. Other examples of stringent regulations include limiting technology development in the domains of autonomous driving and flying drones. Such regulations need to be revisited and redesigned to facilitate innovative ideas and business models.

Another barrier to entrepreneurship is the lack of a start-up culture. Career aspirations of university graduates are still largely anchored in starting their careers in large corporations (e.g., Samsung, LG, Hyundai) that provide prestige or government institutions that provide job security. It is estimated that while 61 percent of Korean entrepreneurs have a bachelor's degree, only 3 percent hold PhD degrees (McKinsey & Company 2015). However, those with more advanced academic qualifications are even less willing to take risks and engage in entrepreneurial initiatives, especially because they are likely to attract more attention from large corporate recruiters. While change is slowly occurring, the prejudice that starting a career at Samsung Electronics is better than one at a start-up whose name is not as well known remains strong. According to the Global Entrepreneurship Monitor's Report (2018, 73), Korea's societal value of entrepreneurship (i.e., the extent to which entrepreneurship is considered a good career choice) ranks 49 out of a total of 52 countries in the report. It is therefore imperative to plant the seed of an entrepreneurial spirit in the younger generation as well as in society in general.

References

Amsden, Alice H. 1997. "Bringing Production Back In—Understanding Government's Economic Role in Late Industrialization." *World Development* 25 (4): 469–80.

Asan Nanum Foundation. 2017. *Startup Korea!* (Seoul: Asan Nanum Foundation, July 2017). https://asan-nanum.org/download/19031.

Board of Audit and Inspection of Korea. 2017. "Status Audit of Venture Business Support Programs." [In Korean.] https://www.bai.go.kr/bai/cop/bbs/detailBoardArticle.do;jsessionid=HIOfv8Txp5j7RUodZNULX2lu.node02?bbsId=BBSMSTR_10000000009&nttId=121147&pageIndex=1&tabOkFlag=&mdex=bai19.

Brander, James A., Qianqian Du, and Thomas F. Hellmann. 2015. "The Effect of Government-Sponsored Venture Capital: International Evidence." *Review of Finance* 19 (2): 571–618.

Chiappori, Pierre-Andre, and Bernard Salanié. 2000. "Testing for Asymmetric Information in Insurance Markets." *Journal of Political Economy* 108 (1): 56–78.

Choi, Mun-Hee. 2018. "Stock Market Experts Warn Biotech Bubble Will Burst Soon." *BusinessKorea*, April 19, 2018. http://www .businesskorea.co.kr/news/articleView.html?idxno=21741.

Global Entrepreneurship Monitor. 2018. *Global Report 2017/18*. London: Global Entrepreneurship Research Association. https:// www.gemconsortium.org/report/gem-2017-2018-global-report.

Guttman, Amy. 2018. "South Korea Triples Its Financial Commitment to Startups." *Forbes*, February 28, 2018. https://www.forbes .com/sites/amyguttman/2018/02/28/south-korea-triples-its-financial -commitment-to-startups/#54b29b8155fc.

Han, Byung Hwa, and Sang Woong Han. 2018. "Bio Bubble in the Small and Medium Capitalization Market, A Serious Harm to Market Integrity." [In Korean.] Eugene Investment & Securities Co., April 18, 2018.

Kim, Do-Nyun. 2017. "Korea Inc. Is Warming up to Local Start-Ups." *Korea Joongang Daily*, December 3, 2017. http://koreajoongangda ily.joins.com/news/article/article.aspx?aid=3041564.

Kim, Hicheon. 2010. "Business Groups in South Korea." In *The Oxford Handbook of Business Groups*, edited by Asli M. Colpan, Takashi Hikino, and James R. Lincoln, 157–79. Oxford: Oxford University Press.

Kim, Hicheon, Robert E. Hoskisson, Laszlo Tihanyi, and Jaebum Hong. 2004. "The Evolution and Restructuring of Diversified Business Groups in Emerging Markets: The Lessons from Chaebols in Korea." *Asia Pacific Journal of Management* 21 (1–2): 25–48.

Kim, Kyu-Rhee. 2020. "15 Years Since the Adoption of Kosdaq's Technology Evaluation Fast-Track. . . Successful Scale-Up, Inadequate Qualitative Growth." [In Korean.] *Maeil Economy*, January 19, 2020. https://www.mk.co.kr/news/stock/view/2020/01/60808/.

Kim, Young-Won. 2019. "Korea, Always in Search of the Next Unicorn." *Korea Herald*, January 31, 2019. http://www.koreaherald .com/view.php?ud=20190131000831.

Korean Venture Capital Association. 2014. "Venture Capital Market Brief (October 2014)." http://www.kvca.or.kr/Program/board/ listbody.html?a_gb=board&a_cd=15&a_item=0&sm=4_1&page =1&po_no=1231.

———. 2017a. "Venture Capital Market Brief (December 2017)." http://www.kvca.or.kr/Program/board/listbody.html?a_gb=board& a_cd=15&a_item=0&sm=4_1&page=1&po_no=4706.

———. 2017b. "2017 KVCA Yearbook & Directory."

———. 2019. "2019 KVCA Yearbook & Directory."

———. 2020. "Venture Capital Market Brief (June 2020)." [In Korean.] http://www.kvca.or.kr/Program/board/listbody.html?a_gb=board&a_cd=15&a_item=0&sm=4_1&page=1&po_no=5449.

KPMG Enterprise. 2018. *Venture Pulse Q1'18: Global Analysis of Venture Funding.* https://home.kpmg/xx/en/home/insights/2018/04/venture-pulse-q1-18-global-analysis-of-venture-funding.html.

Liang, Lien-Wen, Bor-Yi Huang, Chih-Feng Liao, and Yu-Ting Gao. 2017. "The Impact of SMEs' Lending and Credit Guarantee on Bank Efficiency in South Korea." *Review of Development Finance* 7 (2): 134–41.

McKinsey & Company. 2015. *The Virtuous Circle: Putting Korea's Startup Ecosystem on a Path to Sustainable Long-Run Growth.* https://www.mckinsey.com/featured-insights/asia-pacific/virtuous-cycle.

Nam, Doo-Hyun. 2018. "70% of Biotech Firms Enjoy Stock Price Gains in 2017." *Korea Biomedical Review*, January 2, 2018. http://www.koreabiomed.com/news/articleView.html?idxno=2250.

OECD (Organization for Economic Cooperation and Development). 2014. "Industry and Technology Policies in Korea." OECD Publishing, Paris.

———. 2018a. *Entrepreneurship at a Glance 2018.* Paris: OECD Publishing.

———. 2018b. *Financing SMEs and Entrepreneurs 2018.* Paris: OECD Publishing.

———. 2018c. *OECD Economic Surveys: Korea.* Paris: OECD Publishing.

Park, Jae Young. 2017. "Policy Directions to Revitalize Entrepreneurship." [In Korean.] National Assembly Research Service, December 1, 2017. https://www.nars.go.kr/report/view.do?cmsCode=CM0155&brdSeq=22054.

Saito, Kuniyoshi, and Tsuruta Daisuke. 2014. "Information Asymmetry in SME Credit Guarantee Schemes: Evidence from Japan." RIETI Discussion Paper Series 14-E-042, Research Institute of Economy, Trade and Industry, Japan, July 2014.

Song, Jung-A. 2017. "Kosdaq On a Run But Its Problems Go Deep." *Financial Times*, November 21, 2017. https://www.ft.com/content/1f43c95c-ce7e-11e7-b781-794ce08b24dc.

Statistics Korea. 2020. "Job-to-Job Flows in 2019." http://kostat.go.kr/portal/eng/pressReleases/5/1/index.board?bmode=read&bSeq

=&aSeq=390165&pageNo=1&rowNum=10&navCount=10&
    currPg=&searchInfo=&sTarget=title&sTxt=.
Venture Square. 2020. "Startup Investment Report 2019." [In
    Korean.] Venture Square, February 10, 2020. https://www
    .venturesquare.net/801809.
Yang, Hyunbong. 2017. "Current State and Measures to Improve
    Efficiency of the Startup Policy." [In Korean.] i-KIET Policy and
    Economics Issues, November 11, 2017. http://www.kiet.re.kr/
    kiet_web/index.jsp?sub_num=9&ord=0&pageNo=6&state=view&
    idx=53729.

Appendix A

Rank	Company	Industry	Year established*	Market value (billions US$)
1	Samsung Electronics	Semiconductors	1969	297.88
2	SK Hynix	Semiconductors	1949	55.80
3	Celltrion	Biopharmaceutical	1999	35.79
4	Samsung Biologics	Biologics	2011	30.38
5	Hyundai Motor	Automotive	1967	29.80
6	Posco	Iron and steel	1968	26.76
7	LG Chem	Specialized chemicals	1947	25.66
8	Samsung C&T	Trading	1938	25.04
9	Naver	Computer services	1999	24.61
10	KB Financial Group	Banking, financial services	1963	23.93
11	Hyundai Mobis	Auto and truck parts	1977	21.98
12	Samsung Life Insurance	Life and health insurance	1957	21.87
13	Shinhan Financial Group	Investment services	1982	20.43
14	Korea Electric Power	Electric utilities	1915	19.88
15	SK Holdings	Oil and gas operations	1953	19.64
16	Samsung SDS	Computer services	1985	18.64
17	SK Innovation	Oil and gas operations	1962	18.39
18	LG Household & Health Care	Household/personal care	1947	17.79
19	SK Telecom	Telecommunications services	1984	17.78
20	Amorepacific	Household/personal care	1932	17.47
21	LG Electronics	Consumer electronics	1958	16.89
22	LG Corporation	Household appliances	1947	14.01
23	Lotte Chemical	Specialized chemicals	1976	13.99
24	Hana Financial Group	Banking, financial services	1971	12.95
25	KT&G	Tobacco	1883	12.94
26	S-Oil	Oil and gas operations	1976	12.74
27	Samsung SDI	Electronics	1970	12.48
28	Netmarble Games	Mobile and web games	2000	12.26
29	Samsung Fire & Marine	Property and casualty insurance	1952	12.08

(*continued*)

Rank	Company	Industry	Year established*	Market value (billions US$)
30	KIA Motors	Automotive	1944	11.85
31	Amorepacific Corporation	Cosmetics, perfume	1945	11.04
32	Kakao	Internet	1995	9.49
33	Woori Bank	Banking, financial services	1899	9.34
34	LG Display	Electronics	1985	8.82
35	NCSoft	Computer and video games	1997	8.69
36	Hyundai Heavy Industries	Heavy equipment	1973	8.61
37	Korea Zinc	Diversified metals and mining	1974	8.52
38	Industrial Bank of Korea	Banking, financial services	1961	8.10
39	Samsung Electro-Mechanics	Electronic components	1973	7.43
40	E-mart	Discount stores	1993	7.19
41	KT Corp	Telecommunications services	1982	6.78
42	Hyundai Robotics	Industrial robots	1984	6.70
43	Hyundai Steel	Iron and steel	1953	6.42
44	Hankook Tire	Auto and truck parts	1941	6.26
45	Coway	Home wellness appliances	1989	6.25
46	Lotte Shopping	Department stores	1970	6.22
47	Hyundai Glovis	Transportation	2001	5.97
48	Mirae Asset Daewoo	Investment services	1970	5.79
49	Hanonsystems	Automobile air-conditioning systems and modules	1986	5.76
50	Kangwonland	Real estate development	1998	5.69
51	Hanmi Science	Pharmaceutical	1973	5.57
52	Hanmi Pharmaceutical	Pharmaceutical	1973	5.49
53	GS Holdings	Oil and gas operations	1966	5.44
54	Hanwhalife	Insurance	1946	5.07
55	LG Uplus	Telecommunications services	1996	5.04
56	Orion	Confectionery, food	1956	4.77
57	Hanwha Chemical	Diversified chemicals	1974	4.63
58	Korea Aerospace Industries	Aerospace	1999	4.59

Rank	Company	Industry	Year established*	Market value (billions US$)
59	Hyundai Engineering & Construction	Construction services	1950	4.59
60	CJ Cheiljedang	Food processing	1953	4.56
61	Lotte	Conglomerate	1967	4.41
62	CJ Corp	Food processing	1953	4.37
63	Korea Investment Holdings	Investment services	1968	4.34
64	Dongbu Insurance	Auto and commercial insurance	1969	4.34
65	Korea Gas	Natural gas utilities	1983	4.22
66	Hyosung	Diversified metals and mining	1966	4.06
67	Samsungcard	Credit cards	1983	3.92
68	NH Investment & Securities	Investment services	1969	3.75
69	Hotel Shilla	Hospitality	1973	3.55
70	S1	Security	1977	3.54
71	OCI	Green energy and chemicals	1959	3.53
72	OrangeLife	Insurance	1991	3.45
73	KCC	Building materials	1958	3.44
74	Hanssem	Kitchen and bathroom cabinets	1973	3.43
75	Samsung Engineering	Engineering and construction	1978	3.34
76	Shinsegae	Retail	1955	3.32
77	Samsung Securities	Financial investment	1982	3.31
78	Hyundai Marine & Fire	Property and casualty insurance	1955	3.28
79	BNK Financial Group	Banking, financial services	1967	3.20
80	Korean Air	Airline	1962	3.02
81	Doosanbobcat	Construction and engineering	1958	2.97
82	CJ Logistics	Logistics	1930	2.96
83	Macquarie Korea Infra-structure Fund	Infrastructure fund	2002	2.90

(*continued*)

Rank	Company	Industry	Year established*	Market value (billions US$)
84	Samsung Heavy Industries	Engineering/naval engineering	1974	2.84
85	LGInnotek	Electronic components	1970	2.81
86	Daewoo Shipbuilding & Marine Engineering	Heavy equipment	1973	2.78
87	Kumho Petrochemical	Petrochemical	1976	2.77
88	Hanwha	Trading companies	1952	2.77
89	BGFretail	Retail	1989	2.75
90	Hyundai Industrial	Rubber	1979	2.73
91	Posco Daewoo	Trading companies	1967	2.66
92	Panocean	Shipping	1966	2.62
93	Yuhan	Pharmaceutical and chemical	1926	2.56
94	Dongsuh	Food/packaging/logistics	1968	2.52
95	Daelim	Petrochemical	1939	2.44
96	Meritz Securities	Securities and financial services	1973	2.44
97	GS Retail	Retail	1971	2.37
98	Ottogi	Food	1971	2.31
99	Greencross	Biopharmaceutical	1969	2.28
100	Ssangyong Cement	Cement	1962	2.27

NOTE: Ranking is as of March 30, 2018; market value is based on the exchange rate as of March 30, 2018.

* In the event of a corporate name change due to events such as mergers and acquisition or divestiture, this year refers to the year the original firm was founded.

SOURCE: Korea Exchange database, revised.

11 Financing Innovative Enterprises in China

A Public Policy Perspective

Lin William Cong, Charles M. C. Lee, Yuanyu Qu, and Tao Shen

Innovation and entrepreneurship rank highly on the strategic agenda of most countries today. As global competition intensifies, most national policymakers now recognize the central importance of technological advancements to long-term economic growth and societal prosperity (Abramowitz 1956; Solow 1957). Research shows that younger firms contribute disproportionately to job creation, because they are more likely to experiment with disruptive technologies and business models that lead to positive knowledge spillovers (Bloom, Schankerman, and Reenen 2013; Kogan et al. 2017). The cultivation and development of dynamic young firms are especially important to emerging economies where new entrants with transformative business models can take advantage of the rapidly changing landscape in mobile-commerce and web-based technologies.[1]

Acknowledgements: Tao Shen thanks the National Natural Science Foundation of China (grant ID 71603147) for financial support; Will Cong thanks the Initiative on Global Markets and the Polsky Center at the University of Chicago Booth School of Business for research funding; Yuanyu Qu thanks the National Natural Science Foundation of China (grant ID 72003025) for financial support. We appreciate helpful discussions with Richard Lim of GSR Ventures and Pooja Malik of Nipun Capital.

---

[1] Mobile phone adoption is disproportionately important to emerging economies. Between 2014 and 2020, an additional 1.1 billion individuals will acquire a mobile phone for the first time. At current rates of adoption, China and India will soon each have more internet users than the entire population of the United States and Western Europe combined (OECD 2016).

No country is playing a greater role in the redrawing of the global innovation map than China. The 2018 edition of the Global Innovation Index (GII) ranked China 17th among the 126 countries by total innovation score—the highest score received by a country not from the high-income category.[2] In the three years 2015–17, total venture capital and private equity (VCPE) funds investing in China-based start-ups reached $403.6 billion, making China second only to the United States as a destination for the deployment of VCPE funds.[3] In March 2018, China's Ministry of Science and Technology issued a report listing 164 Chinese "unicorns" (privately owned firms worth more than $1 billion each), with a combined worth in excess of $628 billion.[4] In comparison, figures show that there were 132 US-based unicorns valued at around $700 billion as of the end of 2017. By these measures, China is already a central hub of global innovation, particularly in high-tech industries. Yet, while much of this innovation is taking place through entrepreneurial ventures, little is known about how these initiatives are being financed and what financial constraints Chinese entrepreneurs face.

This study examines the current state of affairs in the funding of private innovations in China from a public policy perspective. We frame our analyses in the context of economic theory that underpins entrepreneurial risk-taking activities. We also survey recent academic findings on the subject and provide some evidence on how Chinese entrepreneurs are being funded. Finally, we discuss the implications of these findings for China's public policies, particularly the rules and regulations that govern its access to public equity markets.

---

2   The GII composite score is a broad-based measure of country-level innovation, computed using 79 indicators that span both innovation-related input and outputs. This annual report is jointly produced by Cornell University, INSEAD, and the World Intellectual Property Organization. The upper echelons of the GII ranks are dominated by high-income countries (as measured by per capita gross domestic product). Among the top 30 countries ranked by total GII score, China alone is an upper-middle-income country; only two other upper-middle-income countries (Malaysia and Bulgaria) ranked in the top 40. For a detailed discussion of the conceptual framework behind the GII, see Casanova, Cornelius, and Dutta (2018).
3   The distinction between venture capital and private equity activities is blurred in China. We therefore refer to both together as VCPE investing. In the following section we present more details on total VCPE investments.
4   The 2017 China Unicorn Enterprise Development Report was jointly released by the Torch High Technology Industry Development Center of the Ministry of Science and Technology and the Greatwall Strategy Consultants in Beijing on March 20, 2018.

Our study has three specific objectives: (1) to evaluate the relative size and importance of the channels through which private initiatives for innovation in China are being funded, (2) to survey the academic evidence on potential financing constraints being faced by private initiatives in innovation, and (3) to discuss public policy implications that may arise from these findings, as well as to outline the type of future research that may best inform Chinese policymakers.

We begin in the following section with a review of the channels through which external funding now reaches entrepreneurs in China. We show that VCPE funding has increased exponentially in recent years: much of it is domestic, but a sizeable amount comes from overseas.[5] Furthermore, government entities and state-owned enterprises (SOEs) are also significant direct investors in many start-ups. Our evidence suggests that "mid-stage" financing, covering the expansion and growth stages of a firm's life cycle (see figure 11.1), may not be a major problem for Chinese entrepreneurs. On the other hand, compared to start-ups in the United States, it may still be more difficult to secure early-stage (seed) funding in China. Specifically, our analyses focus sharply on "late-stage" financing and the exit strategies available to Chinese entrepreneurs. In particular, we identify a number of problems with China's antiquated initial public offering (IPO) regulations, which loom as significant obstacles to entrepreneurship and innovation in China.

In the subsequent section, we further explore the problems engendered by China's IPO regulations. In contrast to the registration-and-disclosure system that exists in most countries, the IPO process in China is strictly regulated. Candidate firms are required to meet strict pre-specified profitability and revenue thresholds. Firms meeting these standards typically face a further waiting period, as the China Securities Regulatory Commission (CSRC) reviews and adjudicates on every applicant. This process is arduous, the outcome is far from certain, and there is mounting evidence that the ultimate decision is not determined solely by economic merit.[6] A reason for this is the tightly controlled government policy that allows only a certain number of firms to issue an IPO in a

---

5 Although it is not our focus, debt financing could also be important for funding innovation, at least in public firms. Chen et al. (2021) use the property right and bankruptcy law enactments' shock to assets pledgeability to show that patent activities increased after these two law enactments in 2006.

6 Studies that suggest political connections play a role in China's IPO allocation decisions include Fan, Wong, and Zhang (2007); Francis, Hasan, and Sun (2009); Piotroski and Zhang (2014); Li and Zhou (2015); and Lee, Qu, and Shen (2020).

given time period (the IPO "quota"), often leading to large backlogs of firms awaiting review, especially after an IPO "suspension" period.[7]

Based on our survey of the academic evidence, as well as further empirical analyses conducted in this study, we identify a list of economic problems and consequences that are directly attributable to China's current IPO regulations:

1. Long wait times and substantial uncertainty regarding outcomes among candidate firms seeking access to domestic equity markets.
2. A bias against high-growth technology firms, which typically have lower profits, less developed businesses, and more intangible assets.
3. Substantial underpricing of IPOs, resulting in exceptionally large initial day returns that dwarf those seen in more developed markets.
4. An exodus of high-quality, particularly high-technology, candidate firms to foreign equity markets.
5. Costly reverse merger (RM) transactions in which highly qualified but less politically connected private firms pay more than $400 million each, on average, for a listed shell company.
6. Virtually no delisting or retirement of failed companies from public equity markets (in fact, these failed businesses continue to propagate by leveraging their listing status to acquire new lines of business, thus maintaining control and circumventing the IPO process).
7. Large cross-sectional price distortions among publicly listed firms (including systemic risk associated with IPO regulations and enormous premium packages for the smallest listed firms, which trade more on their expected shell value than on corporate profits).
8. Listing delays in the IPO process that lead directly to a reduction in firms' innovation activity, as measured by patent quantity and quality (such effects begin during the delay period and endure for many years after listing).
9. Potentially inflated market prices for all publicly listed firms, as well as higher levels of speculative trading by domestic investors.

---

7   Between 2004 and 2016, the CSRC suspended all IPO activities on five occasions. The specific timing of these IPO suspensions and reboots can be found on a CSRC authorized website, "IPO Normalization Will Face Twists and Turns," Shichang [in Chinese], http://stock.cnstock.com/stock/smk_gszbs/201701/40136 51.htm. These suspensions lasted between six and 15 months each, and typically led to large review backlogs. For example, as of the end of October 2016, there were 806 companies meeting China's prespecified listing standards and awaiting CSRC processing. For reference, an average of only 7.7 companies were approved for listing every month in the first 10 months of 2016.

In this chapter's final section, we summarize our findings, discuss policy implications, and explore potential venues for future research. We conclude that China's IPO regulations in the past decades present a serious impediment to two important near-term goals espoused by the Chinese government: (1) to bring more high-technology firms back to mainland stock markets, and (2) to be included at a meaningful weight in international stock indices, particularly the MSCI Emerging Market Index.

Considering the problems identified above, we recommend a move toward a registration-and-disclosure system for Chinese IPOs, like those employed by most other countries. In such systems, investors monitor firm quality and market forces adjudicate firm value. This way, firms that receive enough support from the investment community will attain IPO status. The role of regulators is to ensure adherence to established ordinances, which are largely disclosure centric.

We acknowledge the need to protect retail investors and minority shareholders. But this protection should not come by limiting the access of start-up firms to public equity markets. Instead, the protection can be in the form of more stringent enforcement of insider trading laws, increased corporate transparency and quality of disclosure, and changes in the judicial system that would facilitate swift recourse through private litigation in the event of majority shareholder misconduct. None of these reforms would require regulators to adjudicate firms' investment value, a task that we believe is best left to markets.

Financing Entrepreneurship in China

Funding sources that are available to a company vary over its entrepreneurial life cycle. Figure 11.1 provides a graphic representation of the different funding sources commonly available to a business enterprise at each life-cycle stage. In the following discussion, we group the various funding sources in terms of their impact on the three stages of a company's life cycle: that is, the early/seed stage, medium/growth stage, and late/expansion stage.

Chinese initiatives addressing companies' funding needs include financing for R&D of small to medium technology enterprises (Innofund), venture capital and private equity funding (VCPE), corporate investment by a strategic partner (CVC, e.g., Tencent and Alibaba), government-led private equity/venture capital funds (GVC), direct investments by state-owned entities (SOE), and direct listing on the National Equities Exchange and Quotations (NEEQ).

FIGURE 11.1 Funding sources for companies over their life cycle

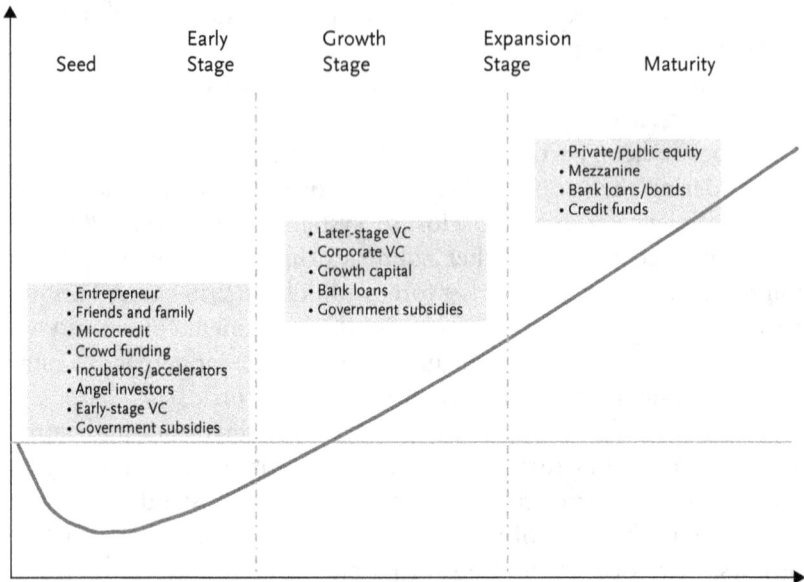

SOURCE: Adapted from Casanova, Cornelius, and Dutta (2018).

Early-stage financing

In the earliest part of its life cycle (the "seed" stage), a start-up typically relies on the entrepreneur's personal savings or funds from friends and family. In China, as in most other emerging economies, start-ups have limited access to bank loans. This is partly due to the fact that a typical start-up does not have sufficient tangible assets to pledge as collateral. Even when such assets exist, many banks are reluctant to lend to start-up businesses because of insufficient credit information or ill-defined legal rights to secure transactions in the event of default. Therefore, unless other external financing becomes available, many start-ups fail to grow and reach positive cash flow status after the entrepreneur exhausts funding from personal connections. Casanova, Cornelius, and Dutta (2018) refer to the trough in this graph—the time between idea origination and the first venture capital (VC) check—as the "Valley of Death."

In more advanced economies such as the United States, would-be entrepreneurs can tap a broad set of early-stage external financing sources such as incubator and accelerator programs. Some may have access to angel investors, microcredit, or crowdfunding sources; others may be fortunate enough to receive funding from early-stage VC firms or government subsidies. Although peer-to-peer lending is available in China through several financial technology start-ups, our discussions with Chinese entrepreneurs and VCPE investors give a sense that the procurement of early-stage financing remains more challenging in China than in the United States.

One Chinese initiative to address early-stage funding for research and development (R&D) is the Innovation Fund for Small and Medium Technology-based Enterprises (the SMTE "Innofund"). This fund was established by the State Council in May 1999 with a mandate to "facilitate and encourage the innovation activities of small and medium technology-based enterprises (SMTEs) and the commercialization of this research by way of financing, trying to bring along and attract outside financing for corporate R&D investment of SMTEs" (Guo, Guo, and Jiang [2016]). Eligible applicants are businesses with less than 500 employees, at least 30 percent of whom have received college-level education. The annual R&D investment of the firm must exceed 3 percent of total sales, and the number of employees engaged in R&D must be at least 10 percent of the total workforce. From 1999 to 2011, the fund provided more than ¥19.2 billion (approximately $3.1 billion) to 30,537 projects. Accordingly, the program created more than 450,000 new jobs and generated ¥209.2 billion in sales, ¥22.5 billion in tax income, and ¥3.4 billion in exports. As of the end of 2008, 82 out of the 273 publicly listed companies on the SME Board of the Shenzhen Stock Exchange were once supported by Innofund.[8]

Guo, Guo, and Jiang (2016) investigate the effects of this program on firm innovation outputs. The authors find that Innofund-backed firms generate higher innovation-related outputs, including both commercialized outputs as measured by sales and exports from new products, as well as technological outputs as measured by the number of patents. These results hold in the cross-section (when compared to counterparts not supported by Innofund), as well as in the time series (when compared to the same firms prior to securing Innofund support). Overall, this study suggests that government support of R&D through the fund is effective in stimulating innovation in China.

Wang, Li, and Furman (2017) also study the Innofund program and report more circumscribed findings. Using internal administrative data

---

8 See http://www.innofund.gov.cn/.

on applications to the program, their study aims to: (1) identify the application features associated with higher chances of obtaining grants, and (2) parse out the causal impacts of receiving a grant on firm performance. Although the authors find that firms with observable merits are more likely to receive funding, they also show that bureaucratic intervention can play a role in the screening process. For example, after acknowledging other factors, firms with political connections are still more likely to receive the funding. Furthermore, after controlling for the applicant's ex ante characteristics, they find no evidence of a causal relation between the receipt of grants and better firm performance. This result suggests that while Innofund was able to identify firms with more promising projects, the grant itself had limited causal impact on subsequent performance. In other words, selection, rather than treatment effects, is likely to drive the positive impact on innovation and firm performance documented in Guo et al. (2016).

In sum, early-stage financing is a significant challenge for entrepreneurs. Companies at the idea stage are much less likely to draw the attention of VC funds when competing against those with working prototypes or other evidence of technological feasibility. In fact, it is possible for early-stage start-ups to be struggling for funding, even as VC capital reaches all-time highs.[9] These concerns suggest a greater role for government-based incubator programs, such as Innofund or other organizations that can also provide mentorship, advice, and connections. Unfortunately, there is a paucity of research on the efficacy of early-stage funding programs, which is an opportunity for academics to contribute to the debate going forward.

Mid-stage financing

Firms that manage to survive the early stage will find many more dance partners in the funding arena. Mid-stage financing is the traditional domain of VC funds. In addition to the usual players, venture investing in China features significant government involvement. Government

---

9   Khosravi (2018) notes that during the first quarter of 2018, more than \$21 billion in VC funding was deployed across 1,200 deals in the United States, but the money was divided among fewer companies. In fact, in the same quarter U.S. VC funds actually reduced their investments in seed and early-stage firms. The author argues that a key reason for this phenomenon is that given their fee structures, most VC firms simply do not have sufficient economic incentive to invest time and capital in relatively small/early-stage companies.

entities (both central and provincial) have their own VC funds, in which they act as the general partner (GP). We will refer to these entities as government VC funds. Many other government entities or SOEs also engage directly in venture investing. Large corporations, most notably Tencent and Alibaba, have been active in corporate venture investing. And finally, in recent years, small Chinese start-up firms can also apply for listing on the National Equities Exchange and Quotations (NEEQ), which is similar to the over-the-counter market in the United States.[10] We provide some evidence on the scale and impact of each of these mid-stage initiatives.

Table 11.1 reports the number of VCPE investment events in Chinese start-up firms during the 2006–17 period and their dollar value. This information is extracted from the PEdata database, in which each bilateral investor-investee transaction is defined as a separate investment event. All Chinese start-up firms in the database are included in the table. We define Chinese firms as those whose headquarters are in China. Similarly, Chinese VCPE firms are those headquartered in China, while foreign ones are those headquartered overseas. Investment values are reported as of each financing round. When several funds participated in the same round but PEdata did not parse out the amount for each fund, we assume that the funds contributed equally. We report total annual investments, as well as the cumulative amount invested over the entire 12-year period. The table shows that venture investing in China has grown quickly in recent years. Of the total $740.74 billion invested by VCPE entities, $403.68 billion (54.5 percent) took place in the past three years. Foreign participation over this period totaled $99.5 billion, but most of the funding ($641.2 billion, or 86.6 percent) came from Chinese sources. In 2017, VCPE investments totaled $152.29 billion, which was 1.75 percent of the total market capitalization of the listed stocks on the Shanghai and Shenzhen stock exchanges at the end of the year.

To better understand funding sources used by China's leading private technology firms, table 11.2 presents a list of the top 20 privately owned Chinese tech firms ("unicorns") in 2017. The list is derived from the Ministry of Science and Technology, and specifically from a

---

10   The NEEQ facilitates trading in the shares of a company that are not listed on either the Shenzhen Stock Exchange (SZSE) or the Shanghai Stock Exchange (SHSE). Note that listing on the NEEQ is not a financing event. We discuss the current level of trading activity in the NEEQ later in this section.

TABLE 11.1 Venture capital and private equity investment in Chinese start-up firms 2006–17

Year	Chinese VC in Chinese firms ($ billion)			Foreign VC in Chinese firms ($ billion)			Total VC in Chinese firms ($ billion)		
	No. of events	Annual	Cumulative	No. of events	Annual	Cumulative	No. of events	Annual	Cumulative
2006	452	7.57	7.57	254	12.91	12.91	706	20.48	20.48
2007	862	9.82	17.40	292	7.64	20.55	1,154	17.47	37.95
2008	1,008	10.36	27.75	262	6.79	27.34	1,270	17.15	55.09
2009	1,217	19.44	47.19	171	3.13	30.47	1,388	22.57	77.66
2010	2,754	29.32	76.51	257	7.71	38.18	3,011	37.03	114.69
2011	4,273	46.18	122.69	328	8.72	46.90	4,601	54.90	169.59
2012	3,318	37.47	160.15	252	6.22	53.12	3,570	43.69	213.27
2013	3,004	42.11	202.27	220	4.50	57.62	3,224	46.61	259.89
2014	4,608	59.89	262.16	443	17.28	74.90	5,051	77.17	337.06
2015	10,373	115.77	377.93	436	10.84	85.74	10,809	126.62	463.67
2016	9,688	118.07	496.00	334	6.70	92.44	10,022	124.77	588.44
2017	10,241	145.24	641.25	385	7.05	99.49	10,626	152.29	740.74
Total	51,798	641.25		3,634	99.49		55,432	740.74	

NOTE: Values originally reported in yuan were converted to U.S. dollars using an exchange rate of 6.5 (average rate over sample period). For other currencies, the exchange rates were 0.85 for the euro, 0.75 for the pound, 7.5 for the Hong Kong dollar, and 110 for the yen. VC = venture capital.
SOURCE: Information from PEdata database.

TABLE 11.2 Top twenty private tech firms ("unicorns") in China, 2017

	Company	Estimated value ($ billion)	Year	Sector	VCPE	SOE	Type of SOE
1	Ant Financial	75.0	2014	Internet finance	Yes	Yes	CIC; Corp; Pension
2	Didi Chuxing	56.0	2012	Internet services (transportation)	Yes	Yes	CIC; Corp
3	Xiaomi	46.0	2010	Hardware	Yes	No	
4	Alibaba Cloud	39.0	2009	Internet services (cloud)	Yes	No	
5	Meituan-Dianping	30.0	2010	E-commerce	Yes	Yes	CIC; Corp
6	Ningde Shidai	20.0	2011	New energy car	Yes	Yes	Local
7	Jinri Toutiao	20.0	2012	New media	Yes	Yes	Corp
8	Cainiao Network	20.0	2013	Logistics/ transportation	Yes	No	
9	Lufax	18.5	2011	Internet finance	Yes	Yes	Corp
10	Jiedaibao	10.8	2014	Internet finance	Yes	No	
11	Weizhong Bank	9.2	2015	Internet finance	Yes	No	
12	Pingan Health	8.8	2016	Internet finance (health insurance)	Yes	No	
13	Koubei	8.0	2015	E-commerce	Yes	Yes	CIC
14	Jinrong Yizhangtong	8.0	2015	Internet finance	Yes	No	
15	JD Finance	7.7	2013	Internet finance	Yes	Yes	Corp
16	Ele.me	5.5	2008	E-commerce	Yes	Yes	Corp
17	Pin An Good Doctor	5.4	2014	Healthcare	Yes	No	
18	Weima Motor	5.0	2011	New energy car	Yes	Yes	GVC
19	Lianying Health	5.0	2011	Healthcare	Yes	Yes	GVC; Corp
20	Weilai Motor	5.0	2014	New energy car	Yes	Yes	Corp
	Total value	402.9					

NOTE: "Corp" denotes a government-owned corporation; "Pension" denotes a pension fund; "Local" denotes a local government fund. CIC = China Investment Corporation (China's sovereign wealth fund); GVC = government venture capital or private equity fund; SOE = state-owned enterprise; VCPE = venture capital and private equity.
SOURCE: The 2017 China Unicorn Enterprise Development Report of China's Ministry of Science and Technology. Funding information is from the PEdata database.

2017 report that provides each of these firms' estimated market value (in $ billion), founding year, and industry sector. We also secured additional information from PEdata, including whether each firm received funding from VCPE or SOE investors, and the type of SOE.

All 20 "unicorns" are valued at $5 billion or more and their collective valuation is more than $400 billion. The most heavily represented industry sectors are internet finance (7), new energy automobiles (3), e-commerce (3), internet services (2), and healthcare (2). Note that all 20 have received some VCPE funding, and 12 out of the 20 (60 percent) also received equity funding from a government entity. For this reason, China's sovereign wealth fund (CIC) and other SOEs (Corp) are important investors (e.g., Ant Financial, Didi Chuxing, Meituan-Dianping, and Kuobei are companies that have a CIC type of SOE; including these companies, many others have a Corp type of SOE). Local governments, government VC funds, and government-owned pension funds (e.g., China's National Social Security Fund) all participated, which reinforces that government entities are active participants in venture investing in China.

Are government-backed ventures more likely to succeed? Cao, Humphery-Jenner, and Suchard (2013) examine this question and find that the rate of success varies depending on whether the investing entity is managed wholly or partially by a government-owned GP. Companies backed only partially are significantly more likely to achieve an IPO and are more capable of exiting even during market downturns. However, backing by a wholly government-owned GP seems to detract from venture success. Also, collectively, government-backed VC funds deliver lower returns as measured by their average exit multiple. These results suggest that some level of government ownership may help investees navigate China's heavily regulated IPO process. Note that while the inferior overall performance of government VC funds may reflect a lack of investing expertise, it is still consistent with the idea that profit maximization is not their sole goal.

Three other studies shed light on the impact of VC investing in China. Guo and Jiang (2013) find that VC-backed firms outperform those not backed by venture capital in terms of profitability, labor productivity, sales growth, and R&D investment. Their evidence suggests that this performance is driven by both superior project selection and the ex post monitoring efforts of VC funds. Humphery-Jenner and Suchard (2013) examine the role of foreign venture capital in ensuring the success of Chinese portfolio firms. They find that foreign VC firms do not increase the overall likelihood of venture success and that they seem to prefer to exit via a merger and acquisition (M&A) or a secondary buyout rather than an IPO, perhaps because they lack the local knowledge and political connections useful in securing the latter. Zhang et al. (2017) provide further evidence that well-connected venture capitalists can be useful in navigating the IPO process. Specifically, the authors show that late-stage (pre-IPO stage) VC investors earn higher returns than those that enter in the early stages. Furthermore, this result is more prominent

TABLE 11.3 Investments made in Chinese start-ups by Tencent and Alibaba, 2008–17

	Tencent		Alibaba	
	No. of events	Total value	No. of events	Total value
Panel A: Investments made through VCPE funds				
2008	0	0.000	2	0.015
2009	1	0.003	3	0.009
2010	3	0.026	3	0.009
2011	20	0.456	6	0.080
2012	22	0.142	5	0.031
2013	20	0.148	21	2.723
2014	54	2.989	38	3.067
2015	75	3.352	43	5.835
2016	55	3.383	21	0.974
2017	88	8.151	20	2.959
Total	338	18.651	162	15.703
Panel B: Investments made through other corporate entities within each group				
2008	2	0.014	2	0.015
2009	2	0.003	5	0.009
2010	6	0.036	5	0.009
2011	22	0.456	8	0.080
2012	26	0.208	7	0.031
2013	30	0.609	25	2.686
2014	82	3.741	49	3.429
2015	115	3.624	66	6.521
2016	90	3.647	48	2.397
2017	118	10.794	32	8.365
Total	493	23.133	247	23.542

NOTE: VCPE = venture capital and private equity.
SOURCE: Information from PEdata database.

for venture capitalists with strong political connections and suggests that the uncertainty associated with China's IPO approval process can impose real costs on start-up businesses, which would pressure them to engage with well-connected VC investors.

An important recent development has been the emergence of two dominant corporate investors. In the past 10 years (2008–17), Alibaba and Tencent have together invested more than $46 billion in Chinese start-ups. Table 11.3 reports the number of financing events made each year (extracted from PEdata) and the value of these investments (in $ billion). Panel A reports only investments made through their VCPE funds; panel B includes strategic investments made through other corporate entities within each group.[11] Both firms have invested around $23 billion each in Chinese start-up firms. Most of the investments ($18 billion for Tencent and $15.7 billion for Alibaba) were made through their VCPE funds, but a sizeable minority were also made as strategic investments through other corporate entities. The total VCPE investment of these two firms ($34.35 billion) represents 5.5 percent of all Chinese VCPE investments over this period. Clearly, these two leading names are leveraging their domain knowledge and access to the financial market by playing important roles in venture financing for Chinese entrepreneurs.

Although China is transitioning toward a market-based economy, many aspects of its governing apparatus still bear the hallmarks of central planning. The most prominent example is the central government's Five-Year Plans, and what is of particular interest is whether the government's actions outlined in these plans lead to better resource allocation in the domain of entrepreneurial finance. Zhou, Chen, and Sheng (2017) examine how policies in China's 12th Five-Year Plan, published in 2010, affected the performance of VC funds. The plan identified seven strategic emerging industries and outlined a series of policy measures to facilitate the development of these industries.[12] Interestingly, Zhou, Chen, and Sheng (2017) find that these policies significantly *reduced* the exit performance of VC firms that focused on the targeted industries. Furthermore, the erosion in performance is concentrated only in privately owned VC firms and is not evident in government-owned ones. Evidently, government involvement in the form of this edict distorted market incentives, leading to overallocation of VC resources to the targeted industries. This finding supports Ahlstrom, Bruton, and Yeh's (2007) view that government involvement can often have unintended negative consequences for VC firms and entrepreneurs.

---

11   The Tencent group invests through four corporate entities (Tencent, Tencent Linzhi, Tencent Cloud, and Tencent Music) and three VCPE funds (Tencent Capital, Tencent Startup Space, and Tencent Venture). The most important vehicle is Tencent Capital, which accounts for more than 90 percent of the group's investments in Chinese start-ups. The Alibaba group invests through six firms and two VCPE funds. The most important vehicle is Ali Capital, which accounts for more than 90 percent of the investments made by the Ali Group.

12   The seven strategic emerging industries listed in this plan are: energy efficient and environmental technologies, next-generation information technology, biotechnology, high-end equipment manufacturing, new energy, new materials, and new-energy vehicles.

Taken together, the studies above suggest that in China, as in developed countries, VC participation is associated with improved entrepreneurial performance. Some amount of government ownership, in particular, can be helpful when exiting through an IPO. But government involvement through central planning edicts, while well intended, may lead to worse resource allocation decisions by the participants in the domain of entrepreneurial finance.

Late-stage financing

The central issue in late-stage venture financing is the exit strategy, and it is in this area that we find the biggest opportunity for public policy improvement in China. In this subsection, we provide some preliminary evidence on how venture investors currently exit their positions in Chinese start-ups. The findings presented here naturally lead to policy issues surrounding China's IPO regulations, which we will discuss in more detail in the section that follows.

Table 11.4 presents the means of exit for VCPE investors in Chinese start-up firms. An exit event is defined as the unwinding of a transaction previously entered in the database as an investment event. Each investor-investee transaction is a separate event in this database.

Panel A of table 11.4 shows that the most common means of exit is via an IPO (4,415 events, representing 43.1 percent of all exited deals), followed by an M&A transaction (28.9 percent) and an equity transfer (20.7 percent). Panel B further breaks down IPO exits by exchange. The domestic exchanges (SHSE, SZSE, and ChiNext) collectively account for 3,044 IPO exit events, representing 76 percent of total IPO exits. Listings on the U.S. and Hong Kong exchanges together account for 956 exit events, representing 23.8 percent of total IPO exits.[13] These results show that VCPE funds investing in Chinese firms rely heavily on IPOs, M&As, and equity transfers to close their investment cycle. Domestic IPOs, specifically, accounted for over 30 percent of the exit events over the past 12 years.

Table 11.5 presents the number and dollar value of Chinese firms that undertook an IPO or a reverse merger (RM) transaction in the period from 2007 to 2017. We include all firms headquartered in China

---

13 According to PEdata, listing in exchanges is counted as an exit event, except for listing in NEEQ, in which VCPE investors need to sell their shares. As discussed later, listing in NEEQ usually is not a financing event.

TABLE 11.4 Venture capital and private equity exit events, 2006–17

Panel A: Means of exit					
Year	No. of events	IPO	Repurchase	M&A	Equity transfer
2006	138	69	1	50	18
2007	303	204	6	64	29
2008	138	58	7	44	29
2009	296	160	6	85	45
2010	671	488	22	101	60
2011	651	441	24	115	71
2012	613	274	62	163	114
2013	740	72	166	328	174
2014	1,534	388	142	665	339
2015	1,582	595	150	472	365
2016	1,318	566	75	336	341
2017	2,255	1,100	86	537	532
Total	10,239	4,415	747	2,960	2,117

Panel B: IPO exits by exchange							
Year	Total	SHSE	SZSE	ChiNext	NEEQ	U.S.	Hong Kong
2006	50	0	15	0	0	19	16
2007	178	8	49	0	1	77	43
2008	55	0	31	0	0	3	21
2009	155	0	40	50	0	19	46
2010	474	29	139	133	0	107	66
2011	437	43	142	150	0	64	38
2012	260	36	74	122	1	10	17
2013	71	0	1	0	3	24	43
2014	357	77	38	83	2	78	79
2015	518	181	83	178	0	15	61
2016	526	203	103	153	0	15	52
2017	926	412	143	328	0	32	11
Total	4,007	989	858	1,197	7	463	493

NOTE: Panel A reports a breakdown of all exit events by category, where IPO denotes initial public offering, repurchase denotes shares reacquired by the investee, M&A is merger and acquisition, and equity transfer refers to sales from one investee to another. Panel B reports a breakdown of IPO exits by stock exchange: NEEQ is the National Equities Exchange and Quotations; SHSE is the Shanghai Stock Exchange; and SZSE is the Shenzhen Stock Exchange excluding the ChiNext Board. Although the ChiNext Board is officially part of the SZSE, it is reported separately here because its listing requirements are lower and it is an important exit market for venture investors. U.S. IPOs include listings in the NYSE, AMEX, and the NASDAQ. Hong Kong IPOs include only listings on the main board as the Growth Enterprise Market (GEM) is extremely illiquid. Note that the total number of IPOs in panel B does not equal the total in panel A because some exit events occur in other places, such as London or Singapore.
SOURCE: Information from PEdata database.

TABLE 11.5 Initial public offering (IPO) and reverse merger (RM) transactions, 2007–17

	IPOs in Mainland China			IPOs in Hong Kong			IPOs in the United States			RMs in Mainland China		
Year	No.	Amount raised	Market value	No.	Amount raised	Market value	No.	Amount raised	Market value	No.	Initial Market value	Current Market value
2007	123	11.07	180.79	39	3.25	14.93	17	3.65	15.56	8	31.91	36.02
2008	76	2.38	14.79	17	0.87	5.47	4	0.25	1.27	11	11.34	24.49
2009	99	4.29	19.23	42	3.23	17.85	6	1.42	5.49	16	19.25	47.48
2010	347	10.85	66.68	63	3.97	28.39	23	2.68	13.50	12	13.69	27.85
2011	281	6.31	33.47	44	1.81	10.75	8	1.62	9.61	11	18.11	33.13
2012	154	2.28	12.86	33	1.37	8.45	3	0.16	1.02	10	8.51	18.42
2013	0	0.00	0.00	54	2.54	12.92	6	0.48	3.26	19	34.72	50.92
2014	125	1.45	10.34	67	2.95	15.37	10	24.81	203.07	23	39.54	68.51
2015	219	3.48	17.97	62	4.21	21.12	0	0.00	0.00	23	89.52	85.75
2016	227	3.29	20.97	41	2.75	16.20	3	1.54	14.80			
2017	436	4.92	29.34	35	1.58	9.54	5	1.49	12.46			
Total	2087	50.32	406.44	497	28.54	161.00	85	38.10	280.03	133	266.60	392.57

NOTE: All monetary amounts are in billions of U.S. dollars. The IPOs in mainland China include the ones in the Shanghai and Shenzhen Stock Exchanges. The Chinese firms' IPOs in Hong Kong include the ones listed on the Hong Kong Main Board. The Chinese firms' IPOs in the United States include the ones listed on the AMEX, NYSE, and NASDAQ.

SOURCE: Data for IPOs in mainland China are from the China Stock Market & Accounting Research (CSMAR); for IPOs in Hong Kong data are from WIND and CSMAR; and for IPOs in the United States they are from Compustat and SDC Platinum. We follow the sample in Cong, Lee, Qu, and Shen (2020).

that went public through an IPO in Mainland China, Hong Kong, or the United States. For each IPO, we report the total funds raised, as well as the implied market valuation for the firm as a whole, based on the IPO issue price. We also include firms that accessed the Chinese mainland market using an RM transaction as per Lee, Qu, and Shen (2019, 2020).[14] For each RM, we report the market value at the announcement of the RM transaction, as well as the current market value of the firm based on closing prices as of the end of March 2018.

One striking fact seen in table 11.5 is the relatively small sum raised through mainland IPOs. This is because the larger Chinese firms are choosing to list overseas or to circumvent the mainland IPO process by listing through an RM. The lethargic long-term performance of the A-shares market further exacerbates the issue (Allen et al. 2014). The table shows that while most Chinese firms IPO in the mainland (there are 2,087 mainland IPOs, versus 582 listings for Hong Kong and the United States combined), the mainland IPOs are much smaller. In fact, over the sample period, mainland IPOs actually raised less money than the overseas IPOs ($50.32 billion versus $66.64 billion for Hong Kong and the United States combined). Furthermore, consistent with Lee, Qu, and Shen (2019), we find that domestic RMs are also much larger than domestic IPO firms. RMs are not financing events, so we cannot compare the amounts raised. However, table 11.5 shows that the RMs begin their lives at an average market capitalization of $2 billion each, while the average IPO is valued at $0.194 billion each (406.44/2087) based on issue prices. Even allowing for a 100 percent IPO initial day underpricing, the typical mainland IPO is an order of magnitude smaller than the typical RM. The initial market valuation of the 133 RMs is $266.6 billion, which is 65.6 percent of the market valuation of all the 2,087 mainland IPOs combined. These results are quite striking given the fact that overseas listings and RMs are quite costly for issuing firms.[15] Evidently, many large Chinese firms are willing to incur real costs to avoid the arduous mainland IPO process.

Table 11.6 provides additional insights on the type of firms that choose to IPO in a mainland exchange (SHZE or SZSE) or overseas (in

---

14   Following Lee, Qu, and Shen (2019, 2020), our RM sample includes all "clean RM transactions," wherein control of the combined entity is transferred to the owners of the unlisted firm, and the entire exchange takes place in a single transaction.
15   Lee, Qu, and Shen (2020) report that the typical shell value paid in a mainland RM transaction is around $400 million.

TABLE 11.6 Key characteristics of mainland IPOs versus other new listings

	Main- land IPO	IPO in Hong Kong		IPO in the United States		Mainland RM	
	Mean	Mean	Diff	Mean	Diff	Mean	Diff
			Panel A: Mean				
Assets	0.600	0.992	–0.392**	0.365	0.235	0.725	–0.125
ROA	0.159	0.160	–0.001	0.060	0.099***	0.146	0.013*
MB	1.148	1.278	–0.130**	74.206	–73.06***	6.322	–5.17***
Lev	0.447	0.614	–0.168***	0.466	–0.019	0.536	–0.090***
Cash	0.204	0.178	0.026***	0.327	–0.123***	0.173	0.031**
			Panel B: Median				
Assets	0.092	0.205	–0.114***	0.096	-0.004	0.416	–0.324***
ROA	0.146	0.127	0.020	0.111	0.035***	0.113	0.034***
MB	0.876	0.705	0.171***	13.668	–12.792***	2.851	–1.974***
Lev	0.447	0.636	–0.189***	0.440	0.007	0.561	–0.115***
Cash	0.172	0.143	0.029***	0.298	–0.127***	0.141	0.031***

NOTE: Assets are the reported total assets immediately before public listing, expressed in billions of U.S. dollars. ROA is return on asset, defined as net profit + financing expenses + income tax expenses divided by total assets. MB for IPOs is the market-to-book ratio, defined as the implied market value of the firm as a whole based on the IPO issue price, divided by the book value of equity + deferred taxes + investment tax credits received in the prelisting year. MB for reverse mergers (RMs) is the market value at the end of the initial announcement period, divided by prelisting book equity. Lev is book leverage, defined as total liabilities divided by total assets. Cash is cash holdings divided by total assets. The Diff column reports the difference of the Mainland IPOs minus the firms identified in the column heading. ***, **, and * denote statistical significance at the 1%, 5%, and 10% level for a difference-in-mean (panel A) or a difference in median (panel B) test between the Mainland IPO firms and the firms identified in each column heading.
SOURCE: Authors.

Hong Kong or the United States), as well as those that elect to access a mainland exchange through an RM transaction (see footnote 14). Specifically, we report the total assets (immediately before public listing), the return-on-assets (ROA), the market-to-book ratio (MB), the book leverage, and cash holdings divided by total assets. All financial numbers are as of the last prelisting report. Panel A reports the mean for each variable; panel B reports the median. (See table for details on variable construction.)

This table highlights a number of differences between firms that go public through a mainland IPO and those that are listed through other means. Many of these differences reflect the expressed preference of the CSRC IPO review committee for stable, profitable firms that have solid balance sheets with higher tangible assets. Note in particular that

Chinese IPOs in the United States are significantly less profitable (have a lower ROA) but have much higher MB ratios.[16] They have fewer total assets, but a significant part of their assets are in the form of cash holdings. Compared to their mainland counterparts, the Chinese firms that IPO in the United States are much more likely to be fast-growing technology firms. The firms that IPO in Hong Kong seem more similar in profile than those that IPO in the mainland, but we still see significantly higher leverage and lower cash holdings than the mainland IPOs. Consistent with Lee, Qu, and Shen (2019), we find the mainland RM firms are larger, less profitable, more leveraged, and hold less cash than the mainland IPOs.

Finally, table 11.7 presents an overview of the National Equities Exchange and Quotations (NEEQ) market, which was established in 2013 to provide more transparency to early start-up enterprises in China. This market operates in a manner similar to the pink sheet over-the-counter system in the United States. Listing on the NEEQ is not a financing event and liquidity is generally quite thin. In panel A, we provide summary statistics on market liquidity. Total trading volume is further subdivided into trades that involve a market maker and those that were consummated through bilateral negotiations between the parties. In Panel B, for comparison, we also present market liquidity statistics for the A-shares markets (Shanghai and Shenzhen combined). In Panel C, we report a distribution of the number of investors for the NEEQ firms, as of end 2017.

Table 11.7 highlights the thinness of the NEEQ market. As of the end of 2017, 11,630 firms were listed on the NEEQ with a combined market value of $760.07 billion (or 8.74 percent of the market capitalization of the main A-shares markets). Note that the NEEQ market value is likely overstated, as price discovery is minimal and share prices in some cases are self-reported. A better measure of the economic scale of this market is its total trading volume. In 2017, total

---

16   In computing the MB ratios, we use the implied market value of the firm as a whole based on the IPO issuance price. The CSRC has an unwritten requirement that the maximum price-to-earnings (P/E) ratio for a mainland listing be limited to 23 (see below, under "China's Initial Public Offering (IPO) Policies") when establishing the listing price. As a result, the MB ratios for mainland IPOs are artificially depressed. However, even if we assume that the issue price is allowed to double (i.e., if the maximum P/E ratio is raised to 46), the MB ratios in mainland IPOs are still much lower than those in U.S. IPOs. This difference most likely reflects the higher growth potential associated with U.S. IPOs.

TABLE 11.7 NEEQ market overview, 2013–17

		Panel A: NEEQ market liquidity					
Year	No. of firms	Total mkt cap	Avg mkt cap	Annual turnover	Total trading volume	Volume: Market makers	Volume: Bilateral negotiations
2013	356	8.51	0.02	0.04	0.13	0.00	0.13
2014	1,572	70.64	0.04	0.20	2.01	0.33	1.68
2015	5,129	378.22	0.07	0.54	29.39	17.00	12.33
2016	10,163	623.97	0.06	0.21	29.42	14.61	14.80
2017	11,630	760.07	0.07	0.13	34.95	12.07	22.87

		Panel B: A-Share market liquidity			
Year	No. of firms	Total mkt cap	Avg mkt cap	Annual turnover	Total trading volume
2013	2,470	3670.37	1.49	2.34	7,139.20
2014	2,592	5735.99	2.21	2.34	11,342.97
2015	2,811	8224.77	2.93	6.06	39,076.45
2016	3,033	7795.66	2.57	3.23	19,364.67
2017	3,465	8695.24	2.51	2.40	16,492.62

Panel C: Number of investors for NEEQ firms		
No. of investors	No. of firms	Percentage (%)
2	742	6.38
3–10	4,454	38.30
11–50	4,529	38.94
51–100	953	8.19
101–200	551	4.74
200 and above	401	3.45
Total	11,630	100.00

NOTE: Total market capitalization and total trading volume are in billions of U.S. dollars. NEEQ = National Equities Exchange and Quotations. SOURCE: Authors.

NEEQ volume was $34.95 billion, a tiny fraction (0.21 percent) of the volume on the main A-shares markets. Furthermore, most of this volume was generated by trades involving bilateral negotiations between the buyer and the seller (essentially "trades by appointment"). The actual volume that involved market makers was only $12.07 billion. Panel C further shows that 83.6 percent of all the firms on the NEEQ have 50 or fewer investors; only 3.45 percent of these firms have more than 200 investors. In nontabulated results, we also find that the accounting qualities of NEEQ firms are significantly worse than those in the main A-shares markets. In short, while the NEEQ currently provides some visibility to a large number of start-up firms, it is unclear how useful this visibility is in resolving the financing needs of these start-ups.

As we have seen, mainland IPOS have played a surprisingly small role in the exit strategies of the venture financiers investing in Chinese start-ups. More VCPE investments have been closed through M&A and equity transfers than through IPOs (table 11.4). For firms that do elect to go through an IPO process, more money has been raised overseas (in Hong Kong and the United States) than in the mainland. Furthermore, a disproportionate number of high-growth technology firms are listing overseas rather than in the mainland. All these results point to potential problems with the mainland IPO approval process, a subject that we turn to in the next section.

China's Initial Public Offering Policies

The literature on law and economics highlights two main competing theories on the role of laws and institutions in the functioning of markets. The *public interest theory* (Pigou 1938) holds that unregulated markets are prone to failures, and that regulations help protect investors from market failures, such as unscrupulous operators and various negative externalities. Conversely, the *public choice theory* (Tullock 1967; Stigler 1971; Peltzman 1976) sees the government as less benign and regulation as socially inefficient. In one form of the public choice theory, the regulatory agency is "captured" (Stigler 1971) by industry and operates primarily for its benefit; in an alternative form, the regulatory agency operates a "tollbooth" primarily for the benefit of bureaucrats and politicians (McChesney 1987; De Soto 1989; Shleifer and Vishny 1998).

The IPO regulations in China present an interesting setting to examine the predictions of these competing theories. On the one hand, the rationale for China's heavy IPO regulation can be framed in terms of Pigou's *public interest theory*. Given its weak corporate governance structure and limited investor recourse through the court system (e.g., see Allen, Qian, and Qian 2005; Jiang, Lee, and Yue 2010), China needs stringent entry rules to protect investors against unscrupulous operators seeking access to public markets (e.g., Pistor and Xu 2005; Du and Xu 2009). On the other hand, these stringent rules may be better understood in the context of the *public choice theory*, wherein they actually provide minimal benefit to the investing public and are kept in place primarily because they can bestow economic rent upon politicians, bureaucrats, and industry incumbents (e.g., Shleifer and Vishny 1998).

The economic calculus of regulation calls for a policymaker to weigh the benefits of a rule against its costs. While it is difficult to quantify the benefits of China's IPO policies in terms of investor protection, the same cannot be said of its costs. In fact, a large literature now discusses the economic problems and consequences directly attributable to the country's current IPO regulations (e.g., Qian, Ritter, and Shao [2020] provide an updated discourse). In this section, we will survey this evidence and offer our own commentary. We organize this review around nine stylized facts that have emerged from this literature.

1. Long wait times and substantial outcome uncertainty for candidate firms

After 2013, the CSRC posted on its website information reviews of each candidate firm. Lee, Qu, and Shen (2020) collected these data and studied success rates and waiting times. Their results show that between 2014 and 2017, a total of 333 candidate firms received a final decision. Among them, 113 (34 percent) were rejected and 220 (66 percent) were approved for listing. The average waiting time (from the initial submission to the listing date) for the 222 firms that received approval was 24.5 months. Lee, Qu, and Shen (2020) also note that historical wait times prior to 2014 are likely longer due to several extended suspension periods.

In sum, the ones to first submit their IPO applications to the CSRC can expect to wait between one to three years before their files are reviewed, at which time they have a one-in-three chance of being approved. In our discussions with Chinese VCPE firms, we learned that during the wait period it is not advisable for the candidate firm to change its profile substantially (for example, develop new product lines, create new markets), as these changes can jeopardize its candidacy. Essentially, candidate firms need to press the pause button on many aspects of their operations after filing an IPO application.

2. A bias against high-growth technology firms

IPO qualifications on mainland exchanges are tilted heavily in favor of stable firms with steady earnings and conservative balance sheets, and against firms that invest heavily in R&D or have substantial intangible assets. This bias is evident in the pre-specified requirements that must be met by IPO candidates even before they register in the CSRC queue.

For example, minimum requirements for IPO registration, as stated in the CSRC's 2006 directive, include the following bright-line thresholds:

1. The firm must have been in operation for more than three years.
2. There must be no major change in the main business operation, directors, top executives, or controlling shareholders in the past three years.
3. The net income in each of the past three years must be positive, and the cumulative net income in the past three years must be more than ¥30 million.
4. The cumulative operating cash flows in the past three years must be more than ¥50 million; or the cumulative gross revenues in the past three years must be more than ¥300 million.
5. The total equity before IPO must be more than ¥30 million.
6. The ratio of intangible assets to net assets should be less than 20 percent in the most recent years.
7. The firm should not have any unrecovered losses in the most recent year.

These requirements would have disqualified many of the most innovative and impactful technology companies that publicly listed in the United States in recent years, including LinkedIn, Twitter, Tesla, Dropbox Inc., and Spotify Technology. In fact, Eisen (2018) reports that more than three-quarters of the 108 companies that completed IPOs in the United States in 2017 reported losses in the 12 months leading up to their public listing date. None of these companies would have been allowed to list under current Chinese IPO regulations.

The recent establishment of the National Equities Exchange and Quotations (NEEQ) market is a partial response to this problem. The NEEQ (often referred to as the "New Third Board") officially opened on January 16, 2013. Its main function is to facilitate the trading of shares in public limited companies that are not listed on either the Shenzhen or Shanghai stock exchanges. As discussed earlier, over 11,000 companies were registered with the NEEQ by the end of 2017. However, trading is thin on the NEEQ and mostly arises from bilateral negotiations between buyers and sellers rather than from market-making activities. More importantly, although registration on the NEEQ may help increase visibility, it is not a financing event. Given the illiquidity of this market, the NEEQ cannot be viewed as an effective exit option for entrepreneurs and early investors.

3. Substantial underpricing of IPOs

Mainland IPOs are typically accompanied by outsized initial day returns. For example, using a sample between 1992 and 2004, Tian (2011) shows that the average (median) first day return is 247 percent (122 percent). Between 1999 and 2007, Chen et al. (2015) find that the average (median) first day abnormal return is 127 percent (105 percent). These differences across studies reflect different sample periods and some changes in the regulations governing IPO offer prices (Chen et al. 2018). Using a recent sample from 2007 to 2015, Lee, Qu, and Shen (2019) still find an average (median) initial day abnormal return of 117 percent (53 percent).

These numbers are much larger than the initial day returns associated with IPOs in most other countries. For example, Loughran and Ritter (2004) show that initial day returns in the United States was 7 percent in the 1980s; 15 percent during 1990–98; 65 percent during the bubble years of 1999–2000; and 12 percent during 2001–03. Using an international sample of 37 countries from 1998 to 2008, Boulton, Smart, and Zutter (2011) show that, excluding China, the average IPO underpricing ranges from 1.43 percent in Argentina to 58.33 percent in Greece.

The IPO underpricing effect in China is attributable largely to an unwritten rule that calls for issuing firms to cap the maximum price-to-earnings (P/E) ratio when establishing an issue price, that is, the proposed issue price should not exceed 23 times the firm's "normal" earnings. Although the rule is not codified, it is widely acknowledged by all parties (investment banks, issuers, and venture capitalists). Firms that price their shares higher than this ratio jeopardize their chances of an approval.

One clear implication of these results is that electing to IPO on a mainland exchange can be quite costly to the issuer. Although investors with prelisting allocations earn large profits, the issuing firm often receives less than half of the total wealth generated through the listing process. In our view, assuming full disclosure of relevant facts, a firm's value assignment and adjudication is better done by market participants rather than regulators.

4. An exodus of high-quality technology firms overseas

Results outlined earlier show that over the past 11 years (2007–17), total financing received by Chinese firms that did IPO in Hong Kong and the United States exceeded the financing received by firms that did so in the mainland. Strikingly, these results also show that at the time of their IPO, the overseas Chinese firms were less profitable, more leveraged, and had much higher MB ratios. Many of these were high-quality technology firms—most notably, Alibaba and Tencent, and more recently, Sogou Inc.

Higher-quality technology firms want to be recognized as such and be weighted on a more equitable scale. To the extent that they believe the value assigned to them by investors in a foreign exchange better reflects their true worth, they would naturally migrate overseas.[17]

5. Costly reverse merger transactions

Another way to circumvent the mainland IPO process is through a reverse merger (RM). Lee, Qu, and Shen (2020) compiled a comprehensive sample of 134 "clean RM" transactions that took place on mainland exchanges, wherein control of the combined entity is transferred to the owners of the unlisted firm and takes place in a single transaction. The results show that during the 2007–15 period, unlisted Chinese firms paid an average of ¥3–4 billion (more than $400 million) for each listed shell, an amount exceeding two-thirds of the median market capitalization of listed firms at the time of the RM.

Because these shell values are established in arm's-length transactions between listed and unlisted entities, Lee, Qu, and Shen (2020) argue that they provide a "shadow price" for the cost of accessing Chinese equity markets. One immediate implication of these large shell values is that the "gate fee" associated with entry into Chinese equity markets is extraordinarily high and that, in China, a RM is not a low-cost channel through which to become publicly listed. The high price paid for shell companies also raises the speculation that Chinese IPO regulations may be too stringent and socially inefficient. Rather than serving as an effective screening mechanism for weeding out lower-quality firms,

---

17   One reason Alibaba gave for its decision to list in the United States is that investors and analysts "better understand" their business model and value proposition.

these policies may in fact be preventing healthy firms from accessing public equity markets.

Picking up on this theme, Lee, Qu, and Shen (2019) study the choice to go public through RMs versus IPOs in mainland markets. Their results show that prelisting RM firms are larger and more profitable, but less politically connected than IPO firms. Chinese RM firms also have superior post-listing performance, both in terms of operations and stock returns, compared to IPOs matched on industry and size. These results are in sharp contrast to developed countries, where RMs are smaller, riskier, and lower-quality "backdoor listings." Again, the evidence suggests that China's stringent IPO policies are blocking high-quality firms from accessing domestic equity markets.

6. Virtually no delisting or retirement of failed companies

In the normal course of events, listed firms that perform poorly should become involuntarily delisted. However, given China's high shell value, failing firms find other ways to keep their coveted listing status. Lee, Qu, and Shen (2020) show that that the average mortality rate for Chinese listed firms (defined as an involuntary delisting for performance reasons) is only 0.6 percent, or 1/40 the mortality rate for U.S. listed firms over the same period. The few firms that were delisted typically involved fraud or criminal behavior; publicly listed Chinese firms are almost never delisted for performance reasons (Allen et al. [2014] also discuss this phenomenon).

Instead of delisting or becoming a shell, poorly performing firms exploit their listing status by taking over another unlisted business. Lee, Qu, and Shen (2020) show that rather than surrender their listing status through an RM transaction, many floundering businesses "reinvent" themselves through a major asset restructuring (MAR).[18] In fact, they show one in five (19 percent) of the firms in their highest estimated shell value (ESV) decile portfolio—i.e., those firms most likely to become shell candidates—actually undergo an MAR in the next 12 months. Evidently many prime shell targets are electing to

---

18   The CSRC defines an MAR as an event where more than 50 percent of a firm's operating assets has changed, and requires firms engaged in an MAR to report such transactions. Asset swaps that do not result in a change in control will not give rise to a RM, but if the scale of the asset swap is large enough, it will result in an MAR filing.

retain control rather than surrender their listing status. To the extent these floundering firms do not have the best managerial talent, these findings point to a greater economic cost of the current IPO regulations—namely, the ability of poor managers to prolong their tenure by leveraging their listing status through MAR transactions.

7. Large cross-sectional price distortions among listed stocks

Given an average shell value of $400 million, at any given time, around 30 percent of China's publicly traded stocks will be trading below their shell value. This should lead to a number of predictable price distortions among listed stocks. Lee, Qu, and Shen (2020) hypothesize and document several such effects:

a. *Expected shell value (ESV) is a priced factor.* The authors define each firm's ESV as the product of the average prevailing shell value and the predicted probability of shell value (ESP), divided by each firm's market equity. They then examine the returns to a hedged-ESV portfolio, that is, long (short) firms with the highest (lowest) ESV. Their results show that high ESV firms earn higher future returns, even after controlling for other firm characteristics known to be associated with expected returns in China. Specifically, they find that a "long-short strategy based on extreme ESV deciles generates a raw return of 29 percent per annum and an abnormal return of 5.4 percent per annum after controlling for all five Fama-French factors. These findings establish the 'shell effect,' or the shell premium, as one of the most prominent predictive variables for equity returns in the Chinse stock market" (Lee, Qu, and Shen 2020, 4).

b. *ESV returns are sensitive to IPO-related regulatory shocks.* If RMs are driven by IPO rationing, returns to the ESV factor should be responsive to regulatory shocks associated with policy changes affecting IPO and RM activities. In particular, Lee, Qu, and Shen (2020) posit that regulatory changes tightening (relaxing) the IPO quota would be associated with positive (negative) returns to the hedged-ESV portfolio. Conversely, regulatory changes that tighten (relax) access to RMs would be associated with negative (positive) returns to the hedged-ESV portfolio. Using a set of six event studies, they find that the shell premium (i.e., returns to the EVS factor portfolio) increases sharply around the announcement of tightened IPO regulations. The opposite result is observed around events that tighten

RM regulations. These results support the view that the ESV factor captures cross-sectional differences in firms' sensitivity to IPO-related regulatory risk.

c. *High-ESV firms are insensitive to corporate earnings.* If high-ESV firms trade primarily on their expected shell value, their stock price should be less sensitive to corporate earnings. Lee, Qu, and Shen (2020) find that for high-EVS firms, there is a negative relation between reported earnings and the MB ratio, which is in sharp contrast to the positive relation that exists between earnings and pricing multiples for low-ESV firms. This result again suggests that China's IPO policies have a distortive effect on the stock returns of its publicly listed firms.

Taken together, these findings suggest that regulatory risk, as captured by fluctuating shell values, is an important economic driver of cross-sectional returns (particularly the large returns earned by small firms) in China.

8. Listing delays leading directly to a reduction in innovation activities

The IPO approval committee at CSRC controls the aggregate approval rate for IPO applications based on market conditions, as too many IPOs may lead to reduced liquidity and market valuation (Braun and Larrain 2009; Tian 2011). One extreme form of regulation that delays listing is an IPO suspension, which puts a pause on all IPO activities beyond the application submission step. Between 1994 and 2016, there were nine major IPO suspensions lasting from three to 14 months. These suspensions were often determined at ad hoc meetings and not announced beforehand, and therefore not fully anticipated by market participants. Such delays are especially costly to firms already approved to IPO because of foregone strategic opportunities (e.g., to make acquisitions or large investments using public funds) and disruptions to long-term corporate plans to invest and innovate.

Cong and Howell (2021) use a novel identification strategy to examine the effect of uncertainty associated with a listing delay due to China's IPO policy on firms' innovation-related activities. Specifically, they assembled a comprehensive data set from multiple sources including IPO prospectuses, Google Patents, CSRC, and the State Intellectual Property Office, covering 1,567 firms that were approved and ultimately went public on the Shanghai and Shenzhen exchanges between 2004 and 2015. Focusing on four recent suspensions affecting firms approved within the year before each suspension, they exploited the fact that the assignment to the control (firms listed right before the suspensions) and treatment groups (firms listed after the suspensions ended) is stochastic and not driven by firm-specific factors.[19] The authors argue that suspension-affected firms faced a longer time between approval and listing as well as greater operational uncertainty. They then examined the lasting impact of temporal delays to accessing the public markets.

Their results show that an extra month of delay reduces innovation-related outputs (measured using patent quantity and quality) during the suspension and even after the firms ultimately list: it reduces the number of patent applications to the State Intellectual Property Office (SIPO) by more than 10 percent of the mean; it also reduces the number of citations to grant SIPO patents by about 10 percent and the number of invention patents by more than 10 percent. These effects begin shortly after IPO approval and endure for years after listing.

The authors also find a positive treatment effect on leverage, a negative effect on tangible investment and return on sales, and no effect on total sales or earnings, but none of these effects lasts beyond the first year of the IPO. Taken together, these findings suggest that innovation is a cumulative process and that delays in the process can have lasting effects on outputs. Specifically, they provide an estimate of the economic loss, in terms of innovation-related outputs, associated with the detrimental listing delays. They also establish a direct link between frictions in the financing process and output-based measures of firm innovation.

9. Potentially inflated prices and excessive speculative trading

China's restrictive IPO regulations are also associated with another problem: the possibility that stock prices in domestic markets can drift further away from fundamental values. These entry regulations form a costly barrier, insulating the domestic market from arbitrage forces at

---

19   Even though application approval could be driven by specific firms' connections with local politicians (e.g., Piotroski and Zhang 2014), the CSRC and local governments do not intervene in the listing process due to firm-specific reasons (except for illegal activities) once the application is approved.

work in other markets. As a result, institutional ownership in mainland markets is low, and foreign ownership is even lower, leading to much noisier stock prices.[20] This effect can be seen in two related empirical phenomena: (1) a wider corridor for mispricing relative to fundamentals and (2) greater levels of speculative trading.

Evidence of the mispricing precipitated by the artificial entry barrier can be seen in the pricing of cross-listed stocks. A number of Chinese firms are cross-listed in both the mainland and in Hong Kong. For many years, the price of A-shares routinely diverged from (and was typically higher than) the price of H-shares for the same company traded in Hong Kong, even though these shares are equivalent claims on the same underlying cash flows. A useful measure to gauge the price disparity is the Hang Seng Stock Connect China AH Premium Index (HSAHP), which tracks the average price differential of A-shares over H-shares for the most liquid cross-listed companies. When HSAHP is higher (lower) than 100, A-shares are trading at a premium (discount) relative to H-shares.

In 2007–17, the annual average HSAHP ranged from a low of 97.98 in 2014 (the only year below 100) to a high of 148.37 in 2007. In earlier years, the premium tended to be larger. For example, Wang and Jiang (2004) studied a sample of 16 A-H dual-listed stocks from 1996 and 2001 and found that the average daily price premium of A-shares relative to H-shares was about 32 percent. In recent years, the pricing differential appears to have decreased. However, even as we write, a sizeable A-share premium remains. The average daily HSAHP for 2018, as of August 17, was 123.40, suggesting an average premium for A-shares of approximately 23 percent. The continuation of this pricing difference speaks both to the limits to arbitrage at play and the general tendency for domestic Chinese investors to prefer A-shares.[21]

---

20   For example, Jiang, Lee, and Yue (2010, table 8) report that for stocks listed on mainland exchanges, the mean (median) ownership by institutional investors in 2004 was only 8.64 (1.26) percent of the total tradable shares. They argue that this low level of institutional ownership is one reason why stock prices did not fully incorporate the value implications of self-dealing (or "tunneling") by firms' block shareholders. Institutional ownership has increased in recent years, but it is still much lower than in other developed countries.

21   Recent innovations, such as the initiation of the Mainland–Hong Kong Stock Connect program in 2016, could reduce arbitrage costs over time. In brief, this program allows mainland investors to buy/sell Hong Kong–listed shares, and Hong Kong investors to buy/sell mainland shares. However, a number of factors make this trade far from riskless. First, currency is an issue, as A-shares are priced in yuan

Another by-product of market fragmentation traceable to the insular nature of mainland markets is higher turnovers. Pan, Tang, and Xu (2016) report the annual turnover rate of the 20 largest equity markets worldwide at the end of 2012. In the 1990s, the annual turnover rate in China was nearly 500 percent, while the annual turnover rate for other countries rarely exceeded 100 percent. After 2000, the annual turnover rate in China gradually decreased to 200 percent but was still much higher than that of other countries. Pan, Tang, and Xu (2016) attribute this high turnover rate to speculative trading and show that a measure of the abnormal turnover rate negatively predicts future marketwide returns in China. Similarly, Hu, Pan, and Wang (2018) report that the monthly turnover in mainland markets averaged around 20 percent during 1990 to 2015. They find that the monthly turnover exhibits wide fluctuations over time without any obvious time trends. For example, China's monthly turnover rate exceeded 120 percent in 1994, 1997, and 2007, and dropped below 10 percent in 2002, 2012, and 2013. These wide swings seem to reflect ebbs and flows in the level of retail investor interest in mainland equities. To the extent that institutional appetite for equities is different, policies that invite greater institutional participation (particularly by foreign investors) should lead to more stable domestic markets.

Summary

Reflections on public policy implications

In this study, we have reported on the current state of affairs in the funding of entrepreneurship and innovations in China and provided a

---

and H-shares in Hong Kong dollars. Second, investor preference in the mainland still favors A-shares. Even when the same company's H-shares are available at a cheaper currency adjusted price through Stock Connect, not enough mainland investors are selling their A-shares in favor of the Hong Kong offering. Third, only larger and more liquid mainland stocks are available through Stock Connect, and it is extremely difficult to short sell mainland shares. Finally, although both types of shares are legal claims to the same underlying cash flows, no direct arbitrage exists. This is because A- and H-shares of the same company cannot be bought and sold in each other's respective markets. All these factors conspire to generate the 20+ percent premium we observe today. Other studies that examine the A/H pricing puzzle include Chan, Kot, and Yang (2009); Zhao, Ma, and Liu (2005); and Zhang and Zhang (2018).

broad survey of academic findings on the subject. Rather than focusing narrowly on a specific subject in this domain, our goal is to curate a broad set of related results and present them for evaluation from a public policy perspective.

Our analyses reveal an exponential rate of growth in total VCPE funding for "mid-stage" enterprises operating in China, particularly over the most recent three years. In 2017, total VCPE funding for Chinese firms exceeded $400 billion, and was second only to the United States. Most of this funding comes from Chinese rather than foreign sources, with both government entities and Chinese private corporations playing substantial roles. This surge in mid-stage funding has occurred in concert with, and endogenous to, the rise of many highly innovative private technology firms, each with a valuation above $1 billion (the 164 Chinese "unicorns" mentioned at the outset). The level of innovative activities in China, as measured by these metrics, has never been higher.

At the same time, our analyses suggest opportunities for improvement in the early stage of the entrepreneurial life cycle. Compared to their counterparts in the United States, early-stage entrepreneurs in China appear to have less access to microfinancing, crowdfunding, accelerator, and incubator programs (with China's Innofund being a notable exception). Beyond financial support, early-stage entrepreneurs often need advice, mentorship, connections, and other educational components not currently available from programs such as the Innofund. For example, in Canada, a network of government organizations (such as the Ontario Network of Entrepreneurs), working together with regional not-for-profit organizations (such as Haltech, MaRS, Communitech, and Invest Ottawa), have advised and mentored startups to help them commercialize their ideas. The Ontario Network of Entrepreneurs alone helped more than 5,600 entrepreneurs to open new businesses (Khosravi 2018). This could be a potentially interesting direction for Chinese policymakers to consider.

Our analyses also point to opportunities for improvement in the late stage of the entrepreneurial life cycle. Specifically, current regulations governing IPOs are antiquated and in dire need of reform. They require candidate firms to endure long wait times, with a significant risk of delays and rejections. They also hold a bias against high-growth technology firms, which typically have lower profits, less developed businesses, and more intangible assets. Furthermore, evidence now links the outcome of the IPO review to a candidate firm's political connectedness.

Given the problems associated with domestic IPOs, it is not surprising that many Chinese entrepreneurs have sought alternative exit strategies. Over the past eleven years, more money has been raised by Chinese firms in overseas IPOs (in the United States and Hong Kong) than in mainland IPOs. Alternatively, to avoid the IPO gauntlet, many private firms have spent an average of $400 million each to purchase a "shell" company in an RM transaction. These large shell values have in turn led to price distortions in China's equity markets, including extraordinarily large returns to the smallest firms. They also help to explain why failed companies almost never delist from public equity markets—they continue to propagate by leveraging their listing status to acquire new lines of business, thus maintaining control despite a demonstrated track record of failure. At the same time, the private (unlisted) firms that are absorbed by these failed entities are circumventing the IPO process, and are gaining public market access without having undergone the mandatory scrutiny and review.

China's current IPO regulations thus are the most serious impediment to two important near-term goals expressly espoused by the Chinese government: (1) to bring more high-technology firms back to mainland stock markets, and (2) to be included at a meaningful weight in international stock indices, particularly the MSCI Emerging Market Index. We discuss each of these goals in turn.

In March 2018, the State Council passed new regulations allowing for fast-track approval of Chinese Depository Receipts by technology firms that have listed overseas. The CSRC is also actively lobbying for large China private technology firms to list domestically rather than abroad (e.g., Yu and Zhang 2018). Though some firms will respond to the "expedited IPO processing" offers now being extended by Chinese regulators, others may see these policies as addressing the symptoms rather than the root cause. Theory suggests that higher-quality firms will want to be recognized as such and if they believe a foreign listing better signals their worth or foreign markets offer greater depth and liquidity, they may still choose to list overseas. Therefore, only a fundamental overhaul of the IPO review system would provide a clearer and more credible signal to these firms that Chinese equity markets will provide a long-term solution to their financing needs.

With respect to the second goal, China's A-shares market is currently the second-largest market in the world; yet it is also the most underowned (by foreign investors). A key reason for this is its exclusion from closely watched and trusted index providers like MSCI Inc. In 2013,

MSCI put A-shares on a review list but declined to include them in any indexes, citing issues such as capital mobility restrictions and uncertainties around taxes. It continued to reject A-shares in 2015 and 2016. Finally, in June 2017, MSCI announced a 5 percent partial inclusion to be implemented in 2018, as an acknowledgment of China's efforts to reform its capital markets. The partial inclusion means A-share stocks will form roughly 0.73 percent of the MSCI Emerging Market (EM) index and 0.1 percent of the MSCI All Country (AC) World index by the end of 2018. Analysts estimate that this partial inclusion translates into $20 billion in foreign investment in Chinese markets. At full inclusion, China would represent about 20 percent of the MSCI EM index, which would translate into at least an additional $300 billion in foreign investments. However, MSCI is clear that further inclusion, if any, would depend on the pace of market reform in China.

Considering the problems identified above, we recommend a move toward a registration-and-disclosure system for Chinese IPOs, like those employed by most other countries. In such systems, investors monitor firm quality and market forces adjudicate firm value. Firms that receive enough support from the investment community will attain IPO status. The role of regulators is to ensure adherence to established ordinances, which are largely disclosure centric. The new Science and Technology Board (STAR Market) announced in November 2018 by President Xi Jinping follows this direction and aims to address some of the above issues. Firms have started to apply for listing on this board from March 2019. China subsequently revised rules on the GEM board and the Shenzhen Stock Exchange (which were introduced earlier but lacked quality listing and liquidity) and modeled them after the STAR market. Qian, Ritter, and Shao (2020) offer a more detailed discussion.

There are some concerns over the sophistication of current A-share investors, and whether they can be relied upon to evaluate the worthiness of IPO firms. Retail investors do play a large role in the trading of A-shares at the moment, and in view of the many problems associated with current IPO regulations, investor protection arguments can no longer justify retention of the status quo. In fact, it is likely that IPO reform will trigger large inflows of foreign capital as MSCI and other index providers increase their A-share allocation to full weight (see preceding section for details). At the same time, this reform will attract the high-growth technology firms that investors, both domestic and foreign, are most interested in owning. Financial education and investment literacy should improve quickly as domestic equity markets become more integrated with global markets.

Reflections on future research directions

Based on our survey of recent research, we have identified three understudied areas. While these fall under the general rubric of entrepreneurial finance, they seem particularly relevant to the current state of affairs in China.

First, relatively little work has been done on the interaction between financing choices (particularly public market financing) and innovations. Given that most of the industrial innovations are not accomplished by organizations other than small firms backed by VCs (Kortum and Lerner 2000), it is important to understand the role that public markets and arm's-length financiers play in facilitating innovation. For example, Atanassov, Nanda, and Seru (2007) find that firms with arm's-length financing have more patents and more novel patents. What drives this result? Is this finding related to the distinction between exploitative versus exploratory innovation, as discussed in Ferreira, Manso, and Silva (2012)? Does it reflect selection or treatment effects? Some progress is being made in this area (e.g., Bernstein 2015; Acharya and Xu 2017), but more research is clearly needed.

Second, the role of government and interventions is understudied. Researchers have begun to examine the ways in which policymakers can catalyze the growth of VC firms and encourage innovation (Irwin and Klenow 1996; Wallsten 2000). Government interventions can help coordinate innovative effort that exhibits complementarity. At the same time, they can alter agents' incentives to become entrepreneurs and innovate, as well as the informational environment in general (Cong, Grenadier, and Hu 2020; Brunnermeier, Sockin, and Xiong 2017).

Given the prominent role of the government in the Chinese economy, it is crucial to understand the benefits and unintended consequences of government interventions. As we reported earlier in the chapter, government entities and SOEs invest extensively in Chinese start-ups. Government initiatives such as the Innofund have also played an active role in financing R&D activities among small and medium technology firms. Yet, with few exceptions (e.g., Guo, Guo, and Jiang 2016; Wang, Li, and Furman 2017), prior studies have provided little evidence on the usefulness of such programs in improving innovation outputs.

Government-led programs also need to consider nonfinancial policy objectives (such as income inequality, market stability, job creation, or the development of strategic sectors), but interventions designed to serve other objectives may have unintended consequences on the innovation process. Clearly, more research is needed to understand both the benefits and costs of government interventions, whether they are directly targeted at innovations or not.

Third, studies on the impact of new forms of financing innovation and start-ups are emerging. Peer-to-peer lending, crowdfunding, and blockchain-based initial coin offerings are notable examples. How are projects evaluated in this environment? Is information better aggregated for efficient investment or termination of innovative projects? Do crypto-tokens serve special functions that encourage open-sourced, decentralized innovations? How do digital platforms shape entrepreneurship and the real economy? Mollick and Nanda (2015); Cong and Xiao (2019); Cong, Tang, Xie, and Miao (2020); and Cong, Li, and Wang (2021, 2020) are early discussions on this front. In the Chinese setting, many of the new e-commerce and fintech firms may provide the data needed to conduct such studies (e.g., Hau et al. 2019; Cong, Ponticelli, Yang, and Zhang 2020). This could be a rich area for future research.

In sum, current research on financing innovations in China is quite limited. This chapter aims to provide a modest contribution in this area by bringing together a wide set of related literature in economics and finance. Given the government's active role in encouraging entrepreneurship and regulating the financial market, China offers an attractive context in which to advance our understanding of many of the aforementioned issues.

References

Abramowitz, Moses. 1956. "Resource and Output Trends in the United States Since 1870." *American Economic Review* 46 (2): 5–23.

Acharya, Viral, and Zhaoxia Xu. 2017. "Financial Dependence and Innovation: The Case of Public versus Private Firms." *Journal of Financial Economics* 124 (2): 223–43.

Ahlstrom, David, Garry D. Bruton, and Kuang S. Yeh. 2007. "Venture Capital in China: Past, Present, and Future." *Asia Pacific Journal of Management* 24 (3): 247–68.

Allen, Franklin, Jun Qian, and Meijun Qian. 2005. "Law, Finance, and Economic Growth in China." *Journal of Financial Economics* 77 (1): 57–116.

Allen, Franklin, Jun Qian, Susan Chenyu Shan, and Julie Lei Zhu. 2014. "The Best Performing Economy with the Worst Performing Market: Explaining the Poor Performance of the Chinese Stock Market." Working paper, Shanghai Advanced Institute of Finance, Shanghai.

Atanassov, Julian, Vikram K. Nanda, and Amit Seru. 2007. "Finance and Innovation: The Case of Publicly Traded Firms." Working paper, University of Oregon, Arizona State University, and University of Michigan, May.

Bernstein, Shai. 2015. "Does Going Public Affect Innovation?" *Journal of Finance* 70 (4): 1365–403.

Bloom, Nicholas, Mark Schankerman, and John van Reenen. 2013. "Identifying Technology Spillovers and Product Market Rivalry." *Econometrica* 81 (4): 1347–93.

Boulton, Thomas J., Scott B. Smart, and Chad J. Zutter. 2011. "Earnings Quality and International IPO Underpricing." *Accounting Review* 86 (2): 483–505.

Braun, Matías, and Borja Larrain. 2009. "Do IPOs Affect the Prices of Other Stocks? Evidence from Emerging Markets." *Review of Financial Studies* 22 (4): 1505–44.

Brunnermeier, Markus, Michael Sockin, and Wei Xiong. 2017. "China's Model of Managing the Financial System." Unpublished working paper.

Cao, Jerry, Mark Humphery-Jenner, and Jo-Ann Suchard. 2013. "Government Ownership and Venture Performance: Evidence from China." Working paper. https://dukekunshan.edu.cn/dukeiff2015/files/GOandVP.pdf.

Casanova, Lourdes, Peter K. Cornelius, and Soumitra Dutta. 2018. *Financing Entrepreneurship and Innovation in Emerging Markets.* Cambridge, MA: Academic Press.

Chan, Kalok, Hung W. Kot, and Zhishu Yang. 2009. "Short-Sale Constraints and A/H Share Premiums." HKUST working paper, Hong Kong University of Science & Technology.

Chen, Huafeng, Xiaofei Pan, Meijun Qian, Yiping Wu, and Qing Xia. 2021. "Asset Pledgeability and Firm Innovation." Working paper.

Chen, Jun, Bin Ke, Donghui Wu, and Zhifeng Yang. 2018. "The Consequences of Shifting the IPO Offer Pricing Power from Securities

Regulators to Market Participants in Weak Institutional Environments: Evidence from China." *Journal of Corporate Finance* 50 (June): 349–70.

Chen, Yibiao, Steven S.Wang, Wei Li, Qian Sun, and Wilson H. S. Tong. 2015. "Institutional Environment, Firm Ownership, and IPO First-Day Returns: Evidence from China." *Journal of Corporate Finance* 32 (June): 150–68.

Cong, Lin W., Steven R. Grenadier, and Yunzhi Hu. 2020. "Dynamic Interventions and Informational Linkages." *Journal of Financial Economics* 135 (1): 1–15.

Cong, Lin W., and Sabrina T. Howell. 2021. "Policy Uncertainty and Innovation: Evidence from IPO Interventions in China." *Management Science* 67 (11): 6629-7289.

Cong, Lin W., Charles M.C. Lee, Yuanyu Qu, and Tao Shen. 2020. "Financing Entrepreneurship and Innovation in China." *Foundations and Trends in Entrepreneurship* 16, no. 1 (2020): 1–64. https://doi.org/10.1561/0300000095.

Cong, Lin W., Ye Li, and Neng Wang. 2020. "Token-Based Platform Finance." NBER Working Paper 27810, National Bureau of Economic Research, Inc., Cambridge, MA.

———. 2021. "Tokenomics: Dynamic Adoption and Valuation." *Review of Financial Studies* 34 (3): 1105–55.

Cong, Lin W., Jacopo Ponticelli, Xiaohan Yang, and Xiaobo Zhang. 2020. "Digital Platforms and the Real Economy: Regional Entrepreneurship and Industrial Development." Working paper.

Cong, Lin W., Ke Tang, Danxia Xie, and Qi Miao. 2020. "Asymmetric Cross-Side Network Effects on Financial Platforms: Theory and Evidence from Marketplace Lending." Working paper.

Cong, Lin W., and Yizhou Xiao. 2019. "Information Cascade and Threshold Implementation: An Application to Crowdfunding." Working Paper No. 2019-30, Becker Friedman Institute, Chicago, IL.

De Soto, Hernando. 1989. *The Other Path*. New York: HarperCollins.

Du, Julan, and Chenggang Xu. 2009. "Which Firms Went Public in China? A Study of Financial Market Regulation." *World Development* 37 (4): 812–24.

Eisen, Ben. 2018. "No Profit? No Problem! Loss-Making Companies Flood the IPO Market." *Wall Street Journal*, March 16. Accessed August 18, 2018. https://blogs.wsj.com/moneybeat/2018/03/16/spotify-and-dropbox-to-join-a-growing-club-profitless-public-companies/.

Fan, Joseph P., T. J. Wong, and Tianyu Zhang. 2007. "Politically Connected CEOs, Corporate Governance, and Post-IPO Performance of China's Newly Partially Privatized Firms." *Journal of Financial Economics* 84 (2): 330–57.

Ferreira, Daniel, Gustavo Manso, and André C. Silva. 2012. "Incentives to Innovate and the Decision to Go Public or Private." *Review of Financial Studies* 27 (1): 256–300.

Francis, Bill B., Iftekhar Hasan, and Xian Sun. 2009. "Political Connections and the Process of Going Public: Evidence from China." *Journal of International Money and Finance* 28 (4): 696–719.

Guo, Di, and Kun Jiang. 2013. "Venture Capital Investment and the Performance of Entrepreneurial Firms: Evidence from China." *Journal of Corporate Finance* 22 (September): 375–95.

Guo, Di, Yan Guo, and Kun Jiang. 2016. "Government-Subsidized R&D and Firm Innovation: Evidence from China." *Research Policy* 45 (6): 1129–44.

Hau, Harald, Yi Huang, Hongzhe Shan, and Zixia Sheng, 2019. "TechFin in China: Credit Market Completion and Its Growth Effect." Working paper. http://abfer.org/media/abfer-events-2018/annual-conference/international-macroeconomics/AC18P1014_Ant_Financial_and_Growth_Effect_Paper_first_draft.pdf

Hu, Grace Xing, Jun Pan, and Jiang Wang. 2018. "Chinese Capital Market: An Empirical Overview." Working Paper 24346, National Bureau of Economic Research. https://www.nber.org/system/files/working_papers/w24346/w24346.pdf.

Humphery-Jenner, Mark, and Jo-Ann Suchard. 2013. "Foreign VCs and Venture Success: Evidence from China." *Journal of Corporate Finance* 21 (June): 16–35.

Irwin, Douglas A., and Peter J. Klenow. 1996. "High-Tech R&D Subsidies: Estimating the Effects of Sematech." *Journal of International Economics* 40 (3–4): 323–44.

Jiang, Guohua, Charles M. C. Lee, and Heng Yue. 2010. "Tunneling through Intercorporate Loans: The China Experience." *Journal of Financial Economics* 98 (1): 1–20.

Khosravi, Bijan. 2018. "Early Stage Startups Are Struggling, While VC Investment Dollars Are at All Time High." *Forbes*, June 3. https://www.forbes.com/sites/bijankhosravi/2018/06/03/early-stage-startups-are-struggling-while-vc-investment-dollars-are-at-all-time-high/#3b87d277468b.

Kogan, Leonid, Dimitris Papanikolaou, Amit Seru, and Noah Stoffman. 2017. "Technological Innovation, Resource Allocation, and Growth." *Quarterly Journal of Economics* 132 (2): 665–712.

Kortum, Samuel, and Josh Lerner. 2000. "Assessing the Contribution of Venture Capital to Innovation." *RAND Journal of Economics* 31 (4): 674–92.

Lee, Charles M. C., Yuanyu Qu, and Tao Shen. 2019. "Going Public in China: Reverse Mergers versus IPOs." *Journal of Corporate Finance* 58 (October): 92–111.

———. vv2020. "Gate Fees: Shell Values and Regulatory Risk in Chinese Equity Markets." Working paper, Stanford University, University of International Business and Economics, and Tsinghua University.

Li, Guoping, and Hong Zhou. 2015. "Political Connections and Access to IPO Markets in China." *China Economic Review* 33 (April): 76–93.

Loughran, Tim, and Jay Ritter. 2004. "Why Has IPO Underpricing Changed Over Time?" *Financial Management* 33 (3): 5–37.

McChesney, Fred S. 1987. "Rent Extraction and Rent Creation in the Economic Theory of Regulation." *Journal of Legal Studies* 16 (1):101–18.

Mollick, Ethan, and Ramana Nanda. 2015. "Wisdom or Madness? Comparing Crowds with Expert Evaluation in Funding the Arts." *Management Science* 62 (6): 1533–53.

OECD (Organisation for Economic Co-operation and Development). 2016. "OECD Science, Technology and Innovation Outlook 2016: Highlights." https://www.oecd.org/sti/STIO%20Key%20messages _backup.pdf.

Pan, Li., Ya Tang, and Jianguo Xu. 2016. "Speculative Trading and Stock Returns." *Review of Finance* 20 (5): 1835–65.

Peltzman, Sam. 1976. "Toward a More General Theory of Regulation." *Journal of Law and Economics* 19 (2): 211–40.

Pigou, Arthur C. 1938. *The Economics of Welfare.* London: Macmillan.

Piotroski, Joseph D., and Tianyu Zhang. 2014. "Politicians and the IPO Decision: The Impact of Impending Political Promotions on IPO Activity in China." *Journal of Financial Economics* 111 (1): 111–36.

Pistor, Katharina, and Chenggang Xu. 2005. "Governing Stock Markets in Transition Economies: Lessons from China." *American Law and Economics Review* 7 (1): 184–210.

Qian, Yiming, Jay Ritter, and Xinjian Shao. 2020. "Initial Public Offerings Chinese Style." Working paper.

Shleifer, Andrei, and Robert W. Vishny. 1998. *The Grabbing Hand: Government Pathologies and Their Cures.* Cambridge, MA: Harvard University Press.

Solow, Robert M. 1957. "Technical Change and the Aggregate Production Function." *Review of Economics and Statistics* 39 (3): 312–20.

Stigler, George J. 1971. "The Theory of Economic Regulation." *Bell Journal of Economics and Management Science* 2 (1): 3–21.

Tian, Lihui. 2011. "Regulatory Underpricing: Determinants of Chinese Extreme IPO Returns." *Journal of Empirical Finance* 18 (1): 78–90.

Tullock, Gordon. 1967. "The Welfare Costs of Tariffs, Monopolies, and Theft." *Economic Inquiry* 5 (3): 224–32

Wallsten, Scott J. 2000. "The Effects of Government-Industry R&D Programs on Private R&D: The Case of the Small Business Innovation Research Program." *RAND Journal of Economics* 31 (1): 82–100.

Wang, Steven S., and Li Jiang. 2004. "Location of Trade, Ownership Restrictions, and Market Illiquidity: Examining Chinese A-and H-Shares." *Journal of Banking & Finance* 28 (6): 1273–97.

Wang, Yanbo, Jizhen Li, and Jeffrey L. Furman. 2017. "Firm Performance and State Innovation Funding: Evidence from China's Innofund Program." *Research Policy* 46 (6): 1142–61.

Yu, Xie, and Maggie Zhang. 2018. "At the Heart of China's Techno-Nationalism Is a Hit List of 200 Unicorns." *South China Morning Post,* March 31. https://www.scmp.com/business/companies/article/2139684/heart-chinas-techno-nationalism-hit-list-200-unicorns.

Zhang, Renbin, and Tongbin Zhang. 2018. "Understanding AH Premium in China Stock Market." Working paper. Universitat Autonoma de Barcelona and the Shangahi University of Finance and Economics, February 9.

Zhang, Jing, Wei Zhang, Andreas Schwab, and Sipei Zhang. 2017. "Institutional Environment and IPO Strategy: A Study of ChiNext in China." *Management and Organization Review* 13 (2): 399–430.

Zhao, Zhijun, Yue Ma, and Yuhui Liu. 2005. "Equity Valuation in Mainland China and Hong Kong: The Chinese A-H Share Premium." Working Paper 142005, Hong Kong Institute for Monetary Research.

Zhou, Xiangyi, Kun Chen, and Xiao Sheng. 2017. "How Does Industrial Policy Affect Venture Capital Performance? Evidence from China." Working paper.

12 In Need of a Big Bang

Toward a Merit-Based System for Government-Sponsored Research in India

Dinsha Mistree

"The time for incremental change is long over. The current age is one that requires transformational change that comes only with drastic policy reform."
—Prime Minister Narendra Modi, remarks at NITI-Aayog on Indian innovation policy, July 27, 2016

Innovation offers tremendous promise. It has the potential to drive economic growth by attracting investment, creating new jobs, and generally growing the pie for everyone. It can be directed to solve otherwise intractable problems that a society faces. It can be used to make a society self-sufficient across a variety of domains, including food, energy, and water. Innovation can radically reduce the costs of provision of basic services like health, education, and security. Innovation can even foster national pride through high-status pursuits like "cancer moonshots" and space exploration.

Yet even though a government's innovation policy has the potential to advance an entire spectrum of developmental projects, it must be determined through careful prioritization. A state with limited resources cannot pursue too many priorities, especially in a developing country like India, where the state must balance its aspirations for funding high-risk innovation projects (such as an ambitious mission to Mars or decoding the human genome) with the more immediate needs of its populace (providing mass literacy, immunizations, and decent infrastructure). Such pressing needs often change the calculus of innovation funding, as the opportunity cost of any research project must be taken into account. Therefore, government-sponsored innovation projects in developing countries need to offer great promise along with a minimal risk of failure.[1]

Against this backdrop, there seems to be widespread agreement that India's strategy for innovation requires drastic reform. During his tenure, Prime Minister Narendra Modi has repeatedly underscored the need to modernize innovation policy in the country; political leaders from the Congress Party and other regional parties have also made similar declarations. Nearly every *Economic Survey of India* over the past two decades has devoted a chapter to reforming innovation policy, with several high-level government panels being convened on this topic. These political and policy moves tend to focus on choosing priority areas for research. Consider, for instance, the *Economic Survey of India 2017–18*, which calls for research and development (R&D) across six national missions, including dark matter, genomics, energy storage, mathematics, cyber physical systems, and agriculture (Ministry of Finance 2018, chapter 8, "Transforming Science and Technology in India"). It is unclear why or how these six missions were prioritized, but it is safe to assume that these priority areas were set by political officials and generalist bureaucrats rather than scientists. In 2019, the prime minister convened a new panel on science and technology innovation, this time with some of the country's most eminent bureaucrat-scientists. The panel announced nine other national missions that would explore natural language translation, quantum mechanics, artificial intelligence, biodiversity, electric vehicles, bioscience for human health, how waste can be converted to wealth, deep ocean exploration, and how to commercialize innovative solutions.[2] Yet despite the great publicity that came with the announcement, it is unclear what steps the government is actually taking to pursue these national missions.

For government-funded innovation projects to realize their promise, Indian leaders need to get away from the cycle of announcing pet

---

1   This is not to say that governments in developing countries should not pursue innovation. Such an argument holds little weight, particularly when the promise of innovation is so great. Instead, it is critical that a government in a developing country ensures that its spending on innovation is maximized for its intended impact. Wasted resources not only undermine the promise of innovation, but they also impede the prospects of development in other resource-poor domains.

2   Office of the Principal Scientific Adviser to the Government of India, *Report of the Principal Scientific Adviser to the GOI 2019–2020*, https://static.psa.gov.in/psa-prod/publication/PSA%20Annual%20Report_Jan%2011th%2C%202021_.pdf

projects and institute deeper reforms. A first step comes from recognizing that innovation policy is—and should be—a subject of constant discussion. In nearly every major country, government officials (usually politicians) and the scientific community struggle to set innovation priorities. Government officials rarely understand the steps and stages of scientific advancement, whereas the scientific community is poorly positioned to answer normative concerns over what is most important to a society. Every society needs to decide whether innovation policy should focus on maximizing economic returns exclusively or whether the government should also pursue innovations that might increase societal well-being, perhaps by reducing the cost of a vaccine or by landing a person on the moon to inspire the nation. Research priorities thus should be decided in a systematic and institutionalized manner, ideally with as little media attention as possible, to avoid generating more flash than substance.

Apart from identifying priority areas, the current machinery in the Indian government that is tasked with executing innovation policy needs to be overhauled. Excluding spending for higher education, the Indian Department of Science and Technology estimates that the central government, the state governments, and public sector enterprises spent a combined total of ₹60,821 crore (~$8.5 billion) on R&D in 2017–18.[3] In nearly every other country in the world, government funds for innovation are usually disbursed to the private sector or to academic research laboratories. In India, on the other hand, government research laboratories spend nearly all of this money on R&D that is conducted in-house. Unfortunately, these laboratories suffer from hierarchical and inefficient management structures that offer few incentives for the production or commercialization of research. This model is disturbingly inefficient, and the track record of the government research laboratories is woeful compared to their potential.

To address these structural flaws, in this chapter I argue that India's government research laboratories need to be consolidated and converted into research funding agencies along the lines of the National

---

3   See Ministry of Science and Technology (2018). ₹1 crore equals ₹10,000,000 (the exchange rate is ₹71.47 for $1 on February 10, 2019). Military spending only accounts for about ₹14,819 crore (~$2 billion) (Ministry of Defence n.d.). The government has substantially grown the exchequer's revenue base since 2017–18, and expenditures in the upcoming 2019–20 budget are projected to be about 30 percent higher, although it is unclear whether R&D expenditures will grow correspondingly.

Science Foundation in the United States or the European Research Council. In government institutions like these, research priorities are set through deliberations between government officials and researchers, while funds are allocated through competitive, merit-based peer review processes to external organizations, mostly in the private sector and in academia.

The vast majority of the research personnel who currently work in Indian government laboratories can either opt for the private sector or be transferred to technical or medical universities, where they can create smaller and more nimble laboratories for engaging in research. Such a transfer of talent would simultaneously alleviate the tremendous faculty shortage that the Indian higher education system is experiencing because of recent expansions: 35 percent of the faculty slots at the Indian Institutes of Technology (IITs) were vacant as of 2017, and in India's regional technical colleges, known as the National Institutes of Technology, the share of vacancies was even higher, at 47 percent (Gosain 2017). This faculty shortage also afflicts state and central universities throughout India's higher education sector.

Reform efforts must consider ideological factors as well. Even though the Indian innovation space has been built on previous Western practices—and Indian politicians seem more willing than before to incorporate these practices—many reforms in this space have been and can be derailed by becoming pejoratively associated with foreign influence. A reform effort that brings meritocratic practices to India's innovation space must consider the political realities of material and ideological resistance; superior policy alone will not win out.

This chapter is laid out in the following manner. In the next section, I compare R&D spending in India with other countries in East Asia. As a proportion of overall R&D spending, the Indian government bears a far more substantial burden than counterpart countries in Asia. I then discuss the merit-based, peer-reviewed funding system that was developed in the United States and has been adopted in many other Asian countries. Compared to India's current system for funding innovation, this system seems like it would support more nimble and effective research as incentives would be aligned with performance. Also, there could be some positive externalities if government research laboratories were smaller. With some exceptions, Indian government research laboratories measure their success primarily by patents and publications. The private sector and academia not only have the potential to match research laboratory performance in these two metrics, but can also offer other benefits in the forms of more commercializable research (in the case of the private sector) and student training (in the case of academia). In the penultimate section, I consider possible political resistance to reforming the system, paying special attention to *material resistance* from those who currently gain from the status quo as well as *ideological resistance* from those who might reject the introduction of foreign practices in innovation. The fifth section concludes.

Comparisons in Innovation Spending: India versus the Rest

In this section, I consider how Indian innovation spending compares to other innovation-driven economies in Asia and identify how Indian spending patterns diverge from other economies, framing the subsequent policy recommendations.

Indian innovation spending stands out in at least three important respects compared to the leading innovation-driven Asian economies. First, although India's current public and private spending for innovation is in line with its level of economic development, it has stagnated over the past four decades relative to its gross domestic product (GDP).[4] Since 1980, India has generally spent between 0.6 and 0.8 percent of its GDP on R&D, which trails the Asian Tigers as well as the United States (see table 12.1).[5] Interestingly, the country was comparable with South Korea until 1980, and even ahead of China until 2000. But unlike these countries, where R&D expenditures have grown over time relative to GDP, India has experienced no such increase. This suggests that while economic growth will increase absolute levels of R&D spending, policy changes are required to increase R&D expenditures relative to GDP.

This brings up a second difference between India and its comparator countries. Indian policymakers routinely call for R&D spending to increase to 2 percent of GDP, expecting this increase to come from the private sector. However, private sector R&D is sorely depressed in India (see figure 12.1). As as a whole, it contributes only 30 percent to

---

4   See Ministry of Finance (2018), figure 2: R&D Expenditure as a Percentage of GDP (Development Time).

5   No Indian government agency collects information on contract R&D work done in the country by foreign firms. Such expenditures by foreign firms could total as much as 0.5 percent of GDP (Forbes 2016).

TABLE 12.1 R&D expenditure as a percentage of GDP, 1980–2016

	1980	1984	1988	1992	1996	2000	2004	2008	2012	2016
India	0.56	0.78	0.86	0.73	0.65	0.77	0.77	0.87	0.6	0.7
China	—	—	0.67	0.64	0.56	0.89	1.21	1.44	1.91	2.11
Japan	2.19	2.63	2.80	—	2.69	2.91	3.03	3.34	3.21	3.15
South Korea	0.57	1.19	—	2.10	2.26	2.18	2.53	3.12	4.03	4.24
Singapore	0.30*	0.53	0.87	0.94†	1.32	1.82	2.10	2.62	2.00	—
United States	2.32	2.87	2.84	2.74	2.44	2.62	2.49	2.77	2.69	2.74

NOTE: *Data from 1981; †data from 1990.
SOURCE: Data from 1980 to 1996 are a percentage of GNP (rather than GDP) and come from the UNESCO *Statistical Yearbook* (1999). Data from 2000 to 2016 are from the UNESCO Institute of Statistics (various years), available at: http://data.uis.unesco.org/. Estimates for India for the years 2012 and 2016 are from the Ministry of Finance (2018).

FIGURE 12.1 Gross domestic expenditure on research and development, by performer share, in selected nations, 2015

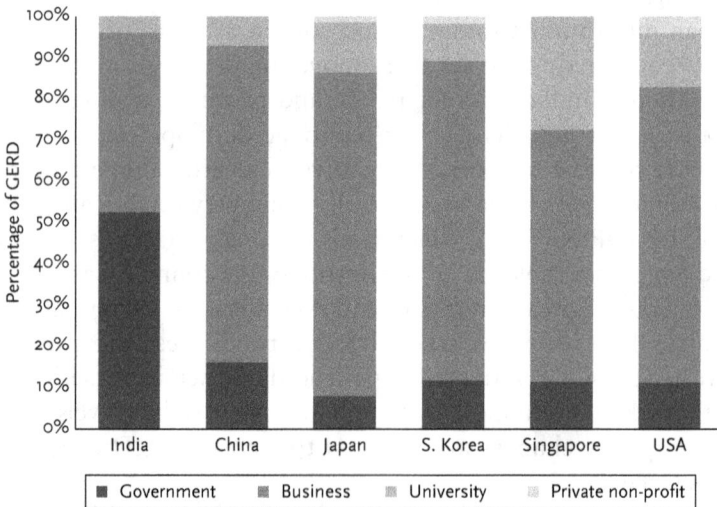

NOTE: GERD = gross expenditure on research and development.
SOURCE: UNESCO Institute of Statistics. Singapore data are from 2014.

the country's R&D expenditures, a paltry amount in the region and much below the global average of 71 percent.[6]

---

6   Five percent of R&D spending is conducted by state-owned enterprises in India (Forbes 2016). In private firms in China, Japan, South Korea, and the United States, the average gross expenditure on R&D is more than 70 percent; in Singapore it is 61 percent.

This lack of private sector spending on innovation is somewhat puzzling, especially when the Indian industry boasts of many globally competitive as well as export-oriented firms—such as those focusing on software exports, pharmaceuticals, and the automotive industry, which all require constant R&D. Essentially, these corporations should be driving innovation spending. Though India has a surfeit of talented scientists and engineers (because of earlier investments in medical education and technical higher education), hundreds of thousands of Indians (in what is popularly known as the IT generation) have migrated to the United States since 1995 (Chakravorty, Kapur, and Singh 2017). Seeking to leverage the talent available in India, foreign firms have only recently set up innovation hubs as well as R&D centers across the country.

The role of businesses in innovation spending cannot be overstated. For comparative purposes, India and South Korea had roughly identical R&D spending patterns until around 1980. Then South Korean businesses dramatically increased their R&D expenditure, and as of 2014, were responsible for 78 percent of the country's R&D spending. Private industry has also contributed to the Chinese growth in R&D spending since 2000 (Forbes 2016).

This brings us to the third and perhaps most important difference between India and other innovation-driven economies. Relative to other innovation-driven economies, the Indian government plays an outsized role in funding R&D. It is not just the main contributor, but also the main user of this R&D funding. In other countries, government spending for R&D is either channeled to the private sector or the higher education sector, usually through competitive, peer-reviewed merit-based research grants. In India, on the other hand, most government funding is sent to government research laboratories: in 2014–15 alone, the eight principal science government agencies received more than $5 billion in government outlays (₹35,034 crore) (Ministry of Finance 2018). Much of this money is spent within the government, with only a small amount used for external research.

What are the returns for this spending on innovation? Many of India's biggest projects are often derivative of other countries' discoveries. Among the most notable of these is India sending a rover to Mars in 2014, replicating what had been done by the Soviets, the United States, and the European Space Agency.[7] In his Independence Day speech in

---

7 For a thoughtful review of recent developments in Indian space policy, see Greene (2017).

2018, Prime Minister Narendra Modi announced that India would be landing a man on the moon by 2022, an initiative already achieved by several other countries (Rajagopalan 2018). Despite its interest in exploring space, India seems to avoid international research collaborations. It does not support the International Space Station or other cross-national space research agendas. Indian research laboratories also completed their own sequencing of the human genome in 2009, six years after the United States had done it in partnership with the United Kingdom, France, Germany, Japan, and China (NIH 2016). If India seeks to pursue cutting-edge innovation, the government should consider collaborating with other countries on big innovation projects.

Apart from the derivative nature of these initiatives, it is also worth considering how well these research laboratories perform according to their own metrics. Consider the Council of Scientific and Industrial Research (CSIR), which in 2017–18 received approximately ₹4,582 crore (~$641 million) in government budgetary support, as well as another ₹863 crore (~$121 million) from other sources (CSIR 2018). This funding supported more than 12,000 researchers across a network of national laboratories. The *CSIR Annual Report 2017–2018* suggests that its main metrics of performance are publications and patents. During this time period, CSIR generated 5,336 research publications and filed for 373 domestic and foreign patents.[8]

For the sake of comparison, we analyze the Indian government spending of about ₹503 crore (~$98.6 million) on the Indian Institute of Technology-Bombay (IIT-Bombay) in 2017–18, approximately one-ninth the amount spent on CSIR (IIT Bombay 2017). The university also brought in about ₹312 crore ($43.6 million) in R&D receipts as well as tuition payments and donations. Over the course of a single year, IIT-Bombay produced 2,685 research publications and filed 116 patents. Given the amount of money the government spent at CSIR and at IIT-Bombay, more publications and patents came from out of IIT-Bombay (see table 12.2). Crucially, IIT-Bombay also graduated 2,577 students and educated thousands of others over the course of the academic year.

How did the 550 faculty at IIT-Bombay outperform the 12,000 researchers at CSIR? IIT-Bombay's superior performance is not necessarily surprising, as universities offer advantages for pursuing innovation that simply cannot be found in typical government research laboratories.

---

8 Some of these patents are double-counted in both domestic and foreign totals.

TABLE 12.2 Council of Scientific and Industrial Research (CSIR) versus Indian
Institute of Technology (IIT)–Bombay, 2017–18

	CSIR	IIT-Bombay
Government spending (₹ crore)	4,582	503
Separate R&D funding (₹ crore)	863	312
Research publications	5,336	2,685
Patents filed	373	116
Research publications / Government funding (Publications per ₹ crore of gov't spending)	1.16	5.34
Patents filed / Government funding (Patents per ₹ crore of gov't spending)	0.08	0.23
2018 graduates	0	2,577

NOTE: For CSIR's R&D funding, ₹156 crore came from foreign or private sources, and the
remaining ₹707 crore came from other government sources (e.g., state-owned enterprises).
IIT-Bombay did not break apart R&D funding between various sources. IIT-Bombay also
received ₹17 crore in donations from alumni.
SOURCE: *CSIR Annual Report 2017–18*; *IIT-Bombay Annual Report 2017–18*

Specifically, universities encourage flatter hierarchies—decentralized
organizational structures that are thought to be more advantageous
for innovation. IIT-Bombay also competitively allocates a portion of its
resources to encourage patenting and publications. And setting aside
patents and publications, universities produce skilled graduates who
can further advance innovation. Recognizing these advantages, many
countries have shifted from pursuing innovation through government
research laboratories to increasing R&D funding to the private sector
and universities.

Reforming the Research Laboratories

Nearly every other innovation-driven economy has moved away from
funding government research laboratories to funding R&D in higher
education or in the private sector. What will it take for India to do the
same?

To understand why India's research laboratories have survived, it
is necessary to put into perspective how they came about. For much
of the country's early history, India focused on achieving social objectives, with economic growth being an incidental concern (Rodrik and
Subramanian 2005). Nevertheless, funding for research and innovation has always been a hallmark of Indian government spending. Following a global standard practice at that time (from the 1940s to the
1960s), resources for innovation were channeled to what India's first

prime minister famously termed the *temples of modern India*: newly created public sector undertakings like government research laboratories, state-led infrastructural projects, and state-owned enterprises.[9] However, this government funding for innovation was not meant to directly translate to economic growth; it was mostly allocated to sectors where discoveries are hard to commercialize, like basic science, atomic energy, and space exploration.

These public sector undertakings reflected the best practices for innovation policy from this era: large teams of researchers working in strict, vertical hierarchies would carry out scientific and industrial R&D. As with other segments of the bureaucracy, employees would enjoy fixed salaries based on their length of tenure and have long-term job security. There was minimal circulation of researchers between government labs and higher educational institutions, and even less between the public and private sectors. When government researchers discovered marketable opportunities, they would form hierarchical, state-owned enterprises where all equity was controlled by the state. In line with other "license raj" policies, the government did not incentivize private sector R&D and frequently stymied any innovation efforts challenging these public sector undertakings.

But beginning in the 1950s, other countries started to transition from funding public sector undertakings to supporting R&D in the private sector and in higher education. This transition started in the United States, which, during World War II, relied on vertical bureaucracies to pursue research. The Manhattan Project is a classic example: a few leaders at the top made most of the decisions and research was "siloed" into a few critical areas to minimize the likelihood of leaking secrets. Several reformers spoke out against this model in the postwar years. Vannevar Bush, arguably the most important administrator in American science history, ultimately proposed a model based on five fundamentals that led to the creation of the National Science Foundation (NSF):

> First, whatever the extent of [government] support may be, there must be stability of funds over a period of years so that long-range programs

---

9 Nehru coined the term "temples of modern India" during an October 1954 speech at the groundbreaking ceremony for the Bhakra-Nangal Dam. The term came to be associated with the Nehruvian political economy, which broadly involved state-led industrial projects. For further reading on this period, see Khilnani (1999).

may be undertaken. Second, the agency to administer such funds should be composed of citizens selected only on the basis of their interest in and capacity to promote the work of the agency. They should be persons of broad interest in and understanding of the peculiarities of scientific research and education. Third, the agency should promote research through contracts or grants to organizations outside the Federal Government. It should not operate any laboratories of its own. Fourth, support of basic research in the public and private colleges, universities, and research institutes must leave the internal control of policy, personnel, and the method and scope of the research to the institutions themselves. This is of the utmost importance. Fifth, while assuring complete independence and freedom for the nature, scope, and methodology of research carried on in the institutions receiving public funds, and while retaining discretion in the allocation of funds among such institutions, the Foundation proposed herein must be responsible to the President and the Congress. Only through such responsibility can we maintain the proper relationship between science and other aspects of a democratic system. (Bush 1945)

In accordance with these principles,[10] the NSF submits a budget request to Congress every year for various research initiatives, after discussions with administrators and leading researchers in each field. Congress then allocates the money with a few earmarks; it does not determine in which geographic locations the NSF can fund research and it has a minimal say in the NSF's research priorities.[11] In fiscal year 2017, the NSF received $7.472 billion, of which more than $6 billion was directed into the NSF's Research and Related Activities Account, and the remaining was used to fund major research equipment, education, and operations (NSF 2017). The Research and Related Activities Account supports already-approved research as well as proposals across various disciplines of scientific inquiry. University research laboratories, researchers in the private sector, or other government scientists can submit proposals within a certain time frame. These proposals must include information about results from previous awards. To approve

---

10 The NSF was created after World War II. Many in the government recognized the need to fund science and technology for the country's advancement but were concerned that science could become politicized. Ultimately, the NSF model was the compromise. For a brief history of its creation, see Kevles (1977).

11 The NSF administration is supposed to take geographical distribution into account, but they are left to determine the best distributions (Kevles 1977).

the proposals, the NSF relies on a scholarly peer review process. These panels consist of scholars within each discipline (usually brought from outside the NSF as well as some from within), who identify the strongest proposals based on their practicality, their intellectual merit, and whether the research will have a broad impact that extends beyond academic debate. Through this competitive and relatively apolitical process, only the most promising research gets funded. Further, the annual reporting system helps to ensure continuous progress is being made. Final reports are provided both for the NSF and the public.

There are slight variations to this basic model of merit-based grants. The National Aeronautics and Space Administration (NASA), for instance, will oftentimes express interest in the development of a certain technology, perhaps a new design for a spacesuit or a new material for a spaceship. The agency will specify the problem or the kind of research needed and open a competitive proposal process. Outside bidders will then submit proposals to conduct the required research. Although some research and engineering is handled in-house at NASA, a large portion of its budget is earmarked for merit-based grants. The Defense Advanced Research Projects Agency (DARPA) has also sponsored "Grand Challenges" to spur the development of autonomous vehicles.[12]

Whether the research problem is specified by the granting agency or not, peer-reviewed merit-based grant processes offer three clear benefits for improving R&D outcomes in India. First, the private sector and universities tend to pursue innovation through decentralized organizational structures. Scholars and policymakers widely agree that flat organizations enable researchers the flexibility to adopt the most optimal paths for research, as it is the researchers—rather than some senior administrator—who are best positioned to decide the next steps in the innovation process. This is perhaps why we see greater research productivity per capita from IIT-Bombay than we observe from CSIR.

A second benefit derives from the nature of merit-based competition. When a merit-based process works well, resources are efficiently allocated to the most promising research. This competition for resources— as opposed to automatically sanctioned funding—increases accountability as researchers must not only come up with strong proposals, but

---

12   In this model, DARPA announced a grand prize and encouraged merit-based competition. Student teams raised money from their universities and through corporate sponsorships. Students and faculty who were involved in the early DARPA Grand Challenges were some of the pioneers in this space (see Davis 2006).

must also deliver if they want their peers to approve future proposals. Competition for resources usually spills into other domains as well, for example, researchers will seek stronger collaborators and students; universities and the private sector will compete to attract those who can bring in more research money; and typically researchers will derive greater autonomy within their organizations when more research money is available. [13]

A third benefit comes from the multiplying effects that are unique to the private sector and to higher education. The government should transfer resources for R&D to the private sector, as it is better positioned than government laboratories to commercialize any technologies that are discovered. Also, just a small amount of seed money from the government might stimulate other private sector investment, as is the case with many early-stage research discoveries. Likewise, when the government instead transfers resources to the higher education sector, the multiplying benefits are manifest. In the United States and in Europe, peer-reviewed, competitive merit-based funding—combined with university autonomy—leads to much stronger university outcomes, including research productivity (Aghion et al. 2010). Research funding that is directed to universities not only increases research output in the immediate term, but also funds students who are simultaneously trained in research. There is immense value in such training. An innovation like a new technical protocol to protect sensitive data might have a shelf life of only a few years (or even a few months), while a student who is properly trained in the field of data security can continue to develop solutions for a generation to come. Perhaps not surprisingly, many other research laboratories and funding agencies within the U.S. government use this merit-based grant process; it also is a popular model for funding R&D in Europe and is growing in popularity in East Asia.

We should see better outcomes if the Indian government transitions its research funding away from the typical government laboratory system toward a merit-based system where smaller groups at universities and in the private sector bid for research proposals. Achieving such a transition, however, can be politically fraught, especially considering the many government researchers entrenched in relatively stable positions. For such a transition to take place, they will need to be convinced that the opportunities from the merit-based system will be greater than

---

13   For the considerable effects of merit-based grant systems on university productivity and autonomy, see Aghion et al. (2010).

the positions that they currently enjoy. In the next section, we consider two forms of political resistance: *material resistance* and *ideological resistance*.

Transitioning the System

How might a merit-based grant process be installed in India? In an ideal world, government research laboratories would either be converted into or replaced by agencies involved in merit-based research allocation processes, modeled on global best practices. The granting agencies would have to be politically insulated, but they should also empower part-time proposal reviewers and not just full-time administrators.

Governments across Asia and in the rest of the world who have come to adopt merit-based funding for innovation have encountered political resistance to these transitions, specifically of two types. The first type of resistance is material; it emerges from those who materially benefit from the status quo. When a country transitions to merit-based allocation of resources, government research laboratories often stand to lose. Instead of spending their resources in-house, they will need to send these resources out. The second type of resistance is ideological. In many countries, there has historically been an intense resistance to Western—and specifically American—scientific practices. India has been no different, with sustained and full-throated calls to maintain Indian scientific practices since the country's independence in 1947. A reformer who is focused on bringing merit-based practices to India must be prepared to encounter both types of resistance. In this section, we analyze how other countries have mitigated—or altogether side-stepped—these political forces, with special attention to how reform can be achieved in India.

Addressing material resistance

In the case of the United States, the transition from vertical government research laboratories to merit-based research funding happened following the end of World War II. Scientists and technocrats had seen firsthand the virtues and limitations of bureaucratized research and decided to transition R&D away from government research laboratories. Even though there were some concerns, there was also little material resistance to the reforms. Prior to World War II, government research laboratories were very small but they ballooned during the war as

American military leaders realized the importance of technology for success in battle. However, few researchers who had joined during the war actually expected to remain with the government research laboratories when the war ended.[14] Instead, many of them pursued careers in academia or in the private sector.

More senior administrators who might have wanted to keep the structure in place encountered strong resistance from the political network, led by Vannevar Bush, whose recommendations shaped government policy in favor of merit-based research. By the end of the 1940s, Bush had basically acquired celebrity status and enjoyed direct communications with the U.S. president as well as key leaders of Congress.

In India, the material resistance is likely to be far more substantial. The government spends more than $8 billion annually on government research, which supports tens of thousands of scientists and engineers within the Indian bureaucracy. Many of these research laboratories have long institutional histories, with lineages tracing back to the 1950s. Equally important politically, the leaders of these government research laboratories hold high-level positions within the government and regularly interact with political leaders. Any reform efforts thus have to be balanced with efforts to mitigate the losses in resources and power that these actors would face.

In seeking to minimize material resistance, the transitions by East Asian economies might prove particularly instructive. In Singapore, the National Science and Technology Board (NSTB) was founded in 1991 with a specific mission: to increase gross expenditure on research and development (GERD) to at least 2 percent of GDP; to encourage the private sector to account for at least 50 percent of GERD; and to increase the number of research scientists and engineers to a minimum of 40 per 10,000 in the labor force (Loh 1998). Notably, these goals did not focus on the number of papers or patents or licensing deals, measures that the Indian government research laboratories currently use to gauge their success. As a first step, the Indian government should define and pursue its innovation policies based upon these economic metrics instead of focusing on papers, patents, and licenses.

As Singapore developed its R&D capabilities, the NSTB was reorganized in 2001 and renamed the Agency for Science, Technology, and

---

14 On a personal note, both of my maternal grandparents joined Oak Ridge National Laboratories during World War II. Like many others, they were keen to leave for opportunities in the private sector following the conclusion of the war.

Research (A*STAR) in 2002. In 2006, the Singapore government created the National Research Foundation to coordinate innovation policy across various domains, and to assume the responsibility of A*STAR. The foundation faced little material resistance at its creation. It largely serves as a coordinating and agenda-setting body, but also allocates merit-based grants. The foundation gives considerable policy leeway to its subsidiary branches to pursue their agendas. It was developed as the funding pie was growing, and since its creation, government spending on R&D has tripled. As a result, few government researchers in Singapore lost out when it came into existence. Barring an economic miracle, however, it is doubtful that India can triple its own government funding for R&D over the next 15 years.

South Korea also offers several lessons from when it transitioned its system to a merit-based granting process. Initial government funding for R&D focused on military applications, and the forming of the first two government research laboratories: the National Defense Research and Development Institute and the Korea Atomic Energy Research Institute in the 1950s.[15] By the 1960s, Park Chung Hee was championing Western-style technological advancement, which would become a core platform for Korean national identity as well as economic development. The government sought to develop a domestic capacity that could absorb and improve upon foreign technologies. It began by focusing on light industry like textiles and simple electronics, relying upon foreign partners to develop turnkey operations. By the 1970s, Korea sought to shift to more capital- and technology-intensive industries. A few large private firms led this shift, with the government playing a supporting role by developing a number of research institutes in the fields of heavy machinery, chemicals, and electronics. Government researchers at these institutes usually partnered with researchers in the private sector on very specific projects. Researchers would also circulate between the government and the private sector; equally important, these institutes lured back Korean engineers and scientists from abroad.

In the 1980s, foreign technology transfer was no longer as desirable or as accessible, and so large Korean firms ramped up their own spending on R&D. Researchers found attractive career options outside of the government, in many cases continuing the projects that they

---

15   The budgets and expectations for both remained relatively modest as the government would mostly come to rely on military technology from the United States (see Chung 2011).

had already been pursuing. By the 1990s, Korea boasted one of the strongest industrial platforms of any developing country, but business groups backed more than 80 percent of all patents filed, and as the private sector grew, it took the lead in R&D spending (Mahmood and Singh 2003). Much of this spending remains concentrated among a few key business groups. In the 2000s, the Korean government sought to reformulate its priorities in spending, seeking to focus on basic sciences and higher education. They combined two of the leading government research organizations and set up a merit-based model for funding research as well as higher education. However, the private sector continues to dominate R&D spending.

Learning from Singapore and Korea, the Indian government should formulate a strategy to grow private sector R&D spending. India has already encouraged private sector R&D through generous tax breaks, although the generally idiosyncratic structure of the Indian taxation regime means that large companies, especially foreign R&D outfits, often have to jump through too many hoops to avail these benefits. Streamlining these processes would encourage the growth of the private sector R&D.

Perhaps more importantly, the government should follow Korea's example and consider meaningful partnerships with the private sector R&D outfits that are already in the country. Unlike Singapore, India might not be able to recruit top-tier foreigner researchers at this stage, but the Indian government should encourage its nonmilitary research laboratories to align their research agendas with industry demand, especially in the private sector.[16] To this end, the government should create systems of lateral entry and exit for its researchers so that they can explore already-existing opportunities in the private sector. Establishing a research network that extends beyond the government is vital for any transition to a merit-based system.

---

16 Memorandums of understanding (MOUs) are another popular metric in India, with the CSIR, government research laboratories, and universities boasting about the number of MOUs that they have signed with other governmental bodies or foreign institutions. It is unclear what precisely is included in each MOU or whether the MOUs actually contribute to the growth of R&D in any meaningful sense. As such, MOU counts alone are poor measures of the quality of collaboration. For a list of MOUs signed by CSIR, see "MoUs/ Agreements Signed by CSIR with Foreign Institutions/Agencies," CSIR, https://www.csir.res.in/sites/default/files/Agreements%20and%20MoUs%20signed%20by%20CSIR%20with%20Foreign%20Institutions%28Latest%29_0.pdf.

India has a special advantage compared to Korea and Singapore in making its transition to a merit-based system. India boasts one of the world's largest higher education systems and is particularly adept at technical education. But the growth of these systems in recent years has outpaced the supply of educators, with the Indian technical education system experiencing a huge shortfall in faculty positions. Government researchers should therefore be encouraged to transition to careers in academia. They can continue their research, hopefully by competing for merit-based grants, while simultaneously training their students to also conduct research. Researchers would strengthen these universities, and the government-sponsored research platform could transition to a merit-based system. But this transition will only happen if the government sets appropriate incentive structures.

Allaying ideological resistance

For many developing countries, science and technology policy is shaped by nationalist concerns (Shin 2006). India is no different. British rule in India had extensively relied upon scientific advancement, or at least the claim of scientific advancement (Prakash 1999). After its independence, India's nationalist leaders struggled to lay out a cohesive science and technology platform. Some were keen to continue with Western practices for science and technology. Most prominently, Nehru's vision for India's future rested squarely on achieving industrialization through Western technological advancement.[17] Indian research laboratories were modeled on British structures. Each of the five initial IIT campuses sought to emulate a foreign technical educational structure: the German structure (IIT-Madras), the Soviet structure (IIT-Bombay), the British structure (IIT-Delhi), the American structure (IIT-Kanpur), and a UNESCO-recommended structure (IIT-Kharagpur).

At the same time, a separate set of India's founders sought to define Indian nationalism by celebrating and protecting precolonial indigenous practices in the realm of the sciences, while rejecting foreign (and specifically British) practices. Mohandas Gandhi's own writings were filled with skepticism about Western scientific and technological practices, which he viewed as instruments of subjection having limited

---

17   Before studying law, Nehru earned an honor's degree in natural science from Cambridge in 1910.

potential for improving the well-being of the average Indian (Nandy 1981). Many government officials shared Gandhi's views and sought to complicate Nehru's vision. For instance, officials were concerned that simply turning over the IITs to foreign professors would undermine Indian technical education, and so they restricted foreigners from becoming university administrators. The government also set up special provisions for the practice of ayurveda, yoga, naturopathy, unani, siddha, and homeopathy (AYUSH).[18]

This ideological resistance to Western science has fluctuated over time and seems to matter more in certain domains than in others today. This is perhaps most prominent when it comes to AYUSH: the government—and its research laboratories—continuously produce remedies without subjecting them to systematic scientific studies.[19] Though the government supports clinical trials of AYUSH medications, Western outlets have mostly rejected their validity. However, in other fields, such as steel production, pharmaceutical manufacturing, and information technology, India seems all too willing to leverage and adopt Western practices and is consequently at the forefront of technological development. The success of entrepreneurs in these spaces has become a source of great national pride.

Because of the important place that science and innovation holds in the context of Indian national sentiment, it is critical to recognize that ideological concerns could potentially derail attempts to Westernize government-sponsored innovation policies. Broadly conceptualized,

---

18   Support for AYUSH has been consistent throughout independent India's history, although in recent years the ruling Bharatiya Janata Party has further promoted these practices. It has formed an independent ministry to oversee AYUSH and integrated AYUSH with other major health programs. From 2018 to 2020, the government sponsored the National AYUSH Mission to the tune of ₹2,400 crore (~$340 million), but it is doubtful that any of this money was used to conduct rigorous scientific research on AYUSH.

19   The experience of Indian research into indigenous medical practices stands in stark contrast to China. In 1995, a CSIR laboratory released an antimalarial drug, which did not seem to have any medical impact. Indian research organizations refused to subject AYUSH to systematic scientific research, unlike in China, where government-supported systematic scientific research of traditional Chinese medicine helped in the development of artemisinin, which has become a mainstream antimalarial drug today. Government scientists in India have claimed that another herbal remedy can get diabetes patients off insulin in six months, and have also commercially released a product called "Memory Plus," despite no scientific evidence of the efficacy of either medication (Patwardhan 2016).

there are two possible ways to ideologically brand a shift toward a system of merit-based resource allocation for innovation in India.

The first way to brand such reforms would focus on their "universalistic" appeal.[20] According to this logic, if India is to take its rightful place as a global leader in innovation, it must understand and modernize its system by adopting global best practices. Many of India's innovation institutions are already modeled on Western and specifically British structures, albeit from the 1930s and 1940s. Additionally, many of India's researchers have trained abroad and have sought to bring Western practices of innovation to India. Some commentators have also observed that there is a growing celebration of the transformative power of Western-style technology and innovation in India, and these changes could overcome any particularistic ideological resistance (Irani 2019).

Alternatively, merit-based reforms could be branded as "particularistic," meaning that they could be portrayed as indigenous to India. Recent efforts to introduce cultural change—such as the Swachh Bharat Mission and the Right to Compulsory Education—have been championed by the government in large part because they are framed as Indian-led projects.[21] Previous efforts to improve sanitation or increase mass education were derailed much earlier due to ideological resistance from government officials. Though both the Swachh Bharat and the Right to Compulsory Education movements received foreign funding and technical support like their predecessor attempts, the big difference was that these received government buy-in as well.

Reformers must carefully consider which ideological framing would be most effective at bringing merit-based practices to India's government research laboratories. The sources of anti-Western bias are not well understood in India. As in other parts of the world, anti-Western views in India seem to stem from several sources ranging from nationalist sentiment to anticapitalism/antimodernity to fear of traditional

---

20   This framing of universalistic versus particularistic appeal is drawn from Shin (2006).

21   Both the Swachh Bharat Mission to promote the usage of toilets and the campaign to make compulsory education a fundamental right were heavily encouraged and supported by international actors, but in both areas they repeatedly tried and failed to realize large-scale cultural change. The movements have been criticized for various shortcomings in implementation, but both received considerable government buy-in, especially compared to their predecessor missions. On compulsory education, see Weiner (1991).

ways of life and culture being usurped.[22] For a reform effort to be successful, reformers must identify and address specific sources of ideological resistance to Westernizing Indian R&D.

Summary

The Indian government's anachronistic system of R&D needs to change. In an era when innovation is pursued by small teams who are competing against one another, the Indian government continues to allocate money to highly bureaucratized government research laboratories that do not have the correct incentive structures in place. These research laboratories need to be disassembled, and funding for R&D should be distributed to smaller teams through peer-reviewed, merit-based mechanisms. The Indian government can leverage the experiences of countries in the West and in Asia that have already adopted these mechanisms as it designs its own system.

Reformers promoting such a profound institutional change should expect two forms of political resistance. First, there are many who benefit from the current status quo and are a source of material resistance. To mitigate potential material resistance, as in other countries, the government should consider adopting different measures of success for its research laboratories. It should particularly encourage government researchers to collaborate with private industry and academia. This will not only to make the quality of the research stronger, but will also create a network of researchers that cuts across government, academia, and the private sector, generating alternative career opportunities for government researchers. The government should also encourage lateral entry and exit for its researchers, ideally with more exits than entries.

A second form of political resistance can potentially arise from ideology. If merit-based peer review systems for pursuing innovation are to be adopted, then reformers need to determine whether to advertise these reforms as Western or indigenous. There are pros and cons for both approaches—and a deeper study is required to fully understand the political circumstances of the ideological resistance—but the wrong decision could derail reforms even before they start.

Crafting a plan for reforming government-supported innovation—and designing a political strategy for such reform—is particularly vital for India. There is a widespread expectance that innovation will drive

---

22   On anti-American views in the Korean experience, see Shin (1996).

economic growth and social development, but there is also widespread recognition that the current system is not delivering the results that it should, as the quotation from Prime Minister Narendra Modi at the beginning of this chapter highlights. Reforms to date have focused on announcing national missions without addressing the underlying weaknesses in the ways that innovation areas are identified and pursued. Without a big bang change, India is unlikely to live up to its developmental potential.

References

Aghion, Philip, Mathias Dewatripont, Caroline Hoxby, Andreu Mas-Colell, Andre Sapir, and Bas Jacobs. 2010. "The Governance and Performance of Universities: Evidence from Europe." *Economic Policy* 25 (61): 7–59.

Bush, Vannevar. 1945. *Science—The Endless Frontier*. A Report to the President of the United States of America. Last accessed May 13, 2019. https://www.nsf.gov/about/history/vbush1945.htm.

Chakravorty, Sanjoy, Devesh Kapur, and Nirvikar Singh. 2017. *The Other One Percent: Indians in America*. New York: Oxford University Press.

Chung, Sungchul. 2011. "Innovation, Competitiveness and Growth: Korean Experiences." World Bank, Washington, DC. Last accessed May 13, 2019. http://siteresources.worldbank.org/EXTABCDE/Resources/7455676-1288210792683/Sungchul-Chung.pdf.

CSIR (Council of Scientific and Industrial Research). 2014. *CSIR Annual Report, 2013–2014*. New Delhi: CSIR. Last accessed May 13, 2019. https://www.csir.res.in/about-us/annual-reports.

———. 2018. *Annual Report 2017–18*. New Delhi: CSIR. https://www.csir.res.in/sites/default/files/turnjsmagazine/140258/turnjs magazines/sourcepdf/CSIR%20Annual%20Report%202017-18%20%20English.pdf

Davis, Joshua. 2006. "Say Hello to Stanley." *Wired*, January 1, 2006. Last accessed May 13, 2019. https://www.wired.com/2006/01/stanley/.

Forbes, Naushad. 2016. "India's National Innovation System: Transformed or Half-Formed?" CTIER Working Paper WP/16/01, Centre for Technology, Innovation and Economic Research, Pune, India.

Gosain, Manash Pratim. 2017. "35% of Faculty Posts Vacant in IITs, 53% in Central Universities." *Times of India*, August 20, 2017.

Last accessed May 13, 2019. https://timesofindia.indiatimes.com/india/35-of-faculty-posts-vacant-in-iits-53-in-central-universities/articleshow/60138942.cms.

Greene, Kate. 2017. "Why India Is Investing in Space." *Slate*, March 17, 2017. Last accessed May 13, 2019. http://www.slate.com/articles/technology/future_tense/2017/03/why_india_is_investing_in_space.html.

IIT (Indian Institute of Technology) Bombay. 2017. *IIT-Bombay Strategic Plan, 2017–2022*. Mumbai: IIT, Bombay. Last accessed May 13, 2019. https://www.iitb.ac.in/en/about-iit-bombay/iit-bombay-strategic-plan-2017-22.

———. 2018. *Annual Report 2017–18*. Mumbai: IIT Bombay. https://www.iitb.ac.in/sites/www.iitb.ac.in/files/AnnualReport/2019/Annual_Report_2017_18.pdf.

Irani, Lilly. 2019. *Chasing Innovation: Making Entrepreneurial Citizens in Modern India*. Princeton, NJ: Princeton University Press.

Kevles, Daniel. 1977. "The National Science Foundation and the Debate over Postwar Research Policy, 1942–1945: A Political Interpretation of Science—The Endless Frontier." *ISIS* 68 (1): 4–26.

Khilnani, Sunil. 1999. "Chapter 2: Temples of the Future." In *The Idea of India*, 61–106. New York: Farrar, Straus, and Giroux.

Loh, Lawrence. 1998. "Technology Policy and National Competitiveness." In *Competitiveness of the Singapore Economy: A Strategic Perspective*, edited by Toh Mun Heng and Tan Kong Yam, 44–80. Singapore: Singapore University Press.

Mahmood, Ishtiaq, and Jasjit Singh. 2003. "Technological Dynamism in Asia." *Research Policy* 32 (6): 1031–54.

Ministry of Defence, Government of India. N.d. "Value of Revenue and Capital Expenditure on Defense Research and Development the [sic] by Indian Government from FY 2015 to FY 2018 (in Billion Indian Rupees)." https://www.statista.com/statistics/741949/india-governmental-expenditure-on-defense-research-and-development/.

Ministry of Finance, Government of India. 2018. *Economic Survey of India 2017–18, Vol. 1*. New Delhi: Department of Economic Affairs, Economic Division. https://mofapp.nic.in/economicsurvey/economicsurvey/index.html.

Ministry of Science and Technology, Government of India. 2018. *Annual Report 2017–18*. Accessed February 10, 2019. https://

drive.google.com/file/d/1IPKUdbSxoDa2Zi_ufzC4u-T3jCFz
Pred/view.

Nandy, Ashis. 1981. "From Outside the Imperium: Gandhi's Cultural Critique of the West." *Alternatives* 7 (2): 171–94.

NIH (National Institutes of Health). 2016. "What Is the Human Genome Project?" Last accessed May 13, 2019. https://www.genome .gov/12011238/an-overview-of-the-human-genome-project/.

NSF (National Science Foundation). 2017. "President Signs Omnibus Appropriations Bill into Law; Federal Agencies Funded through September 30." NSF and Congress, May 8. Last accessed May 13, 2019. https://www.nsf.gov/about/congress/115/highlights/ cu17_0508.jsp.

Patwardhan, Bhushan. 2016. "Aryuvedic Drugs in Case: Claims, Evidence, Regulations, and Ethics." *Journal of Aryuveda and Integrative Medicine* 7 (3): 135–37.

Prakash, Gyan. 1999. *Another Reason: Science and the Imagination of Modern India*. Princeton, NJ: Princeton University Press.

Rajagopalan, Rajeswari Pillai. 2018. "What's Next for India's New Space Ambitions?" *The Diplomat*, August 24, 2018. Last accessed May 13, 2019. https://thediplomat.com/2018/08/whats-next-for -indias-new-space-ambitions/.

Rodrik, Dani, and Arvind Subramanian. 2005. "From 'Hindu Growth' to Productivity Surge: The Mystery of the Indian Growth Transition." *IMF Staff Papers* 52 (2): 193–228.

Shin, Gi-Wook. 1996. "South Korean Anti-Americanism: A Comparative Perspective." *Asian Survey* 36 (8): 787–803.

Shin, Gi-Wook. 2006. *Ethnic Nationalism in Korea: Genealogy, Politics, and Legacy*. Stanford, CA: Stanford University Press.

Weiner, Myron. 1991. *The Child and the State in India*. Princeton, NJ: Princeton University Press.

Index

34; institutional reforms within, 120; IPO regulations within, 259–61, 268, 278–92; IPOs as exit strategy within, 271–78; late-stage financing within, 259, 271–78; Law on the Promotion of Application of Scientific and Technological Achievements, 125; lessons from, 156–58; manufacturing sector within, 155, 157; mid-stage financing within, 259, 264–71; National Equities Exchange and Quotations (NEEQ), 276–77, 280–81; National Green Campus Evaluation Standard, 124; National Innovation Demonstration Zone, 120; Organic Light Emitting Display (OLED), 123; private tech firms within, 267–68; Project 985 within, 39–40; R&D spending by, 305, 306; research and development (R&D) funding within, 263; reverse merger (RM) transaction within, 271, 274–75; Science and Technology Board (STAR Market), 291; sophisticated consumer services within, 155–56; star scientists within, 71; State Intellectual Property Office (SIPO), 286; Tsinghua Technology Service, 120; Tsinghua University S&T Development Corporation, 120; turnover rate within, 288; 12th Five-Year Plan, 270; Type 1 economy within, 154; unicorn statistics within, 258, 267–68; venture capital and private equity funding (VCPE) within, 265–66, 270, 271–78, 289; Visionox, 123; world-class university (WCU) strategy of, 120; Zhongguancun Science Park, 120. *See also* Tsinghua University

Chinese Depository Receipts, 290
Christensen, Clayton M., 54, 58
Chung, Unchan, 88
Cirius Technologies, 220
city planning, artificial intelligence (AI) within, 181
Clark, Burton R., 118
classification of services, within policymaking, 170
Cockburn, Iain, 74
collaboration, network connections within, 77
collaborative knowledge building, 26
collaborative research, 74–80
Commercial Code (Japan), 210
competition: artificial intelligence (AI) use and, 182; example of, 54; as innovation driver, 34; merit-based, 312–13; staying under the radar within, 54; within technology industries, 180; unlevel playing field within, 38
competitive entry strategy, 50, 54–55, 58
Cong, Lin William, 7, 285–86
construction, artificial intelligence (AI) within, 181
constructive learning, 27
consumer services, artificial intelligence (AI) within, 181
contract R&D, 29–30
cooperative entry strategy, 50, 52–54
Cornelius, Peter K., 262
corporate-led innovation, 37, 42
corporate venture capital (VC), 8
corporations, 183–87, 244–46. *See also specific corporations*
Council of Scientific and Industrial Research (CSIR), 308–9
Coupang, 246
Crafton, 246
Creative Labs (C-Lab), 245
Creative Square, 245

The authorized representative in the EU for product safety and compliance is:
Mare Nostrum Group
B.V Doelen 72
4831 GR Breda
The Netherlands

www.ingramcontent.com/pod-product-compliance
Lightning Source LLC
Chambersburg PA
CBHW061000280326
41935CB00009B/774